Experimental Psychol

Experimental Psychology

Research Methods and Statistics

R.B. Burns
Deputy Chairman, Postgraduate School of Education,
University of Bradford

C.B. Dobson
Research Fellow, School of Psychology,
University of Bradford

MTP PRESS LIMITED · LANCASTER · ENGLAND
International Medical Publishers

Published by
MTP Press Limited
Falcon House
Lancaster, England

ISBN 0−85200−369−2

Phototypeset by Swiftpages Limited, Liverpool

Printed in Great Britain by
REDWOOD BURN LIMITED
Trowbridge

Contents

Introduction

This book has been written to meet several needs. Firstly there is a need for a book which integrates statistics, research design, experiments and report writing so that none is learned in a vacuum, as commonly is the case, isolated from the others. The aim is to make the student an active learner encouraged to carry out experiments, so experiencing and understanding the design problems and statistical analyses in the practical context where he can see exactly what he is doing and why. The aim is that by the end of the book, the student should be able to evaluate the research of others, to define a problem, formulate a hypothesis about it, design and carry out the experiment, apply the correct statistics, discuss the results and implications, and write it all up in a logical and sensible fashion. The principle is that old pedagogic one of learning by doing.

Secondly, there is a need for an introductory text on statistics, research design and experimental work for the many students who meet psychology and social science for the first time. The initiate in behavioural science needs to gain a conceptual understanding of statistical procedures and design techniques in order to carry out his own investigations and to understand and evaluate constructively the investigations of others. However, experience has shown us that many students (and even some fellow teachers) are somewhat reluctant to study this area as they believe it is difficult and involves mathematics. These opinions create negative attitudes and low expectations of success at the outset. We try to dispel these fears. This text was designed to present material in small steps, each section and each chapter being built on previous sections and chapters. The only maths knowledge required is the basic four rules of arithmetic (i.e. $+$, $-$, $\times$, $\div$), the understanding of what a square root and squaring a number are, and the ability to read tables. By the time the student has read this text he will have had plenty of practice at all this. Even the mathematically inept should be able to understand and even enjoy the material and activities.

Since this book is meant to be a painless and simple introduction to what is a very complex array of concepts, designs and statistics, the authors have attempted to reduce mathematical notation to a minimum, present examples wherever possible, explain in everyday language and provide questions for self-testing. After working through this book, students should have a basic framework of knowledge in the area of research design and statistics which can be deepened and refined in later courses and by reading more advanced texts.

So the text is addressed to a wide variety of students. Primarily, school psychology students and first year college psychology students who have not tackled psychology at school form the primary targets. However, all social sciences and paramedical students needing an introductory text on this area will find it a boon, particularly if they are working alone, for the book has been deliberately designed for the student working in conditions of minimum class teaching support or in self-remedial tuition. We have deliberately made references back throughout the book to previously presented material since this distributed repetition improves retention, understanding and transfer potential. The text organization demands that students proceed through the book chapter by chapter and not dipping in here and there. It is so structured that as the student masters the material in each chapter he is learning a basis for the understanding of future chapters, with design concepts and statistics introduced in a logical sequence, one by one.

Self Test Questions (STQs) have been placed within the text and at the end of most chapters to enable students to find out for themselves if they are following what has been presented. Such STQs also enable students to revise and/or practice some of the skills they are being taught. The answers to the STQs are either given immediately after the STQ, when the consequent material requires it, or at the end of the book, or found by referring back to previous material.

Science is man's most serious business, because the history of science is a history of the development of man's mind. Despite the struggle that the scientific point of view has had – and in some cases is still having – in becoming accepted, the fact is that science and its methods have become vital to man's existence. There is every indication, moreover, that the scientific method is becoming even more vital as our knowledge accumulates at a faster pace than ever. For this reason, if not for intellectual curiosity alone, any serious student should be well versed in the objective methods of science. This knowledge will not only enable him to understand how scientists help to solve man's problems but will also allow him to appreciate more realistically what science can and cannot do.

A personal note to students from the authors
This book will provide you with an opportunity to become acquainted with the methods of science and, specifically, with the experimental method in social science and psychology. Essentially, the method in all the sciences is the same; only the content varies. At the heart of science is the experiment, and the major aspect of the experiment is control; in fact an experiment can be defined as controlled observation.

When you conduct an experiment it may not come out in the predicted direction; often results will be contrary to those hypothesized. This is to be expected and in no way indicates that your research was poorly done. You should not always expect experiments to work; we do not set out to prove a hypothesis but to test it. However, whether the predictions are confirmed or not, you must always try to account for the results and discuss their implications.

As is usually the case in an introductory course you will run, analyze, and report on a number of experiments involving humans. It should be kept in mind that an experiment is not supposed to be a social event nor is it supposed to be humorous. Experimenters should be neat, courteous, and, above all, serious.

ETHICAL CONSIDERATIONS FOR RESEARCH INVOLVING
HUMAN SUBJECTS
Among the points to keep in mind when you are running your experimental subjects are the following: (1) in most cases your subjects are doing you a favour by participating in your experiments; (2) you are temporarily employing the services of your subjects in a situation that is probably foreign to them, and perhaps even threatening; (3) you are acting as a representative of your profession in general, and of your department in particular; and (4) in many cases you will provide the ony contact that many students will ever have with psychology and social science, or at least with experimental psychology.

It is for at least these reasons that you should observe the following principles in all interactions between you and your subjects:

Never cause undue discomfort or inconvenience to your subjects. A comfortable place for subjects to wait for the experiment to begin should be provided and the experimental environment itself should be as comfortable as possible. If the experiment is to be a lengthy one, always inform your subjects of that fact before they agree to participate.

Always assure your subjects that their performance is confidential. Never discuss how your individual subjects performed on different tasks. Such information is easily misinterpreted.

Do not deceive your subjects. Never even imply that you are doing something that you are not. Remember that people are often threatened by psychological experiments; they feel that you are trying to tap the dark recesses of their unconscious mind. Because many individuals are apprehensive about psychological experiments, and because they have many misconceptions, you must go out of your way not to perpetuate any myths about your work. For example, if you are asked by a subject at the conclusion of an experiment whether his or her performance indicated that he or she was 'smart', 'crazy', or some such thing, you must make it clear that such information is not provided by your experimentation.

Always be prepared. Never wait until you are running an experiment to attempt to understand it. Always be prepared well in advance of running your first subject. If some aspect of the experiment is not clear, consult your teacher/tutor. Being unprepared creates an uncomfortable situation for both you and your subject. It reduces the probability of your subject signing up for other experiments, and it creates an unfortunate image of you, your department, and the profession.

Always be on time. Since your subject has extended you a courtesy by agreeing to participate in your experiment, you are obliged to be on time. If for some reason you cannot keep your appointment, make arrangements to notify your subject. On the other hand, if your subject is late or misses an appointment, you should try to understand that being in an experiment at that particular time of day is not something that he or she is used to. Giving subjects some form of appointment card as a reminder should be helpful.

Where possible, inform your subjects about the experiment. Often students will sign up for experiments because they are curious. They want to know what experiments are like and how they would do in them. Their curiosity is often even more intense after they have participated in an experiment, so it is always a good idea to inform students of what was being attempted by each experiment and what was found. But information should not be given until the experiment has been completed by all subjects. One way to do this might be to prepare multiple copies of a brief statement and distribute them to anyone interested. Another way, of course, is merely to post such a statement in a place where those interested can read it.

Be courteous. Common courtesies, such as thanking your subjects for participating, will increase the probability that your subjects will sign up for other experiments. Courtesy also creates a favourable impression of you and your experimental work. In thanking them you are emphasising the value they have been for your experiment and your success on the course.

Finally may we wish you good luck with your studies and hope you find the contents of this text as valuable and interesting as we have tried to make them.

Many individuals both at student and professional level have contributed to the viewpoints and thinking which characterize this text. To these we owe a debt of gratitude. We are particularly indebted to Mrs G. Claridge, our typist, who produced such a splendid manuscript out of our semi-legible handwriting. Finally, to our close families who bore with us patiently during the long periods of concentration we had to devote selfishly to the production of this book, we are profoundly grateful for their support.

R.B.B.
C.B.D.
Bradford 1980

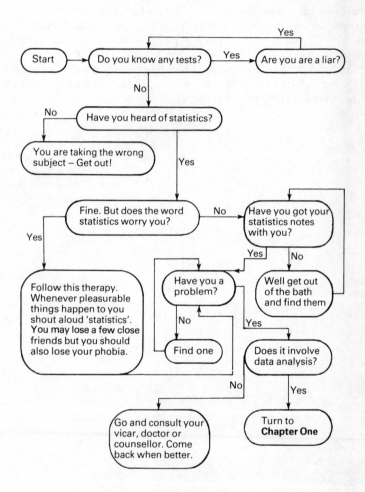

1

Psychology and the scientific method

Introduction
When asked our occupations and we reply that we are psychologists, the frequent response is 'That's interesting, I am a bit of a psychologist myself!' This is a little chastening to our professional pride yet there is an element of truth in the response. George Kelly (1955) echoed the same sentiments when he wrote about his model man – man the scientist, who is continually construing and evaluating his environment to make sense of it. The aspirations of the scientist are in fact the aspirations of all men. In order to live in society, to cope with the mundane aspects of everyday living, each person in his own way must try to understand human experience and behaviour, interpreting feedback from the environment so that he can respond realistically and appropriately, predicting and controlling the course of events in which he is involved. So not only do psychologists, or even teachers, nurses and door-to-door salesmen use psychological knowledge in their daily lives but so does everyone else in their interpersonal relationships. This has caused many people to view psychology as 'common sense messed around a bit' or as an 'abstruse way of stating the obvious'.

However, as in the understanding of most things, understanding human behaviour needs to be effected through as systematic and objective a way as possible, for layman's intuition, subjective judgment and common sense provides in most cases information and theories which are neither 'common' in that it is generally agreed, nor 'sense' in that it is rational. Many of our everyday observations and opinions are distorted in the very act of being made, through subjective bias and prejudice. We stereotype others on scanty evidence, and generalize conclusions well beyond any valid range of generalization. Human beings function on a folklore of unjustified assumptions about behaviour, and woolly armchair philosophizing.

Each day we overhear people making unjustified assertions on often important issues, such as

'Boys are better than girls at maths'

'The Welsh are more musical than the English'

'I am as good a driver when I've had 6 pints as when I'm sober'

'Permissive parents produce children who end up in court'

and so on. Additionally we are confronted daily with claims by so-called experts that have consequences in daily living. Those who can evaluate such claims are better able to separate good solutions from current fads. Newspaper articles and radio broadcasts raise questions about, and discuss such topics as anxiety in children, child-rearing practices, violence on TV, drug addiction, punishment, propaganda, conformity, intelligence, social class and so on. Most of it is generally uncritical, subjective assertions. But in order to understand these topics and find real and valid evidence only a scientific approach to generating and testing ideas will suffice. Too often decisions are made by parents, schools, civil servants, local and central government on important social issues on the basis of expediency, preconception, ideology and bias and not on the basis of the true facts. An understanding of research methods and statistics allows us to evaluate their claims, impressions, ideas and theories and see their implications. Psychologists are interested in all these questions, but the difference between the layman and the psychologist is that the latter employs objective, scientific, controlled experimentation with statistical analysis of data in order to discern what actually is the case, rather than a patchwork of likes and dislikes, rules of thumb, analogy and prejudice.

STQ *Write down in your notebook a couple of sentences explaining why psychology adopts a scientific approach to the study of human behaviour.*

Methods of knowing, or daddy told me
There are four general ways of knowing.

(a) Method of tenacity. Here one holds to the truth because one knows it to be true. The more frequent the repetition of the 'truth' the more the enhancement of the validity of it. It is self-evident then and men will cling to such beliefs even in the face of contrary evidence, e.g. 'The world is flat', 'All Communists are spies'.

(b) Method of authority. A thing must be true if it is in the Bible, or the Prime Minister says it, or teacher said so. The method of authority is not always unsound but we never know when it is or isn't. But we lack individual resources to investigate everything so the presumed competence of authority offers advantages.

(c) Method of intuition (*a priori* method). This claims that reason is the criterion of truth. It 'stands to reason' that learning difficult subjects must build moral character. But whose reason is to carry the judgment, if two eminent persons using rational processes reach different conclusions?

(d) Method of science. This method has one characteristic none of the other methods has, that is, self-correction. The checks verify and control the scientist's activities and conclusions. Even if a hypothesis seems to have support, the scientist will also test alternative hypotheses. Knowledge is attained through the scientific process because science ultimately appeals to evidence; hypotheses are subjected to empirical test. None of the other methods above provides any procedure for establishing the superiority of one belief over another.

What is science?
When many laymen are asked 'What is science?' they usually define science in terms of one of the physical or life sciences such as biology, physics or chemistry. Seldom is psychology identified as a science. When these individuals are told that psychology is indeed a science, they generally express bewilderment or disbelief. Why is psychology not generally associated with the scientific endeavour? If persons who do not associate science with psychology are asked to explain why chemistry is scientific but psychology is not, they will generally make some reference to facts, theories, or laboratory experiments conducted in chemistry – without realizing that psychology involves all of these factors.

Many individuals state that psychological investigations are not scientific. They seem to believe that the approach used in psychology is radically different and that the subject matter does not lend itself to scientific investigation. One possible reason for this belief is that our culture has promoted a number of false stereotypes about what is scientific. Three popular stereotypes have contributed to the pervasive misunderstanding surrounding scientific activity. The first stereotype is the 'white-coat – stethoscope – laboratory' view of the scientist. This stereotype depicts an individual working in a laboratory in which he or she is conducting experiments to generate facts that ultimately will improve mankind. Television commercials frequently use this stereotype to lend credibility to their statements about products. An individual wearing a white laboratory coat and giving the appearance of a scientist states that product X, a hair shampoo, has been shown to be superior to product Y – another hair shampoo.

The second stereotype is the scientist as the 'ivory tower', the brilliant person. Scientists are seen as rather impractical individuals who are concerned with complex theory generation rather than the solution of practical problems confronting mankind. They are perceived as persons in their own little world 'doing their own thing'. Frequently, the scientist working in an academic setting is perceived as conforming to this stereotype.

The third stereotype equates scientific endeavours with technological advances. People marvel at the ability to send a man to the moon, to design complex computers or to produce new power sources. They comment on the tremendous advancement in science that has allowed us to accomplish such feats. In this role the scientist is perceived as a highly skilled engineer striving to improve society.

So what is science?

So far we have looked at what science is *not* rather than what it is. Science has at various times been equated with 'a body of knowledge' : but it is not just knowledge replenishing and correcting itself. It is therefore a process or method for generating a body of knowledge. Science, therefore, represents a *logic of inquiry,* or a specific method to be followed in solving problems and thus acquiring a body of knowledge. Knowledge is not distinct from science – rather, it is the product of science. All knowledge, however, is not scientific knowledge. Knowledge acquired through the scientific method is the only type that is *scientific knowledge.*

The scientific method represents the fundamental logic of inquiry, and technique refers to the specific manner in which one implements the scientific method. To state that psychology uses a different scientific method is inaccurate. However, to state that psychology uses different techniques in applying the basic scientific method is accurate. Variation in technique as a function of subject matter can be illustrated by contrasting the various fields of inquiry as well as by contrasting the techniques used in the various areas of psychology. Consider, for example, the different observational techniques used by the astronomer, the biologist, and the psychologist doing research on small groups. The astronomer uses a telescope and, more recently, interplanetary probes in his or her investigations, whereas the biologist uses the microscope and the small-group researcher may use a one-way mirror to observe subjects' interactions unobtrusively. The scientists in these various fields are all using the same scientific method, the key aspect being controlled inquiry, but the techniques they must use in implementing this method differ. Even within the field of psychology, techniques differ depending on the problem and the subjects, from questionnaires in social psychology to reinforcement in learning theory, and stimulation electrodes in rats' brain in physiological psychology.

Characteristics of the scientific approach
Science has been defined as a specific method of logic of inquiry. This definition suggests that the method of science is somehow unique and different from other methods of inquiry or that it has specific rules or characteristics that have to be followed. Indeed the scientific method does have specific characteristics. These characteristics, while necessary to distinguish science, are not limited to the realm of science. Each of the characteristics could also exist outside of science; however, science could not exist without these characteristics. The three most important characteristics of science are control, operational definition, and replication.

CONTROL
Control is perhaps the single most important element in the scientific methodology, because it enables the scientist to identify the causes of his observations. Experiments are conducted in an attempt to answer certain questions. They represent attempts to identify why something happens, what causes some event, or under what conditions does an event occur. Control is necessary in order to provide unambiguous answers to such questions. Look at this example of how control is necessary in answering a practical question.

A farmer with both hounds and chickens might find that at least one of his four dogs is sucking eggs. If it were impractical to keep his dogs locked away from the chicken house permanently, he would want to find the culprit so that it could be sold to a friend who had no chickens, or to an enemy who does. The experiment could be run in just two nights by locking up one pair of hounds the first night and observing whether eggs were broken, if so, one additional dog would be locked up the second night, and the results observed. If none were broken, the two dogs originally released would be locked up with one of the others, and the results observed. Whatever the outcome, the guilty dog would be isolated. A careful farmer would, of course, check negative results by giving the guilty party a positive opportunity to demonstrate his presumed skill, and he would check positive results by making sure that only one dog was an egg sucker. (Marx and Hillix, 1973, p.8)

The farmer, in the final analysis, controlled for the simultaneous influence of all dogs by releasing only one dog at a time to isolate the egg sucker. To answer questions in psychology, we also have to eliminate the simultaneous influence of many variables to isolate the cause of an effect. Controlled inquiry is an absolutely essential process in science because without it the cause of an effect could not be isolated. The observed effect could be due to any one or a combination of the uncontrolled variables.

In order to test the hypothesis that anagrams formed from unfamiliar words are harder to solve than those formed from familiar words, several variables other than the one we are interested in (i.e. familiarity) must be controlled or else the results may be due to the unmeasured effects of these too. For example all the words must be of equal length because length will influence solution time.

OPERATIONAL DEFINITION
Operational definition means that terms must be defined by the steps or operations used to measure them. Such a procedure is necessary to eliminate confusion in meaning and communication. Consider the statement, 'Hunger causes one selectively to perceive food-related objects'. One might ask, 'What is meant by hunger?' Stating that hunger refers to being starved or some other such term only adds to the confusion. However, stating that hunger refers to 8 or 10 hours of food deprivation communicates a clear idea. In this way others realize what you mean by hunger and, if they so desire, they could also generate the same degree of hunger. Stating an operational definition forces one to identify the empirical referents or terms. In this manner ambiguity is minimized. Again introversion might be defined as a score on a particular personality scale.

REPLICATION
To be replicable the data obtained in an experiment must be reliable, that is, the same result must be found if the study is repeated. That science has such a requirement is quite obvious since it is attempting, in a scientific manner, to obtain knowledge about the world. If observations are not repeatable, then our descriptions and explanations are likewise unreliable and therefore useless.

Reproducibility of observations can be investigated by making intergroup, intersubject, or intrasubject observations. Intergroup observations would consist of attempting to duplicate the results on another group of subjects; intersubject observations involve assessing the reliability of observations on other individual sujects; and intrasubject observations consist of attempting to duplicate the results with the same subject on different occasions.

Science and common sense

In one sense science and common sense are alike, since common sense is a series of concepts or conceptual schemata satisfactory for the practical uses of mankind. But even in practical use common sense may be seriously misleading. It seemed self-evident that punishment must be the most effective way of stopping certain behaviour, that was until Skinner demonstrated the greater effectiveness of extinction allied with positive reinforcement.

Science and common sense differ sharply in five ways.

(a)   The layman uses theories and concepts in a loose fashion, often accepting ludicrous explanations for human behaviour. For instance, 'Being ill is a punishment for being sinful'; 'An economic depression may be attributed to Asian immigrants'. On the other hand the psychologist would systematically create a theory, and subject it to empirical test.

(b)   The layman tests his 'hypothesis' in a selective fashion by choosing evidence to fit the hypothesis. He may believe that male students have long hair. He will verify this belief by noting a large number of instances of it. He will, however, fail to notice exceptions. The more sophisticated psychologist aware of this tendency will test the relationship systematically in the field or in the laboratory.

   The best known of the critics of 'pseudo-science' is Karl Popper, who tells how, as a young man in Vienna, he knew the psychiatrist Adler:

> . . . I reported to him a case which to me did not seem particularly Adlerian, but which he found no difficulty in analysing in terms of his theory of inferiority feelings, although he had not even seen the child. Slightly shocked, I asked him how he could be so sure. 'Because of my thousand-fold experience', he replied; whereupon I could not help saying: 'And with this new case, I suppose, your experience has become thousand-and-one-fold.' (Popper, 1957, p.35)

Without rules operationalizing 'inferiority complex' which could be followed by any trained observer, observations of the concept are not observations in a scientific sense because there are no checks on what is and what is not an instance of the concept.

Science is a 'public' method, open to all who learn its methods, and a similar observation of the same subject using the same operationalized concept should give the same result. Where reliance is placed, argues Popper, on the 'private' opinion of the expert (such as Adler) without strict rules of observation, the test of any hypothesis linking 'inferiority complex' to another concept is unsatisfactory.

Popper proposes in his account of the logic of scientific discovery that theories should be 'falsifiable'. Falsifiability for him is the criterion which distinguishes science from pseudo-science (of which Freudianism, Marxism and astrology are his chief examples). Falsifiability is the doctrine that hypotheses should be submitted to rigorous testing in an attempt to show they are wrong. Science proceeds by refuting hypotheses, by making new observations which when analysed reject the hypothesis which prompted them. Scientists should not look for confirming instances of their conjectures or hypotheses – confirmations are often too easy to find – but submit their hypotheses to the most rigorous test which can be found. His complaints against Marxism amongst other doctrines is that Marxists look for confirming instances and ignore or overlook events and observations which might disprove their theories. The other aspect of Popper's story about Adler is, of course, that Adler was looking for confirming instances of his theory of inferiority complexes and not seeking to test and risk the refutation of his hypotheses as Popper argues science should.

(c)   A third difference lies in the notion of control. The psychologist tries systematically to rule out variables that are extraneous sources of influence. The layman does not attempt to isolate, control, and systematically vary the variables. Chance factors will play a major role in his evaluation of an issue.

(d)   The scientist and layman both look for relationships between variables but the latter will tend to seize on fortuitous occurrences of two phenomena and link them indissolubly as cause and effect. For instance 'Slum environments cause delinquency'.

(e)   Psychologists cannot study propositions that cannot be tested. Science is concerned with things that can be publicly observed and tested. Metaphysical statements cannot, e.g. 'People are poor and starving because God wills it'. All scientific theories must be testable. As Popper (1963) argues, 'a theory which is not refutable by any conceivable event is non-scientific . . . . Every genuine test of a theory is an attempt to falsify it or refute it' (p. 36).

Scientific method does not differ from everyday observation in being infallible, though it is much less so. Rather it differs from everyday observation in that the scientist uncovers his previous errors and corrects them. Indeed the history of psychology has been the development of procedures and instruments that have enabled such corrections to be made. Without the application of a scientific approach to psychology, no valid or reliable results are possible, and the subject cannot develop. We are left at the layman's commonsense level. So the purpose of this book is to provide sufficient basic knowledge and practical skills to enable initiates in the subject in due course to carry out their own controlled investigations.

STQ *Summarize the main characteristics of the scientific approach. How does this approach differ from a commonsense approach?*

Induction and deduction
Science involves both data (observations) and theory (explanations). However, in actual methods of science these form a chicken and egg relationship. Scientists differ about which comes first. Some scientists prefer to start with gathering data; when enough have been obtained patterns of explanation or theory is feasible. There are so many events that are of interest to psychologists that they have to be pulled together in clusters to form manageable sets of generalizations which act as theories. This sequence from individual facts to generalization is termed induction. There is a vital weakness in this inductive method. The flaw is the impossibility of unbiased observation of the basic events/facts. Each observer perceives and interprets what he sees in subtly different ways from any other observer, with past experience, expectation, and personality all influencing the construing of the event.

The reverse approach of starting with theory and working down to data is the deductive approach. The deductive scientist believes that you do not know what data to collect without the guiding framework of some theory, however tentative. The analysis of the data will then allow refinement and modification of the theory to take place. The deductive scientist deduces what should occur in a particular circumstance. The inductive and deductive approaches are only different ways of approaching the same goal and are not as clearly demarcated as the division would suggest. Most psychologists act like an inductive scientist one minute and like a deductive one the next. Skinner's work on reinforcement and learning is an inductive approach commencing with a database which was then employed in constructing theoretical principles. Festinger's theory of cognitive dissonance is a deductive theory.

> **STQ** *Briefly explain the difference between induction and deduction.*

Theory is a statement which explains a variety of occurrences. The more occurrences covered the better the theory, i.e. it is parsimonious. If a theory only explained one occurrence it would a very weak theory. Gravity is a very powerful theory because it explains falling apples, tides, rotation of the earth round the sun etc. Theory is a kind of filing system into which new data can be fitted though sometimes the new data require a new file or a slight change in the order and classifying of the files. As well as organization, prediction is possible by consulting the content of the theory.

A theory can never be proved, only disproved. Data that are partially consistent with it causes the theory to be modified. Data that are consistent with the theory solely lend it support; it postpones the day of its rejection! It follows then that a theory must be testable. If it cannot be tested it can never be disproved. Belief in a theory increases as it survives more and more tests designed to disprove it. But since it is logically possible that some test not yet tried might conceivably find a flaw in the theory, our belief in a theory can never be absolute. Freud's psychoanalytical theories are poor because they cannot be tested or falsified. His concepts are not clearly defined nor can they be operationally defined to allow his hypotheses about human nature to be subjected to scientific scrutiny.

Psychology and the scientific method
Psychologists go about their business much like any other scientists, attempting to establish relationships between circumstances and behaviour and to fit these relationships into an orderly body of knowledge. But some students find it hard to consider psychology a science in the same sense as chemistry and biology. Many humanist psychologists feel the same in that there are aspects of human experience that defy quantification, verbal expression, objectivity and operational definition. How can subjective feelings by a Constable landscape, the imminence of death, job promotion or first romantic

experience be subjected to cold, dispassionate, objective scientific analysis? In any case it can be argued that most data in psychology come not from inert matter as in physics and chemistry but from humans who can think and evaluate.

Most early psychology was based on introspection, i.e. 'looking inside oneself' and describing one's feelings, perceptions etc. This is not a suitable path to valid and reliable psychological knowledge since introspection does not provide public evidence nor can one person infer from his own introspections what others presumably feel and perceive. Even when two people agree to describe a certain perceived event in a particular way there is no proof that there is an exact matching of the subjective perceptions of the two. Introspection, i.e. verbal report, does have a place in psychological investigations but it should be reserved for contexts in which it can be validated by contemporary or subsequent behaviour.

As human behaviour is the major concern of psychologists we run into the problem not faced by physical scientists, that of human variability. A physicist interested in the coefficient of friction for an iron block might measure the time it took to slide down an inclined plane. While the times might vary from trial to trial the variability would be extremely slight. Our physicist would not be making too great an assumption to consider the variability a minor nuisance and eliminate it by taking the average of several trials. On the other hand his psychologist colleague who wants to measure the time it takes a person to press a button in response to a tone would be making a considerably greater error in ignoring human variability. Although it is not likely that the physicist's block was slightly slower on some trials because it wasn't ready, had its mind on other things, was sneezing or was tired, or was slightly faster on others because it had had some practice or wanted to be as cooperative as possible, it is certainly possible for a human subject to react in these and many other ways in an experimental investigation.

As well as variability within the same subject over time, there is variability between subjects too. The physicist can easily construct another iron block of exactly the same shape, size, surface finish and weight as the original, repeat the experiment and replicate his results. No psychologist can recreate an exact replica of another person. Only identical twins have the same genetic material but even these are influenced in subtly different ways by an individually perceived and appraised environment. So there is considerable variation in performance on the same task between individuals. This variability can be tackled in two ways as you will see; firstly by statistical techniques and secondly by controlling it through appropriate research designs.

Psychologists know only too well that subjects may lie, employ defence mechanisms, lack self-insight, give socially approved answers, and try to meet the perceived expectancies of the experimenter etc. However, when a person says something about himself he has the right to be believed. Validation of what a person says is effected by observing what he does but the very act of observing him will alter his behaviour in unknown ways. The fact that a subject lies or provides socially approved answers is a valid psychological piece of behaviour worthy of investigation in any case.

These human restrictions do not imply that the scientific approach to studying human behaviour should be abandoned. Within the limits imposed by having human subjects, psychologists do apply the basic attributes of scientific method so that their findings are as objective, reliable, replicable and quantifiable as possible, employing the hypo-thetico-deductive approach and controlling extraneous variables and systematically manipulating, under defined conditions, the independent variable in question. Even the hardboiled sciences are not totally objective since subjectivity is involved in the very choice of a problem as worthy of investigation and in the discussion of results.

Psychology research is a systematic, controlled, empirical and critical investigation of hypothetical propositions about presumed relations among behavioural phenomena. The basic aim is to discover general explanations (or theories) of behaviour. Explanation, understanding, prediction and control are all involved in theory building.

The approach starts with the psychologist having vague doubts about a relationship between phenomena. He tries to formulate his ideas by reading the literature. This enables a hypothesis to be constructed which is testable. On the basis of the evidence the hypothesis is accepted or rejected. This information is then fed back to the original problem which is then altered as need be. So 6 steps seem inexorably involved in this scientific method:

(1) Identify and survey the problem,
(2) Formulate a hypothesis,
(3) Design the experiment,
(4) Test the hypothesis,
(5) Communicate the results,
(6) Revise the theory (if necessary).

Summary
Scientific method is concerned with techniques for resolving problems. The scientific method has advantages over subjective, intuitive belief in that it relies on systematic observation and is self correcting.

Both inductive and deductive methods are employed, often in a hybrid form, to relate data and theory together. Theory acts as a framework for the organization of data.

Further STQs

(1) *Examine some recent newspapers and select two claims that are not accompanied by supporting evidence. Indicate briefly how support might be obtained.*

(2) *How does the scientific approach differ from the common-sense approach to problem saving?*

(3) *Why are only testable ideas of worth in science?*

(4) *What problems does the psychologist face in attempting to study human behaviour in a scientific way?*

(5) *Do you consider that psychology is a science?*

REFERENCES

Marx, M. and Hillix, W.A. (1973). *Systems and Theories in Psychology.* (New York: McGraw-Hill)

Popper, K. (1957). *The Poverty of Historicism.* (London: Routledge)

Popper, K. (1963). *Conjectures and Refutations.* (London: Routledge and Kegan Paul)

2

Descriptive statistics

Get your psychology class together or go into the coffee bar or wherever some co-operative friends may be found and obtain several sets of data from each person, say shoe size, height, distance they live from college etc.

So now you have some interesting data (possibly even an address or two!). But what can we do with it? Look at all the data you have just obtained on one of these aspects, say distance from college. You may have approached twenty different people and now have twenty pieces of information about distance; additionally another twenty pieces on shoe size, another twenty on height.

We cannot possibly remember each one. Nor do we really want to perform such a feat of memory. We really could do with some way of summarizing the data so that we can describe its essential attributes, and compare it to other similarly derived data.

A Measures of central tendency
1 MEAN (AVERAGE)
We all know that in life's experiences, both objects and people tend to display similar types of behaviour. Where this behaviour is measurable, most of the measurements will cluster round a central point known as the 'measure of central tendency', of which the average is one example. A few scores will, of course, move away (deviate) from the average, above it or below it. It should be noted that the arithmetical average is representative of a set or a group, and as such can be used to summarize the data and to compare it with other similar sets or groups. It must be emphasized that the items which are to be averaged must be of the same kind, otherwise the average will give a misleading impression.

The word 'average' is derived from the Latin word 'havaria', which was an ancient insurance term. When early cargo ships had to throw overboard some of their cargo to lighten their vessels in heavy storms, the owners of the remaining cargo each paid an agreed amount of compensation (havaria) to those merchants who had sacrificed their goods to save the entire cargo. Thus, there is the notion of 'common property' associated with an average which is the product of contributions made by all the objects or people in a set.

Let us now turn to three examples.

Example A. A teacher marked a set of ten test papers in geography and found the following percentages:

55   59   61   57   56   60   62   58   60   59

Example B. The school nurse arrived to measure the height of a group of twenty-five pupils. These were her recordings:

4′ 0″   4′ 11″   4′ 2″   4′ 9″   4′ 8″   4′ 8″   4′ 2″   4′ 7″   4′ 5″   4′ 6″
4′ 6″   4′ 7″   4′ 2″   4′ 2″   4′ 3″   4′ 1″   4′ 0″   4′ 9″   4′ 9″   4′ 5″
4′ 7″   4′ 8″   4′ 6″   4′ 3″   4′ 5″

Example C. An assistant in a shoe shop takes stock of men's shoes made by a certain manufacturer. She has ten boxes and the sizes are:

8   8   7   6   9   8   8   8   7   8

Each set of data in the three examples consists of items of the same genus, and if we add together all the values in each set and divide by the total number of values, we will obtain the arithmetical averages. To arrive at these averages we use the formula:

$$M = \frac{\Sigma X}{N}$$

where M is the shorthand sign for average, Σ means sum of, X refers to the individual items, and N the number of items, scores or people in the sample.

STQ   *Use the formula $M = \Sigma X/N$ and calculate the means of Examples A, B and C above.*

We found them to be 58.7, 4′ 5″ and 7.7 respectively.

The word average which we have employed so frequently above is, however, a generic term. That is, it is a term used to embrace other measures of central tendency, and as statisticians we have to be more precise in our terminology. What we have looked at so far is the *mean,* which is itself divided into three types. The first type is the arithmetic mean (described above as the average), and the two others which need not concern us further are the geometric mean and the harmonic mean. The word 'mean' simply indicates 'centre'.

Sometimes we will find scores arranged in a frequency distribution where each X value may occur more than once. In this situation each value of X must be multiplied by its frequency. Then these fX products are summed to give ΣfX which is divided by the total number of scores. Here is an example:

X	f	fX
10	3	30
9	2	18
8	4	32
7	4	28
6	3	18
5	4	20
4	4	16
3	2	6
2	3	6
	$N = 29$	$fX = 174$

$$M = \frac{\Sigma fX}{N}$$

$$= \frac{174}{29}$$

$$= 6$$

Remember that with frequency distributions $N = \Sigma f$ and *not* ΣX.

Unfortunately, there are a number of occasions when the mean is not the most appropriate statistic to use. Look again at Example A (p. 15). Suppose that the first percentage were not 55 but 98.

STQ *Using the formula given earlier for calculating the mean, find the mean of Example A set of data which now reads:*

---

98   59   61   57   56   60   62   58   60   59

Do you agree that the mean is now 63?

STQ *Look at this mean of 63 in relation to the data and comment on what you notice.*

Hopefully you realized that the mean was larger than any of the other scores save the extreme score.

This example of having one number much greater in value than the other numbers presents a real problem, for it renders the mean untypical, unrealistic and unrepresentative. This problem will become more apparent in the case of the heights in Example B if we suppose that the children whose heights were 4′ 0″ were really 5′ 10″.

STQ *What would be the mean height this time? Is it realistic? It may be mathematically correct but it provides no summary of typical items in the distribution.*

This problem is again highlighted in the following set of values:

$$12 \quad 10 \quad 14 \quad 12 \quad 12 \quad 10 \quad 12 \quad 14$$

The mean is 12 and it is clearly both realistic and representative. We could have a mean of 12 which did not truly represent the items in the set. For example:

$$2 \quad 4 \quad 20 \quad 18 \quad 20 \quad 8$$

If you consider the next example, you will note that the mean is still 12, but it tends to mask the extreme score:

$$4 \quad 4 \quad 8 \quad 10 \quad 10 \quad 36$$

2 MEDIAN

While these examples have been exaggerated in order to be illustrative, they do point to the fact that in any given number of scores, there may be vast differences between the largest and smallest numbers, or the scores may cluster towards one extreme. How, then, do we cope with the unrepresentative mean? This is where the second of our measures of central tendency, the median comes to the rescue.

The word 'median' means 'middle item'. Thus, when we have a series of scores which contains an extreme value or values, it would be sensible to arrange them in rank order so that the highest value is at the top of the list, and the remaining scores are placed in descending order of magnitude with the score of least value at the bottom of the list. The median value will be the central value and where there is an odd number of scores, the central value will be a whole number.

For example, if we have a series of nine scores, there will be four scores above the median and four below. This is illustrated as follows:

$$16 \quad 6 \quad 11 \quad 24 \quad 17 \quad 4 \quad 19 \quad 9 \quad 20$$

Arranged in order of magnitude these scores become:

$$
\begin{array}{l}
24 \\
20 \\
19 \\
17 \\
\underline{16} \quad - \quad \text{median value} \\
\overline{11} \\
9 \\
6 \\
4
\end{array}
$$

STQ *Had we inappropriately used the mean in this instance rather than the median, what would the error difference have been?*

In our example we had a set of odd numbers which made the calculation of the median easy. Suppose, however, we had been faced with an even set of numbers. This time there would not be *a* central value, but a *pair* of central values. No real difficulty is presented here, for the median is to be found half way between these two values.

Let us put the following numbers in rank order and find the median score:

$$16 \quad 29 \quad 20 \quad 9 \quad 34 \quad 10 \quad 23 \quad 12 \quad 15 \quad 22$$

In rank order these numbers appear as follows:

$$
\begin{array}{l}
34 \\
29 \\
23 \\
22 \\
\left.\begin{array}{l} 20 \\ \overline{16} \end{array}\right\} \text{median} \quad = \dfrac{20 \ + \ 16}{2} = 18 \\
15 \\
12 \\
10 \\
9
\end{array}
$$

3 MODE

The third measure of central tendency is the *mode* or modal score, which is the most frequently occurring value in a set of scores. It is a typical result, a common or fashionable one (*a la mode*), but not necessarily a mathematically sophisticated one. The mode in the following example is 24, since four people obtained that score on a test:

23   28   20   (24)   9   (24)   (24)   21   18   19   (24)

The mode lacks the precision of the other two measures and can be misleading. For example, the *frequency* of a score does not necessarily imply a *majority*. It may well be (as in our example) that the majority is made up from the other score frequencies. This will be clearly seen if we space our data as follows and sum each set of scores:

23	28	20		9			21	18	19		=	138
			24		24	24				24	=	96

4 COMPARISON OF MEAN, MEDIAN AND MODE

The choice between the mean and the median as a measure of central tendency depends very much on the shape of the distribution. The median as was shown earlier is not affected by 'extreme' values as it only takes into account the *rank order* of observations. The mean on the other hand *is* affected by extremely large or small values as it specifically takes the *values* of the observations into account, not just their rank order. Thus in (a) below the mean equals the median. But in (b), which is the same distribution except for one extremely large value, the median remains but the mean increases substantially to 20:

(a)   2   4   6   8   10   M = 6   Median = 6
(b)   2   4   6   8   80   M = 20   Median = 6

If a distribution has a few 'extreme' scores, then these can exert a disproportionate effect on the mean; and if you are looking for a simple statistic representing a typical value in order to describe or summarize a distribution, then the mean can be a quite inappropriate measure. In (b) above it is a little difficult to consider M = 20 as being 'typical' of the distribution. In general, if a distribution is substantially skewed, that is, when the bulk of observations are clustered together but a few have much higher or much lower values, then the median is usually preferred to the mean.

As a descriptive statistic, a distribution is said to be '*symmetrical*' if mean, median and mode coincide and the shape of the distribution is identical on both sides of the central value. An idealized form of symmetrical distribution is shown in Figure 1(a). If a distribution has a few very large values it is said to be *positively skewed*. The idealized form is shown in Figure 1(b); this kind of distribution has a tail extending to the right with the mean greater than the median which is greater than the mode. If a distribution has a few very small values it is said to be *negatively skewed*; it has a tail extending to the left as in Figure 1(c) and the mean is less than the median which is less than the mode.

Thus, the mean is affected much more by skewness than is the median, and for skewed distributions the median is preferred. Distributions of income or earnings are usually positively skewed and the median is used to summarize and compare such distributions. However, there are many situations in the social sciences where the data are symmetrically distributed or only moderately skewed and then the mean can be used.

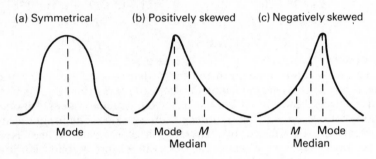

Figure 1 The relationship of the mode, median and mean (*M*)

It is always best from an analytic viewpoint to use the mean wherever possible. The reasons for this will become clear in later chapters, but very briefly they are, first, that many of the summary measures used in descriptive statistics can be and are used in more complex analyses. The development of all these more complex methods relies on mathematical analysis and the mean which is calculated arithmetically is mathematically much easier to manipulate than the median which is found by ordering. Secondly, much of the data used in research derives from samples and from *sampling procedures*. Any sampling procedure leads to '*sampling errors*' for a particular statistic, i.e. we can only estimate the mean or median income or age in a given population within certain *limits of error*. *Sampling theory* shows that this error or '*uncertainty*' is less for the mean than for the median. Thus for most purposes we find that the mean is used in preference to the median, except when the distributions are substantially skewed.

STQ   *Why should M be used rather than the median or mode?*

Generally speaking, the mean should be used where possible because it is the most accurate of the three measures of central tendency. Moreover, in statistics it is generally the mean which is required for further computations, such as those described elsewhere in this book.

B Measures of variability or dispersion

We have looked carefully at three measures of central tendency, or three ways in which numerical data tend to cluster around a central point. Averages or measures of central tendency are a useful way of describing one characteristic of a frequency distribution. But reducing a large set of data to one statistic can lead to a serious loss of information. Consider the three distributions below. Both mean and median are equal for each distribution, i.e. = 10, but a second characteristic differs quite markedly in each:

(a)   8   9   10   11   12
(b) 10   10   10   10   10
(c)   1   5   10   15   19

STQ   *What other characteristic besides central tendency would seem necessary to describe it?*

It is the *variability* of scores around the mean that is required, and we need to know how to measure this variability. This provides another way of summarizing and comparing different sets of data. The notion of variability lies at the heart of the study of individual and group differences. It is the variability of individuals that forms the focus of research. We need some way to describe it. It has by now even with brief acquaintance become obvious to you that we can actually calculate a mean, median and mode for a set of scores even if they have variability or not. If all subjects in a test receive the same score, i.e. no variability, then the mean, median and mode will all be the same, and the same as this score. On the other hand, if there is considerable variation our three measures of central tendency provide us with no indication of its extent. But what they can do is provide us with reference points against which variability can be assessed.

1 RANGE

One method of considering variability is to calculate the *range* between the lowest and the highest scores. In our example the lowest mark might have been 30 and the highest 80, in which case the range would be 80 − 30 = 50. This is not a very good method, however, since the range is considerably influenced by extreme scores. If the candidates in our geography test had included a very weak student and a very bright one, whose marks were 20 and 95 respectively, the range would have been 75. Another method must be found to determine the variability or dispersion of scores.

2 SEMI-INTERQUARTILE RANGE

The semi-interquartile range is helpful here. The scores are set down in order of size and divided into four equal groups. The point which separates the lowest 25% of the scores from the rest is called the lower or first quartile (Q1). The point above which the highest 25% of the scores occur is the upper or third quartile (Q3). A line representing the median will be the second quartile (Q2) – i.e. 50% of the scores will be above, and 50% below, Q2. The interquartile range is obtained by finding the difference between Q3 and Q1; half of this result is termed the semi-interquartile range. A simple example may help to clarify the procedure.

Suppose we have twenty scores. The median (Q2) will occur between the tenth and eleventh scores (i.e. 50% of scores above and 50%

Table 1   The determination of Q3, Q1 and Q for a distribution of scores

Scores	No. of cases (f)	Procedure
50–54	1	1. Find ¼ of the cases ($N/4 = 48/4 = 12$)
45–49	1	2. To find Q1, count from the bottom to
40–44	4	include twelve cases.
34.5 ← 35–39	5	
30–34	3 ←Q3 in	(a) the first-class interval $= 2$ ⎫
25–29	7 this	(b) the second-class interval $= 8$ ⎬ 10
20–24	8 interval	(c) we still need two more to make up
14.5 ← 15–19	9 ←Q1 in	our twelve, so we take two from the
10–14	8 this	third-class interval (i.e. nine cases)
5–9	2 interval	(d) apply the formula:

3. To find Q3, count from the top to include twelve cases.

$$Q1 = 14.5 + \frac{2}{9} \times 5 = 14.5 + 1.1 = 15.6$$

(a) the first-class interval $= 1$ ⎫
(b) the second-class interval $= 1$ ⎪
(c) the third-class interval $= 4$ ⎬ 11
(d) the fourth-class interval $= 5$ ⎭
(e) we still need one more to make up our twelve, so we take one from the fifth-class interval (i.e. three cases).
(f) apply the formula:

$$Q3 = 34.5 - \frac{1}{3} \times 5 = 34.5 - 1.7 = 32.8$$

4. To find the semi-interquartile range (Q), apply the formula:

$$Q = \frac{Q3 - Q1}{2} = \frac{32.8 - 15.6}{2} = 17.2$$

below). The first or lower quartile (Q1) will be found between the fifth and sixth scores, and the third or upper quartile (Q3) will fall between the fifteenth and sixteenth scores. The interquartile range is given by Q3−Q1, and the semi-interquartile range (Q) is half of this, Q3 − Q1 ÷ 2. This may be seen more clearly visualized by referring to Figure 2.

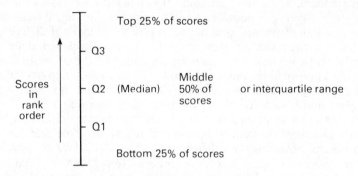

Figure 2 Note that a quartile is a point on a scale, therefore we can say that a person is *at* a certain *quartile,* but not *in a quartile,* though he may be *in* a *quarter*

The example shown in Table 1 will demonstrate by stages how to determine Q3, Q1 and Q for a frequency distribution of scores.

3 MEAN DEVIATION

An alternative way of looking at the variation in a data set is to compare each value in a distribution with the mean. The larger the differences between the values and the mean are on average, the greater is the variation. Thus both the distributions (a) and (b) below have a mean of 10. If we calculate $(X - M)$ for each distribution then the differences are generally larger in (b) than in (a); the largest difference in (a) is between 6 and 10, or between 14 and 10, i.e. − 4 or + 4 whilst the largest difference in (b) is between 2 and 10 or between 10 and 18, i.e. − 8 or + 8.

	Values (X)				Mean	Differences $(X - M)$				
(a)	6	10	10	10	14	$M = 10$	−4	0	0	0	+4
(b)	2	5	10	15	18	$M = 10$	−8	−5	0	+5	+8

The idea of difference or deviation from the mean is fundamental to the measure of variation called the 'variance'. It might seem at first sight that a useful measure of variation would be the sum of these differences, i.e. $\Sigma(X - M)$, but some differences are positive and some are negative; they always cancel each other out and the resulting sum is always zero. Check this in the examples above.

The problem arises because of the 'sign' of the differences; some are negative and some are positive. Two methods can be used to 'get rid of' the sign: one way is simply to ignore them, the other way is to square them. The former solution – which is known as taking the 'absolute' differences – does lead to an acceptable solution. We can sum the absolute differences and divide this by the number of differences (otherwise the result may depend on the number of values and not the variation in values). This statistic, the mean of the absolute deviations, is known as the *mean deviation*. The *mean deviation* has the advantage that it takes into account all the scores and not merely the highest and lowest. To obtain the mean deviation we have to obtain the mean of a set of data first of all, and then find the difference between each item in the distribution and the mean. Note that for the purpose of obtaining these differences, all the deviations are positive, irrespective of whether a score is higher or lower than the mean.

The mathematical formula for finding the mean deviation is:

$$\bar{d} = \frac{\Sigma(X - M)}{N}$$

where $\bar{d}$ = mean deviation
Σ = the sum of
X = various values
M = mean
N = number of values

Here is an example. Find the mean and the mean deviation for the following values: 15   12   9   10   14

To find the mean, apply the formula

$$M = \frac{X}{N} = \frac{15 + 12 + 9 + 10 + 14}{5} = \frac{60}{5} = 12$$

To obtain the mean deviation, calculate the difference of each item from the mean (12) and add them together, then divide by the number of values (*N*).

$$\bar{d} = \frac{\Sigma(X - M)}{N}$$

$$15 - 12 \ + \ 12 - 12 \ + \ 9 - 12 \ + \ 10 - 12 \ + \ 14 - 12 = \frac{10}{5} = 2$$
$$3 \quad + \quad 0 \quad + \quad 3 \quad + \quad 2 \quad + \quad 2$$

mean deviation = 2

4 STANDARD DEVIATION

The mean deviation does 'work' in a practical sense in that for a distribution with no variation the mean deviation will have a value of zero, and the wider the variation in the data, the larger will be the value of the mean deviation. It is intuitively easy to understand and is a useful descriptive measure of dispersion. However, it is very rarely used simply because it leads to difficult and often intractable mathematical problems both for more complex statistical method and for drawing conclusions from samples of data taken from a larger population.

It is theoretically advantageous, and in practice much more convenient, to square the deviations from the mean, sum them and then divide the result by the number of observations. The mean of the sum of squared deviations is known as the *variance*.

$$\text{Variance} = \frac{(X-M)^2}{N}$$

The variance is an important statistical measure in itself and you will come across it later (Chapter 22). As a descriptive statistic, however, it does have the disadvantage that in squaring the differences we also square the units involved, and have a measure involving, say £^{2} or (years of age)^2. To avoid this we derive the *standard deviation* (or SD) which is simply the square root of the variance. Thus the standard deviation (SD) is:

$$\sigma = \sqrt{\frac{(X-M)^2}{N}}$$

The Greek letter σ (lower-case sigma) is used to represent the standard deviation. The SD is considered to be the most important measure of dispersion. The following procedure will produce the standard deviation for the data in the previous example (p. 24).

(a) Obtain the mean of the values ($M = 12$)
(b) Calculate the differences of the values from the mean (3; 0; 3; 2; 2)
(c) Obtain the squares of these differences (9; 0; 9; 4; 4)
(d) Find the sum of the squares of the differences (26)
(e) Divide by the number of items 26/5 = 5.2. This is the variance.
(f) Obtain the square root of the variance which is the standard deviation = 2.3.

The formula for obtaining the standard deviation is:

$$\sigma = \sqrt{\frac{(X-M)^2}{N}} \quad \text{i.e. in our example} = \sqrt{\frac{26}{5}} = 2.3$$

If we are concerned only with finding the standard deviation as a measure of dispersion of the *sample,* this formula will suffice, but if we want to gain some idea of the variability of the population from which the sample was taken, then $N-1$ should be used as the denominator for greater accuracy, thus:

$$\sigma = \sqrt{\frac{(X-M)^2}{N-1}}$$

The reason for the change from N to $N-1$ for samples is that with a small number in a sample $N-1$ will provide a better estimate of the population SD. As you will realize, as sample N gets larger and the difference between size of sample and size of population becomes much reduced the difference between dividing by N or $N-1$ becomes negligible. However, as you will see, research generally involves samples considerably smaller than the population from which it is drawn. Hence the use of $N-1$ as denominator is strongly advised. This formula works well if M is a whole number but so often it is not. That causes unwieldy computations with deviations to perhaps two decimal places then having to square such awkward numbers. Inaccuracy is often introduced here by rounding, so a formula more convenient to use is:

$$\sigma = \sqrt{\frac{\Sigma X^2 - \frac{(\Sigma X)^2}{N}}{N}}$$

where ΣX^2 is the sum of the squared raw scores and $(\Sigma X)^2$ is the sum of the raw scores squared.

This formula is mathematically equivalent to the first formula above. Let us check that we do get the same answer.

X	X^2	
15	225	$\sigma = \sqrt{\dfrac{746 - \dfrac{60^2}{5}}{5}}$
12	144	
9	81	
10	100	$\sigma = \sqrt{\dfrac{746 - 720}{5}} = \sqrt{\dfrac{26}{5}}$
14	196	
$\Sigma X = 60$	$\Sigma X^2 = 746$	$\sigma = 2.3$

This formula too must employ $N-1$ as the denominator when used with samples.

Generally the larger the σ the greater the dispersal of scores; the smaller the σ the smaller the spread of scores, i.e. increases in proportion to the spread of the scores around M as the marker point. But measures of central tendency tell us nothing about the standard deviation and vice versa. Like the mean though the standard deviation should be used with caution with highly skewed data since the squaring of an extreme score would carry a disproportionate weight. It is therefore recommended where M is also appropriate.

STQ **(1)** *Calculate M and σ for the following sample distributions*

(a)   *2   4   6   8   10*
(b)   *10   9   8   7   6   5   4   3   2*
(c)   *2   6   12   20   50*

which has the largest σ and why?

(2) *If you are told that one score in a distribution has a value of 8.0 and σ = 0 which of the following is true?*

(a)   *The M cannot be calculated.*
(b)   *All scores are identical.*
(c)   *N cannot be known.*
(d)   *The distribution is positively skewed.*

(3) *Calculate the σ of the following scores*
        8   10   11   12   12   14   16   18

(a)   *now substract 3 from each of the scores and recalculate. What has happened?*
(b)   *now multiply each original score by 2, and recalculate σ. What has happened in this case?*

(4) *Under what circumstances is the mean a poor choice as a measure of central tendency?*

(5) *When is the median likely to be the best choice of central tendency measure?*

Answers may be found on p. 431.

3

Standard scores

Sometimes we need to compare different individuals on a particular test, and there are occasions when a number of different tests are given to individuals or groups (e.g. personnel selection in the armed forces, vocational guidance, education) and comparisons are made about a person's performance on these tests on the basis of his raw scores. This is not an informed or sensible procedure, but it is one that is often erroneously applied. You may have a school report which shows that you were better at English than you were at history, judged solely on raw scores. Let us look at this more carefully.

Take, for example, a boy who obtains 60 marks in a mathematics examination, and 50 marks in an English examination (Figure 3). Is he more able in mathematics than English? At first sight he is: his mark is higher in mathematics; but since these are different subjects it may be that one teacher is an 'easier' marker than the other. Thus we need to look at how the group as a whole perform in these examinations. To do this we can take each mark (X_x) away from the mean mark (M) from the group or subject. Now, if the mean in mathematics was 40 marks and in English 60 marks, then within this group he is above average in mathematics and below average in English – which more or less answers our original question.

But, what if the mean mark in mathematics is 55 and in English 45? He is now equally above average in each subject but we cannot necessarily regard these differences of 5 marks above average as being equivalent because the variations in the marks, i.e. the standard deviations, may differ between the groups. Thus some teachers may give marks over a limited range, others over a much wider range and the latter is often the case in mathematics.

Assume then that the standard deviation of the mathematics marks for all examinees is 10 marks and that of the English marks is 5 marks; then there would be a wider spread of marks in mathematics than in English and the overall distribution of marks in the two subjects might well be as shown in Figure 3. The effect of the different spreads of

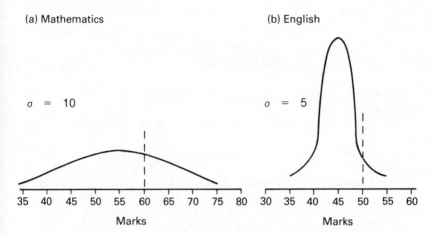

Figure 3 Distribution of marks in mathematics and English examinations

marks is that in mathematics a mark of 60 is quite close (½σ) to the mean of 55 while a mark of 50 in English is comparatively much further away from the mean of 45 (1σ).

Thus, comparing 'raw' scores can be misleading: they have to be put into context and the characteristic of the distribution from which they came must be taken into account. This is done by calculating new 'scores' from the 'raw' data.

We often have to use common scales in many other fields besides psychology. For instance temperature, length, weight etc. There are so many different scales in each, one cannot compare, say, two different temperatures each measured on a different scale and produce a meaningful comparison unless one can turn one into terms of the other or convert both to a common scale. Many of us have been brought up on °F. The only way we can understand the implication of a temperature reported in °C is to convert it into °F. To compare a length measured in yards and in the old Biblical cubits, the best way would be to convert the latter into yards or both of them into metric units. Now we hope you see the problem. It is totally erroneous in test measurement to add and average marks obtained from different distributions which have different means and SDs.

If this is done it is akin to adding °F to °C or yards to metres. Test results should only be combined when, (i) they are from a common scale or, (ii) have been converted to a common scale or, (iii) are all converted into the M and σ of one of the existing distributions. The most common standard scale in test measurement is known as the z score. Such z scores take account of both M and σ of the distribution.

The formula is:

$$z = \frac{\text{Score} - \text{Mean}}{\text{SD of distribution}} = \frac{X - M}{\sigma}$$

The mean of the z score distribution is 0 and the σ is always 1. Let us look at an example.

A student sits a school examination and is awarded marks as follows:

English, 96%; history, 69%; mathematics, 20%; geography, 10%; French, 21%;

At first sight it would appear that the student is best at English and worst at geography. He comes second in history, but performs badly in mathematics and French. Are these deductions, in fact, correct? Are we justified in making these suppositions?

The mean is some help to us in answering these questions, for if we know that the mean for geography is 16.8, then the student is below average. Similarly, while he gives the impression of being poor at mathematics, he would be well above average if the mean were 12.4.

Class positions in examinations are generally calculated on the basis of the total marks obtained in all subjects, and candidate A would be placed higher than candidate B (see Table 2) if their respective totals were 216 and 199. Again, we must question the justice of making such comparisons from raw scores. Let us look at the scores gained by two students, Candidates A and B, on five subjects in an examination; and their corresponding z scores. z Scores are obtained by dividing the deviation score $(X - M)$ by the SD:

$$z = \frac{X - M}{\sigma}$$

Table 2 Examination raw scores and z scores

Subject	Mean	σ	Raw scores		Deviations $(X-M)$		z Scores	
			Cand. A.	Cand. B.	Cand. A.	Cand. B.	Cand. A.	Cand. B.
Geography	16.8	4.1	10	27	−6.8	+10.2	−1.66	+2.49
English	75.3	13.2	96	81	+20.7	+5.7	+1.57	+0.43
French	27.3	4.6	21	36	−6.3	+8.7	−1.37	+1.90
History	43.1	12.4	69	42	+25.9	−1.1	+2.00	−0.09
Mathematics	12.4	3.4	20	13	+7.6	+0.6	+2.24	+0.18
Sums			216	199			2.78	4.91
Means			86.8	79.4			0.56	0.98

From these z scores we learn that candidate A's best subject is mathematics, which came fourth according to his raw scores. History is his second best subject, as it was thought to be from the raw scores. Initially, he was thought to be best at English, but this subject is placed third in terms of standard scores. French becomes the fourth best subject, while geography remains the weakest subject of all. Now examine for yourself the standard scores of candidate B and compare them with his raw scores.

Let us now compare the two students as to their average score. The raw-score totals indicate that candidate A is superior to candidate B because he has the advantage of 17 marks (216−199), or an average superiority of 7.4 marks (86.8−79.4). Turning to the standard scores, candidate B is, in fact, academically superior since he has a lead of 0.42 z over candidate A (0.98−0.56).

You can probably detect the source of the major disadvantage in adding and averaging raw scores from the Table 2. It lies in the size of the σ of each distribution. If you do badly in a test with a small σ it will not affect you as much as doing poorly in a test with a large σ. In raw-score terms this latter situation implies a larger loss of marks, whereas your position relative to others in the group might be very similar in both cases. The converse applies too. Doing well in a test with a large σ will be a better boost to raw-score average than a similar relative position in a test with a small σ. Tests with large σ carry more weight in the summation and averaging of raw scores than tests with small σ because there is a greater range of marks round M in the former. z Scores provide a standard unit of relative worth. + 1z Above the mean in any tests is always a position only exceeded by 16% of the population.

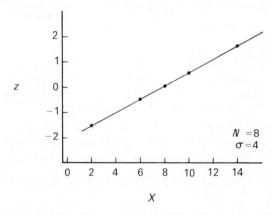

Figure 4 Linear transformation from raw scores to z scores

z Scores represent linear transformations of the original raw scores. In linear transformations the shape of the distribution of standard scores is exactly the same as that of the original scores. Futhermore, linear transformations preserve the relative distance relationships that existed in the original scores. A linear transformation is defined as a procedure in which the equation for changing from one kind of score to another can be graphed as a straight line. To illustrate a linear transformation, we have plotted a transformation in Figure 4.

In Figure 4 note that the transformation line for the *z* scores is a straight line, that is, it is a linear transformation. The graph can thus be used to get *z* scores for any *X* scores. For example, assume we want the *z* for an *X* of 14. It is only necessary to go vertically from score 14 to the transformation line and horizontally to the *z* axis in order to read the corresponding *z* score (1.5).

Because it represents a linear transformation a *z* score distribution is an interval statistic because *z* scores not only indicate the relative position of individuals but also how much better one score is than another in terms of standard deviations.

STQ **(1)** *If a student received a z score of 0, one would know that this student's raw score was_____(below, above, or equal to) the mean.*

(2) *Below are listed the scores made by five students on maths and spelling tests. The maths test had a mean of 30 and a standard deviation of 3. The spelling test had a mean of 45 and a standard deviation of 5. For each, say whether the student did better on the maths or the spelling test or did equally well on both:*

	Maths	Spelling
John	36	35
Peter	33	55
Mike	27	40
Chris	33	45
Betty	36	55

(3) *A student was told that he had made a z score of +1.5 on a test where the mean was 82 and the standard deviation was 6. What raw score did this student obtain?*

(4) *What IQs are represented by the following standard scores? (mean = 100, σ = 15)*

(a) z = 2   (b) z = −1   (c) z = 1.5   (d) z = −0.8   (e) z = 0

(5) *What z scores are represented by the following raw scores from a distribution with M = 70 and σ = 7*
(a) 84   (b) 63   (c) 73.5   (d) 52.5

(6) *If a z score has a value of 4.8 what can you say about the raw score?*

(7) *Explain why a z score from one distribution may be legitimately compared with a z score from a different distribution.*

Answers can be found on p. 431.

4

Normal distribution

So far we have considered data only in terms of its central tendency and its dispersal or scatter. If we plot the data we have obtained from any of our previous observations we would find a host of differently shaped curves when the graph lines were drawn. These graphs are often called frequency distributions. The basic characteristic of a graph is that variables are marked off along two straight lines called axes or abscissa set at right angles to each other, one horizontal, the other vertical. The horizontal axis or baseline is termed the X axis or abscissa; the vertical axis the Y axis or abscissa. The X axis supplies values of the scores with lowest values placed to the left and increasing values to the right. Every possible score should be capable of being located unambiguously somewhere along the X axis. In frequency distributions, the Y axis represents the frequency of occurrences, i.e. values of N.

As we suggested above there are many differently shaped frequency distributions. These can be classified as normal or skewed (Figures 5–7). Normal distributions, as we shall see, are symmetrical, affected only by random influences. Such influences are just as likely to make a score larger than the mean as to make it smaller and will tend to balance out, as the most frequently found scores are in the middle of the range with extreme scores becoming progressively rarer.

Take height, for instance. The distribution of human height is approximately normal. Height is determined by a whole host of variables, both inherited and acquired. Each variable may take on several values which influence height positively, i.e. promote tallness, or negatively, i.e. promote short size. If all the variables are independent of each other, then in any one individual some variables will be positive, some negative, with, on average, an approximate balance of positive and negative values. In some individuals there might be some imbalance of positive and negative values, producing above or below average height. Just occasionally nearly all the variables might have

34

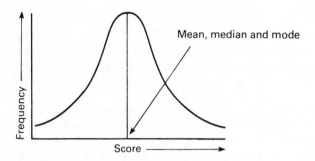

Figure 5 Normal distribution (Gaussian curve)

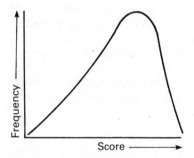

Figure 6 Negatively skewed distribution

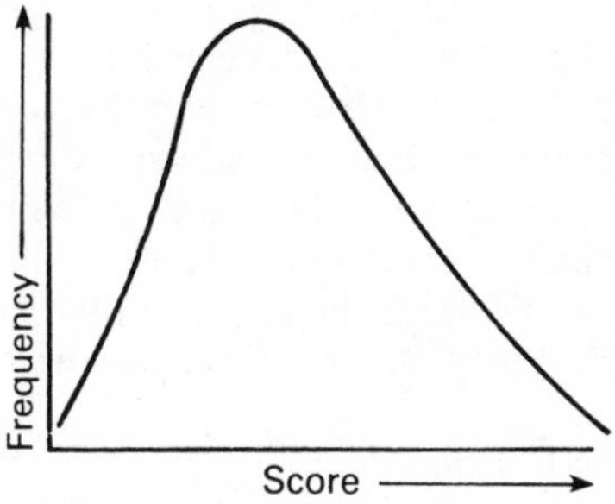

Figure 7 Positively skewed distribution

positive values and this would result in an extremely tall individual. The point to notice is that there are more ways in which the variables can combine to give mostly average values.

Skewed frequency distributions are biased by factors that tend to push scores one way more than another (Figures 6 and 7). The direction of skewedness is named after the direction in which the longer tail is pointing.

STQ *Imagine Figures 6 and 7 were the distributions of scores of two end-of-year tests; what reasons could you suggest that might have caused the skewedness in each case.*

Some of our suggestions are:

For Figure 6 an easy examination; too easy marking; students working hard; a well motivated and/or generally intelligent set
of students etc.

For Figure 7 a hard paper; severe marking; inadequate learning and
        revision; poor motivation; incompetent teaching etc.

Frequency distributions then are convenient ways of describing all
the basic information contained in the repeated measurement of any
variable. They are charts or tables showing the frequency with which
each of a number of values of a variable were observed.

More importantly, we often need to know the shape of a distribution to justify using one or another statistical technique. Many statistical
tests can be used only if the data are 'normally distributed'. A
frequency distribution can be used to decide on the normality of a
distribution. So the most important frequency distribution in our
particular context is the normal distribution or Gaussian curve (Figure
5).

The normal distribution curve is the theoretical distribution of
chance or random occurrences, and is centrally related to probability.
Let us see how probability, chance and normal distribution come
together, for an understanding of these fundamental concepts are
essential for understanding the basis of statistical significance. A consideration of coin tossing, roulette-wheel spinning and dice throwing
should whet the appetite of most of you in what is some rather fundamental theory. Coin tossing comes first!

EXERCISE

Get as many friends together as you can, e.g. the whole of the
psychology class, and ask them each to take out a coin. The coin must
be of the same monetary value for every subject but it does not matter
what value of coin you all use. Next, request all the subjects to toss
their coin so that the tossing is performed as simultaneously as possible. Make a note of how many heads and tails actually occurred. Continue this procedure of tossing the coins simultaneously and recording
the distribution of heads and tails each time, for as long as the good-
will of the group lasts. Let us hope you can obtain at least 100
simultaneous tosses from twenty or more subjects. Now plot your
results on a blank graph. The X axis needs to be labelled at the mid-
point with the theoretical equality of heads and tails possible in your
particular experiment. This is the number of subjects tossing their
coins divided by two, e.g. with 30 subjects the mid-point is labelled
15H 15T (H and T will refer in future to heads and tails respectively).
From this mid-point other points need to be labelled at equal intervals
in each direction, with H decreasing progressively in one direction and
increasing progressively in the other. Remember that each combination of H + T at each point on the X axis must equal the number of
people who participated. So at one unit on each side of the mid-point

we would write the label 16H 14T and 14H 16T respectively if 30 subjects had been used, and so on until the end points of 30H 0T and 0H 30T were labelled in our fictitious example. The *Y* axis is labelled with the frequency with which each combination of H + T occurred. These frequencies have already been printed on the axis for you. Referring to the recordings you made after each toss, count up the number of occasions (i.e. frequency) each particular combination of H + T occurred and place a small neat cross at the intersection of the frequency and the combination. When all the combination frequencies are plotted, draw a graph to join all the crosses. What sort of shape of graph have you produced? Try to explain why you have obtained that particular shape. Usually after a relatively large number of simultaneous tossings the graph produced approximates to a normal distribution curve (Figure 5). If you did not obtain an approximation to such a bell-shaped curve can you explain why? For example, bias might have entered into the experiment through the use of some irregularly worn coins, or some subjects' inability to toss a coin, or relatively few simultaneous tosses or even the deceitful use of two-headed coins!

However by now you should have grasped the point that the normal distribution curve is the distribution of chance or random occurrences. It must be noted, however, that in discussing the normal distribution curve we are dealing with a 'model'. There is not just one normal curve but a whole set of curves which meet the general criteria for normal distribution. Many of the measurements we make in psychology are often regarded as normal since the normal curve has

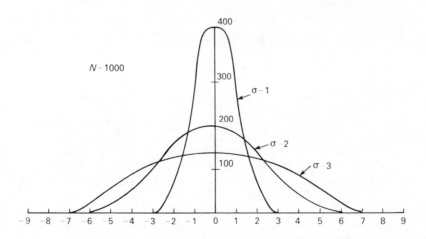

Figure 8 Normal curves based on three different sigmas

known mathematical qualities, which are of considerable value in making statistical inferences.

The shape of the normal curve is affected by the standard deviation of the distribution, i.e. the greater the spread of scores the flatter the curve. Figure 8 shows three normal curves each with the same N but different standard deviations.

The normal distribution or Gaussian curve is the distribution of an infinite number of scores each determined by an infinite range of chance happenings. You may now want to ask how on earth can we plot data on the X and Y axes when the range of each is theoretically infinite. Well, for the Y axis we work in proportions of the total area under the curve which conventionally is taken as 1.00. For the X axis we employ z scores which have a mean of 0 and a standard deviation of 1. This prevents the distribution of scores from getting unmanageable. The number of standard deviations a case is above or below the mean is called the z score of that case.

Normal distribution curves possess some notable characteristics which are always present, otherwise normality would not exist. Figure 9 depicts these constants.

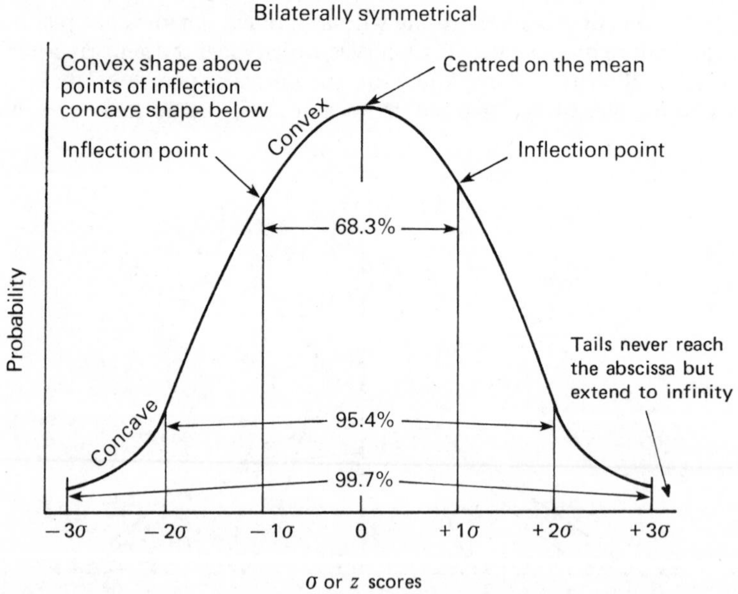

Figure 9 The shape and important characteristics of the normal, or Gaussian, distribution

The following points should be carefully noted:
(a) The distribution is bilaterally symmetrical and bell shaped.

(b) The mean, median and mode all coincide; this is the only situation where this congruence occurs.

(c) The tails of the curve never quite reach the X axis but continue outwards to infinity yet simultaneously get progressively and infinitely closer to the axis.

(d) In practical terms the range of the distribution is 6 standard deviation units, i.e. 3 σ (or $3z$) on each side of the mean. The proportion of cases beyond $\pm 3\sigma$ is so small that it is common practice to use $\pm 3\sigma$ as arbitrary limits in illustrative diagrams.

(e) The distribution has been so thoroughly studied that the proportion of the area under the curve that lies between the central (mean) value and any z score is known; tables (usually entitled 'Areas under the normal curve') have been drawn up (Table A in Appendix 1) giving these proportions, which have tremendously important applications. There are three such proportions of area that you should come to know well. These are:

between $+1\sigma$ and -1σ from the mean $=$
    68% approximately of the area under the curve
between $+2\sigma$ and -2σ from the mean $=$
    95% approximately of the area under the curve
between $+3\sigma$ and -3σ from the mean $=$
    99% approximately of the area under the curve

(f) Since the area under the curve represents the total number of cases plotted then the particular percentages quoted above can be translated into the percentage of cases lying within the designated areas, and then into the number of cases if the total number is known.

Table A (Appendix A) is a very important one as it enables research workers to determine the area within any designated segment of the normal distribution curve, and by implication therefore, if we know the total number of cases plotted we can also determine the number of cases within that segment.

Turn to Table A (Appendix A) now. It shows for each z score (column 1) the proportion of the area that, (i) lies between 0 and z (column 2) and, (ii) lies beyond z (column 3). These areas are shaded in the diagrams heading the respective columns. Since the normal distribution is symmetrical the proportions for $-z$ are exactly the same and if the area one is interested in extends on both sides of M (or 0) then it is necessary to add the two relevant areas together. Here are some examples for you to follow.

(i) What proportion of the total area lies between 0 and $+1.5\sigma$? To find the answer look up 1.5σ in the z column. Then look across to the next column (column 2) which is headed with the shading between 0 and z. The answer is 43.32% (since the figures are given as proportions of 1).

(ii) What proportion of the total area lies beyond -2.30σ? Look up $2.3z$ (forget the negative sign). Refer to column 3 headed by shading beyond z. The answer is 1.07%.

(iii) If one of the z scores is positive and the other is negative we find the proportion of the curve between them by adding values from column 2 in Table A. What proportion of the curve lies between σ of -1.6 and σ of $+0.5$? Column 2 indicates that the proportion between $z = -1.6$ and the mean is 0.4452, and from the mean to $z = +0.5$ is 0.1915. Therefore, the proportion between $z = -1.6$ and $z = +0.5$ is $0.4452 + 0.1915$, or 0.6367. This means that 63.67% of the cases in a normal distribution will fall between these z scores (Figure 10).

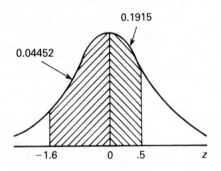

Figure 10 Area under curve for example (iii)

(iv) When we want the proportion of the normal curve falling between two z scores with the same sign we subtract the area for the smaller z score from the area for the larger z score. For example, let us find the proportion of cases between a z of -0.68 and a z of -0.98 in a normal distribution. Column 2 in Table A indicates that the area between the mean and a z of 0.98 is 0.3365, while the area between the mean and a z of 0.68 is 0.2517. Thus, the area between $z = 0.68$ and $z = 0.98$ is found by subtracting the area for the smaller z score from the area for the larger z score; in this case, $0.3365 - 0.2517 = 0.0848$. We would expect 8.48% of the cases in a normal distribution to fall between these z score points (Figure 11).

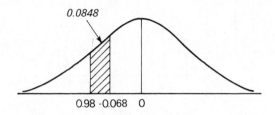

Figure 11 Area under curve for example (iv)

(v) If we have plotted the heights of a random sample of the population involving 10 000 persons how many lie between -1.00σ and $+1.00\sigma$? Using the table we note that 34.13% of the area lies between 0 and $+1\sigma$, thus 68.26% of the area is involved so 68.26% of the cases must be included, i.e. 6826 persons.

STQ *Try these on your own. The answers are on page 432. But don't look yet!*

   (i) What proportion of the total area lies between 0 and $+2.6\sigma$?

  (ii) What proportion of the total area lies beyond -1.8σ?

 (iii) What proportion of the total area lies between -1.96σ and $+1.96\sigma$?

 (iv) With a normal distribution involving 20 000 cases how many lie beyond $+2.65\sigma$?

  (v) Can you explain in simple terms why the median and mode coincide with the mean?

 (vi) Now check the approximate percentages given for areas between $\pm 1\sigma$ $\pm 2\sigma$ and $\pm 3\sigma$ on page 404 by referring to Table A Appendix A.

If we know the σ of any normal distribution we can assign scores along the X axis corresponding to the z scores we have been using so far. For example Figure 12 depicts a normal distribution with a mean of 50 and a standard deviation of 10.

As you see, for every unit of z the score increases or decreases by 10 marks, i.e. $+1z$ is 10 marks higher than M since we regard the z as a standard deviation unit. If the $\sigma = 15$ then each z unit is 15, and a

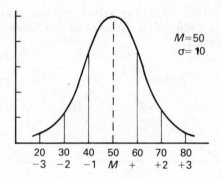

Figure 12

point $+2z$ on a normal distribution with $M = 70$ would be 100, i.e. (2 × 15) + 70. Each full z unit is equivalent to the size of the standard deviation.

STQ (1) *Given the following data, determine the raw scores at each of the z scores*

(a) *M =   30 σ =   6: z of −2, +1.5, −0.5.*
(b) *M = 110 σ = 20: z of +0.5, −3, +1.2.*

(2) *With a M = 100, N = 10 000 and σ = 15, how many of the random sample will score:*

(a) *between 100 and 130,*
(b) *over 130,*
(c) *below 80.*

(3) *A set of scores is normally distributed with M = 100 and σ = 15, what percentage of scores lie*

(a) *between M and −1σ*
(b) *between M and ±2σ*
(c) *between −1.5σ and +0.8σ*

(4) *Using the same distribution as in 1(b) above and knowing that 10 000 scores are plotted, how many subjects scored*

(a) *between ±3σ*
(b) *between M and +1σ*
(c) *above +3σ*
(d) *over a score of 115*
(e) *below 85.*

(5) *Find the proportion of the area under the normal curve between the mean and the following z scores:*

(a) −2.10
(b) +0.45
(c) +1.33
(d) −1.95
(e) −0.28
(f) −2.56
(g) +1.05

(6) *Given a score located 1.65 standard deviations above the mean in a normal distribution, determine the following:*

(a) *area between the mean and the score*
(b) *total area to the left of the score*
(c) *total area to the right of the score*

(7) *Given a score located −1.90 standard deviations units below the mean in a normal distribution, determine the following:*

(a) *area between the mean and the score*
(b) *total area to the left of the score*
(c) *total area to the right of the score*

(8) *On a classroom test, the mean was found to be 62 and the standard deviation 5. The teacher gave the top 10% of the group an A. What was the minimum score needed to get an A? Assume a normal distribution.*

(9) *If the bottom 5% received a failing grade on the above test, what was the highest failing score?*

(10) *A teacher wishes to identify the middle 50% of a group on a test where the distribution is known to be normal.*

(a) *What z score range would include the middle 50%?*
(b) *If the mean is 60 and the standard deviation 9, what raw scores would set off the middle 50%?*

(11) *If the mean, median and mode of a distribution are known to be of the same value, what type of distribution are we likely to be dealing with?*

The answers are on page 432.

5

Probability and significance

In considering the normal distribution curve, we have seen that chance or randomness is the basis of the distribution of possible outcomes. We saw in coin tossing too that some combinations of H and T occurred fairly often but other combinations were less frequent, the frequency decreasing with the increasing discrepancy between the most likely split (50%/50% or in probability terms 0.5 H/0.5 T) and the obtained split. Most frequent combinations tended to be close to the 50%H/50%T split; infrequent combinations were those with a low percentage of either H or T. It is this gradual decrease in frequency of occurrences from the middle outwards in both directions that gives the normal distribution its characteristic shape.

What we did not attempt to do in the last chapter was to place probability figures on any of the H/T combinations. That is, what were the chances of any particular combination occurring on any particular toss? A visual inspection of a normal distribution curve subjectively provides an impression of decreasing probability from the mean outwards and you perhaps noticed this phenomenon during the recording of that plethora of coin tossings you performed. However, we need to be able to place some probability value on each possible outcome, as it is through this means that we are then able to assess whether an experimental result is at such a level of probability that it is only one of many outcomes regularly to be expected by chance, or whether the improbability of gaining such a result by chance renders us capable of saying 'yes, this is so rare that it is likely to have been produced by what we have done in the experiment.'

How can we work out the probability of an outcome? Let us return to coin tossing then. I will take a coin from my pocket and I shall toss it to decide who will buy the beer if you and I meet up at university. Heads you pay, tails I pay!

H   Heads!   Hards lines, better luck with the second drink!
H   Heads!   Bad luck, like to try again for the third pint?

H   Heads!   Well you've got to win some time.
H   Heads again!   Well, well!

Now let us assume that you started off believing in the fairness of the coin. At what point in such an unbroken series of heads would you suspect me of cheating? In Table 3, put a ring around the toss at which you became convinced of 'foul play'.

Table 3

Toss	1st	2nd	3rd	4th	5th	6th	7th	8th	9th	10th
	H	H	H	H	H	H	H	H	H	H

Probability can best be defined as the likelihood of something happening. Probability is usually given the symbol p and can be thought of as the percentage of occurrence of a particular event to be expected in the long run. For example, a fair dice will produce in the long run a 5 on 1/6 or 16.66% of all rolls because each of the six sides are equally likely to come up on each roll, i.e. $p = 0.16$.

> **STQ** *A roulette wheel has 36 numbers on it. On average how many times would we expect any number to occur in 360 spins? In 36 spins?*

In the first case you should have answered ten, and in the second case the answer is one. On average over a large number of spins we might expect each number to occur one time in every 36 spins. This fact is reflected in the odds a casino gives the gambler against the bet on a number. If the gambler bets on a number which wins he receives 35 times the size of his bet. In other words the casino knows that the odds against the number coming up by chance are 35 to 1. The probability of any number's occurrence in any one spin is 1/36 or 0.028.

There is a second likelihood, that of a thing not occurring. This is q; $p + q$ must equal 100%, because a thing does or does not happen. It is more usual to express p in decimal form, i.e. 1.00 rather than 100%, and 0.50 rather than 50%.

So probability can be given a numerical value ranging from 1 to 0. The probability value of 1 means absolute certainty of an event or outcome as when we predict heads when tossing a double headed coin. The probability value of 0 implies the absolute impossibility of an event such as obtaining tails on tossing a double headed coin. Most events of course are more or less probable, less than certain, but more than impossible, and hence have a value less than 1 but greater than 0. You have an intuitive idea of the probability of obtaining a particular run of heads by chance alone. When the probability is fairly high you are willing to believe that chance alone accounts for the results. When it is low you are inclined to believe that some other fact is operating to affect the results. It is possible if not probable that we can get a very long run of heads by chance alone, we argue, but at some point we have to draw the line and start to believe in foul play rather than chance. At what point did you definitely believe the coin to be biased? What is the probability of getting such a run of heads by chance alone? In Table 4 the actual probabilities of getting a run of heads for each size of run are shown.

Table 4 Probabilities of obtaining run of heads

Toss	1st	2nd	3rd	4th	5th	6th	7th	8th	9th	10th
Probability	0.500	0.250	0.125	0.063	0.031	0.016	0.008	0.004	0.002	0.001
No. of times likely to occur by chance in 100 or 1000 occasions	50 in 100	25 in 100	12.5 in 100	6.3 in 100	3.1 in 100	1.6 in 100	8 in 1000	4 in 1000	2 in 1000	1 in 1000

You probably notice that on the first toss the probability is 0.5 i.e. a 50/50 chance of obtaining heads or tails. For succeeding heads the probability is half the preceding probability level. These probability levels are based on the assumption that chance factors only are operating, i.e. the coin is symmetrical, uniform and is not double headed! Thus the coin has no tendency whatsoever to fall more often on one side rather than another; there.are absolutely even chances of heads and tails.

We have just considered a sequence of tosses but we can attach probability values to the sort of simultaneous tossing outcomes you performed earlier. Your actual distribution of tossings should have approximated to a normal distribution. When we plot the *possible* outcomes of such simultaneous tossing we also obtain a normal distribution. Consider two coins being tossed simultaneously. There are four possible outcomes:

	Coins	
	A	B
Outcome 1	H	H i.e. both heads
Outcome 2	H	T ⎤ two ways of getting one head and one tail
Outcome 3	T	H ⎦
Outcome 4	T	T both tails

We can put this another way as in Table 5, i.e. there is a 1 in 4 or probability of 0.25 of getting two tails. Can you work out the probabilities of the other outcomes? If three coins are tossed simultaneously the distribution is as shown in Table 6.

Table 5 Distribution of outcomes of falls of 2 coins tossed simultaneously

Two coins	Two heads (2H)	One heads (1H) and One tails (1T)	Two tails (2T)
Number of chances in four	1	2	1

Table 6 Distribution of chances of falls of 3 coins tossed simultaneously

Three coins	3H	2H 1T	1H 2T	3T
Number of chances in eight	1	3	3	1

Tossing four, five, six, seven, eight, nine and ten coins at a time, the probabilities of the distribution of falls in each case are as shown in Table 7.

Just to ensure you have grasped the concept of probability, look at Table 7. There are 10 chances in 1024 of obtaining 9H/1T from tossing 10 coins simultaneously, i.e. 1 in 102 or a probability of approximately 0.01. Similarly there is a probability of 0.25 approximately for obtaining 5H/5T when tossing 10 coins simultaneously.

We have plotted on Figure 13 the possible distribution of throws when 10 coins are tossed simultaneously. We have joined the midpoints of each column with an unbroken line. The height of each column thus represents the number of chances in 1024, corresponding to the conditions set out along the base. We are back to our normal distribution again, but we know the probability of each outcome now. The shape of the unbroken line only approximates to a normal distribution curve. If we were to increase the number of coins tossed simultaneously the curve would become smoother, but the plotting of heads and tails combinations will never produce the really smooth curve associated with normal distribution since heads and tails are discrete categories. With continuous data such as the heights or IQs of the population the curve is a smooth one representing a continuous relationship between two variables.

The procedure for computing probabilities that has been presented in this section rapidly becomes unwieldy as the number of coins, or pairs of scores, is increased. Fortunately, these probabilities have been worked out for us. They are presented in Table A column 3 in the Appendix A. These figures show the probabilities at each σ (or z) unit

Table 7   Probabilities of falls of 4 to 10 coins

4 Coins	4 H	3 H 1 T	2 H 2 T	1 H 3 T	4 T						
No. of chances in 16	1	4	6	4	1						
5 Coins	5 H	4 H 1 T	3 H 2 T	2 H 3 T	1 H 4 T	5 T					
No. of chances in 32	1	5	10	10	5	1					
6 Coins	6 H	5 H 1 T	4 H 2 T	3 H 3 T	2 H 4 T	1 H 5 T	6 T				
No. of chances in 64	1	6	15	20	15	6	1				
7 Coins	7 H	6 H 1 T	5 H 2 T	4 H 3 T	3 H 4 T	2 H 5 T	1 H 6 T	7 T			
No. of chances in 128	1	7	21	35	35	21	7	1			
8 Coins	8 H	7 H 1 T	6 H 2 T	5 H 3 T	4 H 4 T	3 H 5 T	2 H 6 T	1 H 7 T	8 T		
No. of chances in 256	1	8	28	56	70	56	28	8	1		
9 Coins	9 H	8 H 1 T	7 H 2 T	6 H 3 T	5 H 4 T	4 H 5 T	3 H 6 T	2 H 7 T	1 H 8 T	9 T	
No. of chances in 512	1	9	36	84	126	126	84	36	9	1	
10 Coins	10 H	9 H 1 T	8 H 2 T	7 H 3 T	6 H 4 T	5 H 5 T	4 H 6 T	3 H 7 T	2 H 8 T	1 H 9 T	10 T
No. of chances in 1024	1	10	45	120	210	252	210	120	45	10	1

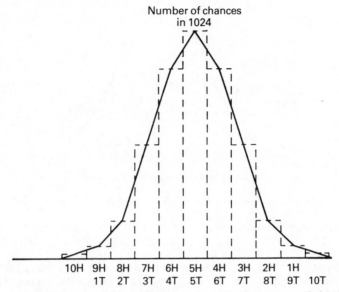

Figure 13 Possible distribution of throws when 10 coins are tossed simultaneously

along the baseline of the normal distribution curve. This means that we can look up the probability of obtaining *by chance* any particular score whose deviation in z score terms from the mean can be calculated. Since we are dealing with a standard score on a standard distribution the probability of any particular deviation above or below the mean is always the same. From henceforth probability will be designated by the symbol 'p'.

Look at Figure 14; it is a normal distribution curve with the three standard deviations above and below the mean marked on as you saw in Chapter 4. In addition the approximate p levels of each point is added. At M there is a probability of 0.5; at $\pm 1\sigma$ from M the probability of obtaining a score by chance at that point is 0.32; a score occurs by chance at -2σ and $+2\sigma$ with a probability of 0.023 and so on. In other words as with our penny tossing the rarer the combination of H/T or the rarer the score the lower the probability level and the nearer the tails of the distribution the event is placed. The greater the deviation of the score from the mean the less frequently it is likely to occur.

STQ *Do you notice any similarity between the p values and the areas contained within the curve beyond that point? Refer to page 38 to refresh your memory.*

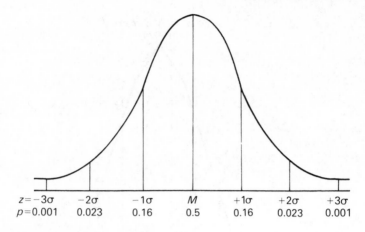

z = -3σ   -2σ   -1σ   M   +1σ   +2σ   +3σ
p = 0.001   0.023   0.16   0.5   0.16   0.023   0.001

Figure 14 Approximate *p* values

Since 68% of the area of scores lie between ±1σ from the mean then 32% of the area or scores must lie beyond those points. Thus the probability of drawing a score at random from the normal distribution at + 1σ is 0.16 (16%) and at −1σ is also 0.16 or 16% (32% divided equally in each tail of the distribution). Similarly a score at + 2σ or −2σ has a probability of 0.023 because approximately 95% of all cases lie between + 2σ and −2σ, hence the probability of obtaining a score with such a deviation from the *M* is 1.0 −0.95 (100% − 95%) = 0.05 (5%). This 0.05 covers both tails of the curve so must be halved when considering only one side of the distribution. The 0.05 therefore reduces to 0.025 for a score at + 2σ and 0.025 for a score at −2σ. The slight difference between the theoretical probability of 0.023 and the approximation of 0.025 we have just worked out exists because the 95% limits are not ±2σ exactly but ±1.96σ. You can check this for yourself in Table A in Appendix A. The whole number ±2σ is easier to remember as a major defining point on the normal curve than ±1.96σ though as we become more confident in dealing with the normal curve and significance tables (Chapter 6) these other numbers, less convenient to remember, will begin to take root. Table A in Appendix A, as well as providing us with detailed information about areas under any part of the normal distribution curve, provides the probability level for any point. This is obtained by reading the second column away from the column containing the *z* value of the required point i.e. column 3. For example to find the probability of obtaining a score that is + 1.5σ from the mean on a normal distribution curve we read across to the second column where we find the value 0.0668. This is the probability of drawing by chance (at random) a score at that point, i.e. about 7 times in 100.

STQ *Using Table A (Appendix A) find the probability of obtaining by chance a score of:*

(i)   *62 when M   =   74 and σ   =   6*
(ii)   *48 when M   =   36 and σ   =   8*
(iii)   *110 when M   =   100 and σ   =   15*
(iv)   *+1.3z; +2.5z*
(v)   *−2.8z; −0.6z*

Answers are to be found on p. 432.

6

Statistical significance

By now you should have grasped the principles that:

(a) The normal distribution curve depicts the distribution of chance occurrences round a mean.
(b) Some occurrences occur more frequently by chance than other occurrences.
(c) Each occurrence can be assigned a probability value, i.e. the likelihood of its occurring by chance.

In evaluating experimental results we need to know whether the results might be expected fairly frequently on a chance basis or whether it is a chance, rare event, with a consequent low probability. Remember some of our coin-tossing exploits. In one experiment (p. 37), you noticed how infrequently a large disproportionate split occurred (e.g. 29H and 1T) when tossing coins simultaneously; in another (p. 46) you found that an unbroken line of seven heads on tossing the same coin repeatedly was quite a rare event too.

But in both these cases such outcomes will still occur by chance on occasions, however infrequently! But how far must an outcome be away from the expected, how infrequent must it be, or how far removed from the mean of a normal distribution before we say that, although it *can* occur by chance occasionally, the fact that we have obtained this outcome in a 'one-off' experiment suggests that this is *not* a chance variation but is due to our systematic manipulation of the independent variable?

Now that we are able to allocate probability levels to all points or scores on the normal distribution curve, the next step is to decide at what level of probability we believe that a result is more than likely due to the experiment than to chance, always remembering that *every outcome is possible* on a chance basis even if the odds are as high as those required for winning the football pools.

The social science investigator is particularly interested in the probability of a particular sample result occurring by chance. He wants to know the odds against a chance occurrence. If the odds *against* occurrence by chance are greater than a certain figure, he decides that his result is *statistically significant*. In practice he focuses his attention on certain conventionally accepted probability levels, which you will repeatedly encounter in research reports. These specify the probability of a chance occurrence of findings for a sample. The highest probability he generally considers is $p = 0.05$ or 5 occurrences by chance in 100; the odds against this chance occurrence are 95:5 or 19:1. A lower level he sets is often $p = 0.01$ or 1 occurrence by chance in 100; the odds against this chance occurrence are 99:1. And an even lower level is $p = 0.0001$ or 1 occurrence by chance in 1000; the odds against chance are 999:1. In general the *lower* the probability of a chance result (low p value) the more confidence the researcher has in his results. The three p values of 0.05, 0.01 and 0.001 are conventionally accepted as the major thresholds for decisions about statistical significance. But why have research workers picked on these levels? The problem is not unlike that facing the gambler playing roulette who has to decide whether to maximize his possible profits on a single number (odds of 35:1 against) or to opt for less by betting on, say, all red numbers as opposed to black numbers (odds of 1:1, or evens). As scientists, psychologists generally opt for high odds, they want to minimize the possibility of claiming a significant result when the result is probably a chance one. They consider the error of drawing a false conclusion that a relationship exists between variables more serious than the error of failing to uncover some actual relation. So the minimum level usually acceptable is the 0.05 or 5% level. But remember that even here results will occur by chance 5 times in 100. By saying our result is significant at the 0.05 level we are saying it is very unlikely to be due to chance though that suspicion must always be in the back of our minds. That is why even more rigorous levels of 0.01 and 0.001 are also employed. At both these levels chance results are even more unlikely. Hence we can be more confident in rejecting the view that chance has caused the result and assume that the result is statistically significant. But even here chance does still operate on rare occasions and we do not know on which! So statistical analyses of results can never definitely prove a hypothesis, only support it at certain levels of probability. The significance levels of 0.05 and 0.01, while seemingly chosen arbitrarily, do correspond reasonably well to two and three standard deviations from the mean respectively in a normal distribution.

You can see in Table 8 how the four commonly employed levels of statistical significance are expressed. Three significance levels are depicted *viz.* 0.05, 0.01, and 0.001, as well as the cryptic NS which means 'not significant'. The sign $<$ simply means 'less than', i.e.

$p < 0.05$ means 'the probability of a chance occurrence of less than 0.05 or 5 times in 100.

STQ *What does $p < 0.01$ and $p < 0.001$ imply? Write down your answers and compare them with ours.*

$p < 0.01$ means probability of a chance occurrence of less than 1 in a 100 ($p < 0.001$ – less than 1 in a 1000). The probabilities of a chance occurrence of greater than 0.05 are usually designated 'not statistically significant' or 'NS'.

STQ *Can you explain to yourself why such results are regarded as not statistically significant?*

You may also encounter two other forms of expressing statistical significance, (i) probability may be expressed as a percentage which is termed a significance level, e.g. $p < 0.01$ becomes the 1% significance level, (ii) it may also be expressed as odds against chance though this is not common. For example $p < 0.05$ is odds against a chance of more than 19 to 1 as we saw above.

These various ways of expressing statistical significance are to be summarized in Table 8 by you.

STQ   **Table 8** *Try to complete the table below yourself.*

Level	Probability limits	Frequency of a chance occurrence	Significance levels	Odds against a chance occurrence
NS	$p > 0.05$			
Low	$p < 0.05$			19:1
	$p < 0.01$		1%	
High	$p < 0.001$	1 in 1000		

A completed table will be found on p. 432.

Selecting a level of significance

So far we have not tackled the question of why we would be prepared to risk one level of probability rather than another when deciding whether to reject the null hypothesis. What risk would you be prepared to accept that the scores resulting from your experiment occurred randomly as stated by the null hypothesis and were not significant at all? Of course, we would like to be 100% certain that the difference in scores was significant. But, you can never be 100% certain that it is not a freak chance occurrence. How small should the significance level be – that is, how small should the probability of an event be before we reject the possibility of its having occurred by chance?

There is no simple answer. It is up to you to decide what odds you are prepared to accept when deciding whether the results of your experiment are significant (i.e. significantly greater than chance). We must make a decision about how much of a difference we demand before we are prepared to accept it as statistically significant. This decision involves political, social, educational, philosphic and economic considerations as well as statistical ones.

In order to answer this question, we must consider the consequences of the decision to act as though the event had or had not occurred. A somewhat fanciful example might make this point clear. Assume that you are presented with a box of 200 pistols, exactly ten of which you know to be loaded, and allowed to take one of them out. The probability that this pistol is loaded is, thus, 10/200, or 0.05. Would you act as if it were loaded or as if it were not? In deciding, you would take into account not only the probability that the gun is loaded but also the consequences of your acting as if it were loaded. If you were asked whether you would be willing to hold the gun to your head and pull the trigger, you would act as though it were loaded. On the other hand, if you were asked whether you would be willing to use it to defend yourself in a duel, you would act as though it were not loaded. This approach is perfectly rational; though the probability is the same in both cases, the consequences are not. Thus, to answer our question, we must consider the consequences of accepting or rejecting the null hypothesis.

Imagine a medical situation where you were testing a powerful drug with nasty side effects and found a small improvement in patients taking the drug as compared with a control group. If the difference between the groups could have occurred randomly by chance 5 in 100 times, would you accept that the difference was significant and introduce the new drug? Would you change your odds if you knew that without the drug most of the patients would die anyway? And how would you feel about going on your package trip to Torremolinos if an aeroplane you were going to fly in had a 1% probability of developing engine failure on take off?

Again imagine you were an educational psychologist testing whether a new reading scheme might help backward children and you carried out an experiment in which you compared the progress of a group of such children using your new scheme against the progress of a similar control group using traditional methods. Suppose you found a difference in reading improvement scores between the two groups in favour of the new scheme. Suppose the probability that this could have occurred by chance was 10% (i.e. a 10 in 100 or a 1 in 10 probability that there were only random differences rather than a significant difference caused by the reading scheme). Would you accept that the difference was significant and introduce the new reading scheme, and at what cost in terms of materials and teacher training?

These examples bring home the fact that choosing a significance level is always a matter of deciding what odds you are prepared to accept in a particular situation that your results are due to chance. In the case of the reading scheme, no child would probably suffer all that much if it was all due to chance after all, so, as long as it was not too expensive, you would probably go ahead and introduce the new scheme.

On the other hand, you might feel more doubtful about introducing a powerful drug with nasty side effects if there was a 1 in 20 chance that it was doing no good at all; although you might accept these odds if it were the only hope of saving people's lives. I do not think any of us would fly in a plane with a 1 in 100 chance of crashing!

In social science (possibly because it is felt that nothing too terrible can happen as a result of accepting a result as significant) it is a convention to accept that odds of either 1 in 100 (i.e. 1%) or 5 in 100 (i.e. 5%) are adequate grounds for rejecting the null hypothesis that the results are random, and instead accepting the experimental hypothesis. They are reasonable gambles in most situations.

All this goes to show that significance testing in psychological research needs to be tempered with a good deal of personal judgement and common sense. In common with the general strategy of science, the usual practice is to set a sufficiently high significance level to *minimize* the possibility of accepting chance results. But by doing this there is always a danger of overlooking a genuine result. A good researcher will keep this in mind when testing statistical hypotheses using a particular significance level. He looks for evidence for general trends in results as well as statistically significant or statistically insignificant findings.

7

Sampling

A The reason for sampling

We are all guilty on many occasions of making generalizations about groups of people or inferences about individuals based on very limited experience or knowledge of them. We might meet one member of a group, say a Welshman who can sing, and this causes us to attribute such vocal ability to all natives of that principality. One student once said to me, 'I do not like Norwegians, I met one once'. Likewise we read in newspapers that 'people have no moral values now' or that 'politicians are corrupt'. Such generalization is invalid yet generalization is necessary in research.

In any study it is seldom that the investigator is interested only in the sample of subjects on which the results were obtained. Typically one usually wants to state that the results hold for the much larger population from which the sample was drawn. This process of extending one's finding from the sample to the population is referred to as generalization. Generalization is a necessary scientific procedure since rarely is it possible to study all members of a defined population.

In their role as guinea pigs for experimental investigations, people are referred to as subjects. The use of this term is a little unfortunate since it can also denote a field of study, e.g. mathematics, geography. However, provided you are alert to this ambiguity, it is unlikely to cause much trouble. In reading text books, research reports and the like you will frequently find that the symbol S is used to denote a subject. The symbol E may be used for the experimenter.

B Population

When you are wearing your statistical hat you must always remember that a population is a complete set of all those things (people, numbers, societies, bacteria etc.) which completely satisfy some specification; for example, all colour-blind, English, male, comprehensive-school pupils.

A statistical population is a defined group, not a demographic concept. A population is defined as the total number of potential units for observation. It can have relatively few units (e.g. all the students in the social science faculty); a large number of units (all the British electorate); or an infinite number of units (e.g. all the possible outcomes obtained by tossing a coin an infinite number of times). So a population is an entire group of people or objects or events that all have at least one characteristic in common, e.g. Manchester United supporters club, brand X cigarettes, road accidents, flat-footed policemen, council-house tenants.

Any measure of a defined population is called a parameter. The average height of all British Members of Parliament is a parameter of that population of MPs.

C Sample

A sample is a subset or subgroup of a defined population. Any measure of a sample is termed a statistic, so the average height of a representative sample of British policemen is a statistic. To obtain a sample the first task is to define or specify the population, and then secondly, by an appropriate method, select a sample from this population. The concept of representativeness is not implicit in the concept of a sample. One of our great concerns in this current chapter will be to distinguish between samples which are in some sense representative of a population and those which are not, and to demonstrate ways of drawing samples that will be representative.

If sample data (statistics) are to be used as a basis for generalizations about the population it is essential that the sample is representative of that population. A representative sample is a true replica of the population, reflecting accurately the proportion or frequency of relevant characteristics in the defined population. The key word in the sample – population relationship is representativeness. We cannot make any valid generalization about the population from which the sample was drawn unless the sample is representative. But representative in terms of what? Weight, IQ, political persuasion, cleanliness? The answer is that the sample must be representative in terms of those variables which are known to be related to the characteristics we wish to study. The size of the sample is important too, as we shall see, but it will suffice for now to remember from our Welshman who could sing and from the student who disliked his one Norwegian contact that we are on very dangerous ground trying to generalize from a sample of one. Usually the smaller the sample the lower the accuracy, but size is less important than representativeness. There is a famous example of a sample of ten-million voters supposedly representative of the electorate in the USA used to poll voting intentions for the presidential election in 1936. The forecast, despite the sample size, was disastrously out because the sample was contacted by telephone. Telephone ownership biased the sample in favour of the middle class who were mainly Republican. The Republican candidate went to bed on the eve of polling day contented with the prospects of an overwhelming victory. He awoke to find that his Democratic opponent (Truman) was to be the new president! So telephone directory lists form very poor bases for sampling, as do voting lists unless this is the population defined by the researcher. Can you think why voting lists (electoral roll) can be a poor basis for sampling the adult population?

A sample may need to be relabelled a population if its function changes. Of course if this happens the relevant statistic then becomes the parameter. An example may help to make this clearer. We might define a population as all nine-year-old children in the British Isles. A sample of this population could be any smaller group less than the total – say nine-year-old children attending one school. On the other hand the focus of our research interest might change from the population as a whole to this one school. We might want to investigate certain characteristics of the children in this school in order to aid decisions about the curriculum of the school. In this case our population is re-defined as all nine-year-old children attending the school and samples of this population are now defined as any smaller group of children in the school. In other words the definition of a population sets limits on the statements about characteristics which we wish to make – i.e. it enables us to *define* our parameters. If a sample is redefined as a population the *statistics* we obtain for it are now similarly redefined as population *parameters*.

Whereas a parameter is of interest in its own right, as a measure which provides a description of a characteristic of a population we are interested in, the function of a statistic is to give us some idea of the probable value of the corresponding parameter. In statistician's jargon, we say the statistic *estimates* the parameter, since rarely can we ever measure the population to determine the parameter exactly.

STQ   **(1)** *Psychologists have few population lists they can use and the tendency is to grab whatever sample is handy (opportunity sampling). As a result much research is carried out on captive groups of pupils and students, who are a biased sample of the general population. Can you think in what ways they are biased?*

(2) *A research worker interested in studying ego strength among 12-year-old males found that the average*

> *ego-strength level in a selected group from the Gas Works High School was higher than that of all the 12-year-old males in the whole city. Name:*
>
> *(a) the statistic*
> *(b) the population*
> *(c) the sample*
> *(d) the parameter*

Answers on page 432.

Only large-scale national investigations have the resources to employ sophisticated sampling techniques, e.g. Government surveys, NFER; and moreover using the individual as the sampling unit causes untold problems, for one of the sample might be in Aberdeen, another in Exeter, with the rest scattered in between. In sampling a school population there may be chosen one child in that class, two children in this and so on. As a result the class unit or school unit have been used as the sampling unit for logistical purposes. Hence there are a number of valid ways in which representative samples may be drawn and it is at these we will now look.

D Techniques of sampling

1 THE RANDOM SAMPLE

Once the population has been carefully defined a representative sample can be drawn. The first step towards representativeness is achieved by *random* sampling. Random sampling is that method of drawing a sample so that each member of the population has an equal chance of being selected. This will become clear by the following example. Suppose the population in which we are interested was the first-year group of a ten-form entry secondary school, but of the total population of 300 children we could test only one-third, i.e. 100. Since the population is clearly defined it can, in principle, be listed, i.e. a list including each child's name or code number. This list is called the sampling frame. One method of drawing the random sample is to write each name or code number onto a slip of paper then shuffle the slips in a container. The slips are then drawn out at random. At this stage there are two possibilities open. We can either replace the slip once it has been drawn or we can retain it and continue drawing slips from the remainder until the required sample size of 100 is obtained. This latter procedure does obviously alter the chances of being selected as the sampling proceeds, i.e. at the commencement in our example the first name has a 1 in 300 chance, but the last choice has a 1 in 201 chance.

Table 9 Random sampling numbers

2017	4228	2317	5966	3861	0210	8610	5155	9252	4425
7449	0449	0304	1033	5370	1154	4863	9460	9449	5738
9470	4931	3867	2342	2965	4088	7871	3718	4864	0657
2215	7815	6984	3252	3254	1512	5402	0137	3837	1293
9329	1218	2730	3055	9187	5057	5851	4936	1253	9640
4504	7797	3614	9945	5925	6985	0383	5187	8556	2237
4491	9949	8939	9460	4849	0677	6472	5926	0851	2557
1623	9102	1996	4759	8965	2784	3092	6337	2624	2366
0450	6504	6565	8242	7051	5501	6147	8883	9934	8237
3270	1772	9361	6626	2471	2277	8833	1778	0892	7349
0364	5907	4295	8139	0641	2081	9234	5190	3908	2142
6249	9000	6786	9348	3183	1907	6768	4903	2747	5203
6100	9586	9836	1403	4888	5107	3340	0686	2276	6857
8903	9049	2874	2104	0996	6045	2203	5280	0179	3381
0172	3385	5240	6007	0671	8927	1429	5524	8579	3196
2756	4979	3434	3222	6053	9117	3326	4470	9314	9970
4905	7448	1055	3525	2428	2022	3566	6634	2635	9123
4974	3725	9726	3394	4223	0128	5958	9269	0366	7382
2026	2243	8808	1985	0812	4765	6563	5607	9785	5679
4887	7796	4339	7693	0879	2218	5455	9375	9726	9077
0872	8746	7573	0011	2707	0520	3085	2221	0467	1913
9597	9862	1727	3142	6471	4622	3275	1932	2099	9485
3799	5731	7040	4655	4612	2432	3674	6920	7210	9593
0579	5837	8533	7518	8871	2344	5428	0048	9623	6645
5585	6342	0079	9122	2901	4139	5140	3665	2611	7832
6728	9625	6836	2472	0385	4924	0569	6486	0819	9121
8586	9478	3259	5182	8643	7384	4560	8957	0687	0815
4010	6009	0588	7844	6313	5825	3711	1847	7562	5221
9455	8948	9080	7780	2689	8744	2374	6620	2019	2652
1163	7777	2320	3362	6219	2903	9415	5637	1409	4716
6400	2604	5455	3857	9462	6840	2604	2425	0361	0120
5094	1323	7841	6058	1060	8846	3021	4598	7096	3689
6698	3796	4413	4505	3459	7585	4897	2719	1785	4851
6691	4283	6077	9091	6090	7962	5766	7228	0870	9603
3358	1218	0207	1940	2129	3945	9042	5884	8543	9567
5249	4016	7240	7305	5090	0204	9824	0530	2725	2088
7498	9399	7830	7947	9692	4558	4037	8976	8441	7468
5026	5430	0188	6957	5445	6988	2321	0569	9344	0532
4946	6189	3379	9684	2834	1935	2873	3959	5634	9707
1965	1344	7839	7388	6203	3600	2596	8676	6790	2168
6417	4767	8759	8140	7261	1400	2828	5586	2338	1615
1843	9737	6897	5656	5795	0188	1189	4807	4260	1192
6558	6087	5109	9661	1553	6681	6688	4475	3701	2888
7990	3100	9114	8565	3175	4315	4593	6478	3453	8802
0723	0015	5905	1609	9442	2040	6376	6567	3411	9410
9008	1424	0151	9546	3032	3319	0014	1928	4051	9269
5382	6202	2182	3413	4103	1285	6530	0097	5630	1548
9817	2615	0450	7625	2033	5484	3931	2333	5964	9627
0891	1244	8240	3062	4550	6454	6517	8925	5944	9995
3721	4677	8487	6739	8554	9737	3341	1174	9050	2962

Each digit is an independent sample from a population in which the digits 0 to 9 are equally likely; that is each has a probability of 1/10.

For drawing large samples this manual technique would be rather laborious so the alternative is to use a random number table (Table 9). This consists of blocks of numbers in random order. The table can be entered at any point and can be worked through horizontally or vertically. In our example each member of the population would be given a three figure number from 001 to 300. Selection of the random sample of 100 takes place by entering the table and selecting three-digit numbers as they occur. Repetitions or numbers outside the population range are disregarded. For example, commencing with the left-hand column and working down the numbers drawn run as follows: 279, 294, 410, 306, 680, 244, 240 etc. This method can be speeded up by the use of computers which select at random, e.g. Ernie with Premium Bond winners.

So by 'random' we are implying 'without bias' and the sample is drawn unit by unit, all members of the population having an equal chance of selection. Results may be generalized to the population but even a random selection is never a completely accurate reflection of the population from which it was drawn. There is always some sampling error and the generalization is an inference, not a certainty.

Try this exercise to prove to yourself that sampling error does occur even with random sampling. In Table 10 there are ten columns. For each column, draw ten single-digit numbers at random from Table 9. (The first column is done for you).

Table 10 Samples of random numbers

	1	2	3	4	5	6	7	8	9	10
	9									
	7									
	6									
	7									
	3									
	8									
	4									
	1									
	3									
	2									
Total	50									
Average $\frac{50}{10}$ = 5.0										

(a) To draw these random samples write the numbers 1 to 50 on separate slips of paper representing the rows of Table 9 (p. 61) and 1 to 40 on separate slips of paper representing the columns of Table 9. Place each set of slips in a separate box and shuffle them around. Draw out one slip from the first box and one from the second. The number of the first slip locates the row for your first random number and the second slip locates its column. Take the first number in the set of four in the table you have located. Thus if the numbers you draw first are 15 and 2, your first random number will be 1; if you then draw 30 and 6, your next random number is 7. After drawing each slip replace it in its box. Continue the drawing process until you have selected all the random numbers you need.

(b) When you have drawn the remaining nine samples of ten random numbers, compute the arithmetic average for each column. This is found by adding all the numbers and dividing this total by the number of numbers in each column, in this instance, ten. (Return to Chapter 2 if hazy.) The average of the first column has also been computed for you.

Since in Table 9 each number from 0 to 9 occurs an equal number of times, the population average (a parameter) must be the average of the sum of the numbers 0–9.

$$\text{i.e.} \quad \frac{0+1+2+3+4+5+6+7+8+9}{10} \quad = \quad 4.50$$

Now we can see if any sampling error has occurred in your random samples in Table 10. Are any of your sample means exactly 4.5? This is not likely though many will be close to it. When we tried it our sample averages ranged from 2.9 to 6.2, with 4.3 as the sample average closest to the population average. In other words there is always some error. We shall see later (Chapter 8) how this error can be estimated. Now compute the average of the ten sample averages. Hopefully this average is a more accurate reflection of the population mean than most of the sample averages. This illustrates a further point: that usually the larger the sample the smaller the sampling error.

The notion of randomness is difficult to define. Dictionaries suggest such synonyms as accidental, haphazard, aimless. But these are not much help for statisticians since research workers are quite systematic about randomness; they plan random procedures. The word random is used because people do not know enough. In ignorance we have to say events are random when we cannot predict their outcome. For example we cannot predict whether a tossed coin will come down heads or tails. Paradoxically, though an individual event is hard to predict, we can predict the outcome of a large number of events, so that if we toss the coin 10 000 times we can predict fairly accurately the total number of heads and tails.

STQ *Given a population of 100 mice in a cage, would the following constitute methods for selecting a random sample of twenty mice for a maze-running experiment?*

(a) Shove a hand in the cage and grab the first twenty mice that you can.

(b) Unbolt a swinging door in the side of the cage and take the first twenty mice to emerge.

Do these procedures qualify as random sampling? Why or why not?

Neither method would constitute a random sample. The first might lead to the selection of the twenty mice least able to avoid the experimenter. These may be the most unhealthy, the most petrified or even the most curious mice. The other method might lead to the selection of the twenty mice with the greatest problem solving ability or greatest mobility.

The only sure way of picking an unbiased population is to number the whole population of mice and then select the mice corresponding to the first twenty numbers found in a table of random numbers.

2 SYSTEMATIC SAMPLING

If the defined population can be listed then the sample can be drawn at fixed intervals from the list. In an earlier example on random sampling we wanted to select 100 pupils from 300, a 1 in 3 ratio. In systematic sampling a starting number between 1 and 3 is chosen randomly and selection continues by taking every third person from that starting number. So if the 3 was the starting number successive selections would be 6, 9, 12, 18 etc.

STQ **(1)** *If no. 2 was the starting point on a selection ratio of 1 to 5 what are the next four successive selections?*

(2) *There is a fundamental difference between random and systematic sampling. One of the conditions of random sampling is that the selection of one individual should be independent of the selction of another. Systematic sampling does not satisfy this condition. Can you explain why?*

The selected starting number fixes which successive numbers are taken and those which can never be selected.

The major disadvantages of systematic sampling is where a periodic cycle exists in the sampling frame or population list which would bias the sample. For example if all school classes were 25 pupils strong with boys listed before girls then a sampling interval of 25 would generate an all male sample.

3 STRATIFIED SAMPLING

We saw earlier that random sampling involves some degree of sampling error. One way to reduce this error and increase precision without increasing sample size is by employing prior information about characteristics of the population. This involves stratified sampling. Suppose we had a population of 20 persons – 12 men and 8 women – and we wished to select a sample of 10 containing 6 men and 4 women, we could select 1 in 2 from each sex or stratum. This will provide a better estimate because the right proportion from each stratum is obtained. There is always a risk with random sampling of getting a 'wild' sample of 10 men. In this way sampling error is reduced by stratification, for the sample cannot differ from the population with respect to the stratifying factor(s), so the distribution of sample means are not spread out as much as in a random sample. A stratum is fairly homogeneous with respect to the characteristic on which the stratum is based therefore variance must be restricted and as a corollary sampling error too.

So in this design the researcher divides his population into layers or *strata*. The characteristics which define these strata are usually those variables which are known to relate to the characteristic(s) under study. Thus a population can be divided on the basis of (say) social class membership, sex, level of intelligence, level of anxiety if these are known to be important. Having stratified the population, a simple random, or systematic, sample is drawn from each stratum.

The number of subjects drawn from each stratum will depend on whether the sampling is done proportionately or disproportionately. Proportionate stratified sampling requires that the proportion of subjects in the sample should reflect the proportion of subjects in the population. Suppose the population was defined as all secondary-school children in one county, and this population was divided up, or stratified, by type of school. If 5% attend public schools, 20% grammar schools, 25% comprehensive schools and 50% secondary modern schools, then these are the proportions of the population that should appear in the sample. Similarly if in each type of school 50% are male and 50% female then this too is reflected.

Suppose, for the sake of argument, the total population of

secondary-school children in the county was 100 000, and that because of limitations of time and finance etc. the sample was limited to 1000. This indicates a sampling ratio of 1 in 100 for each stratum. The number of children attending each type of school in the population and in the sample is shown in Table 11. Since a proportionate stratified sample reflects the actual proportions in the population, greater representativeness is achieved than in a simple random sample.

Table 11 Numbers in population and sample in a proportionate sampling design

Type of school	Per cent in population	Total in population	Total in sample	Male	Female
Public	5	5 000	50	25	25
Grammar	20	20 000	200	100	100
Comprehensive	25	25 000	250	125	125
Modern	50	50 000	500	250	250
Total	100	100 000	1000	500	500

Furthermore it can be shown that, provided the principle of stratification is not completely irrelevant to the study, e.g. type of school bears no relation to the parameter we wish to investigate, then the error in the estimate of this parameter will be less than in a non-stratified sample. But against this advantage must be set the disadvantage that the size of the sample in such strata can still be too small for adequate analysis on their own. Note that in our example the public-school sample is only 50. This means that we would still be severely limited in investigating the characteristics of public-school children separately. Stratification with proportionate sampling increases the representativeness of the total sample. But the total sample size still imposes severe limitations on any one stratum that may be involved in it.

4 MULTI-STAGE CLUSTER SAMPLE

If a researcher is studying a population which is spread over the whole of the country, e.g. psychology A-level students, then before selecting on a random basis this would involve listing them all – a mammoth task. The sample itself would be spread widely to one or two students in each college. Add on the constraints of time, finance and administration and a random sample is just not a feasible proposition for most research workers. One alternative is to sample natural groups or clusters rather than individuals, i.e. in our example whole classes of A-level students chosen randomly from the population of psychology

A-level classes. This retains the principle of randomness and only lists for the selected units required.

Examples of clusters are:

(a) classes in school
(b) trade union branches
(c) local government electoral wards
(d) branches of an industrial firm.

So the stages of sampling in our example might be as follows:

(a) Randomly select '*N*' LEAs from the list of all LEAs,
(b) Randomly select from within each chosen LEA '*M*' schools/colleges from the LEA's list of schools/colleges that teach psychology A-level,
(c) Randomly select from within each chosen institution individuals from the class lists of psychology A-level classes.

5 OPPORTUNITY SAMPLING

This form of sampling involves considerable error but is often used because no other alternative is open to the research worker. This happens when, owing to constraints of finance, and even permission, research is carried out on conveniently accessible groups, such as students in one's own college, people living in your neighbourhood etc. There is no proper sampling involved and no possibility of generalization to a wider population.

Students found in the library one afternoon, housewives interviewed in a supermarket one morning, or workers contacted at a union branch meeting are not likely to be representative of college students, housewives, or trade unionists. Such samples are non-probability samples because the chance of selection is unknown.

In some investigations it may be impossible to indentify members of the population, particularly where illegal activities are concerned e.g. drug taking. There is also the problem of contacting such people too. One method is the snowball technique, which starts with a small number of informants and from them other members of the population can be identified. It is the 'chain letter' principle.

Other opportunity samples involve volunteers such as was used by Milgram (1963) but we never know whether volunteers differ in some way from those who don't.

Quota sampling, often used in market research, comes under this heading also. Strata are determined as under 3 above, but instead of selecting at random the researchers knock at doors or accost people in the High Street until enough people within each stratum have been obtained. But of course people willing to co-operate may have different characteristics from those refusing; the High Street may produce mainly housewives, and the railway station working-class persons, business men or housewives, depending on time of day.

E Size versus representativeness

In general the larger the sample the better, simply because a large sample tends to have less error, as we found in the exercise using the table of random numbers. This is not to say that a large sample is sufficient to guarantee accuracy of results. Although for a given design, an increase in sample size increases accuracy, it will not eliminate or reduce any bias in the selection procedure. We have already noted an example of this in the 1936 Presidential election in the USA. As another example, if a 1 in 2 sample of the whole country consisted of one sex only it would be large, but unrepresentative. Size is therefore less important than representativeness. A general adage for research on this basis would be that 'no data are sounder than the representativeness of the sample from which they were obtained, no matter how large the sample!'

Another consideration is whether sub-groups are to be analysed in the study, and if so, to what extent. Many investigations not only make general comparisons between the major groups studied, but gain valuable information by dividing these into sub-groups, for example by sex, age, social class etc. These sub-groups could become too small to be representative or to allow statistical procedures to be applied with confidence. In fact some sampling designs commence from considerations of how large sub-groups are to be and then consider how such sub-groups can be obtained by random sampling.

In deciding size, non-response should be taken account of. This is particularly important in follow-up investigations, and in studies using pupils and students, for absentee rates can be up to 25%. This would effect representativeness. For example, in studying delinquency, learning problems, school phobia etc. the absentee group is obviously an important section of the potential sample.

F Sampling strategy

Below is a rough sequence to act as a guide for sample planning:

(a) Clearly define the population about which you intend to generalize from your results.
(b) Estimate roughly the size of sample required taking into account possible sub-groups and the time and resources available.
(c) Consider firstly a random sample procedure if a complete sampling list or frame is available.

(d) If simple random sampling is not practical decide if stratification would increase convenience/efficiency.

(e) If not (d) try a multi-stage design.

(f) If not (e) then even an opportunity sample may yield information of value, particularly for exploratory studies or case studies. This type of sample is the most frequent one used because of the difficulties of obtaining proper representative samples. Psychologists know what sort of sampling procedures they ought to employ but money, time, and other logistic problems temper ideals with realism, and as one writer said random samples are as common as white blackbirds! Most of the psychology in research journals and in the textbooks is based on opportunity samples and is perhaps largely the psychology of the student population.

We have attempted briefly to show why the experimental approach to the study of human behaviour provides more valid and reliable information than intuition. However, there are disadvantages which represent a trade-off between the precision that comes from experiments and the loss of real-life richness through the artificiality that control and standardization bring in.

Completing the following (Table 12) will provide a useful summary of the sample designs which have been considered in the previous two sections. The type of sample is indicated in column 1. You should complete column 2, describing how each sample is drawn, and column 3, the advantages and disadvantages of each method. In completing column 3 keep in mind such things as representativeness, error, appropriateness and/or convenience to the researcher.

Table 12 Summary of research design

Column 1	Column 2	Column 3
Type of sample	*How sample is drawn*	*Advantages and disadvantages*
1 Simple random		
2 Systematic		

Table 12 (Continued)

Column 1	Column 2	Column 3
Type of sample	*How sample is drawn*	*Advantages and disadvantages*
3 Stratified		
4 Multi-stage cluster		
5 Opportunity		

EXERCISE

Table 13 is a sampling frame showing the population of first-year children in a secondary school measured on five dimensions. From this population you are now to draw samples using some of the methods outlined in this chapter. Follow these instructions:

(1)   Random sampling

Enter the random number table (Table 9, p. 61) at any point and read off the first 20 two-digit numbers (let 00 represent 100). Continue to select numbers until you have 20 different two-digit numbers. Record on the scoring sheet (Table 14) how many of your sample fall into the categories given. Calculate average scores for reading, family size and self attitude.

(2)   Systematic sampling

Select 20 subjects by systematic sampling. This will require you to choose every fifth person. Hence select randomly any number between 1 and 5 and proceed from there. Again compare your averages with the overall group and the previous random sample.

(3)   Stratified sampling

Consider the ways in which the population varies and decide on the aspect(s) which will be most relevant to a fair sampling for attitude to

Table 13 Sampling frame

Number	Sex	Standardized reading score	Social class of father	No. children in family	Attitude to self rating
01	G	105	IV	4	3
02	G	98	III	2	7
03	G	102	III	3	6
04	G	120	IV	1	8
05	G	94	III	2	5
06	G	87	V	6+	1
07	G	101	I/II	1	7
08	G	103	III	2	6
09	G	124	III	3	6
10	G	120	III	5	5
11	G	98	IV	4	4
12	G	97	III	3	5
13	G	102	V	2	4
14	G	110	IV	1	9
15	G	94	III	4	4
16	G	108	V	2	6
17	G	100	III	1	6
18	G	96	V	3	5
19	G	98	IV	2	3
20	G	102	III	4	4
21	G	89	III	2	4
22	G	104	IV	3	6
23	G	110	III	2	3
24	G	119	I/II	2	6
25	G	96	III	3	7
26	G	105	IV	2	7
27	G	104	III	3	4
28	G	93	V	4	3
29	G	98	IV	1	8
30	G	108	III	3	6
31	G	102	III	5	4
32	G	99	V	2	4
33	G	86	III	3	4
34	G	104	III	1	7
35	G	96	IV	2	5
36	G	110	III	3	8
37	G	123	III	4	6
38	G	115	V	1	7
39	G	112	IV	3	5
40	G	97	III	2	5
41	G	93	I/II	6+	8

Table 13 (Continued)

Number	Sex	Standardized reading score	Social class of father	No. children in family	Attitude to self rating
42	G	98	V	2	3
43	G	107	IV	2	6
44	G	100	IV	2	6
45	G	104	III	3	5
46	G	97	III	2	4
47	G	96	IV	4	2
48	G	101	IV	3	5
49	G	108	III	1	7
50	G	92	III	2	5
51	G	118	III	5	7
52	G	104	III	2	6
53	B	94	III	3	5
54	B	106	III	3	7
55	B	115	III	2	8
56	B	88	V	4	2
57	B	97	IV	2	4
58	B	96	V	6+	4
59	B	105	III	3	6
60	B	107	III	2	7
61	B	107	III	1	8
62	B	103	III	4	7
63	B	98	III	3	5
64	B	112	I/II	1	7
65	B	94	IV	2	5
66	B	97	IV	3	4
67	B	103	IV	1	7
68	B	107	III	2	8
69	B	100	V	3	4
70	B	91	V	5	3
71	B	101	IV	3	5
72	B	105	III	2	7
73	B	89	III	5	3
74	B	106	IV	1	7
75	B	120	III	4	6
76	B	101	IV	2	6
77	B	104	III	3	7
78	B	98	IV	4	5
79	B	103	V	3	4
80	B	85	III	6+	3
81	B	110	III	1	8
82	B	108	IV	2	6
83	B	112	I/II	1	9

Table 13 (Continued)

Number	Sex	Standardized reading score	Social class of father	No. children in family	Attitude to self rating
84	B	99	III	4	6
85	B	95	IV	3	5
86	B	123	III	5	6
87	B	118	V	2	7
88	B	99	IV	4	3
89	B	95	V	2	6
90	B	102	III	1	8
91	B	103	IV	3	5
92	B	102	V	6+	5
93	B	95	III	2	6
94	B	99	III	3	6
95	B	96	IV	3	4
96	B	105	IV	4	4
97	B	99	III	2	5
98	B	110	I/II	3	9
99	B	98	III	2	7
100	B	97	III	3	4

self. You will then be in a position to define each of your strata in terms of one or more of the variables. For instance you might decide that the variable 'number of children in family' would strongly affect the attitude scores. You might therefore classify your population into smaller families (one to three children) and larger families (four or more children). You would then list the population of each stratum and randomly select ten from each.

You could of course decide upon much more complex strata such as low reading score and smaller family, low reading score and larger family, high reading score and smaller family and high reading score and larger family.

When you have selected your strata and sampled them randomly such that the total sample size is 20, calculate the mean attitude score and compare it with your previous samples.

4 OPPORTUNITY SAMPLING
Scan the lists quickly and select the first 20 pupils you find which conform to your definition above of large family size and small family size. Calculate the average attitude score and compare with the rest. Is this sample as representative of the population as your random sample?

Table 14 Scoring sheet

Type of sample and size		Whole population (N = 100)	Random (N = 20)	Systematic (N = 20)	Stratified (N = 20)	Opportunity (N = 20)
Sex	G	52				
	B	48				
Standardized reading score	85 − 89	6				
	90 − 94	8				
	95 − 99	28				
	100 − 104	24				
	105 − 109	14				
	110 − 114	8				
	115 − 119	5				
	120 − 129	6				
Social class	I/II	6				
	III	50				
	IV	28				
	V	16				
Number of children in family	1	15				
	2	32				
	3	28				
	4	14				
	5	6				
	6 and more	5				
Attitude to self score	1	1				
	2	2				
	3	9				
	4	18				
	5	19				
	6	21				
	7	18				
	8	9				
	9	3				
	10	0				

Table 14 (Continued)

Type of sample and size	Whole population (N = 100)	Random (N = 20)	Systematic (N = 20)	Stratified (N = 20)	Opportunity (N = 20)
Average attitude score	5.5				

Table 15   Attitude scores

Sex	1	2	3	4	5	6	7	8	9	10	Row totals
Girl	1	1	5	10	10	12	8	4	1	0	52
Boy	0	1	4	8	9	9	10	5	2	0	48
Column totals	1	2	9	18	19	21	18	9	3	0	100

IQ scores

	1	2	3	4	5	6	7	8	9	10	
85 – 89	1	1	2	2	—	—	—	—	—	—	6
90 – 94	—	—	2	1	4	—	—	1	—	—	8
95 – 99	—	1	3	8	8	4	3	1	—	—	28
100 – 104	—	—	—	6	5	7	5	1	—	—	24
105 – 109	—	—	1	1	—	5	6	2	—	—	15
110 – 114	—	—	1	—	1	—	1	2	3	—	8
115 – 119	—	—	—	—	—	1	3	1	—	—	5
120 – 124	—	—	—	—	1	4	—	1	—	—	6
Column totals	1	2	9	18	19	21	18	9	3	0	100

Social class

	1	2	3	4	5	6	7	8	9	10	
I/II	—	—	—	—	—	1	2	1	2	—	6
III	—	—	3	8	9	13	11	6	—	—	50
IV	—	1	3	5	8	5	3	2	1	—	28
V	1	1	3	5	2	2	2	—	—	—	16
Column totals	1	2	9	18	19	21	18	9	3	0	100

Table 15 (Continued)

Number of children in family

1	—	—	—	—	—	1	7	5	2	—	15
2	—	—	3	5	6	10	6	2	—	—	32
3	—	—	—	7	10	6	3	1	1	—	28
4	—	2	3	4	1	3	1	—	—	—	14
5	—	—	2	1	1	1	1	—	—	—	6
6 and over	1	—	1	1	1	—	—	1	—	—	5
Column totals	1	2	9	18	19	21	18	9	3	0	100

	Means Population	Girls	Boys
Reading score	104.6	104.9	104.2
Family size	2.79	2.7	2.9
Attitude to self score	5.5	5.3	5.7

Table 15 provides some basic population data for comparison purposes. Now write a brief summary of the differences you note in the scores produced by the various sampling techniques and try to explain why you believe such differences arose.

STQ (1) *Below are examples of the selection of samples. Decide for each which sampling technique was used.*

(a) *Restricted to a 5% sample of the total population, the researcher chose every 20th person on the electoral register.*

(b) *A social worker investigating juvenile delinquency and school attainment obtained his sample from children appearing at the juvenile court.*

(c) *A research organization took their sample from Public Schools, Direct Grant Schools and Comprehensives so that the samples were exact replicas of the actual population.*

   (2) *Explain how you would acquire a random sample of first-year college students in a city with two colleges.*

   (3) *Explain why a random sample from a population in which certain subjects were inaccessible would be a contradiction in terms.*

---

(4) *If, from an extremely large population, a very large number of samples were drawn randomly and their mean values calculated which of the following statements are true?*

(a)   *The sample means would each be equal to the population mean.*

(b)   *The sample means would vary from the population mean only by chance.*

(c)   *The sample means, if averaged, would have a grand mean grossly different from the population mean.*

(d)   *The sample means would form a distribution whose standard deviation is equal to σ.*

(e)   *The sample means would be very different from each other if the sample sizes were very large.*

Answers are to be found on p. 432.

REFERENCES

Milgram, J. S. (1963). Behavioural study of obedience. *J. Abnormal Psychol.*, **67,** 371–378

8

Standard error

Standard error

You probably remember the exercise we conducted when explaining random sampling procedure. You were asked to draw samples of ten numbers from the random number table and compute the means of each of these samples of ten numbers. Turn back to p. 62 and refresh your memory. Like us you no doubt obtained a range of means round the 'true' mean of 4.5 and you became aware that despite random sampling procedures some chance or random error was involved.

This sampling variability of a mean score which is the extent to which a mean score can be expected to vary as different samples of the same size are randomly selected from the same population is expressed by its standard error. The standard error of any sample measure such as a mean is the standard deviation of the distribution of measures that would result if large numbers of different samples of the same size were randomly selected from the same population.

If this were the best of all possible research worlds, there would be no random error. And if there were no random or chance variation or error, there would be no need for statistical tests of significance. The word 'significance' would be meaningless, in fact. Any difference would always be a 'real' difference, the sort of difference we look for in an experiment. But such is never the case. There are *always* chance errors (and biased errors, too), and in psychological research they often contribute substantially to the total variance. Standard errors are measures of this error, and are used, as a sort of yardstick against which experimental or 'variable' variance is checked.

The *standard error* is the standard deviation of the sampling distribution of any given measure – the mean or the correlation coefficient, for instance. In most cases, population values (parameters) can never be known; they must be estimated, from sample measures, usually from single samples.

So the standard error is a measure of chance fluctuation of

experimental measurements. It is a measure against which the out-comes of experimental manipulations are checked to discern whether any difference between (say) two sample means is a 'real' one or simply one of those many relatively small differences that arise by chance as a function of sampling procedures.

The standard error is a fundamental instrument in research since most statistical inference boils down to a family of fractions based on the model:

$$\frac{\text{statistic}}{\text{standard error of that statistic}}$$

It is possible to obtain the estimate of the amount of sampling error for a mean on the basis of only one sample. If we know the size of the sample and the standard deviation of scores in that sample we can predict the standard deviation of sampling errors. This expected stan-dard deviation of sampling errors is the standard error of the mean, often represented either by the symbol SE_m or as σ_m. In formula form it is written

$$SE_m = \frac{\sigma}{\sqrt{N-1}}$$

Even when the sampling process is conducted along approved lines to ensure no bias in selection, it does not follow that the sample(s) drawn are completely representative. As we noted in our sampling exercise, the sample means do vary but at least there is no consistent or systematic difference. Each difference is a chance due only to 'error' inherent in sampling since unless the entire population is to be tested, there must be some slight fluctuations around the 'true' mean. Such errors are unavoidable and in the long run cancel out because they are random and therefore normally distributed. Random error must be carefully distinguished from constant or systematic error which func-tions in one direction only and which must be eliminated in various ways as we shall discuss in Chapter 17. Consider a project involving measuring the height of random samples of the adult male population. We might draw a large number of samples of 20 men. Only rarely would such a sample consist of men all above average height or all below average height. Most often men below and above average height would be included so that virtually all sample means would tend to deviate from the 'true' mean only by a relatively small amount. But each would contain random error even so, error being the deviation of the sample mean from the true mean. Increase the sample size and the concentration of sample means round the true mean becomes even more marked, since it becomes less likely to ran-domly select men who are all tall or all short as the sample size increases. The SE_m decreases as sample size increases, that is a larger random sample is more likely to be representative or provide a better estimate of the population than a small one. The smallness of the SE_m is a measure of the reliability of that mean.

If we did not carry out a random sample to gain one of the samples, but went to the barracks of the Scots Guards for our 20 men, we would obtain a mean that was considerably different from the population mean. This deviation would be systematic error, not random error, since we have systematically biased the sample.

The SE_m is much smaller than the σ because sampling means are not as spread out as the original scores. The equation makes it clear that as N increases so sampling error is reduced. Look at these hypothetical examples and note how the SE_m changes with increasing sample size.

$$SE_m = \frac{\sigma}{\sqrt{N-1}} = \frac{10}{\sqrt{100}} = 1.0$$

$$= \frac{10}{\sqrt{400}} = 0.05$$

$$= \frac{10}{\sqrt{900}} = 0.033$$

Horowitz (1974) demonstrated this concept of the distribution of sample means by artificially generating a population of 1000 normally distributed scores so that the mean and standard deviation of the entire population would be known. This is almost never the case in actual research situations, of course. His 1000 scores ranged from 0 to 100 and had a mean of 50 and a standard deviation of 15.8. The scores were listed on 1000 slips of paper and placed in a container. Ninety-six students, each drew samples of ten slips from the container, and calculated the mean. On each draw from the container, a slip was taken out, its number noted, and then replaced. The slips were mixed somewhat and another number was removed, and so on. After each student calculated the mean of the ten scores in her or his sample, Horowitz plotted the sampling distribution of these 96 means (Table 16). In Table 16 the intervals between which means might fall are on the left and the number of means falling within each interval is on the right. The distribution is almost perfectly symmetrical, with almost as many scores in any interval a certain distance below the true mean of the population (50) as above it. Also, the mean of the 96 sample means (49.99) is quite close to the actual mean of the population (50). But the main thing you should notice in Table 16 is the great variability among the sample means. Although each sample of ten was presumably random and not biased in any way, one sample had a mean of 37.8 while another had a mean of 62.3. Obviously these are very disparate means, even though they were sampled from the same population. If you were doing an experiment and found two very different sample means like this and were trying to decide whether they came from the same underlying distribution or two different distributions, you might think that such a large difference would indicate that they came from different distributions. In other words, you would think that the experimental treatment produced scores reliably different (from a different distribution) than the control scores. Usually this is a good rule – the larger the difference between means in the conditions, the more likely they are to be reliably different – but as we have seen here even random sampling from a known distribution can produce sample means that differ greatly from each other and from the true population mean, which is known in this case. This is a lesson that should be kept in mind while pondering small differences between means.

Table 16 The distribution of sample means for the 96 samples taken by students in Horowitz's class. Each sample mean was based on 10 observations (after Horowitz, 1974, Table 8.1)

Interval	Frequency	
62.0 – 63.9	1	
60.0 – 61.9	1	
58.0 – 59.9	3	
56.0 – 57.9	7	
54.0 – 55.9	9	Mean of sample means = 49.99
52.0 – 53.9	12	Standard deviation of sample means
50.0 – 51.9	15	(SE_m) = 5.01.
48.0 – 49.9	15	
46.0 – 47.9	13	
44.0 – 45.9	9	
42.0 – 43.9	6	
40.0 – 41.9	3	
38.0 – 39.9	1	
36.0 – 37.9	1	
	96	samples

Suppose we draw a random sample of 100 12-year-old children in such-and-such a school system. It would be difficult or impossible, say, to measure the whole universe of 12-year-old children for reasons we need not go into here. We compute the mean and the standard deviation from a test we give the children and find these statistics to be M = 110: σ = 10. An important question we must now ask ourselves is 'How accurate is this mean?' Or, if we were to draw a

large number of random samples of 100 pupils from this same population, would the means of these samples be 110 or near 110? And, if
they are near 110, how near? What we do, in effect, is to set up a
hypothetical distribution of sample means, all computed from
samples of 100 pupils each drawn from the parent population of
twelve-year-old pupils. If we could compute the mean of this population of means, or if we knew what it was, everything would be simple.
But we do not know this value, and we are not able to know it since
the possibilities of drawing different samples are so numerous. The
best we can do is to *estimate it with our sample value, or sample mean.*
We simply say, in this case, let the sample mean equal the mean of the
population mean – and hope we are right! Then we must test our
equation. This we do with the standard error.

A similar argument applies to the standard deviation of the whole
population (of the original scores). We do not know and probably can
never know it. But we can estimate it. And we estimate it with the
standard deviation computed from our sample. Again, we say, in
effect, let us assume that the standard deviation of the sample equals
the standard deviation of the population. We know they are probably
not the same value, but we also know, if the sampling has been random, that they are probably close. This is why the SE_m formula
employs the σ of the sample and not that of the unknown population.

The SE_m is often termed the sampling error. In fact this is how you
first met it in Chapter 7. Just as the standard deviation is a measure of
the dispersion of the original sample scores, the standard error of the
mean is a measure of the dispersion of the distribution of sample
means. It is *not* the standard deviation of the population of individual
scores.

Returning to our random sample of 100 12-year-olds with $M = 110$
and SD = 10 the $SE_m = 10/\sqrt{99} = 1.005$.

This figure of 1.005 is the standard deviation of sampling means of
random samples of 100 12-year-olds on that particular test. Now how
do we interpret it? Well we know that if we had taken a large number
of similar random samples and plotted their means we would have
produced a normal distribution. This normal distribution has a much
narrower spread than that proposed by the original raw scores. The
mean of the population or the mean of all sample means will form the
pivotal or central point on the baseline and the values for sample mean
will extend over the $\pm 3\sigma$ range as in any other normal distribution.
The proportion of sample means found under any part of the curve
can be found as before by reference to Table A in Appendix A. In
other words the normal distribution of sample means is no different in
characteristics from the normal distribution of raw scores.

> **STQ** *Do you remember the approximate percentages of scores found*
>
> *(i)   between ±1σ*
> *(ii)   between ±1.96σ*
> *(iii) between ±2.58σ*

Look up Table A (p. 404) if you are not sure.

The distribution of sample means follows the same pattern. 68% of all sample means from a defined population will fall between ±1σ from the 'true' mean. Likewise 95% and 99% of all sample means lie between ±1.96σ and ±2.58σ respectively from the 'true' or population mean. The standard deviation of this distribution, let us repeat, is the standard error of the mean (SE_m).

Do you recall the probability of obtaining a score at 1.96σ and 2.58σ? Refer back to p. 53 if you are hazy. The probabilities are the same for obtaining a sample mean at those distances from the true mean. That is, a sample mean will occur by chance 95 times in 100 between ±1.96σ and 99 in 100 between ±2.58σ along the baseline. If you cannot follow any of this argument you must retrace your steps and reread Chapter 6.

The normal distribution of sample means provides again a theoretical probability distribution that acts as a mathematical model against which we can set our research findings just as we did in our penny tossing (Chapter 5). We are enabled to state the probability that a particular observation, say in this instance a sample mean, has occurred by chance. In other words we are interpreting the probability of obtaining mean scores in this chapter in the same way as we interpreted the probability of obtaining individual scores in Chapter 6.

Of course we can only specify certain limits for the estimate of how far one sample mean, perhaps the only one we have and are ever likely to have, is close to the 'true' mean. We can never be certain.

Thinking now in terms of errors rather than mean values, you can realize that at the centre of the normal distribution of sample means we have zero error. This occurs with maximum frequency – i.e. of all our estimates of the population mean the correct value will occur with highest frequency. As we move to the 'tails' of the curve, the errors get larger. But their frequency correspondingly decreases. In other words in our very large number of samples, the size of the error we are likely to find is inversely related to the number of samples in which it occurs. As the size of the error goes up, its frequency goes down. Minimum errors are likely to occur most often; maximum errors are likely to occur least often; in between we have errors of varying frequency of occurrence.

Let us make a final return to our 100 twelve-year-old children, for whom with a $M = 110$, $\sigma = 10$ the SE_m was 1.005. We can now calculate that 95% of all similar samples will have means that lie within $\pm 1.96\sigma$ of 110, i.e. 1.96 $\times$ 1.005 in either direction. Since 1.96 $\times$ 1.005 equals 1.97, the boundary scores for the 95% limits are 111.97 and 108.03.

STQ   *Can you now calculate the boundary scores within which 99% of sample means will lie?*

Suppose we did obtain quite a number of other samples, most of whose means lay close to 110 but suddenly out of the blue we found one which was quite different, a mean of 114 in fact. We can calculate its z score distance from the centre of the sampling distribution of means by the z score formula:

$$z = \frac{X - M}{\sigma}$$

$$z = \frac{114 - 110}{1.005} = \frac{4}{1.005} = 3.98$$

The probability of obtaining a sample M at this point is well beyond the 0.01 level in fact three times in 100 000. Check this in Table A (Appendix A).

This would be so rare a sample mean as to suggest that either it is a biased on non-random sample, or that the samples do not come from the same sampling distribution, i.e. they are from a different population of children, perhaps an older age group for example.

Here is another example to illustrate the value of standard error. Imagine that an IQ test with $M = 100$ and $\sigma = 15$ was given to a random sample of 100 children from a low class city area. The mean IQ obtained was 96. Is this strong evidence for concluding that children of that area are below average in intelligence? In essence we are asking, is this obtained mean just one of the plethora of possible random fluctuations round the true population mean? Is it a sampling deviation from the true mean of 100? The SE_m in this case is $15/\sqrt{100} = 1.5$. The obtained mean of 96 expressed as a deviation from the true mean in SE_m units is $4/1.5 = 2.66$. That is, the obtained mean is 2.66 standard deviation units below the true mean. From Table A, Appendix A, we can see that similar sample means would occur with a $p < 0.0039$, i.e. would arise less than four times in 1000 samples. Accordingly we conclude that children from this particular city area are not average in intelligence but are as a group significantly different and in saying this there is less than a 0.4% chance of being wrong.

Other statistics beside the mean have standard errors since they too provide estimates of population parameters, and in each case the standard deviation of the sampling distribution is known as the standard error of that statistic, e.g. standard error of a median; standard error of a proportion; standard error of a correlation.

STQ **(1)** *A random sample of 226 British policemen have a mean length of foot of fifteen inches with a standard deviation of 1. What is the SE_m?*

(2) *Which sample size will provide the smallest SE_m assuming the same σ: 25, 100, 5, 70.*

In the previous section we saw that the crucial test in considering whether a sample mean came from the same sampling distribution as the other sample means was that of comparing the extent of the deviation of the sample mean from the 'true' mean to the standard error. We formed a ratio by dividing the difference between the sample mean and true mean by the SE_m which provides us with the deviation in standard-error units. In our example (p. 84) we had $4/1.5 = 2.66$. This ratio is an example of a number of similar ratios which follow the model of testing an obtained statistic against the standard error of that statistic to find out the extent of its deviation from the population estimate. As we know from Chapter 7 if large numbers of similar samples were drawn, the different values of their means would be normally distributed about the population, true or expected mean, with a standard deviation equal to the estimated standard error. However, samples can be of different sizes and sample size influences the size of SE_m. So if we calculated SE_m from samples of differing sizes the estimated SE_m would change and small sample sizes can produce far from negligible differences in SE_m from those produced by large samples (look back at the calculations on p. 80). The estimated SE_m is then not constant from sample to sample. So the ratios $(M(\text{sample}) - M(\text{true}))/SE_m$ are not constant either. These ratios, highly important ones, are called t ratios or critical ratios. The distribution of these ratios each with a different SE_m as the denominator due to sample size difference, departs from normal distribution. There is in fact a different t distribution for every sample size. With small samples t departs appreciably from normality with relatively more extreme values. As sample size increases so the t distribution becomes more and more similar to the normal or z distribution. Table B, Appendix A, is a table of the distribution of t for various sample sizes. Sample size is indicated by degrees of freedom in the table. For now take degrees of freedom (df), as N-1.

We will consider degrees of freedom later on (Chapter 16).

Look at Table B now. With 6 *df*, deviates of 2.447 units (i.e. $t =$ 2.447) are necessary to include 95% of the area (i.e. 5% level) compared to 1.96 units in a normal distribution. However, as sample size increases to 30, deviates of 2.045 are required and for samples in excess of 120 the normal distribution of z and the t distribution are approximately the same. The values in each column in the t table are those which must be achieved for a particular *df* at a specified level of significance.

STQ   *Using Table B find the value of t required for significance in each of the following cases. (Assume two-tailed test).*

(i)	*N*	=	21	$p<0.05$
(ii)	*df*	=	60	$p<0.01$
(iii)	*df*	=	30	$p<0.05$
(iv)	*df*	=	4	$p<0.001$
(v)	*df*	=	∞	$p<0.05$

Answers on p. 433.

Degrees of freedom

Imagine that you are holding a dinner party for twelve people. You wish to seat them round a table each in a pre-arranged place. When you have labelled the places for eleven of the guests, the twelfth or final person must sit at the only place left. We have no 'freedom' about where we will place him. So we can say that although there are twelve people (N) there are only eleven ($N-1$) degrees of freedom. The final place is always determined no matter how many people we are trying to seat. This principle applies in statistics whether we are concerned with ΣX, M or the variance.

Let us consider ΣX and M first of all. Suppose we have a sample size $N = 10$. The mean value can be calculated and all but one of the scores can be altered to other values without altering the mean. One score's value is, however, determined by the remaining nine because of the necessity that their total scores sum to $N \times M$. Thus one score is not free to vary but is controlled by what the other nine values are. The number of degrees of freedom are 1 less than N or $N - 1$. In another example if one had three numbers, which sum to 24 and hence a mean of 8, with two of the numbers known, i.e. 10 and 6, then the third is fixed, i.e. 8. If we alter the 10 to 11 and the 6 to 7 then we have determined that the third must be 6 if the ΣX and M are to remain the same.

In experiments with two groups of subjects each group must lose one degree of freedom. To show this let us return to our dinner party. We are old fashioned enough to try and seat men and women in alternate seats round the table. In this case, once you had seated five men and five women, everyone would know where the last man and the last woman would have to sit. This is like the case where there are two groups of six subjects, N_1 and N_2. In fact, for each group there are only five degrees of freedom ($N_1 - 1$ and $N_2 - 1$).

You have probably noticed that in many of the formulae you have met, e.g. σ, SE_m, the denominator has been $N-1$ rather than N. We use $N-1$ when we are dealing with samples and N when we are dealing with a population. Samples will only provide estimates of population parameters and if we divided by N we would bias the estimate. Think of it this way: samples are relatively small, populations are relatively large. If we divide a large number the difference between using $N-1$ or N is minute but if we divide a small number the choice of $N-1$ or N can make a large difference to the answer. To divide sample data by $N-1$ will provide an estimate of the population which has no systematic tendency to be either greater or less than the relevant population parameter.

Degrees of freedom are usually symbolized as *df*. In many statistical tables results are evaluated not against N but against *df*, e.g. tables of *t* are summaries of separate distributions for each *df*. With a large *df* the *t* distribution approaches the normal distribution.

REFERENCES
Horowitz, L. M. (1974). *Elements of Statistics for Psychology and Education.* (New York: McGraw-Hill)

9

Hypothesis formation

A What is an hypothesis?

A hypothesis is a hunch, an educated guess which is advanced for the purpose of being tested. If research were limited to gathering facts, knowledge could not advance. Without some guiding idea or something to prove, every experiment would be fruitless, since we could not determine what was relevant and what was irrelevant. Try this everyday example of hypothesis formation. Suppose the only light you had on in the bedroom was the bedside table lamp. Suddenly it went off. You would no doubt ponder the reason for it. Try to think of several reasons now and write them down.

There could be a number of causes. I wrote, (i) lamp bulb failure, (ii) plug fuse failure, (iii) main power fuse failure. Whatever you wrote is an implied hypothesis, an educated guess. In practice you would test each one in turn until the cause was located. Let us imagine the cause was a fuse failure in the plug. Because the lights came on after I changed the fuse only lends support to the hypothesis. It does not prove it. The fault could have been caused by a temporary faulty connection which in turn caused the fuse to blow. In mending the fuse I corrected the connection by chance as I caught the wire with my screwdriver unbeknown to me. Proved carries the connotation of finality, and certainty. Hypotheses are not proved by producing evidence congruent with the consequences – they are simply not disproved. On the other hand if the observed facts do not confirm the prediction made on the basis of the hypothesis then it is rejected conclusively.

B Why do we need hypotheses?

In Chapter 1 we saw that the use of the scientific method follows a series of logical steps. The impetus for any inquiry involves the identification of a problem which needs a solution. However, it is not enough to just identify a problem. The statement of a problem is often vague, diffuse and unmanageable. It must be refined and narrowed so that it can be researched. A hypothesis is the basic way one can state a problem in clear, succinct and operational terms which enables it to be tested. Hypotheses, then, state the expected or predicted relationships between variables.

A theory as developed by a scientist is, like the theory of the layman, a set of generalizations believed to have some value in predicting important events. But the scientist and the layman differ in the way in which they derive their theories – the theory of the scientist is derived from well established knowledge and is formulated in as precise terms as he can find; that of the layman is rooted in casual observation. A theory may be formulated in a set of carefully worded statements, or, if the state of knowledge is far enough advanced, in a set of mathematical equations. From the theory which he has formulated the scientist derives hypotheses, which are simply statements of some of the consequences that can be expected of the theory if it is true. He can then investigate these hypotheses in order to determine whether the theory he has formulated stands up when it is used for making predictions.

C Hypothetico-deductive approach

This mode of accounting for problems is the characteristic pattern of scientific thinking. It possesses three essential steps:

(a) The proposal of a hypothesis to account for a phenomenon.
(b) The deduction from the hypothesis that certain phenomena should be observed in given circumstances.
(c) The checking of this deduction by observation.

Hypothetico-deductive arguments have a clear logical structure which can help one to see the pitfalls that the unwary researcher may fall into. We start with a suppostition or assertion H_1 which has a number of deducible consequences – C_1, C_2, C_3. By testing these consequences

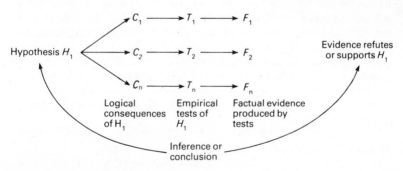

Figure 15 Hypothetico-deductive approach

by appropriate empirical procedures a conclusion is drawn. This is used to confirm or refute the hypothesis. The diagram (Figure 15) illustrates this process.

But notice the status of the conclusion drawn. It is an inference, not a proof. The researcher who tests and confirms one consequence of a hypothesis may think that he has established the cause of the phenomenon he is investigating. But this reasoning is faulty.

The reseacher may show that C_1, C_2, C_3 support H_1 or confirm it to a certain extent, but other hypotheses *may* also account for these consequences. What the evidence C_1, C_2, C_3 can do is refute the hypothesis. If one single consequence of it turns out to be unsuported then the hypothesis must be wrong. This distinguishes the scientific hypothesis from everyday speculation and conjecture. A scientific hypothesis is one that can be disproved. We shall see what this implies later when we discuss the null hypothesis. (Chapter 10).

Let us look at another example. An educational psychologist may have reasoned that poor family background causes poor reading attainment in children. He may have tried to produce empirical evidence that low family income and overcrowding are associated with poor reading attainment. If no such evidence was forthcoming then, as we have seen, the hypothesis must be decisively rejected. But if the predicted relationship was found could the researcher conclude that his hypothesis was correct – i.e. that poor family background does cause low reading attainment? The answer must be 'no'. It might equally have been the case that bad teaching is to blame which may also be associated with the consequences of a poor home background, because schools in poor neighbourhoods may attract only the less competent teachers. In other words there may be alternative hypotheses which explain the phenomenon of reading backwardness equally well. These alternative hypotheses will have other deducible consequences, e.g. if poor teaching in poor neighbourhoods causes backwardness in reading, then in-service training of teachers in schools in poor neighbourhoods will improve reading attainment among the children in these schools. To underline the main point once again, the scientific process never leads to certainty in explanation – only the rejection of existing hypotheses and the construction of new ones, which stand up best to the test of empirical evidence.

STQ *Write a brief paragraph to explain why hypotheses can never be proved.*

D How do we formulate hypotheses?

The formulation of hypotheses follows logically on from the review of literature on the problem. But problems are not the only source of hypotheses. They are often derived from theory too, since theory guides research and provides predictions which need testing. Hypotheses are the working instruments of theory. But regardless of the source of the hypothesis it must meet one criterion. The hypothesis must be stated so that it is capable of being either confirmed or refuted. A hypothesis which cannot be tested does not belong to the realm of science. Hypotheses must be operational.

Consider the following hypothesis: 'Is a person's authoritarian behaviour directly related to his attitudes concerning punishment received from his parents?' Although this statement of purpose is quite detailed, it conveys little information unless the meanings of 'authoritarian behaviour', 'attitudes concerning', 'punishment' and 'received' are clearly defined. Even though these terms have meanings known to most individuals, they lack sufficient precision for use in scientific investigations.

The investigator can define the terms more specifically by using other terms, that is, by substituting words about words. He may, for example, define authoritarianism by using phrases which include 'respect for order', 'stereotyped thinking', 'need for authority' and 'dependence'. The meaning is no clearer, however, unless each of these terms is further broken down into a description of states which can be directly observed. To avoid this dilemma of indefiniteness, the investigator can relate how authoritarianism will be measured. He can employ an operational definition in which a process is substituted for the conventional definitional description, i.e. by a score on a particular scale of authoritarianism.

The term authoritarianism has now been operationally defined so that everyone understands what the author means. Other testing instruments can be used to define operationally 'attitudes toward the parental punishment'. To cite another example, 'gifted' can be operationally defined as follows: 'If and only if a child scores at or above a point two standard deviations above the mean on the Stanford Binet'.

If we want to study the relationship between childhood aggression and exposure to violent television programmes, we need to define both the variables under study, i.e. aggression and television violence, operationally. The former might be simply a tally of the observed aggressive acts of children such as hitting, kicking, biting others, damaging, or destroying property. Or it might be based on an analysis of projective test material, i.e. aggressive feelings as revealed on the TAT.

Another way to develop an operational definition of aggression would be to have a panel of judges watch a film of each child in a free-play situation and then rate the child's aggressiveness on a seven-point scale. Or we could tell each child several stories about other children in frustrating situations and ask the child what he or she would do in each situation. We could then use the number of 'direct-attack' responses as a measure of aggressiveness. Another alternative would be to observe children as they play with a selection of toys we had previously classified as aggressive – such as guns, tanks, and knives – or non-aggressive – such as trucks, tools and dolls. We could then measure the percentage of time that the child played with each type of toy. You can undoubtedly think of many other behaviours that would be an indication of a child's aggressiveness.

The defining of violent television programmes may be somewhat harder to agree on. What constitutes violent television? Is the Saturday-night soccer match violent? Are Popeye cartoons violent? Is Starsky and Hutch violent? Are news and current affairs programmes on Cambodia, Vietnam and Northern Ireland violent? Not everyone would agree on these.

The problem here is that there is a difference in precision between what the general public will accept in defining a term and what experimental psychologists will accept. An operational definition of the variables means that psychologists must specify the operations they would go through to determine if a television programme were violent and outline the specific steps they would take to classify television programmes.

For example, if you were conducting our television experiment, you could operationalize the concept of a violent television programme by showing each programme to a randomly chosen group of 100 people and requiring that 75% of them indicate a programme is violent before you operationally define it as violent. Another alternative would be to devise a checklist with such items as: 'Is there physical contact of an aggressive nature?' 'Has an illegal act taken place?' 'Did one person act so as to make another feel inferior?' Perhaps you would require that each programme have at least five out of ten such items checked 'yes' in order for it to be considered violent.

A great many important psychological questions require complex operational definitions: do people whose mothers were affectionate make more successful marriage partners? Do students learn more from popular professors? Does a worker's morale affect work output? Does anxiety cause depression? Prior to doing an experiment to answer any of these questions, you would need operational definitions for the terms affectionate, popular, morale, and anxiety.

STQ *Try to formulate operational definitions of 'affectionate', 'popular', 'morale' and 'anxiety'. How do you propose to measure such concepts?*

The use of operational definitions enables the researcher to indicate the exact means used to determine unobservable states referred to in the statement of purpose. Even though an operational meaning may be clear, the acceptability of a measure used to determine such conditions as 'attitude towards punishment' and 'authoritarianism' may be questioned by the discerning reader. By indicating the exact nature of measurements made or things studied, however, the researcher has achieved clarity if not acceptance. Greater progress can be made toward the establishment of a solid foundation of knowledge if both researcher and critic are aware of the extensional meanings associated with terms used in stating hypotheses. Without operational definitions, scholarly disputations are reduced to words about words.

E Research and operational hypotheses

Many research workers see an hierarchy of hypotheses in a research study, each hypothesis being a tighter and more testable statement than its predecessor. They often term the original hypothesis derived from the hazy problem as the Research Hypothesis. When this latter is re-expressed in operational terms it becomes the Operational Hypothesis.

For instance, Christopher Columbus had a theory that the world was round. From this theory he hypothesized that if he sailed due West he would arrive at the Indies. This hypothesis would have been rather difficult to arrive at and, in addition, more difficult to accept as testable, had it not been for the general theory engendering it. When Columbus set sail from Spain his actions were directed by this hypothesis and so it is called an operational hypothesis.

In between his chain of thought beginning at his theory and ending with his operational hypothesis there was an intermediate stage of thought called a research hypothesis where he no doubt formulated from the theory a more general and hazier hypothesis, such as 'If the world is round then a traveller will eventually come back to his starting point'. This intermediate hypothesis is easier to construct from its parent theory than is the more precise and ultimate operational hypothesis but the research hypothesis suffers from the fact that it too is in too general terms to test. In order to test it one would have to choose a particular traveller, and a particular starting point, and point him in a certain direction and stipulate the opposite direction as the one from which he would eventually appear from his world circumnavigation.

As another example suppose we have decided to investigate Eysenck's theory of personality in relation to academic attainment in higher education students. The research hypothesis might read as follows:

that extraversion and neuroticism are related to academic performance of students in higher education. This research hypothesis is still
not in a form that can be tested; it needs to be operationalized, i.e. the
phenomena referred to in it need to be defined in terms of observations that can be made.

In our research hypothesis about the relationship between personality and academic attainment, suppose that the measures used
were the Eysenck Personality Inventory (the EPI), which is designed
to measure the variables 'extraversion' and 'neuroticism' and degree
result which will give a measure of academic attainment.

STQ   *Write down now two operational hypotheses which could
be derived from the research hypothesis.*

In this instance you could have postulated that 'Extraversion, as
measured by the Eysenck Personality Inventory, will be significantly
related to degree classification. Or 'neuroticism, as measured by the
Eysenck Personality Inventory, will relate significantly with degree
classification'.

Look at this sequence of hypothesis refinement moving from the
general to the operational.

Problem or General Hypothesis	You expect some children to read better than others because they come from homes in which there are positive values and attitudes to education.
Research Hypothesis	Reading ability is related to attitudes towards education in nine-year-old children.
Operational Hypothesis	There is a significant relationship between reading ability as measured by standardized reading test X and attitudes to education as measured by attitude test Y for nine-year-old children living in a major conurbation in West Yorkshire.

F Criteria for judging hypotheses

(a) Hypotheses should be stated clearly, in correct terminology, and
    operationally. General terms such as personality, school attain-
    ment, social class etc. should be avoided. The statement demands
    concise technical language and the definition of terms. More ap-
    propriate therefore are – 'personality as measured by the Eysenck
    Personality Inventory'; 'school attainment as measured by

English Progress Test E (National Foundation for Educational Research)'; 'Social class as defined by the Registrar General's classification of head of household's occupation. Such hypotheses as 'creativity is a function of self actualization' and 'democratic education enhances social learning' are too vague.

(b) Hypotheses should be testable. Since hypotheses are predictors of the outcome of the study, an obvious necessity is that instruments should exist (or can be developed) which will provide valid measures of the variables involved.

(c) Hypotheses should state relationships between variables. A satisfactory hypothesis is one in which the expected relationship between the variables is made explicit.

(d) Hypotheses should be limited in scope. Hypotheses of global significance are not required; those that are specific and relatively simple to test are preferable. It is of course possible to state a rather broad research hypothesis and derive a number of operational hypotheses from it.

(e) Hypotheses should not be inconsistent with most known facts. All hypotheses should be grounded in past knowledge, i.e. the knowledge gained from a review of the literature. They obviously cannot be consistent with all known facts since many studies give contradictory results. In these cases the hypothesis may be formulated to resolve the contradiction. For example, differences in the relationships found between personality and attainment in different age groups might be due to methodological errors or might be explained by a new hypothesis that the form of the relationship changes with age. There is also certainly room for the use of imagination in the extrapolation of known facts to new populations. But the hypothesis should not lead the cynical reader to say to himself 'whatever led you to expect that' or 'you made this one up after you collected the data'.

STQ *Now consider the following examples in terms of the five criteria above. Look at each hypothesis and say whether it satisfies all the criteria; if it does not say why not.*

EXAMPLE 1
Among fifteen-year-old male school children, introverts as measured by the Eysenck Personality Inventory, will gain significantly higher scores on a vigilance task involving the erasing of every 'e' on a typescript than extraverts.

EXAMPLE 2
Progressive teaching methods have led to a decline in academic standards in British primary schools.

EXAMPLE 3
The introduction of psychology into the curricula of secondary schools will produce better citizens.

EXAMPLE 4
A hungry rat will learn a maze task quicker than a better fed rat.

   Possible answers to examples 1−4 above.

EXAMPLE 1
'Among 15-year-old male school children, introverts, as measured by the Eysenck Personality Inventory, will gain significantly higher scores on a vigilance task involving erasing every 'e' on a typescript than extraverts.'

In this example the hypothesis is formulated in concise language in which the terms are defined: there is a stated relationship between the variables of extraversion, introversion and vigilance, which is testable; it is not too broad in scope, and is consistent with most known facts. All five criteria are therefore satisfied.

EXAMPLE 2
'Progressive Teaching methods have led to a decline in academic standards in British primary schools.'

Two variables − progressive teaching methods and academic standards − are related, thus satisfying the third criterion. However, general terms are used − how are progressive teaching methods to be defined? Can they be tested? What academic standards are involved? Over what period of time is the comparison to be made? Are all age groups within British schools involved? What evidence is there for this decline? It is clear that only criterion 3 is satisfied in this example.

EXAMPLE 3
'The introduction of psychology into the curricula of secondary schools will produce better citizens.'

The major disadvantage of this hypothesis, in its present form, is that it is virtually untestable. To find out whether social science courses and citizenship are related would require that pupils who have taken social science courses have grown to adulthood, criteria of citizenship would have to be formulated against which each subject could be evaluated and, most difficult, it would have to be determined what part the social science course had played in each individual's citizenship rating. Furthermore, terms such as 'better citizen' involve value judgements which are unlikely to be acceptable to all investigators – i.e. any one operational definition of the term is unlikely to satisfy many people.

EXAMPLE 4
'A hungry rat will learn a maze task quicker than a better fed rat.'

This is a totally inadequate hypothesis. We need to define 'hungry rat' and 'better fed rat' perhaps in terms of hours since last fed. What does 'learn' imply? Is is the first occasion correct or until the task is performed five times correctly in succession?

G Unconfirmed hypothesis
But what if the hypothesis is not confirmed? Does this invalidate the prior literature? If the hypothesis is not confirmed then either the hypothesis is false or some error exists in its conception. Some of the previous information may have been erroneous or other relevant information overlooked; the experimenter might have misinterpreted some previous literature or the experimental design might have been incorrect. When the experimenter discovers what he thinks is wrong a new hypothesis is formulated, and a different study conducted. Such is the continuous on-going process of the scientific method. Even if a hypothesis is refuted, knowledge is advanced.

Further STQs
(1) *Construct research and operational hypotheses for the following problems.*

    (a) Does learning how to learn transfer to new situations?
    (b) Does teacher feedback cause changes in student performance?
    (c) Does group decision-making lead to less risk taking?

(2) *Why is knowledge advanced if a hypothesis cannot be supported?*

10

Hypothesis testing

You will recall (Chapter 9) that the refuting or supporting of a hypothesis is a major element in scientific methodology. A hypothesis is a reasonable conjecture about a particular state of nature. Two different ways of stating a hypothesis exist to match the two major approaches in research design, those of, (i) looking for differences between groups, and (ii) looking for relationships between groups. So we have hypotheses which make statements about differences or which make statements about relationships. For example, a hypothesis which states that there is a difference between the performance of primary-school boys and girls in reading skills is obviously a different hypothesis and requires different statistical measures from a hypothesis that states that there is a relationship between self-esteem and academic performance in secondary school pupils.

It was argued in Chapter 9 that there are various levels in hypothesis statements, each producing a more rigorous and operational statement than the previous form.

STQ *Can you recall the three levels of hypotheses? Look back to Chapter 9.*

We conceptualized the following three levels:

(a) The general hypothesis is frequently a statement of the problem area in general terms,
(b) The research hypothesis then restates this in a concise, succinct, specific way,
(c) The operational or experimental hypothesis puts the research hypothesis into operational terms so that variables are defined unambiguously and can be measured.

This brings us to the important point that in statistical analysis we do not actually test the operational hypothesis we are advancing but its logical opposite – the null hypothesis. In other words we do not test the hypothesis that a population correlation or difference does exist, but instead we test the hypothesis that there is no population correlation or difference. Why do we do this?

The reason is based on simple logic. Suppose we hypothesize that there should be a difference between the mean scores of boys and girls on a field dependence/independence test with a range of marks from 0 to 20. This hypothesis would be satisfied by any difference in the mean scores from 0 to 20. More realistically, the difference might be 3, 5, 7 or 9 marks – any of these would satisfy the hypothesis. On the other hand, if we state the hypothesis in the null hypothesis form, i.e. that no difference exists, we have only one value to deal with: zero. We can then say that the null hypothesis is refuted if any difference occurs over and above zero. This, of course, would be a valid statement to make about differences in the total population. In practice in psychological research we are generally dealing with a sample of data from the population which we use to estimate the population values of our variables. Any estimate of a population parameter involves sampling error. So what we are actually doing in stating a statistical null hypothesis is saying that there is no difference between the mean values over and above the difference brought about by random sampling error. Statistical theory enables us to specify the limits of this sampling error around any estimated population value, including zero (we dealt with standard error in Chapter 8). We can thus set precise limits – significance levels – for the rejection of a null hypothesis. This is the basic principle on which all statistical tests are founded.

Setting aside the question of sampling error for a moment, supposing we are able to reject a null hypothesis. We can then confirm an alternative hypothesis that a difference does exist. This is of course the hypothesis that we are primarily interested in; but we now call it the alternative hypothesis to emphasize the point that we reach it via the null hypothesis and not the other way round.

The null hypothesis is thus a proposition which states essentially that there is no relationship or difference. When proposed the null hypothesis is saying to you, 'you are wrong, there is no relationship (or difference) – disprove me if you can'. As Fisher (1951) argues, 'every experiment may be said to exist only in order to give the facts a chance of disproving a null hypothesis'. The operational, or alternative, hypothesis is often designated H_1 and the null hypothesis as H_0.

Since we are usually dealing with samples and not populations the null hypothesis does *not* imply that there is *no* relationship or *no* difference, i.e. it does not mean absolute equality. It means that there is no relationship or difference greater than that due to chance or random fluctuation.

The sequence of hypothesis formulation is depicted below.

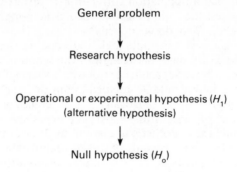

General problem

↓

Research hypothesis

↓

Operational or experimental hypothesis (H_1)
(alternative hypothesis)

↓

Null hypothesis (H_0)

The null hypothesis is a succinct way to express the testing of obtained data against chance expectation. The null hypothesis is the chance expectation. The standard error is a means of testing the null hypothesis. Indeed, it expresses the null hypothesis since it is a measure of expected chance fluctuations around a mean of zero.

How do we know when the relationship or difference is large enough to be significant to exceed chance expectation? Well, we use the levels of significance (0.05, 0.01, 0.001) which we discussed in Chapter 6. Tables exist (Appendix A pp. 403–17) which tell us whether our results reach these levels or not.

Operational or experimental (the alternative) hypotheses should be stated in a way similar to the following, 'that there is a significant relationship (difference) between . . .'. Null hypotheses should take the following form, 'that there is no significant relationship (difference) between . . .'. By placing the term 'significant' in the proposition we are emphasizing the fact that our test of the null hypothesis invokes the test against a stated and conventionally acceptable level of statistical significance. Only if such a defined level is reached can we discard the null hypothesis and accept the alternative one, always remembering that we are never proving a hypothesis, only testing it, eventually rejecting or accepting it at some level of probability.

EXAMPLE

Suppose an experiment tests the retention of lists of words under two conditions:

(1) The lists are presented at a fixed pace determined by the experimenter.
(2) The lists are perused at a rate determined by the subject attempting to memorize them – self-pacing.

The null hypothesis simply predicts that the two conditions, fixed and self-pacing, will not produce any real difference in list retention. The experimental or operational hypothesis predicts the alternative – that the two conditions will produce a genuine difference in list retention.

These hypotheses cannot be tested simply by noting whether or not the mean retention scores are identical or different in the two experimental conditions. Different mean scores may be thought to support the alternative hypothesis, but a difference in scores might be due to chance fluctuations alone. Conversely identical mean scores might be thought to support the null hypothesis, but the identity might be a coincidental correspondence produced by variability of scores around two real and genuinely different levels of performance.

For such reasons the null hypothesis is couched in the following form: the two conditions will not differ by an amount which is greater than that to be expected by chance alone, i.e. there is no significant difference.

The alternative hypothesis is couched in this form: the two conditions will differ by an amount which is greater than is to be expected by chance alone, i.e. there is a significant difference.

In evaluating the null hypothesis it is possible to work out the probability that an observed difference is due simply to chance, because we can use a theoretical sampling distribution.

So the procedure adopted for evaluating an experimental hypothesis is as follows:

(a) Set up the null hypothesis, i.e. any observed difference between conditions is entirely attributable to chance fluctuations.
(b) Calculate the exact probability that the observed difference could have been derived by chance alone.
(c) Accept the null hypothesis if this probability is higher than a certain value (i.e. the chosen level of significance). Reject the null hypothesis if the probability is below a certain level (i.e. the chosen level of significance).
(d) Accept the experimental hypothesis if the null hypothesis has been rejected. Reject the experimental hypothesis if the null hypothesis has been retained.

A summary of the logic of statistical inference

The rationale behind statistical inference then is as follows:

(a) Whenever a difference between the two experimental conditions is observed, one or the other of the following statements necessarily holds true:

(i) *Null hypothesis.* The difference is due entirely to random error or chance.

(ii) *Experimental hypothesis.* The difference is not due entirely to random error; that is, it is due in part, at least, to some constant effect; either an experimental effect or systematic error. (Chapters 14 and 17 cover experimental error.)

(b)   The probability that random error alone produced a difference as large as the one we observed is sufficiently low that we reject this possibility; that is, we reject the null hypothesis.

(c)   There, we accept the experimental hypothesis.

The first statement is necessarily true, for it merely presents a partition of possibilities and asserts that one and only one of the alternatives can represent the true state of affairs. Note that the statement of the experimental hypothesis does not distinguish between an experimental effect and experimental error. This distinction cannot be made on the basis of statistical inference but must be made on the basis of a consideration of the design of the experiment. Statistical inference deals with random error only, and not with systematic error (vide Chapter 14).

The second statement is based on, (a) some very straightforward probability calculations, and (b) a decision as to how low the probability of an event has to be before we will be willing to reject the possibility of its having occurred by chance.

The third statement simply follows logically from the others. It may seem that we are approaching the problem backwards, however. For, while it is the experimental hypothesis in which we are really interested, instead of proving it directly we prove it by disproving the null hypothesis. Is this roundabout procedure actually necessary? The answer is yes, and the reason is that only the null hypothesis is sufficiently precise to permit us to compute the probabilities that are required to decide whether it is likely to be true or not. The null hypothesis states that exactly 100% of the effect is random. In order to compute probabilities, we need an exact hypothesis like this. We can say that the probability of getting heads with a fair (100% random) coin is 1/2 or 0.50, but we cannot say what the corresponding probability is for a biased coin without knowing how great the bias is. Thus, we test directly the status of the more precise hypothesis and infer the status of the experimental hypothesis we are really interested in.

STQ   *Look back at Chapter 5 and the coin-tossing example in which you ended up owing me a large number of pints because the coin came down heads in an unbroken succession of tosses.*

> *Can you now answer the following questions?*
>
> *(a) What is the null hypothesis of this experiment?*
> *(b) What is the alternative hypothesis?*
> *(c) What was the probability of obtaining the run by chance alone at which you personally rejected the null hypothesis? (Refer to Table A, Appendix A.)*

We would have answered the above STQ as follows

(a) That the coin is fair, or not biased.
(b) That the coin is unfair, or biased.
(c) Each of you may have chosen a different probability, but in science there are commonly accepted conventions about what particular probability to accept as evidence for rejecting the null hypothesis. The lowest level commonly used is the 0.05 level, or the 5% level. What it means is that the null hypothesis will be rejected when the probability of the result having arisen by chance alone is as low as or lower than 0.05. So, the null hypothesis is rejected if the result we obtain would only be expected to arise by chance alone on five or less occasions if we were to repeat the experiment exactly on a hundred occasions.

Incidentally, was your personal level of significance about the same as the commonly accepted 0.05 level? That is, did you reject the null hypothesis (of a fair coin) at about the point where the probability of a run of heads from a fair coin dropped below 0.05 or 5%? Did you choose some other level? Why not adopt the level you opted for?

In one sense there is no reason. Levels of significance are fairly arbitrary as we have seen. However, it is impoortant to have a public standard to go by so that we all know what we mean when we describe a result as significant. Otherwise one person may call a result significant when it could have occurred by chance on 50 out of every 100 occasions of testing (i.e. a 50% level of significance), whereas another person may be reluctant to call a result significant unless it could only have occurred by chance on less than one in a thousand occasions of testing (i.e. a 0.1% level of significance). So a fixed level of significance between the extremes helps to temper the optimists and encourage the pessimists.

> **Further STQs**
> (1) *Formulate null hypotheses for the following experimental hypotheses.*
>   *(a) That there is a significant difference in the mean score on Raven's Progressive Matrices between males over*

> the age of retirement and males between the ages of 55
> and 65 still at work.
> *(b)* That there is a significant relationship between scores
> on Witkin's Embedded Figures Test and extraversion
> as measured by the EPI in psychology A-level students.
>
> **(2)** *Assuming the relationship in 1(b) above was found to be
> significant, make a statement about the implications for,
> (a) the null hypothesis and (b) the experimental hypothesis.*
>
> **(3)** *What level of 't' (two tailed) would you require to reject the
> null hypothesis with df = 20 and p < 0.01?*
>
> **(4)** *What does any null hypothesis predict?*

TYPE I AND TYPE II ERROR
Statistical inference can lead to two kinds of error: rejecting the null
hypothesis when it is true and accepting it when it is false. The first
kind of error is called a type I error; it is the optimistic error of 'seeing
too much in the data'. The second kind of error is called a type II error; it is the pessimistic error of 'not seeing enough in the data'. The
significance level affects the probabilities of both types of error; as the
significance level is made smaller, the probability of a type I error

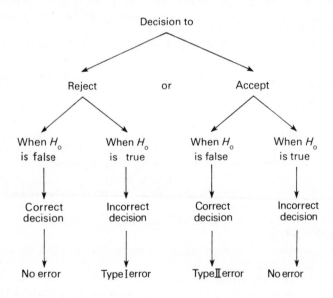

Figure 16 Statistical decisions

decreases, and the probability of a type II error increases. We ordinarily set the significance level low, so as to provide more protection against a type I error than against a type II error. There are two reasons for this. One is that the consequences of a type I error are generally more serious. When you reject the null hypothesis, you usually take positive action – for example, publishing the results; or advocating some sort of social action. When you accept the null hypothesis, on the other hand, you usually do not take positive action. The other reason for setting the significance level so as to provide more protection against a type I error is that we have no other protection against this error. Because of these considerations, then, the minimum significance level is most commonly 0.05.

Thus, if the probability that random error alone produced a difference as large as the one observed is 0.05 or less, we will reject the null hypothesis, and if it is larger than 0.05 we will retain the null hypothesis. So by now I hope you can detect the analogy between gambling and hypothesis testing. By setting a particular significance level the researcher is *gambling* that he will distinguish chance results from genuine ones. If he sets his level too high, i.e. a very low probability value, then he may decide that a difference is a chance result when it is in fact a genuine one. If he sets it too low he may be in danger of accepting a result which is really a chance effect.

STQ **(1)** *A naive experimenter conducts an experiment, which is actually done properly. But having calculated the final statistic he uses z not the 't' distribution. There is a df of 8 and it was only just possible to reject the null hypothesis at the 1% level. What type of error is being invited?*

(2) *If one experimenter sets a significance level of $p < 0.01$ and another is prepared to accept a significance level of $p < 0.05$ which of the two is more likely to make a Type I error and which more likely to make a Type II error? And why? If you are unsure read through the previous section again.*

In science it is a virtue to be conservative; it prevents us from jumping to the wrong conclusions too often. How can we tell when a type I or type II error has arisen? Unfortunately there is no way. This is why replication of experiments is a wise process, for when several sets of results point the same way we diminish greatly the likelihood of error.

The selection of a particular level of significance should be performed before the experiment is conducted just as anyone who bets on the horses must do so before the race is run. You cannot go and place your bet after the race. Yet many sane researchers try to do this in their statistical operations. For instance let us imagine that you decided on a level of 0.05 for rejection of the null hypothesis before collecting the data. After the results are analysed you find that instead of reaching a z value of 1.96 (i.e. the 0.05 level) you obtained 1.957. Strictly speaking you should retain the null hypothesis. But it is so easy to make it a significant result by rounding up, or retrospectively reducing the required significance level, or by stating that the result 'approached significance'. This latter ploy enables an honest retention of the null hypothesis, yet enables you to act almost as though you had rejected it. If we go around manipulating the elements in an experiment, after the event to suit our wishful thinking, then there was no reason to do the experiment in the first place, and we might just as well believe anything we want to believe.

STQ **(1)** *When is a type I error made?*
(2) *Why can it be arranged that a type I error is more serious than a type II error?*
(3) *How can the risk of making a type II error be minimized?*

Answers are to be found on p. 433.

One-tailed and two-tailed hypotheses

There is one further point about the way an experimental (or alternative) hypothesis is formulated which has implications for the way in which you look up probabilities in statistical tables. This is whether the experimental hypothesis is unidirectional (known as one-tailed) or bidirectional (known as two-tailed), a tail referring to an extremity of the distribution. A unidirectional hypothesis is one that, as its name implies, makes a prediction in one particular direction. In a memory experiment this might be that categorized word lists will result in more words being remembered. But there are some hypotheses which make a bidirectional prediction by predicting that the effect of an independent variable may go in either direction. In our example, this would mean predicting that categorized word lists will result in either more words being remembered or less words being remembered, i.e. predicting that categorization will have some effect, but not being prepared to say what.

It is obviously preferable to be able to give an explanation of human behaviour in terms of predicting behaviour in one direction, than to state vaguely that there will be an effect of some kind. However, there are times, particularly during the more exploratory phase of a research programme, when you might just want to see whether a variable has any effect, for example, whether some teaching method has an effect, good or bad, on children learning to read.

One-tailed and two-tailed hypotheses also have implications for statistical analysis. This is in connection with the probabilities that the differences in scores in an experiment will occur randomly. The point is that, for a hypothesis which predicts a difference in only one direction, there is a specific probability that that difference will occur randomly by chance. But, if a hypothesis makes a prediction that a difference might occur in either direction, then the probability is divided equally at each tail. For example, the 5% level in a two-tailed test is split 2.5% at each tail beyond 1.96 z when N is large. But on a one-tailed test the 5% is all at one tail, or end of the distribution. Consider the following example.

Suppose we have a sample of 100 eleven-year-old children who have experienced discovery learning methods at primary school and we want to find out whether this experience has affected their performance in arithmetic as assessed by an arithmetic test. Suppose further that we are in the fortunate position of knowing the performance of all eleven-year-old children in the country on the arithmetic test. We hypothesize that the mean score on the arithmetic test for the sample will differ from the population mean value. We decide to reject the null hypothesis at the $p < 0.01$ level. Our basic data are as follows:

Sample size   =   100
Mean for population   =   25
Mean for sample   =   24
Standard deviation for sample   =   3
Estimated standard error of population mean   = $\dfrac{3}{\sqrt{100-1}}$ = 0.302

We can test the null hypothesis by seeing how many standard errors our observed sample mean value is from the population mean value. The value we obtain for this difference is $(25-24)/0.302 = 3.31$. Now we know that all values that are more than 2.58 standard errors from the mean have a probability of occurrence by chance of $p < 0.01$. As our obtained value is 3.31 standard errors from the population mean this means that at the $p < 0.01$ level the null hypothesis is rejected.

But now let us go a step further. You will notice that in our example we have not said whether the children's experience of discovery learning methods is likely to produce an improvement or a deterioration in their arithmetic attainment. We have simply said it will produce a difference; our hypothesis is non-directional. And to test it we used the areas at both ends of the normal distribution. For obvious reasons we call such a test a 'two-tailed' test. Supposing we have strong grounds for believing that discovery learning methods will improve arithmetic performance. In this case we have a directional hypothesis and we can specify the direction in which rejection of the null hypothesis will occur. Instead of taking into account both tails of the probability distribution we now have to deal with only one. To find out the probabilities for rejection of this type of hypothesis we mark out the areas in the positive half of the curve equal to probabilities of 0.05 and 0.01. These are shown in Figure 17.

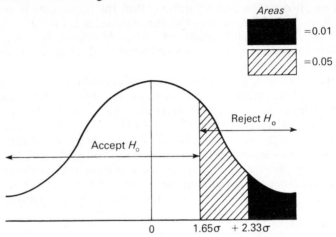

Figure 17 One-tailed significance levels

In this case to reject the null hypothesis at the $p < 0.01$ level we have to find a value that is greater than the population mean value by only 2.33 standard errors. This is the critical value. Similarly to reject the null hypothesis at the $p < 0.05$ level our sample value needs to exceed a critical value of only 1.65 standard errors. Thus our directional null hypothesis about the effect of discovery learning on arithmetic attainment is now even more strongly rejected. In other words if we can confidently state the direction of a null hypothesis we do not need such large observed differences to reject it at particular significance levels.

It should be clear from the above that stating a null hypothesis in a directional form loads the dice in favour of its rejection. Can you see why? If not, complete Table 17 (p. 110) by referring to the Table B in Appendix A and calculating the relevant areas. For this reason most researchers opt for caution by keeping the hypothesis non-directional and consequently using a two-tailed significance test by which to evaluate it. Virtually the only situations where directional tests are used are when a procedure, such as a new drug, has been designed to

Steps in testing a hypothesis	Statistical decisions	Posssible research errors
Construct null hypothesis	Decide alternative hypo- thesis – directional or non-directional	Scientific reasoning
Choose significance level	If set level high (e.g. $p < 0.001$)	Type II error (alternative hypothesis wrongly rejected)
	If set level low (e.g. $p < 0.01$)	Type I error (alternative hypothesis wrongly accepted)
Choose statistical test	Select powerful test	Assumptions for the test may not be met by data
	Select test lacking in power	Results statistically insignificant
Draw conclusion	Results are statistically significant	Conclusion of no practical importance

Figure 18 Steps in testing a hypothesis

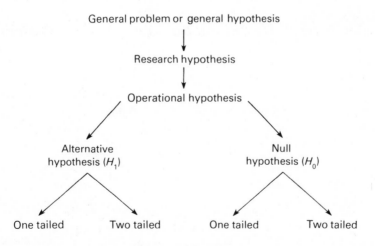

Figure 19 The refinement of the general problem

produce changes in a patient population in a particular direction. And it is extremely unlikely that it will have adverse effects. Sometimes however, this caution may not be as admirable as it seems. You will remember that if we set a significance level too high there is always a danger that we accept a null hypothesis that is in fact false; that is we make what is termed a type II error. There might be cases then in a particular research field where a lot of evidence has accumulated about the direction of a difference to use a one-tailed test. The use of a one-tailed test makes it easier for us to reject a false null hypothesis, but as a corollary make a type I error for support is easier to come by for the alternative hypothesis.

STQ **(1)** *Complete Table 17.*

p	*t-value two-tailed*	*t-value one-tailed*	
0.05		*1.65*	*Assume N = 1000*
0.01	*2.58*		
0.001		—	

(2) *What are the advantages and disadvantages of, (a) one-tailed tests, and (b) two-tailed tests?*
(3) *What is the relationship between significance level, one- and two-tailed tests and type I and type II errors?*

Answers are to be found on p. 433.

REFERENCES
Fisher, R. (1951). *The Design of Experiments.* (New York: Hafner).

11

Variables

What is an experiment?

Imagine you are a student taking a course in experimental psychology (not too hard to imagine is it!) and the tutor told you to undertake the following task. 'Take this rat that hasn't been fed since 5 p.m. yesterday and time him at running this maze!' Will you be performing an experiment? Before you try to answer we shall sketch out the major criteria for an experiment. An experiment occurs when the environment is systematically manipulated in order to observe the effect of this manipulation upon some behaviour. Aspects of the environment that are not of interest, and hence not manipulated, are held constant so as not to influence the outcome of the experiment. To answer the question above, we must introduce two special terms – independent and dependent variables – to describe how the environment is manipulated and how behaviour is observed.

Many students are surprised to discover that the actions described above are not an experiment. All experiments require at least two special features called independent and dependent variables. A variable is a property that can take on different values. To speak tautologically, a variable is something that varies. Examples of importance in psychology are intelligence, anxiety, age, social class, sex, self concept, aspiration, achievement etc. A variable must have a minimum of two values e.g. sex, but most are characterized by continuous values, e.g. test scores. An experiment occurs when the environment is systematically manipulated in order to observe the effect of this manipulation on some aspect of behaviour. The part of the environment that is manipulated is the Independent Variable (IV). The particular behavioural effect of this manipulation is the Dependent Variable (DV) i.e. what is measured.

$$IV \text{ manipulated} \longrightarrow \text{measured changes in } DV$$

The IV is that variable which is manipulated by the experimenter. The number of food pellets given to a rat, the loudness of a tone, the inducement of a set are all *IV*s. *IV*s are selected on the basis that the experimenter thinks they will cause changes in behaviour. For instance increasing the number of food pellets given to the rat should increase its bar pressing behaviour; increasing noise levels should decrease attention to other signals. When the *IV* does cause a change in behaviour we can then say that the behaviour is under the control of the *IV*. Failure of the *IV* to produce variations in behaviour is usually due to an insufficiently strong variation of the *IV*. For instance if the increase in the number of food pellets offered to the rat is quite small, then the rat's behaviour may not change because the variation in the environment has not been detected.

The *DV* is that observed and recorded by the experimenter. It depends on the behaviour of the subject. The time to solve anagrams, the number of times a rat presses a bar, the number of nonsense syllables recalled are all *DV*s.

The dependent variable in our introductory example is the time taken to run the maze. But in order to have an experiment there must be at least two ways, often called conditions or levels, of manipulating the environment. Often these two might be simply the presence and absence of manipulation. In our example there is only one level, that of starvation, since 5 p.m. the previous night. Running the maze will certainly give us a time value *but* would the rat have done better, the same or worse if he had not been starved or if other periods without food had been employed? We do not know. So we need at least two levels of hunger to see the effect on time taken.

For a variable to qualify as an *IV*, it must be manipulable. The variable must be presented in at least two forms even if this boils down to a presence versus absence type of variation.

The number of *IV*s the experimenter actually varies at will is small. In the main most variables have to be taken at such levels as they occur in nature. Thus age, achievement and type of delinquency are not under the experimenters control. He has to take existing groups which fall into these categories.

Variations in the *IV* are called levels, so that for instance, sex has two levels. There are several ways in which the desired variation in the independent variable can be achieved.

PRESENCE VERSUS ABSENCE

The presence versus absence technique for achieving variation is exactly what the name implies. One group of subjects receives the treatment condition and the other group does not. The two groups are then compared to see if the group that received the treatment condition differed from the group that did not. A drug study can illustrate this type of variation. One group of subjects is administered a drug and a second group is administered a placebo. The two groups of subjects are then compared on some measure such as reaction time to determine if the drug group had significantly different reaction times than did the placebo group. If they did, then the difference is attributed to the drug.

AMOUNT OF A VARIABLE

A second basic technique for achieving variation in the *IV* is to administer different amounts of the variable to each of several groups. We might vary the amount of time subjects were exposed to three different stimulus figures to investigate the influence of exposure duration upon perceived length. Subjects exposed to the stimulus figures for periods of 30, 60, 120, 240, 480, 960, and 1920 msec are then required to estimate whether the stimulus figure they have just seen was longer or shorter than a standard stimulus figure. Note that in this experiment the presence – absence form of variation could not be used since subjects must be exposed to the stimulus figures for some period of time in order to have a basis for making their comparative judgements. Other studies may include a group that does not receive any amount of *IV*. Such studies combine the technique of varying amount with the presence versus absence technique. A drug study represents an excellent candidate for combining these techniques as do many other types of studies. One group would receive a placebo and three additional groups would receive three different amounts of drug being investigated. In such a study you could not only tell if the drug had an influence on the subjects' responses but also whether the different amounts of the drug influenced their responses. But whatever variable is selected as the *IV*, it must be capable of being translated into concrete experimental operations. Learning, guilt, frustration, self esteem and so on must be defined operationally. This problem of operation definition is discussed in relation to hypotheses in Chapter 9.

So far the manipulation of the *IV* has been discussed in terms of the manipulation of events. Another way variation can be introduced is by manipulating instructions. For example, in a memory experiment one group might be asked to rehearse the presented words in the period between learning and recall, while another group might be requested to think of other words which would remind them of the original words. There are two dangers inherent in the manipulation of instructions. First some subjects (Ss) might be inattentive and not hear, or understand the full set of instructions. Secondly there is always the possibility of subtle inter-subject variations in the interpretation of the instructional message. Both these dangers introduce uncontrolled variation or experimental error into the experiment.

The selection of the dependent variable

So the psychological experiment is conducted to answer a question, 'What is the effect of . . .?' and to test the corresponding hypothesis, 'a certain change in X will result in a certain change in Y'. In order to answer the question and test the hypothesis, a variable – the *IV* – is varied in order to determine if it produces the desired or hypothesized effect. The issue of concern for the experimenter is to make sure that he or she actually obtains an indication of the effect produced by the variation in the *IV*. To accomplish this task, the experimenter has to select a *DV* that will be sensitive to, or be able to pick up, the influence exerted by the *IV*. If the *DV* has a limited range it is easy to reach the maximum or minimum values with minimal manipulation of the *IV*. Any further manipulation of the *IV* cannot be registered through changes in the *DV* since the latter's limits of movement have been reached already. When it is impossible to sink any lower on a scale, we have the 'floor effect'; similarly the impossibility of recording a higher score than maximum is the 'ceiling effect'. Unfortunately there is no golden rule that will enable us to select the most sensitive *DV*. In any case no *DV* will reveal sufficient variation if the variations or levels of the *IV* are insufficient in the first place.

The *DV* must also be operationally defined so that we are quite sure what we are measuring. Implicit in this too is that some accepted mode of measuring the *DV* exists. Many *DV*s in which psychologists are interested are hypothetical constructs, e.g. learning, intelligence, short term memory etc. These must be operationalized as observable and measurable behaviours that allow inference back to the construct. For example, it is impossible to study the learning process directly. If, on the other hand, a student sits down and studies certain material for an hour and then can answer questions he previously could not, we say learning has taken place. In this case learning is inferred from an increase in performance.

The *DV* must also be reliable and valid. The measures available to assess the *DV* must be reliable and valid. These two terms will be considered in detail later on (Chapter 25). For now it suffices to say that reliability is the consistency with which a result will repeat itself, all other things being equal. Validity implies that the measurement technique/instrument is actually assessing what it purports to measure.

STQ	**(1)**	*Differentiate between the IV and DV in a concise sentence.*
	(2)	*In what ways is it possible to manipulate the IV.*
	(3)	*What do you understand by the 'ceiling' and 'floor' effects?*

Let us have a look at *IV* and *DV* in the context of a hypothesis. We will start with a problem. Do men prefer blondes? It is impossible to design an experiment to answer this problem without being a great deal more precise and specific about the relevant issues. What does 'prefer' mean? Which men are referred to? Can you write some research hypotheses that are capable of being operationalized for this problem. Refer to Chapter 9 if you wish to refresh your memory about hypotheses.

We came up with the following:

Hypothesis 1: Male college students will be more likely to ask a blonde female student for a date than female students with other hair colour.

Hypothesis 2: Wealthy men over the age of 40 are more likely to have blonde mistresses.

Hypothesis 3: A greater proportion of blonde than non-blonde women between the ages of 20 and 26 will be married.

Hypothesis 4: A woman who dyes her hair blonde will have a better sex life than one who does not.

All these hypotheses relate to the general problem given above. Yet they all focus upon different aspects of the problem. It is certainly possible that some of these hypotheses might be true, implying an answer of yes to our problem, while others might at the same time be false, implying that men do not prefer blondes. This is one of the most frustrating aspects of scientific research. There usually is no simple yes or no answer to any general problem. It all depends upon how the specifics of the problem are formulated.

Not all hypotheses are equal in the eyes of the scientist. The more specific and hence the more testable the hypothesis, the more the scientist likes it. An adequate hypothesis already contains some specification of independent and dependent variables. Hypotheses that fail to meet this criterion are only problems in disguise.

STQ *Which of the above hypotheses cannot yet be tested experimentally?*

Look at Hypothesis 4. What do we mean by a 'better sex life'? (You may have your own ideas on this but keep them to yourself!) The point is as yet Hypothesis 4 is not sufficiently precise to enable an experiment to be formulated which could put it to the test.

FROM HYPOTHESIS TO EXPERIMENT
The first step in going from a hypothesis to an experiment is to state the independent and dependent variables. The independent variable

for our remaining three hypotheses is hair colour. However, this can be manipulated in several ways. The most obvious way is to randomly select women only on the basis of hair colour. This may not always be the best way, since a sample will differ on many other dimensions: personality, height, bust, etc. If our random sample is sufficiently large, these other characteristics tend to balance out, but the precision of our experiment is nevertheless decreased. If we used the same woman with different coloured wigs, this would keep all the other variables constant.

The dependent variable for Hypothesis 1 is the number of times a blonde was asked for a date versus the number of times a non-blonde was asked. There are several ways in which the independent and dependent variables could be combined into an experiment. We might have a male subject watch colour videotape interviews with several women who differ in hair colour and then ask him which one he would prefer to date. The use of videotape prevents verbal and non-verbal differences from situation to situation that would probably occur if the subject were exposed to the women in the flesh. Even a highly trained female interviewer would find it difficult to conduct exactly the same conversation with each and every subject. The female experimenter could wear different wigs and visit a number of student unions. We could then count the number of times she was asked out when she wore each wig. Using the same experimenter will control for differences in personality, etc. Other experiments are possible. The important thing to remember is that even though a hypothesis is far more specific than a problem, there still remains a wide range of possible experiments to test the hypothesis. No single experiment is the perfect test of any hypothesis.

For Hypothesis 2 the dependent variable is the proportion of mistresses who are blonde. Clearly this is a difficult phenomenon to carry into the laboratory. Indeed, we would probably encounter severe sampling problems in trying to test this hypothesis outside the laboratory. Not all hypotheses are equally testable. Having a sufficiently precise hypothesis does not guarantee that available techniques can test that hypothesis. So we will put aside the second Hypothesis as being beyond the reach of the tools of psychology.

Hypothesis 3 does not require any laboratory study. The investigator can measure the dependent variable by interview or questionnaire to see how many married women are blonde. Of course, since there are not the same number of blondes as of other hair colours in the population, the investigator would also have to obtain data about the number of blondes, etc., in that age range. Then the proportions of women with different hair colour who are married could be calculated. Note that there are no control variables with the exception of the limited age range specified in Hypothesis 3. It is the job of the experimenter to select the best test of the hypothesis given available resources. Even if the ideal experiment could be formulated to test some hypothesis, practical considerations often would prevent us from carrying out this experiment. Limitations of time, space, equipment, subjects and so forth all bear on the design of an actual experiment. Every experiment is to some extent a compromise.

STQ   *Identify the IV and DV in each of the following research hypotheses.*

(a)   *Working-class children will learn nonsense syllables slower than middle-class children.*

(b)   *Girls who follow science courses in the sixth form are more aggressive than girls following non-science courses.*

(c)   *The degree of illusion created by the Muller – Lyer illusion depends on whether it is presented vertically or horizontally.*

(d)   *Adults find it easier to remember a list of meaningful words than to remember a list of nonsense syllables.*

CONTROL VARIABLES

A control variable is a potential *IV* that is held constant during an experiment. It is not allowed to vary. For any one experiment the list of control variables it is desirable to control is large, far larger than can ever be accomplished in practice. The problem is that such variables have their potential effects on the *DV* so that it becomes impossible to separate out those variations in the *DV* that are due to the *IV* and those that are due to other variables. The potential effects are unsystematic too, sometimes causing improvements and at others deficits, so their influence is unmeasurable. Consider for example a simple experiment in which pupils are required to solve five-letter anagrams. Here one would want to control age, intelligence, and previous experience with anagrams. Even time of day is important in affecting efficiency. Other variables such as motivation, and interest, can hardly be controlled though they will play an important part. The list could obviously be extended. In practice the experimenter will try to control as many of these salient factors as possible so that the effect of uncontrolled factors will be slight relative to the effect of the *IV*. Most control variables are subject variables, i.e. variables that are attributes vested in each subject and which they bring with them into the experimental context, e.g. age, experience, social class, sex, motivation, expectation etc. For example if one group of subjects contains more intelligent people than another group, differences in performance may be due not to the *IV* but the intelligence. When two variables are mixed up in this way they are confounded with each other. Similarly other control variables are context variables and they may confound the results. If a varying amount of a tranquillizer is given to create different levels of anxiety, heavy doses may cause sleepiness so that performance on the *DV* is affected by an unknown combination of sleepiness and anxiety level. Specific methods of control will be dealt with in Chapter 17. Look at these two examples.

(i)   Among boys there is a correlation between physical size, and social maturity while for girls, in the same age group, there is no such relationship.
Control variable: Age.

(ii) Under reinforcement conditions of verbal praise, middle-class children learn significantly faster than working-class children.
Control variable: Verbal praise.

STQ *Check your ability to select IV, DV and control variables in the following.*

(a) A car manufacturer wants to know how bright brake lights should be in order to minimize the time required for the driver of the following vehicle to realize the car in front is stopping.

(b) A behaviour therapist reinforces a patient by nodding, smiling and extra attention every time the patient says something positive about himself and pays no attention (extinguishes) to negative verbal material about himself.

(c) A pigeon is trained to peck at a disc every time a red light comes on but not when it is a green light.

(d) A social psychologist tries to discover if men car drivers conform more to stop signs at crossroads than women car drivers.

(e) With IQ held constant, boys with perceptual motor training will perform better on hand–eye co-ordination tasks than boys without this training.

INTERVENING VARIABLES

All the variables so far discussed have been under the control of the experimenter. Each *IV* and control variable can be manipulated and each variation observed on the *DV*. However, what the experimenter may be trying to find out in some experiments is not necessarily concrete but hypothetical. The intervening variable is a hypothetical one whose effect is inferred from the effects of the *IV* on the *DV*. Significant effects suggest support for the hypothetical construct. Look at the following hypotheses.

(1) As measured task interest increases measured task performance increases.
IV: Task interest.
DV: Task performance.
Intervening variable: Learning.

(2) Subjects blocked from achieving goals exhibit more aggressive acts than those not so blocked.
IV: Blocking or not blocking.
DV: Number of aggressive acts.
Intervening variable: Frustration.

(3) People given more positive feedback experiences will have more positive attitudes to others than people given fewer positive feedback experiences.
IV: Number of positive feedback experiences.
DV: Attitudes to others.
Intervening variable: Self esteem.

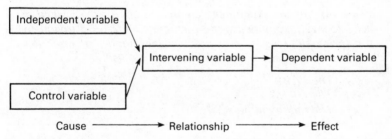

Figure 20 Relationship between variables

A variable can be an *IV* in one study and a *DV* in another; for example we can study the results of the possession of various levels of motivation or we can look at the determinants of motivation. Variables are the gears and cogs of an experiment. Their selection, control, manipulation and measurement is what makes the experiment run.

> **STQ (1)** *A psychologist designed an experiment to test whether people find it easier to remember meaningful material than nonsense syllables. The subjects were asked to recall lists they had learned and the number of items recalled were recorded.*

(a)　What is the IV?
(b)　What is the DV?
(c)　State the null hypothesis.

(2)　*An experiment was devised to reveal whether practice with multiplication tables improved children's understanding of mathematical principles.*

(a)　What is the IV?
(b)　What is the DV?
(c)　State the alternative hypothesis.

(3)　*In an investigation of the effect of home background on school attainment which two of the following are DVs:*

(a)　Size of family.
(b)　Form position.
(c)　Age of father.
(d)　Social class of family.
(e)　Scores on reading test.
(f)　Parents' education aspirations for child.

(4)　*In an experiment conducted to discover whether behavioural therapy or psycho-therapy is better as a treatment for curing smoking as measured by the number of cigarettes smoked daily after the end of treatment:*

(a)　The IV is?
(b)　The DV is?
(c)　The null hypothesis is?

Answers are to be found on p. 433.

12

Levels of measurement

A fundamental step in the conduct of research is measurement. Measurement is the use of rules to assign numbers to objects or events. The rules determine the level of measurement that is obtained and the operations that can be performed on the numbers. It is necessary to classify the dependent variable according to the level of measurement obtained in order to select an appropriate statistical test. There are four levels of measurement.

1 Nominal measurement

Nominal means to name; hence a nominal scale does not actually measure but rather names. Observations are simply classified into categories with no necessary relationship existing between the categories. Nominal is the most primitive level of measurement, and only requires that one can distinguish two or more relevant categories and know the criteria for placing individuals or objects into one category or another. The only relationship between the categories is that they are different from each other.

For example we can classify people as male or female, right handed or left handed, psychologists or non-psychologists. Other nominal classifications are political parties, social class levels, the numbering of bus routes or the jerseys of footballers.

Numbers are often used at the nominal level but only as a way of identifying categories. All members of a category are assigned the same number, and no two categories are assigned the same number. For instance in preparing data for a computer, the numeral 0 might be used to represent males and 1 to represent females. The 1 does not indicate more of something than the 0; it is simply a labelling system. So the numbers assigned to categories cannot be added, multiplied or divided etc. The numbers assigned to football players consitute a nominal scale but we cannot say the player with the number 10 on his back is twice as good a player as the one wearing the number 5 jersey!

The only permissible thing to do is to count the number of cases within each category so that they can be displayed in a table (Table 18).

Table 18   Voting preferences

	Preference		
	Liberal	*Labour*	*Conservative*
Before broadcast	400	750	850
After broadcast	500	700	800

Table 18 depicts the number of voters in a sample of 2 000 registering a preference for a political party before and after a party political broadcast for the Liberals (fictitious data). The analytical procedures available for nominal data are:

(a) Reducing to proportions and percentages then making comparisons.

(b) Applying chi-square (Chapter 20) or the sign test (Chapter 18).

2 Ordinal measurement
Ordinal measurement implies the ability to put the data into order and rank them, i.e. from largest to smallest, or vice versa. For example normal, neurotic, and psychotic all describe degrees of maladjustment. If one accepts that a single dimension underlies a classification then it is useful to treat the results as ordinal rather than nominal data. So subjects in the normal, neurotic and psychotic categories can be assigned the scores of 1, 2, and 3 respectively. There is no underlying assumption that the differences between successive ranks are equal. All one is determining is the relative position of individuals or objects with respect to some attribute. We frequently use rankings in judging characteristics, e.g. sociability, Miss World contests, or performance in athletics, music festivals etc. The empirical procedure used for ordering objects must satisfy the transitivity principle. That is if $a>b$, and $b>c$ then $a>c$. Of course other words may be substituted for 'greater than' such as 'stronger than', 'has more of some attribute than' etc. The rank numbers assigned indicate position order and nothing more. There is no implication that equal differences exist between ranks. Thus there is no way of knowing how much better one person is than another merely by inspecting differences in ranks.

The use of the sequence first, second, third . . . nth represents the systematic progression of an ordinal scale. The statistical procedures available for ordinal data are, (i) Spearman's rank-order correlation (Chapter 21), (ii) Wilcoxon (Chapter 18), and (iii) Mann – Whitney (Chapter 16).

3 Interval measurement

An interval scale provides equal intervals from an arbitrary origin, so that order and distance relationships have meaning. One unit on the scale is equal in size to any other unit.

For interval data there are equal intervals between successive values. For example, the difference between 70 °F and 90 °F is the same as the difference between 40 °F and 60 °F. Because there is no true zero point we cannot say the 90 °F is twice as hot as 45 °F. Likewise there is no zero intelligence. A student may occasionally receive a score of zero on (say) a statistics test! This does not mean he has zero knowledge, nor does it mean that a student who obtained a score of 40 has twice as much knowledge of statistics as one who received a score of 20.

With interval scaling the whole range of parametric statistical procedures is available. All reputable ability, and aptitude tests, personality and attitudes scales are regarded as providing interval data. But there are reasons to doubt this assumption. There is no way of knowing whether the difference between IQs of 100 and 105 is the same as the difference between IQs of 120 and 125. We are even more doubtful of interval equality on attitude scales. Probably if we were very rigorous we would never accept that psychological data were at better than ordinal level. However statistical procedures appropriate to interval data have been applied to such tests and scales over several generations and in terms of outcome they seem to work. It seems reasonable then to assume that the tests and scales designed according to accepted technical procedures and standards can be treated as interval scales.

4 Ratio measurement

This is the highest form of measurement. A ratio scale has equal intervals between successive units and an absolute zero. Thus a 12 stone person is twice as heavy as a 6 stone person. It is doubtful whether any psychological test produces ratio data, since if there is no such thing as zero personality, IQ or attitude then there can be no ratio scale. Ratio scales are really encountered only in the physical sciences, e.g. 9 ohms is three times the resistance of 3 ohms. Length and time are ratio scales too, so that 6 ft. is twice as long as 3 ft. and 6 minutes is twice as long as 3 minutes.

LEVELS OF MEASUREMENT AND MEASURES OF CENTRAL TENDENCY

Usually only one measure of location is used in analysing the distribution of a variable. The selection of which one to use in any particular context is partly a matter of judgement based on a knowledge of the characteristics of the statistic and the research question in hand.

Fundamentally, the use of a particular 'average' is determined by the scale of measurement which can be assumed for the data. The position is summarized in Table 19. For data on a nominal scale, there is no choice, the mode is the only appropriate measure. For ordinal scale data a choice is available and either the median or the mode may be appropriate, but the median is preferable for it retains more of the information contained in the data set by taking into account the rank order of the values.

As for data measured on interval or ratio scales, any of the measures may be used and the comparative merits of the mean and the median then become important.

Table 19 Measures of central tendency that may be used with given scales of measurement

	Mode	Median	Mean
Nominal	Yes	No	No
Ordinal	Yes	Yes	No
Interval/ratio	Yes	Yes	Yes

Summary of the four levels of measurement

Nominal	Allocates data into labelled categories
Ordinal	Rank orders data as points on a scale
Interval	Allocates data on a continuous numerical scale with equal intervals between points
Ratio	As interval with absolute zero

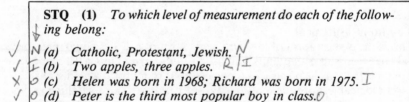

STQ (1) *To which level of measurement do each of the following belong:*

(a) Catholic, Protestant, Jewish.
(b) Two apples, three apples.
(c) Helen was born in 1968; Richard was born in 1975.
(d) Peter is the third most popular boy in class.
(e) Time taken to solve anagrams.
(f) Judging an art competition.
(g) Recording the height of students.
(h) A pass/fail dichotomy on a test.

al8xxateaddbdbd22zx

zxz—.

(i) Recording mechanical aptitude scores. O
n(j) Numbering of houses along a road. O

(2) Complete the following table by writing yes or no in the columns. Three have been filled in as starters.

Scale	Labels	Order	Equal intervals	Absolute zero
	Property possessed by scale			
Nominal	Y	N	N	No
Ordinal	N	Y	N	N
Interval	N	Yes	Y	N
Ratio	Yes	Y	Y	Y

Answers are to be found on p. 434.

13

Writing an experimental report

This section is concerned with writing up practical work. There is an art in this and you will find that it comes easier with practice. It must be appreciated from the outset that practical work must be written-up systematically and with great care, so that the reader is not faced with the prospect of having to sort out ambiguities or misunderstandings. You must be prepared to write up a report a couple of times at least before you are satisfied that there is no further room for improvement. Researchers who are experts in writing up their results often have to make several drafts before writing up the final report. Extremely valuable and interesting practical work may be spoiled at the last minute by a student who is not able to communicate his results easily.

The time factor is important. Writing up experiments cannot be rushed without doing an injustice to the results and conclusions of these experiments. Careful thought has to be given to the best way to present the results and to interpreting them. Unless enough time is devoted to the writing up, serious errors can be made. The purpose of writing up one's findings is to enable others to replicate the work if they are interested or to modify aspects of it. It therefore follows that each part of the experiment should be reported carefully and accurately. There are various methods which may be employed in writing up practical work, but the following is recommended as being one which students find easier to use and which sets out the stages of the report in a logical fashion. Tutors and examiners like to see material presented in a logical sequence.

1 Title

Here is an example of a point referred to above about re-writing aspects of the report. The title should be as short as possible but it should retain meaning. You may have to make several attempts at writing down the title until you are satisfied with it. The title should reflect the main idea, topic or theme of the experiment. A reader needs to see at a glance what the experiment is about and consequently we cannot reiterate too strongly the points about brevity and meaning. It is useful to decide what the hypothesis aims to test, as this can provide a basis for formulating a title.

2 Summary

In printed research papers, this may be referred to as the abstract, and it may appear at the beginning or end of the paper. For our purposes it seems sensible to call it the summary as this acts as a reminder to us that its purpose is to present an overview of the design, contents and results of the experiment. Another reason for placing the summary early in the write-up is to enable the reader to determine whether or not it is worth his while to plough through the whole report. This raises another point.

The summary (ideally) should be an amplification of the title, which by itself could be misleading. A researcher may be interested in a particular topic and diligently traces a number of learned journals which supposedly contain articles relevant to his subject. His eyes light on a title which he considers will be informative, only to find on reading the summary that it has not the remotest connection with his research interest. As with the title, brevity is the key word. The summary should be as short as possible and should contain only one paragraph. Essentially, it should refer to the hypothesis, the experimental design, the results, and the most significant findings all concisely reported. Clearly, the summary cannot be written until all the other parts of the report have been completed.

3 Aim of experiment and background

Aim and 'background' logically fit together. It is our experience that students have a 'hunch' that if you manipulate variable X a change will take place in variable Y. When we ask why the student should suppose that this should be so, some rather naive, unfounded assumptions are made. Invariably there is little or no reference to either theoretical or practical accounts in the text books. In other words, the student embarks on an experiment without having engaged in the necessary reading. Background reading – what others have done or failed to do – should be the starting point or source of psychological enquiry.

This section of the write-up should present the reason for doing the experiment at all (rationale) and it should relate to other previous work in the same area. Names of other researchers will be mentioned, with the year of their research in brackets after their name. These names and corresponding years will also appear in the section on references at the end of the report, to enable interested readers to follow up their work and consult the original papers.

It is useful to conclude this section with a statement of the hypothesis or hypotheses which will be tested in the experiment, and which arise out of a consideration of the background material. Do you remember what we said earlier about the different kinds of hypothesis?

4 Conditions

Results obtained in experiments can sometimes be affected by unacceptable conditions, and their authenticity is thereby either enhanced or diminished accordingly. Spurious results lead to incorrect conclusions, in spite of the fact that great care may have been taken in choosing subjects, selecting the most appropriate experimental design, and applying the correct statistical procedure. Results obtained under one set of conditions may not be faulty in a particular instance, but may be faulty when produced under different conditions.

It is therefore essential that you give a detailed description of the conditions which operated at the time of your experiment, but only those conditions which were relevant to the outcome of the experiment need to be stressed. You may need to refer to environmental conditions such as place, time of day, room temperature, etc., if you think these could be important factors. Subject variable, such as fatigue, co-operativeness etc., may also deserve some mention.

Learning lists of words in a memory experiment could quite easily be affected by the time of day and the room in which the experiment was conducted. For example, subjects might be more alert in the morning than in the afternoon, and the room in which they undergo the memory task may be next to a workshop where lathes are turning. These two factors could influence the results, and for this reason should be included under the headings of conditions.

Again it should be emphasized that conditions which appear to have no relevance to the experiment need not be reported. Tutors and examiners are aware of the difficulties which students face in trying to obtain ideal conditions, and allowances are made for this. What we are suggesting, quite simply, is that the experimenter must exercise discretion in reporting experimental conditions – including crucial factors and avoiding trivial ones. It is not necessary, as students are keen to suggest, that all conditions must be reported.

5 Subjects and experiments

You should state the number of subjects who took part in the experiment, and you may find it necessary to give a little more information about them if you think it could be relevant to the progress of the experiment and the subsequent results. For instance the age range of your subjects could be important, and in certain types of experiments (e.g. interpersonal attraction) the sex of the subjects could be most influential. The same applies to the experimenter(s) – is their age important, or their sex? Is the experimenter known to the subjects, and could this be relevant?

One final but extremely significant piece of information should be given about the subjects, i.e. how were they obtained? Were they enlisted because they were friends? Were they 'captive' and somewhat unwilling subjects? Were they chosen 'because they were there'? In other words did your subjects constitute an opportunity sample, or did you have the good fortune to be able to take a random sample? Do you remember what we said in Chapter 7 about sampling and being able to generalize our results to the population from which the sample was taken? This kind of information needs to be included at this point.

6 Apparatus and equipment

You should include this heading in your report even when no apparatus has been used, in which case you should write the word 'nil' beneath the heading. If you make use of *standard* equipment (i.e. equipment which is usually basic in psychology laboratories) there is no need to offer a description, since most psychologists will be familiar with a memory drum, a pursuit rotor, and a tachistoscope!

If you construct equipment or manufacture material specifically for your experiment, then it is essential that you describe it in some detail. When you have done this, re-read what you have written and ask yourself whether another person, unfamiliar with your work, would be able to re-construct your equipment or material.

A photograph or photographs of new equipment will be welcomed by a reader who is unacquainted with your work, and examples of your actual material should be appended to the report where possible. For example to refer to a list of anagrams without specifying their length, their difficulty or even their number is singularly unhelpful. Moreover if material is available in the report, you will have little difficulty describing your work and discussing it with a tutor or examiner. Some students feel that if they write 'nil' under this heading because they have not used equipment they will be penalized by an examiner. There is a tendency for students to associate sophisticated equipment with a superlative exp/:riment. The reverse is often the case, however, for some students become so engrossed in the technicality of modern equipment that they forget they are supposed to be engaged in a psychological experiment. You may be an expert at handling a three-channel polygraph linked to a tape-recorder and a computer, but unless you can see these act only as a means to a psychological end, you must not regard yourself as a competent student of human behaviour.

7 Method
Some researchers would regard this as being the most important section in the report. Since in theory, the purpose of writing a report is to enable others to replicate your work, great care must be taken in describing your methodology clearly, concisely and logically. You will need to furnish information as to how each stage of the experiment was conducted. Once again, we must emphasize that this will demand much patience on your part, and you must be prepared to re-write the section several times before producing an acceptable version.

You will need to state which experimental design you used and it is a good idea to say *briefly* why you used it. Remember that your choice of design dictates the statistical procedure you will later apply to your results. Having described your apparatus and equipment in the previous section, you must now explain how it was used, mentioning the number of trials per subject, the rate of presentation of material, the instructions given to the subjects, etc. Since the instructions to subjects are so important, they could be set out en bloc and/or underlined, or even printed on a separate sheet and inserted at a suitable place in the report.

When you have written a draft of this section, show it to a friend. Ask him to read it through and then tell you how he interprets your method. This procedure often highlights any aspects which are not clear or where there are ambiguities. You may even notice certain omissions in your report – items which you believed you had included.

8 Results
Clarity! This is the key word in this section. Sound experiments which have produced excellent results are often spoiled at this stage simply because students either do not know the best way to present their results, or do not pay sufficient attention to their presentation. The major failing seems to be in trying to present too much information at once: graphs become confusing and tables are difficult to interpret simply because the student has tried to convey too many results in one display. Present your results clearly, simply and neatly. Your results

should be presented in tables which have appropriate, meaningful, and short headings. There are occasions however when diagrams may be more suitable depending on the kind of data. Short comments on the results are permissible, such as 'introverts scored higher then extraverts on this scale' but do try to avoid detailed and penetrating comments which are better placed in the 'Discussion' section.

9 Treatment of results

In everyday situations people look at sets of figures or scores and draw conclusions from them. Raw data can be misleading, and subjective evaluations which are based on them can be seriously incorrect. This is why we have to apply statistical techniques to our raw data, although so many students seem to find this a tedious undertaking. At face value there may appear to be a significant difference between two sets of scores, since their means may give the impression of being quite close. There may appear to be a correspondence between two sets of variables, but again this assumption would be made after making a visual scan of the data. Statistics provide an opportunity for you to introduce objectivity into your analyses but you must be certain which statistical procedure is most appropriate for your kind of data. If you were careful to select the correct experimental design at the outset, you should have little difficulty deciding which statistical procedure to employ. Are your data ranked? Are you concerned with response frequencies? Are you looking for differences or relationships? Once you have adopted the correct experimental design, and you can answer questions such as those outlined above, you should know which test to use, and whether it should be parametric or non-parametric. It is desirable to write out the full procedure step by step so that others can check your work. Sometimes fruitful information can emerge from a step in the calculation which would otherwise be lost if only the answer were given. Significance levels should be quoted and a *brief* statement (one sentence) should be offered to say whether the results were significant, and whether the null and alternative hypotheses were supported or rejected.

Some students become anxious if they conduct an experiment and find that they are not able to apply statistical procedures to their results, because their results do not lend themselves to this kind of treatment. It may be that a graph or chart would be more suitable and more meaningful. If this is the case, then do not hesitate to present your results in this format, providing they are clearly displayed and convey accurate information.

Finally, it should not have to be said that you should check thoroughly all mathematical functions before writing this section in its final form. Embarrassing errors can often be eliminated at this stage, such as $r = 4.32$ which should read $r = 0.432$, or $p<0.5$ which should read $p<0.05$.

10 Discussion of results and conclusion

The purpose of this section is to enable you to assess your results and draw sensible conclusions from them. It is quite common to find students who have painstakingly undertaken an interesting experiment, produced a set of results, and applied appropriate statistical procedures but are incapable of explaining their significance. What do the results mean in terms of your hypothesis? What implications or inferences can be made from your results? Are you able to summarize your conclusions, perhaps suggesting ideas from your experiment which could be developed by another person?

Do not be afraid to mention any failings in your experimental design, your sampling difficulties, or your procedure. Tutors are impressed by students who are capable of analysing and criticising their experimental methodology. Do not overdo it, though, and remember that it is not possible (or even desirable) to try to explain away all discrepancies.

Conclude this section by recapitulating the major conclusions and results of the experiment, and re-state the hypothesis in its original wording, pointing out whether or not it was supported.

11 References

You must record all the references you have mentioned in your experiment, but no others. Accuracy is important as other people may wish to follow up your work by reading some of the references in the library, and much time can be wasted if a librarian has to search for a non-existent manuscript, or one which is contained in an entirely different journal. References are written in a standard format. They appear in alphabetical order according to the name of the author. When a reference is made to the title of a book, you should underline the *title*, but when you refer to an article in a journal it is the name of the *journal* which is underlined. The parts which you underline would appear in italics in a printed experimental report. The following are examples of the format.

Hunter, I. M. L. (1966). *Memory.* (Harmondsworth: Penguin)
Bower, G. H. (1970). Organisational factors in memory. *Cognitive Psychology,* **1,** 18–41

This model for writing an experimental report is of course only one particular model. Another common pattern is the following one which may be found in some journals, namely:

> Summary
> Introduction
> Method
>
> > a. Sample
> > b. Instruments/apparatus etc.
> > c. Design
> > d. Conditions
>
> Results
> Discussion
> References

But whatever model or pattern you use, the basic criterion is that it should provide a logical sequence, concisely expressed, enabling another interested person to understand what has been done, why, and with what results.

You should now read the following pages which give an example of how an experiment was conducted in a classroom with sixth formers, and the report of the experiment written up in the form suggested above. The write-up is authentic in all its details and shows that experiments can be performed in school or college and written up in an orderly and intelligible fashion. You must use this chapter as a continual reference point when you are writing up your experimental reports.

Report on a classroom experiment

1. TITLE – SOCIAL CLASS STEREOTYPES
2. SUMMARY

It was hypothesized that sixth-form students would attribute certain characteristics to people of different social classes according to pre-conceived and, therefore, probably biased notions.

Forty-eight sixth formers, randomly assigned to four groups, were each given a card bearing a set of six statements describing an imaginary person. Statement 4 differed slightly for each group.

Subjects were then presented with pairs of alternative (extreme) personality statements and asked to underline whichever statement from each pair best suited, in their opinion, the person described on the card.

It was found that certain items showed significant differences in response between groups; other items revealed interestingly directional responses. It was therefore concluded that the hypothesis has been supported.

3. AIM

The aim was to investigate the social class stereotypes of sixth-form student groups. Research has been undertaken to examine how people perceive others as individuals and in groups. For example, a study concerning ethnic and racial groups in South Africa was undertaken by Pettigrew, Allport and Barnett (1958). A similar study was carried out by Hovland and Sherif (1952) in connection with the social problem of desegregation in the USA. The public have always tended to hold strong views about conscientious objectors in time of war and a study connected with this topic was reported by Crespi (1945).

Where the views of people are particularly strong — i.e. where they feel personally involved in a situation — they tend to hold relatively extreme views and therefore to pass extreme judgements. An instance of this is mentioned by Tajfel and Wilkes (1963) in which they used photographs of youngish men in order to elicit from their subjects free descriptive statements about other people. The paper by Tajfel and Wilkes is referred to in *Experiments in the Social Sciences* (see references). Both the research paper and the book provided background for the present experiment and gave rise to the hypothesis that 'Sixth form students will attribute certain characteristics to people of different social class according to preconceived and therefore probably biased notions'.

4. CONDITIONS

The experiment was conducted in a school classroom with groups of sixth formers as part of their General Studies programme. The physical conditions were normal.

5. SUBJECTS AND EXPERIMENTERS

Thirty-eight male sixth formers performed the experiment as part of their General Studies Programme. In addition there were ten lower-sixth form A-level Psychology students. Approximately half of the sample were arts students and half science. There were two experimenters drawn from the teaching staff of the school.

6. APPARATUS

(a) Four sets of cards were produced (see Figure 22) taken from Brown, Cherrington and Cohen (1975). Each card contained six statements giving factual information about a fictitious male (Mr X). The statements on each of the four sets of cards were identical with the exception of Statement 4, where the variation was as follows:

Card 1.   Owns a large country house.
Card 2.   Owns a semi-detached house.
Card 3.   Lives in a council house.
Card 4.   Lives in a crowded tenement.

(b) A Personality Inventory sheet containing twenty pairs of alternative (extreme) statements (Items 1–20) relating to the personality of the fictitious 'Mr X' (see Figure 23). The twenty statements had been randomized by Brown *et al.*

Card 1	Card 2
Is 43 years old Has a wife and three children Served in the forces Owns a large country house Enjoys pictures Is keen on sport	Is 43 years old Has a wife and three children Served in the forces Owns a semi-detached house Enjoys pictures Is keen on sport
Card 3	Card 4
Is 43 years old Has a wife and three children Served in the forces Lives in a council house Enjoys pictures Is keen on sport	Is 43 years old Has a wife and three children Served in the forces Lives in a crowded tenement Enjoys pictures Is keen on sport

Figure 22 Statements about 'Mr X'

(c) There were four sets of data sheets relating to each of the four cards. Each sheet was divided into two columns headed 'L' and 'R' indicating responses to statements in the left-hand and right-hand columns of Figure 23. The left-hand side of the sheet was numbered 1–20 to identify each pair of statements.

7. METHOD

The experiment was conducted with different groups during one week's General Studies lessons. The nature of the experiment (investigation into stereotyping etc.) was not discussed at this stage, but left until the following week when all the subjects had completed the experiment.

Subjects were given cards at random (1, 2, 3 or 4) and also the Personality Inventory of Mr X. They were instructed to read the description on the card and then to underline whichever one of each pair of personality statements (Items) they considered most appropriate to the Mr X described on their card. They were asked to work through the Items as quickly as possible since first impressions were required and they were asked not to discuss the experiment with other subjects. They were asked to hold up the card and the Inventory as soon as they had finished and the documents were collected immediately by the experimenters.

The data sheets (see 6(c) above) were used by the experimenters to record the responses of the subjects. A response in the left-hand column on the Personality Inventory (Figure 23) was indicated by a tick on the 'L' column of the data sheet and vice versa. The total number of ticks was transferred to Table 20 as shown below.

8. RESULTS–DATA SHEET

Table 20 Responses to statements on four cards

	Card 1		Card 2		Card 3		Card 4	
	Country house		Semi-detached		Council house		Tenement	
Items	L	R	L	R	L	R	L	R
1	11	1	11	1	9	3	9	3
2	3	9	1	11	3	9	5	7
3	4	8	9	3	8	4	4	8
4	8	4	12	0	7	5	7	5
5	10	2	4	8	7	5	8	4
6	7	5	3	9	10	2	11	1
7	4	8	7	5	5	7	6	6
8	5	7	7	5	4	8	9	3
9	12	0	11	1	8	4	9	3
10	2	10	2	10	5	7	4	8
11	9	3	5	7	7	5	8	4
12	3	9	5	7	4	8	3	9
13	7	5	7	5	7	5	9	3
14	4	8	7	5	6	6	3	9
15	1	11	2	10	5	7	9	3
16	7	5	9	3	7	5	6	6
17	10	2	9	3	5	7	4	8
18	11	1	11	1	11	1	9	3
19	7	5	9	3	8	4	9	3
20	4	8	9	3	6	6	5	7

9. TREATMENT OF RESULTS

Table 21 % L + R Responses

	Group 1 + Group 2		Group 3 + Group 4	
	L	R	L	R
1	92	8	75	25
2	17	83	33	67
3	54	46	50	50
4	83	17	58	42
5	58	42	63	37
6	42	58	88	12
7	46	54	46	54
8	50	50	54	46
9	96	4	71	29
10	17	83	38	62
11	58	42	63	37
12	33	67	29	71
13	58	42	67	33
14	46	54	38	62
15	13	87	58	42
16	67	33	54	46
17	79	21	38	62
18	92	8	83	17
19	67	33	71	29
20	54	46	46	54

Table 22 Chi-square Analysis

1	2.40
2	3.10
3	6.93
4	6.84
5	6.53
**6	14.11
7	1.70
8	4.90
9	5.80
10	3.10
11	1.00
12	1.00
13	1.00
14	2.00
**15	14.11
16	1.60
*17	8.92
18	2.28
19	1.08
20	4.68

$$* \; p = 0.05$$
$$** \; p = 0.01$$

(a)   The total number of 'L' responses on each Item in respect of the subjects who had used cards 1 and 2 (country house/semi-detached) were combined and converted into a percentage. The same procedure was applied to the 'L' responses of subjects using cards 3 and 4 (council house/tenement). From these data the percentages for the 'R' responses were easily calculated. The percentage responses for the two groups are shown in Table 21.

(b)   In order to gain a more sophisticated and precise response profile, chi-square (χ^2) was applied to the data for each of the twenty Items in

Consider the 20 pairs of alternatives below. For each pair, underline the one statement which you feel best applies to the person described on your card. If you are not sure make a guess.

1	Mainly optimistic	Mainly pessimistic
2	Regards his work lightly	Conscientious in his work
3	Spends much time with his children	Usually leaves his children to their own devices
4	Tends to be thrifty	Rather reckless with money
5	Rarely helps with the housework	Often helps in the house
6	Lives mainly in the present	Plans for the future
7	Attentive to his wife	Apt to take his wife for granted
8	Quite fond of gambling	Opposed to gambling
9	Self-reliant	Dependent on others
10	Somewhat untidy	Meticulous in his habits
11	Largely self-centred	Great concern for others
12	Active church member	Not bothered about religion
13	Loud and boisterous	Quiet and reserved
14	Shares his wife's interests	He and his wife go their own ways
15	Left in politics	Right in politics
16	Slow and deliberate	Quick and impulsive
17	Somewhat ambitious	Has few ambitions
18	Rather patriotic	Not very patriotic
19	On friendly terms with his neighbours	Tends to remain aloof from his neighbours
20	Scrupulously honest	Not averse to petty dishonesty

Figure 23 Personality Inventory of Mr 'X'

Table 20. In this way it was possible to compare the observed frequencies of responses with those that might have been expected assuming chance alone. The results of the χ^2 analysis are shown in Table 22; these results would be significant at the 5% level if they reached 7.81 and highly significant at the 1% level if they reached 11.34. (Refer to chi-square in Chapter 20 of this book.)

10. DISCUSSION OF RESULTS AND CONCLUSIONS

(a)   The chi-square analysis produced three significant items – numbers 6, 15 and 17.

Item   6. Owners of country and semi-detached houses are thought to tend to plan for the future whereas council-house and tenement dwellers are seen as tending to live for the present.
Item 15. Council-house and tenement dwellers are seen as tending to the left in political views while members of the other two groups were perceived as tending to the right.
Item 17. Country-house and semi-detached-house owners were seen as more ambitious than the others.

(a)   While the χ^2 analysis revealed only three *significant* Items, it highlighted other Items which failed to reach significance, but which gave some indication of interesting differences in attitude between groups (see Items below). For the purpose of analysis it was assumed that the people in the country houses and semi-detached houses would fall within one socio-economic range, while the council house and tenement dwellers would belong to a different group. Any discussion of results tended to relate to these two main classes of people rather than to the four sub-groups although where clear differences in attitudes were noted in relation to the sub-groups these are reported (e.g. Item 3). From Tables 21 and 22 the following Items warrant comment:

Item   3. The extreme sub-groups (country house and tenement dwellers) are seen as spending less time with their children than the other two sub-groups.
Item   4. This seems to indicate that sub-groups 1 and 2 are thought to be more thrifty than the others, but the semi-detached owners are seen as the most thrifty of all.
Item   5. Owners of country houses are viewed as not helping with house-work, but those who live in semis are often thought to help with domestic tasks – rather more than those in the remaining sub-groups.
Item   9. Here the members of the first two sub-groups are seen as more self-reliant than those in the other sub-groups. The tenement and council-house dwellers are viewed as being fairly dependent on others.
Item 10. Those in sub-groups 1 and 2 are characterized as more meticulous in their habits, while the other groups are considered untidy.
Item 20. The sub-group seen as scrupulously honest is that of the semidetached owner. Country-house dwellers were thought not to be above petty dishonesty.

(c)   From the Items discussed above it would appear that the hypothesis – 'that sixth-form students will attribute certain characteristics to people of different social classes according to preconceived and therefore probably biased notions' – is confirmed.

It must be borne in mind that the Items discussed here are based on the responses of students in this particular sample and that these responses were given by the students according to their own stereotyped conceptions of social class characteristics. Thus evaluations made in respect of each of the Items considered above must be seen in the context of this particular sample.

(d)   It would have been interesting to analyse the responses given by each student to determine whether he personally attributed 'good' characteristics to those in groups 1 and 2 or to those in groups 3 and 4 and then to establish the student's own placing on the socio-economic scale.

It was felt that personal knowledge of someone in one of the groups would influence the response and from this particular knowledge one would tend to generalize about the group as a whole.

There were one or two students who did not fully understand the meaning of the word 'tenement', but this was not discovered by the experimenters until after the experiment when it was too late to remedy the situation; consequently it was felt that the results might have been influenced to a slight degree.

11. REFERENCES

Brown, G., Cherrington, D. H. and Cohen, L. (1975). *Experiments in the Social Sciences*. (New York: Harper and Row).

Crespi, L. P. (1945). Public opinion towards conscientious objectors: intensity of social rejection in stereotype and attitude. *Journal of Psychology*, **19**, 251–276

Hovland, C. I. and Sherif, M. (1952). Judgemental phenomena and scales of attitude measurement: item displacement in Thurstone Scales. *Journal of Abnormal Social Psychology*, **47**, 822–32

Pettigrew, T. F., Allport, G. W. and Barnett, E. O. (1958). Binocular resolution and perception of race in South Africa, *British Journal of Psychology*, **49**, 265–78

Tajfel, H. and Wilkes, A. L. (1963). Salience of attributes and commitment to extreme judgement in the perception of people. *British Journal of Social and Clinical Psychology*, **2**, 40–49

> **STQ   (1)**   *Look back now at the section entitled 'Discussion of Results and Conclusions'. It could be a useful exercise to hold a class discussion on the nine items listed in this section in an attempt to answer the question of why the scores on these items turned out the ways they did. For example, in Item 3, why may it be that those who live in a country house or tenement were thought to spend less time with their children? Is it because the men in the first group are too busy with business affairs which they conduct at home? Or do such houses employ people to look*

> *after the children? Is the tenement dweller the kind of person who spends little time in the house? Or does he regard looking after children as his wife's responsibility? Take the discussion from here.*
>
> **(2)**   *Could you replicate this experiment with subjects of your own choice? It would be interesting to compare your results with those shown here and to try to account for any differences. For example, the sample reported here consisted entirely of male subjects. Would an all-girl group, or a mixed group produce significantly different results?*

Reading research reports

Now that we have seen that experiment 'write-ups', research reports and articles follow a more or less standard pattern, a brief outline is in order about how to read research articles meaningfully and critically. In studying psychology any student will benefit from using original sources from time to time and reading the original article. Research reports may appear forbidding to the beginning student. Technical language is frequently used, charts and graphs may be confusing, the concise form of reporting seems cold, and mathematical equations may be intimidating.

A research article may be read with any one of three aims: (1) acquaintance, (2) comprehension, or (3) critical evaluation. After preliminary selection based on the title or abstract, the student should approach each article with acquaintance as his first objective, comprehension as his second, and, if he has sufficient background and interest, critical evaluation as his third objective.

If the aim of the reading is acquaintance with a research paper, the student should first read the introductory paragraphs to determine the nature of the problem being investigated. Then the method and discussion should be scanned briefly. Finally, the summary statements should be carefully scrutinized. (In many journals, a summary statement appears in the form of an abstract at the beginning of the article.) By following this procedure, the student will achieve at least a cursory acquaintance with the contents of the article and perhaps acquire a 'feel' for what it is all about. The beginning student should not become over-involved in the fine details of research presentation, lest he lose sight of the general conclusions and their implications.

With acquaintance as a basis, the student can now concentrate on acquiring a more profound comprehension of the work. In order to do this, he must scrutinize rather than scan the article. That is to say, he will ask a number of questions in the course of his reading. Some of the typical questions students have found useful in scrutinizing research articles are outlined in the following paragraphs.

The introduction will generally provide information to answer the following questions: What is the author trying to do? Is he trying to discover new relations among events? Is his work aimed at testing a hypothesis (a hunch) by systematic observation? Is he trying to confirm findings reported at an earlier time? Is he interested in determining the generality of a principle? Is he questioning a popular conception that has not been subjected to systematic examination through controlled experiments or careful observations? Is he interested in determining the fruitfulness of a method?

The methods section will generally provide answers to questions of this sort: How does the author convert his hunches or his beliefs into testable hypotheses? What operations does the experimenter employ to answer the questions to settle his doubts? How does the author specify the variables? For example, how does he justify his selection of an ink-blot test as a measure of sexual interest? How does he select his subjects – are they randomly selected or selected according to some other criteria? What kinds of manipulations of the subjects does he introduce? How are the control samples selected? Are the control samples adequate? What sort of design is used? Is it appropriate? Are the statistics to be applied appropriate to the design and level of data?

The results section will provide answers to these typical questions: What are the raw data from which the results are refined? Are they ratings, scale scores, speech samples, self-reports, physiological measurements, test scores, census data, and so on? Have the data been processed to give summary statistics, such as averages? Are the results significant or not? What are the implications for the null hypothesis?

The discussion section will usually provide answers to questions of this type: Are the results in line with predictions from the author's initial hypotheses? How does the author relate his findings to conclusions reached by other investigators? How does he explain differences between his data and the predictions generated by his hypotheses? How does he integrate his findings with other current attempts to answer the same or similar questions?

Having achieved comprehension, the student is in a position to evaluate critically the research report by asking a few additional questions. Such questions cannot be asked by the beginning student; they are based in part on familiarity with research design, statistical methods, and the logic of experimentation. However, students at any level of sophistication may use common sense as the basis for criticism.

The student will ask the following questions to help him achieve a critical evaluation: Are the investigator's research hypotheses clearly linked to the questions raised? Are the specifications of the variables reasonable? Is he justified in specifying, for example, that a score on a personality test is equivalent to 'ego-control'? Is he concerned with representativeness both in selecting his subjects and in specifying the behaviours to be observed? In what ways are his controls adequate, and in what ways inadequate? Are the statistical tests appropriate to the data? May conclusions other than those of the author be derived from the same data? In what way are the findings significant, i.e. do they contribute in any important way to our understanding of conduct? Can the efficiency of prediction and control of behaviour be increased as a result of the application of the findings?

It is not unusual for the student to hesitate before critically evaluating a research article. This hesitancy is understandable; for years he has practised accepting the written word as the final authority. The reluctance to criticize may be eliminated if the student will bear in mind that a research article, simply because it is in print, is not the last word, nor is it perfect. In keeping with one of the purposes of this book – to help the student solve the problems that arise in connection with his experimental efforts – the student should recognize that any research study provides only tentative and imperfect answers to questions. It is not improper for the student to be sceptical, to doubt, and to raise questions. By asking penetrating questions, new hypotheses emerge and new research is undertaken. This is as it should be: new research is the hallmark of science.

To summarize: the student should first attain cursory knowledge of an article by scanning the introduction, reading the summary and conclusions, and superficially examining the rest. Reading for comprehension and for critical evaluation may follow. Some suggestive questions have been listed above as an aid to the student who seeks comprehensive understanding of research articles.

14

Experimental design and the control of error
I. The between-groups unrelated design

The purpose of experimental design is to minimize uncontrolled variation (experimental error), thereby increasing the likelihood that an experiment will produce reliable results. Entire books have been written about experimental design. Here we will cover only a sample of some common techniques used to improve the design of experiments. While this treatment is necessarily less complete than that of an entire text devoted to the subject, it should give you an understanding of the aims of the psychologist designing an experiment, even though it will not give you all the techniques that could be used.

A Experimental error

Experimental error occurs when a change in the DV is produced by any variable other than the IV. What we are wholly interested in is the effect of the IV on the DV. When other variables that are casually related to the DV are confounded with the IV, they produce experimental error; they produce differences on the DV between the experimental conditions that add to or subtract from the difference that would have been produced by the IV alone. Experimental error covers up the effect you are interested in and can make it difficult or impossible to assess.

Let us imagine that we obtain some Ss, assign half to a formally taught psychology course and half to the same course taught by programmed instruction, and at the end of the term, measure all Ss on an attainment test. There are a number of variables which, unless we are careful, may be confounded with the IV. One is time of day; one course may be taught in the middle of the morning, when students are alert, and the other at the very end of the day. Another is intelligence; students in one course may be brighter than those in the other. Since both of these variables are likely to affect the attainment score obtained at the end of the term, allowing either to be confounded with the IV is likely to result in experimental error.

There are two kinds of experimental errors; constant or systematic error and random error. An understanding of these kinds of errors and of ways to deal with them constitutes a fundamental basis of experimental reasoning.

(a) Systematic or constant error is an error or bias that favours the same experimental condition every time the experiment is repeated. Any error due to time of day would be a constant error, for whichever course is taught at the more favourable time of day is taught at that time for all Ss in that experimental condition.

(b) A random error is an error which, on repetitions of the experiment, sometimes favours one experimental condition and sometimes the other, on a chance basis. If Ss are assigned to conditions randomly, then any error resulting from differences in intelligence will be random error. Very often, the error from any particular source has both constant and random components. This would be true of the error produced by intelligence if the Ss volunteered for the conditions and if the brighter Ss usually, but not always, chose the same experimental condition. We shall continue to consider just the pure cases of constant and random error, and it is perfectly legitimate to do so. But we do this with the understanding that the error from any particular source may involve these components in any proportions.

The effect of a constant or systematic error is to distort the results in a particular direction, so that an erroneous difference masks the affairs. The effect of a random error is not to distort the results in any particular direction, but to obscure them. In designing an experiment, controls are employed to eliminate as much error as possible and then randomization to ensure that the remaining error will be distributed at random and thus interpretable statistically. Controlling or randomizing sources of constant error eliminates bias.

B Sources of experimental error

There are four sources of experimental error; sampling, assignment, conditions and measurement. Experimental error can be introduced in sampling the Ss from the population, in assigning the Ss in the sample to the experimental conditions, in administering the experimental conditions, and in measuring the DV. Error from any of these sources may be either constant or random. We will look at the first three sources in Chapters 14 and 17, but will leave measurement error (and its corollary reliability) to a later time (Chapter 25).

1 ERROR DUE TO SAMPLING

We have already considered sampling techniques in Chapter 7. It was apparent from there and also in chapter 8 on standard error that random error is difficult to avoid even with the best sampling techniques and that systematic (constant) error is always a threat.

Error due to sampling could arise in the teaching-method experiment above (p.143) if, as is usually the case, we did not test all the Ss in the population to which we wish to generalize the results and if, as is usually the case, the size of the experimental effect differs from S to S. Perhaps a psychology course taught by formal methods is of greater benefit to brighter students. Thus, while the true difference between the methods in the population as a whole might be a slight difference in favour of the formal method, the difference in a sample of bright students might be quite large, and that in a sample of less-bright students might be negligibly small. These discrepancies from the true difference constitute error. If the sampling procedure is random, sometimes brighter students will be drawn and the error will be in one direction, and sometimes less-bright students will be drawn and the error will be in the other direction. The error will be random. If subjects can volunteer and all bright students opt for the same teaching method then constant error is introduced. To control error due to sampling, the procedure of stratified sampling can be used.

> **STQ** *Write down your definition of a stratified sample. (We met it in Chapter 7.)*

What one does in stratified sampling is to stratify, or classify, the population with respect to the variable one wishes to control, and then to draw Ss from these classes so that they are represented in the sample in the same proportions in which they occur in the population. For example, 16% of the general population have IQs below 85, 34% have IQs between 85 and 100, 34% have IQs between 100 and 115, and 16% have IQs above 115. Thus, in a sample of 50 Ss, stratified with respect to IQ, there would be 8, 17, 17, and 8 Ss, respectively, in each of these classes.

Of course, not just one but many variables contribute to sampling error. Because stratification controls only one, or at best a few, variables, it reduces rather than eliminates sampling error. Consequently, after stratifying on one or a few variables and eliminating any error they might produce, you sample randomly from within strata to randomize the remaining variables and any sampling error associated with them. The name of the complete procedure is thus stratified random sampling. To randomize error due to sampling we can also use simple random sampling.

> **STQ** *Do you remember what a random sample is? Refer back to pp. 60–64 if you cannot answer.*

You know now that to sample randomly you draw Ss from the population in such a way that, (a) each S has an equal chance of being included in the sample, and (b) the selection of one S does not in any way influence the selection of other Ss. One way to sample 50 Ss randomly would be to put the names of everyone in the population into a hat – a large one – shake it thoroughly, and draw out 50 names without looking. This would be a cumbersome procedure, at best, as are all procedures for sampling randomly from a population of any size. If a sampling frame is available the use of random number tables is urged. (This has been discussed in Chapter 7.)

Randomization is the most important and basic of all control methods, providing control not only for known sources of variation but for unknown ones too. In fact it is the only technique for dealing with the latter source. Randomization prevents bias from systematic error. It is like an insurance policy, a precaution against disturbances that may or may not occur, and, clearly stated procedures involving tossing coins, random number tables, or picking numbers out of a hat should be employed.

2 ERROR DUE TO ASSIGNMENT

Error due to assignment could arise in the teaching-method experiment above if Ss in the two conditions differed initially in intelligence, as they no doubt would. The observed difference at the end of the experiment would then be the true difference resulting from manipulating the *IV* plus or minus this initial difference. This error would be a constant error if the procedure for assigning Ss to conditions were in some way biased. Perhaps Ss were allowed to choose which course they would take, and brighter Ss tend to take the formally taught course. Such an error would always tend to favour the taught-course performance when a comparison is made. Control of experimental error due to assignment is effected by the subject allocation design of the experiment. There are three basic designs:

(a)   Independent group or between subjects or unrelated design.
(b)   Within subjects, related or repeated measures design.
(c)   Matched pairs related design.

In almost all experiments we have to make a decision whether to employ the same subjects in each condition or level of the *IV*, or to use different subjects for each condition.

C Between-groups design

There are some kinds of experiment in which it is very difficult to use the same people for all conditions. What about an experiment testing the relationship between sex and induced learned helplessness? There is simply no way (apart from a split-second sex change!) in which the same people can perform in both the male and female groups. So there have to be different people (men and women) in the two groups. This design is known as a between-subjects or an unrelated design because the comparison is between two independent groups of unrelated people.

There are other experiments too in which it is easier to use different people for the different experimental conditions. These include experiments involving very long tasks which would exhaust the patience and lower the motivation of subjects if the same people had to perform all the conditions. Another reason is that if you use different people you avoid the possibility of practice effects transferring from one task to another.

Then there are some experiments which may depend on, at least temporarily, misleading people about the true purpose of the experiment. To take an example, people may be asked to look at a list of words and put them into certain categories. Then they are suddenly asked to remember the words when they were not expecting to. This is known as incidental learning as opposed to intentional learning, and depends on subjects not knowing about the memory task beforehand. If you wanted to investigate incidental learning under two conditions you could not use the same people because the second time round they would anticipate that you were going to spring a 'surprise' memory task on them. So you have no alternative but to employ different Ss for the different experimental conditions. But individuals do differ markedly from each other.

The only way to deal with this is to allocate the different people at random to the different experimental conditions. Here random means that it is purely a matter of chance which people end up doing which condition or level of the *IV*. The reasoning is that, if subjects are randomly allocated to experimental conditions on a chance basis, then people of different ages or abilities are just as likely to be found in all the experimental groups. For example, you might find that all the subjects who arrive first to volunteer for an experiment are the most highly motivated people who would tend to score more highly quite regardless of experimental condition. So they should not be placed in the same group. It would be better to allocate alternate subjects as they arrived, or perhaps to toss a coin to decide which group each subject should be allocated to; in which case – unless your coin is biased – the allocation of subjects to groups should be truly random.

The groups should also be assigned their level of the *IV* by a random procedure i.e. toss a coin to decide which group shall be the experimental one and which the control group. Random assignment exerts control by virtue of the fact that the variables to be controlled are distributed approximately the same in all groups. In this way their influence is a constant across the groups, since they cannot produce any differential influence on the *DV*. Remember though that bias can exist even after randomization has been applied since chance variation between groups will still occur. Do you recall the variation between means of randomly selected samples (Chapter 7)?

Look at the following example of randomization. We are to conduct our study on comparing the two psychology teaching methods referred to earlier (p. 143). Since intelligence is correlated with learning ability this factor must be controlled. We do not want all the bright subjects in one group since any mean difference (variation in *DV*) will include an unknown component caused by differences in intelligence between the groups. Let us imagine that the first time we did the experiment we were completely unsophisticated about experimental design and placed the first ten students who turned up in Group A and the second ten in Group B. The results of the experiment revealed that Group B learned significantly faster than Group A. But a knowledgeable colleague points out that he recently tested the very

Table 23 Group assignment based on arrival sequence

Group A		Group B	
Subjects	*IQ scores*	*Subjects*	*IQ scores*
1	97	11	106
2	97	12	108
3	100	13	110
4	103	14	113
5	105	15	117
6	108	16	119
7	109	17	120
8	110	18	122
9	113	19	128
10	116	20	130
Mean IQ Score	105.8		117.3

Mean difference between the two groups: 11.5

same students on a reputable IQ test and that the first ten students we formed group A from were less bright than those in group B. He then suggests, much to our chagrin, that the mean differences we assumed were due to the variation in level of the *IV* might be confounded by the mean IQ differences of the two groups. Table 23 reveals the IQ scores of the subjects in each group in our experiment.

Let us now imagine that we had been well aware of the intelligence being a possible confounding variable and had our colleague's data on the subjects' IQ at hand. We can now eliminate intelligence as a confounding variable and as a rival hypothesis for explaining the observed performance difference in the two groups by randomly assigning the twenty subjects to the two conditions of the *IV*. Table 24 depicts the IQ data for the two groups after this random allocation. The mean IQ scores become very similar, with only 0.1 IQ point of a difference.

Table 24 Random assignment of subjects to groups

Group A		Group B	
Subjects	*IQ scores*	*Subjects*	*IQ scores*
1	97	3	100
2	97	4	103
11	106	6	108
5	105	12	108
13	110	7	109
8	110	9	113
10	116	14	113
15	117	16	119
19	128	17	120
20	130	18	122
	111.6		111.5
Mean difference between the two groups: 0.1			

This little diversion was designed to illustrate the point that random assignment produces control in between-subjects or unrelated group designs by distributing the variables that need to be controlled in approximately the same manner in all groups. Randomization is the only method for the control of unknown variables. Other control techniques are only of value with known confounding variables. The principle is to randomize wherever and whenever possible, even when applying one of the other control techniques.

This between-subjects or unrelated design requires the use of either an unrelated '*t*' test when the data are interval (i.e. a parametric test) or a non-parametric test such as Mann – Whitney when the data are ordinal in level. But before we consider these two statistical tests and look at experiments that utilize them, another vital statistical concept, again a standard error, must be understood, the standard error of the difference between means.

STQ **(1)** *Briefly outline what you see as the advantages and disadvantages of the independent (between-groups) design.*

(2) *How can we generally avoid error due to assignment?*

15

Standard error of the difference between means

One of the two major types of hypothesis is one which is stated in difference terms, i.e. that there is a significant difference between two independent groups. This difference is essentially a difference between the two sample means. We want to know whether the difference between sample means is a real one or whether it could be reasonably attributed to chance, i.e. does the difference between the two sample means lie within the expected chance distribution of differences between the means of an infinite number of pairs of samples at some level of probability?

Remember what we saw when we drew a large number of samples when discussing random sampling (Chapter 7) and standard error (Chapter 8)? The means of the samples of a population distributed themselves normally around the 'true' population mean. Now in the case of differences between sample means we have the same principle applying. If we plot every difference between every possible pair of sample means, a normal distribution of differences between pairs of means is produced, because on many occasions the differences will be nil or quite slight with larger differences occurring more rarely. We can calculate the σ of this distribution. It is called the standard error of the difference between means. It estimates the dispersal of these mean differences.

Suppose, for instance, that a random sample of adult males produce a mean score of 52 on a visual-tracking test while a random sample of adult females attained a mean of 54. Does this difference reveal a real superiority on the part of females on this task? The answer depends on how this obtained difference of 2 in mean score would vary as further pairs of random samples are tested. Our obtained difference of 2 is only one value of a distribution of differences, a sampling distribution of the difference between means.

STQ *What is the standard deviation of this sampling distribution called?*

The standard deviation of this distribution is termed the standard error of the difference between means. This standard error depends on the sampling distribution or standard error of each of the two sample means. When each sample is selected independently of the other the standard error of the difference between means is symbolized by either SE_{diff} or σ_D. It is expressed as:

$$SE_{diff} = \sqrt{SE_{M1}^2 + SE_{M2}^2}$$

The subscripts indicate sample mean 1 and sample mean 2 respectively. Since $SE_m = \sigma/(N-1)$ then $SE_m^2 = \sigma^2/(N-1)$. We can then substitute into the SE_{diff} formula and obtain the following easier to compute formula, *viz*:

$$SE_{diff} = \sqrt{\frac{\sigma_1^2}{N_1 - 1} + \frac{\sigma_2^2}{N_2 - 1}}$$

the subscripts again referring to the first and second samples respectively. As with the standard error of the mean, a critical ratio is formed to find the deviation in standard error unit terms of the difference between the means.

This ratio is called the *t* ratio.

$$t = \frac{M_1 - M_2}{SE_{diff}} \quad \text{or} \quad \frac{M_1 - M_2}{\sqrt{\dfrac{\sigma_1^2}{N_1 - 1} + \dfrac{\sigma_2^2}{N_2 - 1}}}$$

The obtained '*t*' is compared to the tabled entry of *t* (Table B, Appendix A) for the relevant *df* and level of significance. *df* in a *t* ratio is $(N_1 - 1) + (N_2 - 1)$. If *t* is the same as or greater than the relevant tabled entry then the *t* is significant at that level of significance.

Suppose that the mean scores obtained in the tracking test above were derived from a sample 201 men and 201 women with standard deviations respectively of 4 and 5. The research hypothesis is that there is a true sex difference in performance, the obtained difference of 2 between the means not being a random or chance sampling deviation. The computation in our example is as follows:

$$t = \frac{54 - 52}{\sqrt{\dfrac{4^2}{200} + \dfrac{5^2}{200}}} = \frac{2}{\sqrt{\dfrac{16}{200} + \dfrac{25}{200}}}$$

$$= \frac{2}{\sqrt{0.08 + 0.125}}$$

$$= \frac{2}{\sqrt{0.20}}$$

$$= \frac{2}{\sqrt{0.444}}$$

$$= 4.54$$

This 4.54 is the obtained difference expressed in standard error units. From the *t* table (Table B, Appendix A) with $df = 400$ we can see that there is much less than a 1% chance of differences in means arising of this magnitude from sampling error. The null hypothesis is therefore rejected and the difference in sample means accepted as significant at beyond the 1% level. The research hypothesis that there is a significant difference in performance on this tracking task between the sexes is supported quite strongly.

Let us look at the above result in a more 'visual' way. The SE_{diff} is the estimate of the dispersal of all possible mean differences between an infinite number of similarly drawn pairs of samples. The $SE_{diff} = 0.444$. This is shown on the normal distribution below, which represents a population of differences $M = 0$, $\sigma = 0.444$.

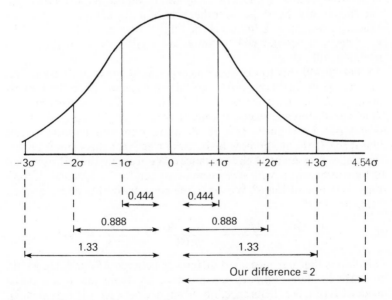

Figure 23 The SE_{diff} shown on the normal distribution

We would expect 95% of sample mean differences to be between −0.888 and +0.888. Our difference of 2 is equal to 4.54σ which is way beyond 3σ from the mean. Obviously something is happening here besides chance! It is, provided we have controlled other variables, the experimental effect.

Here is another example. Suppose we have two randomly selected groups of 100 ten-year-old pupils each. We show a film in intergroup relations to one group, for example, and none to the other group. Next, we give both groups an attitude measure. The mean score of Group A (saw the film) is 70 and the mean score of Group B (did not see the film) is 60. Our problem is this: is the difference of 10 units a 'real' difference, a statistically significant difference? Or is it a difference that could have arisen by chance – more than 5 times in 100, say, when no real difference actually exists?

If the scores of the two groups had been chosen from a table of random numbers and there were no experimental conditions, we would expect no difference between the means. But we have learned that there are always differences that are relatively small, which are due to chance factors. We explored this point in discussing the SE_m in Chapter 8. These differences are random. In this instance let us assume the standard error of the differences between the means is 1.08. By chance alone, there would be random fluctuations in the differences between M_A and M_B. Only rarely would the differences exceed three times the SE_{diff}. Another way of putting it is to say that the standard error of 1.08 indicates the limits (if we mulitply the 1.08 by the z deviate) beyond which sample differences between the means probably will not go.

What has all this to do with our experiment? It is precisely in this way that we evaluate our experimental results as we did in the first example. The standard error of 1.08 estimates random fluctuations. Now our difference was 10, that is, $M_A - M_B = 10$. Could this have arisen by chance, as a result of random fluctuations as just described? It should by now be halfway clear that this cannot be, except under very unusual circumstances. We evaluate this difference of 10 by comparing it with our estimate of random or chance fluctuations. Is it one of them? We make the comparison by means of the t ratio, or t test:

$$t = \frac{M_A - M_B}{SE_{diff}} = \frac{70 - 60}{1.08} = \frac{10}{1.08} = 9.25$$

This means that our measured difference between M_A and M_B would be $9.25z$ or 9.25 standard deviations away from an hypothesized mean of zero (zero difference, no difference between the two means).

We would not have any difference, theoretically, if our subjects were well randomized and there had been no experimental manipulation. We would have, in effect, two distributions of random numbers from which we could expect only chance fluctuations. But here we have, comparatively, a huge difference of 10, compared to an insignificant 1.08 (our estimate of random deviations). Chance is not the only influence here. The influence, presumably, is the effect of the film, the experimental condition, or independent variable, other conditions we trust having been sufficiently controlled, of course.

Again look at a visual representation of this result. Figure 24 represents a population distribution of differences between means with a mean of zero and a standard deviation of 1.08. (The mean is set at zero, because we assume that the mean of all the mean differences is zero). Where would the difference of 10 be placed on the base line of the diagram? In order to answer this question, the 10 must first be converted into standard deviation (or standard error) units. This is done by dividing it by the standard deviation (standard error) which is 1.08 : $10/1.08 = 9.25$. But this is what we got when we computed the

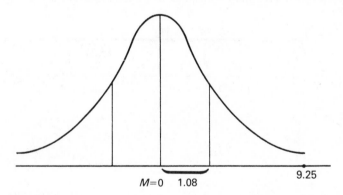

Figure 24

t ratio. t is, then, simply the difference between M_A and M_B 10, expressed in standard deviation (standard error) units. Now we can put it on the base line of the diagram. Look far to the right for the little dot. Clearly the difference of 10 is a deviate. It is so far out, in fact, that it probably does not belong to the population in question. In short, the difference between M_A and M_B is statistically significant, so significant that it amounts to what Bernoulli called 'moral certainty'. Such a large difference as this, or deviation from chance expectation, can hardly be attributed to chance. The odds are actually greater than a billion to one. It could happen. But it is hardly likely to happen.

Again in this case we can reject the null hypothesis that the difference was a chance one and accept the alternate hypothesis that viewing a film on intergroup relations has a significant effect on measured attitude.

The formula

$$\mathrm{SE}_{\mathrm{diff}} = \sqrt{\frac{\sigma_1^2}{N_1 - 1} + \frac{\sigma_2^2}{N_2 - 1}}$$

unfortunately is appropriate only when the samples are large and both groups are of equal size. In some *t*-test situations the samples are small and of different sizes and the way one must cope with this and compensate is by adopting this modified formula.

$$\mathrm{SE}_{\mathrm{diff}} = \sqrt{\frac{\sigma_1^2 + \sigma_2^2}{N_1 + N_2 - 2} \left(\frac{1}{N_1} + \frac{1}{N_2}\right)}$$

The σ^2 in the formula can be restated mathematically as $(\Sigma X^2 - (\Sigma X)^2/N)$ thus the total *t* formula for unrelated groups is:

$$t = \frac{M_1 - M_2}{\sqrt{\frac{\left(\Sigma X_1^2 - \frac{(\Sigma X_1)^2}{N_1}\right) + \left(\Sigma X_2^2 - \frac{(\Sigma X_2)^2}{N_2}\right)}{(N_1 - 1)(N_2 - 1)} \left(\frac{1}{N_1} + \frac{1}{N_2}\right)}}$$

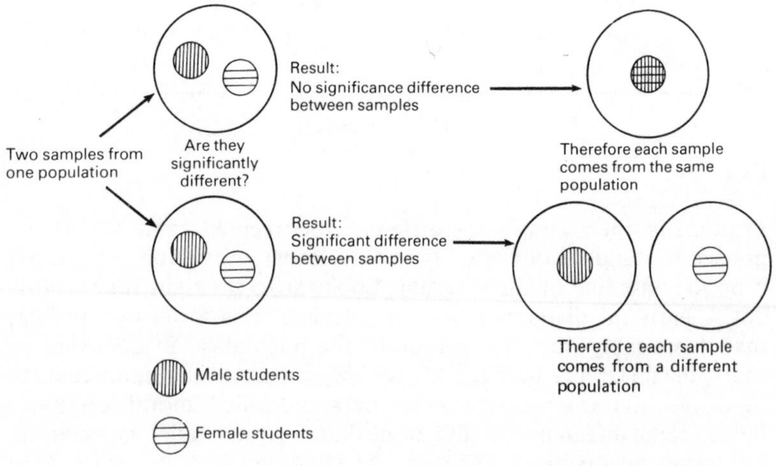

Figure 25 Two samples from the same or different population

One way of looking at the statistical inference of significance in a 'difference' hypothesis is to reason that if the difference is genuine then the two groups are each a sample from two different populations. For example, if we take two random samples of students to test their speed in solving anagrams, one a sample of females, the other a sample of males, then if there is no significant difference in anagram solution times they have likely been drawn from the same population. If there is a significant difference then we can infer that female and male students form different populations as far as the ability to solve anagrams is concerned. This point is illustrated in Figure 25.

STQ (1) *If a near infinite number of pairs of samples were taken randomly from a population and the mean differences between each pair plotted on a graph, what would we term the standard deviation of these plotted differences?*

(2) *An independent group experiment is carried out correctly and yields the following information:*

	M	σ	N
Experimental	15.8	2.5	26
Control	17.6	2.0	21

What could you conclude?

(3) *The results of a two-tailed experiment are:*

$$M_1 - M_2 = 3; \sigma_1 = 4; \sigma_2 = 3; N = 25$$

in each of the two random groups. Calculate t. Would you retain the null hypothesis at $p < 0.05$?

Answers on page 434.

16

Statistical tests for unrelated designs

A Unrelated *t* test (parametric)

Here is a worked example of an unrelated *t* test, taking you right through from the raw data derived in a memory experiment.

Twenty subjects are randomly assigned to two groups. Ten subjects learn lists of letter–digit telephone numbers, and the other ten subjects learn lists of all-digit telephone numbers. Their recall scores are given in Table 25.

Table 25 Recall scores of subjects in letter–digit and all-digit conditions

Subjects	Condition A letter–digits	Subjects	Condition B all-digits
1	11	11	3
2	6	12	2
3	7	13	8
4	4	14	5
5	10	15	5
6	9	16	6
7	8	17	3
8	6	18	6
9	7	19	4
10	6	20	5
	Mean: 7.4		Mean: 4.7

To calculate *t* we have to compare the means of the two groups of subjects.

Let us look at the *t*-test procedure step by step, using the data from our example. First, draw up a table of scores for each condition and find their squares (see Table 26).

The raw scores (X_1) in condition A should be totalled (ΣX_1) and this total squared (ΣX_1^2). Find the squares (X_1^2) of each of the raw scores and

158

the sums of squares (ΣX_1^2). The mean will be calculated at this stage. Apply exactly the same procedure to the data in condition B. You now have available the necessary information to find *t*.

Table 26 Table of results

Scores X_1	Squares X_1^2	Scores X_2	Squares X_2^2
11	121	3	9
6	36	2	4
7	49	8	64
4	16	5	25
10	100	5	25
9	81	6	36
8	64	3	9
6	36	6	36
7	49	4	16
6	36	5	25
$\Sigma X_1\ 74$	$\Sigma X_1^2\ 588$	$\Sigma X^2\ 47$	$\Sigma X_2^2\ 249$
$\{\Sigma X_1\}^2\ 5476$		$\{\Sigma X_2\}^2\ 2209$	
Mean: $M_1\ 7.4$		Mean: $M_2\ 4.7$	

Let us now apply these steps to the data on Table 26.

(a) Sum the X_1 scores in condition A and the X_2 scores in condition B.

$$\Sigma X_1 \;=\; 74 \qquad \Sigma X_2 \;=\; 47$$

(b) Find the means of the scores in each condition.

$$M_1 \;=\; 7.4 \qquad M_2 \;=\; 4.7$$

(c) Square the total scores

$$(\Sigma X_1)^2 = 74 \times 74 = 5476 \qquad (\Sigma X_2)^2 = 47 \times 47 = 2209$$

(d) Sum the squares in each condition

$$\Sigma X_1^2 \;=\; 588 \qquad \Sigma X_2^2 \;=\; 249$$

(e) We are now able to insert the values in the formula to obtain *t*.

$$t \;=\; \cfrac{M_1 - M_2}{\sqrt{\cfrac{\left(\Sigma X_1^2 - \dfrac{(\Sigma X_1)^2}{N_1}\right) + \left(\Sigma X_2^2 - \dfrac{(\Sigma X_2)^2}{N_2}\right)}{(N_1 - 1) \;+\; (N_2 - 1)}\left(\dfrac{1}{N_1} + \dfrac{1}{N_2}\right)}}$$

Applying our data:

$$t = \frac{7.4 - 4.7}{\sqrt{\frac{\left(588 - \frac{5476}{10}\right) + \left(249 - \frac{2209}{10}\right)}{9 + 9}\left(\frac{1}{10} + \frac{1}{10}\right)}}$$

$$t = \frac{7.4 - 4.7}{\sqrt{\left(\frac{588 - 547.6 + 249 - 220.9}{18}\right) \times \frac{1}{5}}}$$

$$= \frac{2.7}{\sqrt{3.806 \times 0.2}}$$

$$= \frac{2.7}{\sqrt{0.7612}}$$

$$= \frac{2.7}{0.872}$$

$$= 3.096$$

To find the degrees of freedom, subtract two from the total number of subjects, which is the same thing as $N_1 - 1$ plus $N_2 - 1$. The reason for this is because there is one less degree of freedom than the number of subjects each group.

The degrees of freedom: $df = (10 - 1) + (10 - 1) = 18$. Look up the significance level of t in Table B Appendix 1. Glance down the left-hand column to find 18 df; look along the row to determine whether the observed value of t (3.096) is equal to or larger than the critical value. The observed value of t of 3.096 is larger than the tabled value of 2.878.

STQ   *How would you relate these results to*
       (a) a one-tailed hypothesis?
       (b) a two-tailed hypothesis?

When the conditions for applying a parametric t-test cannot be met, that is when the data is not interval level, or when the distribution of scores is extremely non-normal or when the σ of the two sets of data are very different a non-parametric test of difference must be employed. The non-parametric parallel to the unrelated t test is the Mann–Whitney test.

EXPERIMENT USING THE UNRELATED OR INDEPENDENT *t* TEST
Aim and background
This is part of a review of the literature on recognition and recall. Read it through carefully, and see if you could find suitable books from the library which would enable you to develop this outline.

To recall something is to call that something back to mind. It is the remembrance of things learned or experienced. Recognition on the other hand is the realization that something is familiar; it is to identify with something known or experienced before.

People normally find it easier to recognize something than to recall something. This is because in recognition the person is presented with some sort of stimulus which immediately restricts the possibilities open to the person. With recognition, an event is present in the here and now with some characteristic, previously stated, enabling recognition to take place.

Due to the above, recognition requires comparatively less energy. It is usually a çase of a decision as to whether something has been encountered before or is a new experience, e.g. we may be unable to recall a person's name or where we met him before – but we may be able to recognize the person as being familiar, that we have met him/her before.

Recall is a much more energy consuming, and often time consuming, process. It requires a more complex decision than yes/no. The number of possibilities are almost unlimited, or at least greater than occurs with recognition. The information has to be searched for through the memory store. Cues may point in a certain direction when trying to recall something, but some effort is still required of the person. Recognition only involves checking that something is stored in the memory, and people with an efficient memory process will be able to check this in a matter of seconds.

From the literature available it seemed that recognition was a much easier process than recall, and it was decided to test this. The following null hypothesis was therefore formed: 'that subjects will not find it significantly easier to *recognize* words than to *recall* them'.

Conditions
The experiment took place during one lunch hour in the psychology laboratory. Environmental conditions were normal.

Subjects and experimenters
There were 50 twelve-year-old boys who took part in the experiment, 25 under each condition. The two experimenters were psychology students.

Apparatus

The recall condition group were supplied with small pieces of paper on which to record their responses. The recognition group were supplied with printed sheets containing ten different words with three slightly different spellings for each. Those subjects without writing instruments were given pencils.

The ten words used in the experiment were:

COMMITTEE	PENICILLIN
PROFESSION	HALLUCINATION
NECESSARY	CORRESPONDENCE
PARALLEL	EMBARRASSED
COMMISSION	PHENOMENON

Method

The first group to undergo the experiment was the recognition group. They were brought into the psychology laboratory and asked to find a seat. The printed sheets were handed out, to the subjects, face down. When the subjects were comfortable and all the sheets had been given out, the following instructions were read out:

'This is an experiment on memory. When you turn over the sheets you will find three different spellings of ten words. We would like you to underline which spelling you think is correct for each of the ten words. Please do not copy or talk amongst yourselves. If you guess the spelling of a word, please put a tick in the appropriate box to the right of the word. Please finish as quickly as possible. You may begin now.'

As each subject finished, his paper was collected. When all the subjects had finished they were thanked for their help and allowed to go. The second group of subjects (the recall group) was brought into the psychology laboratory a few minutes after the recognition group had departed. It was ensured that the two groups were not allowed to interact during this period of time. These subjects were issued with small pieces of paper and the following instructions were read:

'This is an experiment on memory. I am going to read you a list of ten words and I would like you to write down what you think is the spelling for each. Please do not copy or talk amongst yourselves.'

The words were read out one at a time, leaving a suitable gap between one word and the next to allow the subjects to respond. When the papers had been completed, they were collected in and scored for correct and incorrect spellings. The subjects were thanked for their co-operation. The number of correct responses for the recall group and the recognition group are shown in the Results table.

Results

Number of correct responses

Subject	Recall Group A	Recognition Group B
1	0	3
2	1	4
3	1	5
4	0	2
5	2	6
6	4	4
7	1	3
8	0	4
9	1	4
10	1	6
11	2	2
12	6	5
13	0	4
14	4	6
15	0	3
16	2	4
17	1	6
18	2	5
19	1	2
20	1	5
21	2	4
22	0	5
23	2	6
24	1	4
25	1	3
	Σ = 36	Σ = 105

Treatment of results

An uncorrelated t test was employed to test for the differences between the means of the recall and recognition groups:

(a) Sum the X_1 scores in condition A and the X_2 scores in condition B

$$\Sigma X_1 = 36 \quad \Sigma X_2 = 105$$

(b) Find the means of the scores in each condition

$$M_1 = 1.36 \quad M_2 = 4.20$$

(c) Square the total scores

$$(\Sigma X_1)^2 = 36 \times 36 = 1\,296$$
$$(\Sigma X_2)^2 = 105 \times 105 = 11\,025$$

(d)   Sum the squares in each condition

$$\Sigma X_1^2 = 102 \quad \Sigma X_2^2 = 481$$

(e)   We are now able to insert the values into the formula to obtain t

$$t = \frac{M_1 - M_2}{\sqrt{\dfrac{(\Sigma X_1^2 - \dfrac{(\Sigma X_1)^2}{N_1}) + (\Sigma X_2^2) - \dfrac{(\Sigma X_2^2)}{N_2}}{(N_1 - 1) + (N_2 - 1)}\left(\dfrac{1}{N_1} + \dfrac{1}{N_2}\right)}}$$

$$t = \frac{4.20 - 1.36}{\sqrt{\dfrac{\left(102 - \dfrac{1296}{25}\right) + \left(481 - \dfrac{11025}{25}\right)}{(25 - 1) + (25 - 1)}\left(\dfrac{1}{25} + \dfrac{1}{25}\right)}}$$

$$= \frac{2.84}{\sqrt{\dfrac{50.16 + 40}{48}\ (0.08)}}$$

$$= \frac{2.84}{\sqrt{1.88 \quad (0.08)}}$$

$$= \frac{2.84}{\sqrt{0.15}}$$

$$= 7.319$$

with $(25 - 1) + (25 - 1)$ or 48 degrees of freedom, from Table B in Appendix A

$$t = 2.021 \text{ at the } 5\% \text{ level}$$

The observed value of t is greater than the table value, therefore there is a significant difference between the two conditions, and the null hypothesis can be rejected.

Now you should carry out the above experiment and write up a report which should include a review of relevant literature and a discussion both of which we did not include above. That is your task. Use the model in Chapter 13 to help you structure the report.

B The Mann–Whitney test (non-parametric)

Let us imagine that we want to discover the effect of organization on memory. The experiment will adopt a null hypothesis to demonstrate that it will not be significantly easier to remember a set of words which are organized in categories than a set of words that has no organization.

We allocate six subjects randomly to a group where they will learn material *without* the aid of organized categories, and allocate eight subjects to a group where they will use categorized material. The effect of organization on memory will be measured by the number of words each subject recalls.

Table 27 Number of words recalled by each subject in either the 'category' or 'non-category' conditions

Group 1 $N_1 = 6$	Condition 1 'non-category'	Group 2 $N_2 = 8$	Condition 2 'category'
1	13	7	21
2	14	8	16
3	12	9	10
4	18	10	15
5	16	11	11
6	19	12	14
		13	20
		14	17
Means	15.33		15.50

There are very few differences between the Mann–Whitney test and the Wilcoxon test (Chapter 18). The Mann–Whitney uses different subjects and an unrelated or between-groups design, while the Wilcoxon uses the same subjects and a related design. Unlike the Wilcoxon test, which analyses differences in the results between same and matched subjects under two experimental conditions, the Mann–Whitney test notes the differences in the results between all the subjects in both conditions. It should not be used when there are many tied ranks.

Table 28 Calculation of the value of U (the Mann−Whitney statistic)

Group 1 $N_1 = 6$ 'non-category'	Condition 1	Ranks 1	Group 2 $N_2 = 8$ 'category'	Condition 2	Ranks 2
1	13	4	7	21	14
2	14	5.5	8	16	8.5
3	12	3	9	10	1
4	18	11	10	15	7
5	16	8.5	11	11	2
6	19	12	12	14	5.5
			13	20	13
			14	17	10
		$T_1 = 44.0$			$T_2 = 61.0$

(1) Place all the scores in rank order, taking both groups together. Give rank 1 to the lowest score, rank 2 to the next lowest score etc. Add the ranks for each group separately.

(2) Use the following formula to find U

$$U = N_1 N_2 + \frac{N_1(N_1 + 1)}{2} - T_1$$

where N_1 = number of group 1 subjects
N_2 = number of group 2 subjects
T_1 = rank total for group 1.

$$U = 6 \times 8 + \frac{6(6 + 1)}{2} - 44.0$$

$$= 48 + \frac{42}{2} - 44.0$$

$$= 48 + 21 - 44.0$$

$$U = 25$$

(3) Substitute the values of U, N_1 and N_2 in the following formula. Calculate U^1, substituting the values of U, N_1, N_2.

$$U^1 = N_1 N_2 - U$$
$$= 6 \times 8 - 25$$
$$U^1 = 23.0$$

(4) Select a level of significance i.e. $p < 0.05$ (two-tailed). Look up the smaller of U and U^1 in Table D Appendix A. There is a significant difference if the observed value is less than or equal to the

table value. In Table D, the critical value of U for $N_1 = N_2 = 8$ at the $p < 0.05$ two-tailed level of significance is 8. Because our observed value U^1 (23.0) is not equal to, or less than, the table value, there is no significant evidence that the scores under the two conditions differ, and the null hypothesis would be supported.

EXPERIMENT USING THE MANN–WHITNEY TEST

When a problem has to be solved, will a small group of people be more effective than an individual in finding a solution? Some researchers have reported in favour of individual problem solving, while others have supported group problem solving, in fact, much depends on the nature of the problem and the kind of individuals who are trying to seek a solution.

In the present experiment, a student read some of the research which he considered presented a balanced view of both individual and group problem solving practices. The studies of Marquart (1955) and Dunnette *et al.* (1963) represented the superiority of individual problem solving, while those of Lorge and Solomon (1959), Taylor and Faust (1952), and Triandis *et al.* (1963) favoured the group approach. These references are detailed at the end of the experiment.

The student conducted the present experiment to compare an individual's ability to solve a complex problem with that of a group of three persons. How might he have formulated his hypothesis?

Subjects and experimenters

There were eight experimenters, and each chose four subjects.

Apparatus

There were four copies of the problem (see below). Pencils, rubbers and sheets of paper were made available for jotting down ideas. Each experimenter had a watch to time the experiment, which could last up to an hour. The problem to be solved was as follows:

'A jailer once offered three of his prisoners freedom if they could solve a problem. One of the prisoners had normal sight, one was blind in one eye, and the other was totally blind. The jailer told the three men that from three white hats and two red hats he would select one to place on each of their heads. The jailer took each prisoner aside and placed one of the five hats on his head in a manner that prevented the prisoner from seeing the colour of his own hat. This, of course, was not a problem with the blind prisoner. The prisoners were then brought together with their hats on their heads and the prisoner with normal vision was offered his freedom if he could tell what colour hat was on his head. He confessed that he could not. The jailer then offered freedom to the prisoner who was blind in one eye if he could tell the colour of his hat. He too could not tell. The blind man then asked if he would still be given his freedom if he knew the colour of his hat. The jailer smilingly said yes, whereupon the blind man accurately reported the colour of his hat and was given his freedom.

What colour was the blind man's hat and how did he know what colour it was? Hint: always ask what colour hats a prisoner must see on the heads of the other two prisoners before he can know for certain what colour his hat is.'

Method

(1) When the individual subject entered the room, the experimenter gave him a copy of the problem. The subject was instructed to solve the problem using any methods which occurred to him, but he must be prepared to explain how he arrived at his solution. A guess would not be acceptable. No more than 60 min would be allowed.

(2) When the group of three subjects entered the room, the experimenter presented each of them with a copy of the problem. They were instructed to solve the problem as a group and to discuss possible solutions. One of the group would have to explain how they arrived at their solution, as a guess would not be acceptable. No more than 60 minutes would be allowed.

Results

Table 29 Problem solution times

E	Condition A solution of problem (individual)	Condition B solution of problem (group)
1	39 min	60 min
2	28 min	58 min
3	54 min	49 min
4	43 min	40 min
5	41 min	57 min
6	30 min	26 min
7	37 min	52 min
8	44 min	55 min

Treatment of results

A Mann–Whitney U-test was applied to the results in Table 29.

Taking both groups together, rank the times assigning rank 1 to the lowest time:

Table 30 Solution times by ranks

E	Condition A	Condition B
1	5	16
2	2	15
3	12	10
4	8	6
5	7	14
6	3	1
7	4	11
8	9	13

$$T_1 = 50 \qquad T_2 = 86$$

Sum the ranks for condition A (or this would be the smaller sample if the conditions were not equal in size). The sum is known as T_1 Thus,

$$5 + 2 + 12 + 8 + 7 + 3 + 4 + 9 = 50$$

U is found by applying the following formula:

$$U = N_1 N_2 + N_1 \frac{(N_1 + 1)}{2} - T_1$$

$$U = (8 \times 8) + \frac{(8 \times 9)}{2} - 50$$

$$= 64 + 36 = 100 - 50 = 50$$

$$U^1 = N_1 N_2 - U$$
$$= (8 \times 8) - U$$
$$= 64 - 50$$
$$= 14$$

Look up Table D, Appendix A and take which is the smaller of U and U^1. If the obtained value is equal to or less than the table value there is a significant difference.

In our example, U^1 is smaller (14), than U (50). The table value for $N_1 = 8$, $N_2 = 8$ is 13. Since the obtained value (14) is not less than the value shown in the table (13), there is no significant difference between the two conditions.

REFERENCES
Dunnette, M. D., Campbell, J. and Jaastad, K. (1963). The effect of group participation on brainstorming effectiveness for two industrial samples. *J. Appl. Psychol.*, **47**, 30-7.

Lorge, I. and Solomon, H. (1959). Individual performance and group performance in problem solving related to group size and previous exposure to the problem. *J. Appl. Psychol.*, **48**, 107–14.

Marquart, D. I. (1955). Group problem solving. *J. Soc. Psychol.*, **41**, 103–13.

Taylor, D. W. and Faust, W. L. (1952). Twenty questions: Efficiency in problem solving as a function of size of group. *J. Exp. Psychol.*, **44**, 360–8.

Triandis, H. C., Bass, A. R., Ewen, R. B. and Mikesell, E. H. (1963). Team creativity as a function of the creativity of the members. *J. Appl. Psychol.*, **47**, 104–10.

Exercise

Now it is your turn. Try to carry out the above experiment. Read as many of the references as you can and write up a review and introduction to your study. When you have calculated your results and determined their significance, write a discussion section indicating any implications and inferences. Refer to Chapter 13 for a model report and how to write a report.

STQ **(1)**   **(i)** *Using random samples of 750 children an investigator tested the hypothesis that children in Scotland receive significantly less pocket money then children in Wales. Which one of the following tests should he apply:*

(a)   t test for related samples
(b)   z test
(c)   Mann–Whitney test
(d)   t test for independent samples

     (ii) *In the hypothesis above which one of the following procedures should he use:*

(a)   a two-tailed test
(b)   a one-tailed test
(c)   either a one-tailed or a two-tailed test

     (iii) *If he used a significance level of $p < 0.01$ which one of the following consequences is most likely:*

(a)   a type I error
(b)   a type II error

    (2)   *What is the null hypothesis of the Mann–Whitney test?*

> **(3)** *Two random groups of pupils are used to determine whether a programmed text book is worse than an ordinary text book. The following data are the final test scores on a common examination.*
>
> *Programmed text: 57, 78, 45, 33, 52, 58, 28, 76.*
> *Ordinary text: 86, 34, 85, 60, 87, 94, 79, 56, 90.*
>
> *Perform a Mann–Whitney U test and come to a conclusion using the 0.05 level.*

Answers on page 434.

17

Experimental design and the control of error: II. Within-groups related design and matched pairs design

A Within-subjects related design (repeated measures design)
So far we have presented exclusively the advantages of using different rather than the same people for all the experimental conditions.

> **STQ** *Can you list some of these advantages?*

But, against all these advantages, there is one crucial disadvantage about using different subjects for each experimental condition. This is that there may be all sorts of individual differences in the way different subjects tackle the experimental task.

> **STQ** *What major individual differences affect the way different subjects tackle an experimental task?*

There are many; for instance, in a memory experiment some people might be more intelligent than others, some might think the experiment a bore, others that it would get them extra marks, some might not even be able to read the items, some might be old, some young, some take three minutes over each item, others four seconds, some might be anxious, and others might be thinking about the disco they are going to that night. Such variability might affect their ability to remember the items, from nil by a person who cannot read, to 100% by an ambitious person who thinks he is going to get an A grade for his performance. The existence of all these other factors might mean that each subject's behaviour is being affected by variables which have nothing to do with the independent variable the experimenter is intending to manipulate. The danger is that all the people who are likely to do well on memory tasks might happen to be allocated to one experimental condition, e.g. learning lists of meaningful words. This would mean that the memory scores for this condition would be artificially inflated, solely because of irrelevant variables that have nothing to do with the independent variable of learning lists of meaningful words versus nonsense items. But we would never know, nor would we ever be able to disentangle the amount of score inflation due to such uncontrolled variables from the amount effected by the independent variable manipulation.

So how might one try to eliminate the possible effects of individual differences in biasing the results towards higher scores in one condition? An experimental design in which the same people are performing all the experimental conditions is the best method for eliminating such individual differences. This is known as a within-subjects, or related or repeated measures design because the comparison is within the same set of subjects and so their scores are related. Anything peculiar to one individual (like high or low IQ or motivation) is then spread across all conditions. If a person is highly motivated when learning one list of words, thus inflating the scores for that condition, he will also tend to be well motivated when learning other lists of words and so will inflate those scores as well. The point about using a same-subjects design is that any individual peculiarities get equalized out over all conditions. Note that they do not get removed, they simply form a constant on the results of each condition.

The more alike all the subjects are on as many relevant variables as possible the more likely it is that mean differences between groups arise as an outcome of the manipulation of the independent variable. For example, we wish to evaluate the effect of a drug on athletes' performance in a 100 yards sprint. So we obtain two random groups of athletes, one group to be given the drug, the other group to be given a placebo. The mean difference was found to be 0.5 s. However, as

Table 31 Individual times to run the 100 yards for two groups of randomly chosen athletes

Subjects receiving placebo	Time (s)	Subjects receiving drug	Time (s)
Mike	11.7	Don	15.7
Bob	18.2	Hector	13.4
Frank	12.2	Ron	18.0
George	15.4	Tom	12.8
Harry	15.8	Steve	13.6
Gordon	13.2	Alan	19.0
John	13.7	Peter	16.2
Bill	19.1	Dick	11.9
Randolph	12.9	Dan	14.6
Tim	16.0	Paul	18.0

Mean difference = 0.5 sec.

Table 31 shows there was tremendous variability within each group anyway because some could run fast and others were slow, irrespective of drugs. So the mean difference is far smaller than the within-groups differences. Now let us conduct the same experiment on randomly chosen sprinters. The results are depicted in Table 32. Again the mean

Table 32 Individual times to run the 100 yards for two groups of randomly chosen sprinters

Subjects receiving placebo	Time (s)	Subjects receiving drug	Time (s)
Arthur	10.6	Robert	10.9
Simon	10.3	Frank	11.1
Nick	10.3	Walter	10.9
Daryl	10.2	Gary	10.7
Ralph	10.4	Ken	10.9
Will	10.0	Bryan	10.8
Reuben	10.2	Dick	10.7
Edward	10.1	Stan	10.8
Fred	10.3	Richard	10.8
Jack	10.4	Mark	11.2

Mean difference = 0.5 s

difference is 0.5 s but since the individual differences between sprinters in each group are negligible the mean difference looks more like a real difference. By choosing sprinters we have eliminated individual differences to a great extent, so the mean difference is less likely to be due to chance variation.

How can we make subjects even more alike in the two groups? The answer which should be obvious to you all by now is to use the same subjects. This is the ultimate way to minimize individual differences between subjects. A within-subjects design makes it more likely that any differences in performance discerned between levels of the independent variable are true differences.

Table 33 compares the within- and between-subjects assignment for an experiment that has two levels of an independent variable. In the top case each of the ten subjects is assigned to both levels, while in the bottom case a different set of ten subjects is assigned to each level.

One practical advantage of a within-subjects experiment is immediately obvious from Table 33: fewer subjects are required. If N subjects are required to give you an adequate number of data for a within-subject experiment, then $N \times 2$ are required for a two-level, between-subjects experiment. There will also be times when the number of subjects available to you is limited, especially, when the

Table 33 A comparison of the assignment of subjects for a within-subject experiment and a between-subjects experiment

Within-subject design	Independent variable	
	Level 1	*Level 2*
	Subject 1	Subject 1
	Subject 2	Subject 2
	.	.
	.	.
	.	.
	Subject 10	Subject 10

Between-subjects Design (Chapter 14)	Independent variable	
	Level 1	*Level 2*
	Subject 1	Subject 11
	Subject 2	Subject 12
	.	.
	.	.
	.	.
	Subject 10	Subject 20

subjects must meet certain requirements. For example, you may need pilots, or racing-car drivers, or ballet dancers for certain experiments! Or you may want subjects to be afflicted with some disorder like a specific psychosis, or colour-blindness or left-handedness. In such cases, you may not be able to find enough subjects who meet these requirements to use a between-subjects design and you will need to rely on a within-subjects experiment.

In addition to their greater efficiency, within-subjects designs can also be preferable for statistical reasons. In an inferential statistical test, experimenters attempt to infer whether any differences they find among the data samples collected at the various levels of the independent variable are due to real differences in behaviour of some larger population or due to chance. To make this inference most of these tests compare the differences between the average performance at the two levels against an estimate of how variable the performance is within each of the levels. A statistical test is more likely to call a difference real if the difference between levels is large or if the estimated variability within levels is small.

B Error from administration of experimental conditions.
Since there are many practical and statistical advantages to using within-subjects designs, why should we ever use between-subjects

designs? Unfortunately, the within-subject design also carries some rather serious disadvantages.

The basic problem is that once subjects are exposed to one level of the independent variable, there is no way to change them back into the people they were prior to being exposed. The exposure has done something irreversible to the subject, so we can no longer treat him as a pure, uncontaminated, naive subject. How is the subject changed?

One way a subject can change is to learn. Suppose we wanted to know whether it takes someone longer to learn to type on a manual typewriter or an electric typewriter. We decide that because there are likely to be large individual differences in typing ability, we will use a within-subject design. We take ten subjects and find out how many hours they have to practice in order to type 30 words a minute on a manual typewriter. We then switch them to an electric typewriter and find out how many hours they have to practice to type 30 words per minute on that. We find that it takes them an average of 45 hours of practice to reach criterion on the manual, compared with 2 hours on the electric. Can we conclude that the electric typewriter is that much easier to learn on? Obviously not.

During the first part of the experiment, in addition to learning the specific skill of using a manual typewriter, the subjects were also learning a general typing skill. The general skill is confounded with the specific skill. By the time the subjects typed on the electric typewriter, their general typing skill was undoubtedly at a higher level then when they started the experiment. Any time such an effect changes systematically across the trials, we must be careful to keep the effect of our independent variable from becoming confounded with it.

To illustrate how we might avoid confounding variables in this way, let us consider another experiment. Suppose you are interested in the difference in a person's ability to throw darts at a target with the preferred or non-preferred hand. To minimize the effect of prior experience, you decide to use subjects who have never played darts. And to minimize the effect of individual differences in ability, you decide to use a within-subjects design. You choose as your dependent variable the number of darts hitting the target during a 30-second trial. Being a good experimental psychologist, you realize your experiment has a potentially confounding effect: the subjects will learn a general dart throwing skill as they go and will be more likely to improve with each additional trial regardless of which hand they are using. How can you get rid of this confounding effect? The answer is to counterbalance, to control sequencing or order effects. Familiarity, practice, learning, motivational changes, fatigue etc. may often influence performance quite markedly on the second task.

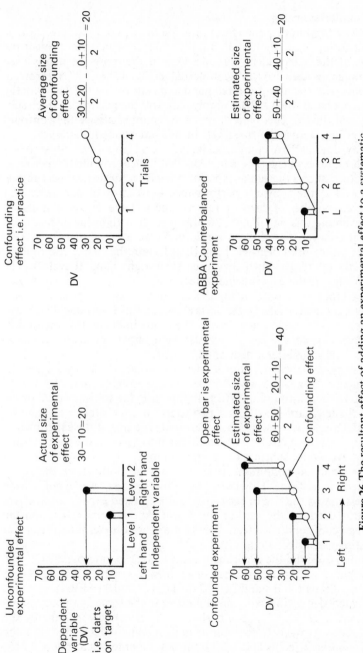

Figure 26 The resultant effect of adding an experimental effect to a systematic confounding effect for a confounded within-subject design and an ABBA counterbalanced design

C Counterbalancing

One way to minimize the effect of a systematic confounding variable like learning is to counterbalance the order in which you present the levels of the independent variable. One of the more frequently used techniques is called ABBA counterbalancing. If we call A throwing the dart with the non-preferred hand and B throwing the dart with the preferred hand, then ABBA simply indicates the pattern in which subjects will throw. This pattern serves to counterbalance the confounding effects across the two levels of our independent variable.

Why does ABBA counterbalancing work? Figure 26 illustrates a two-level experiment. The panel labelled 'Unconfounded Experimental Effect' shows the actual experimental effect for an average subject. At Level 1, the subject's performance is 10 units of our dependent variable (number of darts on target), and at Level 2 it is 30 units. In our example this part Figure 26 illustrates that right-handed subjects who had never played darts would make an average of ten darts on target if they used their left hand (Level 1) on the first 3 min trial, or 30 darts on target when they used their right hand (Level 2). The actual size of the experimental effect is 20.

The graph of 'Confounding Effect' shows a systematically increasing effect due to trials. In the darts example, this effect could be learning, or an increase in general skill. The figure indicates that the subject improves by an average of ten darts on target for each additional 3-min trial no matter which hand is used.

The panel labelled 'Confounded Experiment' illustrates the experimental results we would expect·if the experimental effect were added to the confounding effect. In this case, the subject would throw with the left hand on the first two trials, and with the right hand on Trials 3 and 4. If we were now to estimate the size of the experimental effect from these results without taking into account the confounding effect, we would subtract the average number of successful throws in the left-handed condition from the average number in the right-handed condition. However, by this process we would have overestimated the size of the effect; our estimated experimental effect of 40 is equal to the sum of the actual experimental effect and the average confounding effect. We want a way to determine the actual experimental effect alone.

Suppose we did the experiment using ABBA counterbalancing. The final panel shows the expected experimental results when Level 1 is used on Trials 1 and 4 and Level 2 on Trials 2 and 3 (ABBA). Here the estimated size of the experimental effect is the same as the actual experimental effect. The counterbalancing effectively eliminates the confounding effect without our actually having to determine what the confounding effect is and subtract it out. Counterbalancing will only work if the confounding effect is linear.

An ABBA-counterbalancing technique attempts to counterbalance order effects in a completely within-subject manner: the same subject gets both orders. Other counterbalancing techniques make order a between-subjects variable by counterbalancing order across subjects. In intra-group counterbalancing, groups of subjects are counter-balanced rather than each subject. So for example, with two conditions (i.e. A and B) of the *IV*, half the subjects chosen at random receive sequence AB, and the other half receive BA. A completely ran-domized counterbalancing is possible too with each subject receiving one of the sequences chosen by a random process. However, in all counterbalancing you are making the assumption that the effect of having B follow A is just the reverse of the effect of having A follow B. This assumption is sometimes called an assumption of symmetrical transfer.

As we add more levels to our independent variable, we increase the complexity of a complete counterbalancing procedure. In a complete-ly counterbalanced design, every level has to occur an equal number of times and also follow every other level an equal number of times. Table 34 shows completely counterbalanced designs for two-, three-, and four-level experiments. As you can see, complete counterbalanc-ing can become a monumental task when you have a large number of levels or many independent variables.

Table 34 Completely counterbalanced designs for two-, three-, and four-level independent variables. A, B, C, and D represent the levels

Two levels of independent variable	
Number	*Order of levels*
1	AB
2	BA

Three levels of independent variable	
Number	*Order of levels*
1	ABC
2	ACB
3	BCA
4	BAC
5	CAB
6	CBA

Table 34 Continued

Four levels of independent variable

Number	Order of levels	Number	Order of levels
1	ABCD	13	CABD
2	ABDC	14	CADB
3	ACBD	15	CBAD
4	ACDB	16	CBDA
5	ADCB	17	CDAB
6	ADBC	18	CDBA
7	BACD	19	DABC
8	BADC	20	DACB
9	BCAD	21	DBAC
10	BCDA	22	DBCA
11	BDAC	23	DCAB
12	BDCA	24	DCBA

Counterbalancing will not remove an order effect. Hopefully, it will make it constant in both levels. Moreover demand characteristics are likely to be a big problem in this design since taking several levels of the *IV* may allow a subject a greater chance of correctly guessing what the experiment is about or what the experimenter 'wants', whatever order he takes the conditions in.

> **STQ** (1) *Can you explain why counterbalancing is used in some circumstances?*
>
> (2) *What do you understand by the term 'order effects'? Can you name some order effects?*

D Matched pairs related design

We have previously seen how the probability of a real (experimental) effect is assessed (Chapter 15). Can you recall the principle? It is that of pitting the variation due to the *IV* (e.g. $M_1 - M_2$) against the variation expected by chance, the standard error. If this error variance (denominator) is large relative to the amount of the experimental effect (the numerator) then it is concluded after reference to the appropriate table that the *IV* did not produce a significant effect. It is possible that the *IV* did produce an effect but that this was masked by the large error variance when the critical ratio was evaluated. The best way to detect a real effect then is make the error variance as small as possible. Matching is one technique to achieve this. It creates constancy of influence of any variable on which the subjects are matched.

This design gains the advantage of a between-subjects experiment yet avoids some of the problems of large individual differences between groups of subjects, like the within-groups design yet avoids the latter's order problems. Matched pairs simply means that an attempt is made to have the same kind of subjects undertake the experiment.

To do this you match pairs of subjects on what seem to be important characteristics – sex, age, IQ, memorizing ability, anxiety, or whatever – depending on the experiment. The idea is that, if IQ is important to performance, then you have pairs of subjects at each IQ level and one of each pair is allocated randomly to each group. This means that neither group should have a special advantage since they have equal ranges of IQ among their members.

A matched-pairs design can be treated as a related design, because the purpose of the matching is to end up with related pairs who are matched so closely that, on the characteristics relevant to the particular experiment, they are as near as possible the same person. In the case of a same-subjects design the related pairs are, of course, the same, performing under both experimental conditions.

It is often not possible to match pairs of subjects, either because it is a time-consuming and often expensive business to find matched pairs, or because the experimenter cannot always tell beforehand which are likely to be the important variables to match in a particular experiment.

In the typical between-subjects experiment, you hope that the subjects at each level are pretty much alike, and you have randomization on your side. Random assignment of subjects makes it likely that the groups will be essentially equivalent, and this becomes more likely the larger the groups. However, because this is a random process, there are times when the difference between the subjects assigned to each level, rather than your independent variable, will cause the differences in the dependent variable. That is, your experiment may be confounded by subject differences. By matching your groups of subjects, you can minimize this possibility. But on what basis can you match the groups?

You must match your groups on a variable that is highly correlated with the dependent variable. In our sprinting example (p. 174) it would have been a waste of time for us to match the two groups of runners on the basis of IQ scores. Fast feet are not related to quick minds! However, we could have had each subject run the 100 yards then made up pairs of subjects: the two fastest, the two next fastest, and so on. We could then toss a coin to assign one member of each pair to each of the conditions. In this way, we know that the groups are somewhat equivalent in running speed prior to introducing the independent variable.

Through matching, we decrease the probability of being wrong when we say that the independent variable caused a change in behaviour. Matching provides a statistical advantage in that a statistical test is more likely to say that a given difference in the scores of the dependent variable is due to the independent variable rather than to chance. That is, the tests are more sensitive to any difference associated with the independent variable.

One disadvantage in doing matched-groups experiments is that it takes longer to match the groups, so that experiments sometimes require two sessions, one for the pretest and one for the experiment itself. If you are planning to use many subjects anyway, the chances of getting large differences between groups using random assignment is quite small, and the problem of matching might not be worth the effort.

Matching causes the pool of potential subjects to be smaller too. For example, we can hold constant across each experimental group, by say sex, by only using males, IQ by only using one IQ level, age by only having 21-year-olds, and ethnic group by only using Iranians etc. But it would be difficult to locate sufficient numbers of male 21-year-old Iranian subjects with the same IQ. But it is easy to realize that experimental variation will not include any variation due to sex, or age, or ethnic group, or IQ variation, hence less of the variation is error variation. The implementation of matching is to pair individuals on the basis of certain relevant variables and then by a toss of a coin (randomization) allocate one to each group. Let us return to our hypothetical teaching-method experiment (p. 143) in which IQ is a confounding variable. We could place the subjects in rank order, then take two at a time starting at the bottom and randomly assign each to a group. In this way we roughly match the IQ within each pair. Table 35 illustrates the process.

Perfect matching is rarely possible so even in our example a slight mean difference still exists. One can imagine how difficult it can be to obtain pairs both members of which are exactly the same on the matching variable. The matching procedure of course is taken to the ultimate conclusion in the previous design in that the within-subjects design is the same as matching each individual on all subject variables. Experimental error is considerably reduced because chance fluctuations in the performance of one person at two points in time tend to be smaller than the fluctuations of two people at the same point in time.

The choice of a variable on which to match is an important one. Ss in a matched Ss design should be matched on the basis of a variable that is as highly correlated as possible with the *DV*. Ss might be matched on intelligence if the experiment is one on problem solving, on sex if the experiment is one on the effect of a particular film on attitudes toward dating, and so forth. Matching on intelligence may not be of much help in a study of leadership, for Ss who are perfectly matched on intelligence may be very poorly matched on leadership. Some measure more closely related to the *DV* of leadership, such as number of positions of leadership held in the past, would produce more relevant matching.

Table 35

	Group A		Group B	
	Subjects	*IQ*	*Subjects*	*IQ*
Pair 1	2	97	1	97
Pair 2	3	100	4	103
Pair 3	5	105	11	106
etc.	12	108	6	108
	7	109	8	110
	9	113	13	110
	14	113	10	116
	15	117	16	119
	18	122	17	120
	20	130	19	128
	M = 11.4		*M* = 11.7	
		difference = 0.3		

If a pre-test is necessary to obtain data on which the matching is to be based, such a pre-test must not contaminate the main experiment. For example, in a memory experiment we find that matching on memory ability is the best variable, but the memory pre-test must not be similar to the task in the main experiment or else differential effects on subjects in terms of practice, learning, motivation etc. will influence the experiment.

Error due to conditions could arise in the teaching-method experiment if the courses were taught at different hours or by different instructors. Such error is usually eliminated by control, by making the conditions identical with respect to the offending variables. There are two special procedures for controlling error due to conditions: blinding and standardizing.

E Double-blind

One of the best techniques for overcoming the subjects perception and interpretation of what is being done in the experiment is to apply the double-blind technique. This technique produces a situation in which all the manipulations of the experiment actually appear the same to all subjects in all conditions. When two conditions of the *IV* are being given and it is possible for the experimenter to be prevented from knowing which condition he is giving to which subjects and the subjects equally are unaware of which they are receiving, then this should be done. Experiments to test the effects of drugs use this technique. The experimenter asks doctors to give these pills to half of those patients who complain of a headache and to give nothing to the other half.

STQ *What is the IV and DV in this experiment? What two variables are being confounded here?*

The *IV* must be the amount of drug, the levels being none and one pill. The *DV* is how well S says he feels. Two variables are being confounded here. The Ss in one condition have been given a drug: they know they have been given a drug; the Ss in the other condition have not been given a drug, and they know they have not. Any difference on the *DV* between these two conditions could be attributed to either of these two variables; if the Ss who have been given the drug feel better, the improvement could be due to a chemical change produced by the drug, a psychological change produced by the knowledge that they have been given a drug, or both.

One confounding variable in this experiment, then, is Ss knowledge of whether or not he has been given a pill. In principle, there are two ways of controlling this variable: making all Ss think that they have not been given a pill or making all Ss think they have been given a pill. The first possibility would be difficult to realize in practice, but the second could quite easily be realized by giving chemically inert pills ('placebos') to the Ss who are not to receive the medication. This would 'blind' the Ss to the status of the *IV*.

Even with the variable controlled, however, one other source of possible confounding remains. Suppose that the doctors believe in the efficacy of the headache pills under test and feel guilty about giving out sugar pills to sick patients. Although the sugar pills may look the same as the medicated pills, they can hardly be expected to produce the same psychological effect unless the doctors show the same confidence in giving them to their patients as they do with the medicated pills. By his manner, a doctor can subtly and unconsciously communicate to the patient his knowledge of which pill contains medication and which does not and can thus destroy the attempt to keep the patient ignorant of which treatment condition he is in. Obviously, the doctors in this experiment, as well as the patients, must be 'blinded' to the status of the *IV*. The experimenter can do this by bottling inert and medicated pills identically and mixing them up in the box in which they are delivered to the doctor, so that the doctor cannot know which he is taking out to give to any particular patient. (Of course, the experimenter has to keep track of which pills go to which patients. He can do that by numbering all the bottles, having someone other than the doctor keep track of which pills go into which numbered bottles, and having the doctor keep track of which numbered bottles go to which patients.)

F Standardizing
This term can be applied in two ways. It can refer to the standardizing of the experimental conditions or the standardizing of the marking. It is the former which is to be considered briefly here. Standardizing of the experimental conditions ensures that every subject undertakes the *IV* level applicable to him in the same conditions as everyone else. For example think how the results of an experiment could be interpreted if some Ss had a longer time to complete the task, or got different instructions, or suffered from noisy disturbances while undertaking the task. (Of course experiments can be devised in which these variables could act as the *IV*.) These unstandardized conditions would be reflected in unknown ways in the *DV* variations, and impossible to disentangle from the real effects of the *IV*. So for these types of variables control of error is effected by holding them constant for all Ss.

Holding a variable constant ensures that it will produce no experimental error for the obvious reason that variables which do not change cannot produce changes on any other variable.

STQ   *Can you write down a few variables that need to be held constant in most experiments?*

It is now possible to see what each design and control technique achieves. In the independent groups design no subject variables are controlled. In the matched pairs design one or more between-subject variables such as age, IQ, sex, social class are controlled. In the within-subjects design all between-subject variables are controlled though the variables on which a single person varies from time to time such as fatigue, motivation, are not controlled.

In the between-Ss and matched Ss designs, S variables that have not been controlled are randomized by assigning the members of each pair randomly to conditions. In the within-Ss design, within-S variables that are related to order of presentation, such as fatigue and adjustment to the experimental situation, are, as we shall see, automatically counterbalanced with order of presentation. But the experimenter has no control over other within-S variables, such as anxiety, and he must trust nature to randomize these. The essential difference, then, between the three kinds of design is the degree to which they control error due to between-S variables. Since between-S variables usually contribute most to random error, this is an important difference. On this basis, the identical Ss design is to be preferred to the matched Ss, and the matched Ss to the independent Ss.

Advantages and disadvantages of using same and different subjects.

	Advantages	*Disadvantages*
Between-subjects unrelated design (i.e. different subjects doing experimental conditions).	(1) No order effects (2) Necessary for natural groups, e.g. different ages. (3) Necessary for experiments in which subjects are misled or taken by surprise. (4) Each subject has to do only one experimental condition. (5) N need not be the same for each group.	(1) The use of different subjects introduces an unknown amount of individual differences in performance of the different experimental conditions. (2) Larger number of subjects required than within-subjects design.

	Advantages	*Disadvantages*
Within-subjects related designs (i.e. same subjects doing all experimental conditions).	(1) Eliminates individual differences in performance between experimental conditions. (2) Fewer subjects required than in unrelated design.	(1) Problem of order effects because subjects have to do conditions in a certain order. (Needs counterbalancing.) (2) Cannot be used when subjects have to be different, e.g. men and women. (3) Might mean that each subject has to perform a lot of boring experimental conditions.

	Advantages	Disadvantages
Matched pairs related designs (i.e. different, but matched, subjects doing experimental conditions).	(1) Has all the advantages listed under between-subjects designs because different people are doing the experimental conditions. (2) Attempts to eliminate individual differences by using matched subjects who are likely to perform in the same way. (3) Useful when large values of N are difficult to get hold of. (4) Error controlled by matching and then by random assignment to group, and random assignment of group level.	(1) Although this design attempts to combine the advantages of both within-subject and between-subject designs, one can never be sure that subjects are matched on all the variables which are likely to affect performance. (2) It is often a time-consuming and expensive exercise to try and find suitably matched pairs of subjects. (3) Need to know in advance a variable on which matching is to be based which will not spoil subjects for the experiment yet which correlates strongly with DV.

We have taken you through quite a lot of considerations you might take into account when designing an experiment. To summarize, firstly, there is the use of systematic controls to ensure that all variables except the independent variable are equalized across treatment groups. This may take the form of standardizing experimental conditions and instructions, matching subjects, counterbalancing for order effects. The point is that the experimenter is trying to think about all possible extraneous variables which might affect his results, and then make sure that they are equalized across all the experimental treatments.

The second method is randomization. When you deal with variables by randomly allocating subjects to treatments, or by randomizing the order in which conditions are presented, you are really leaving it to chance that extraneous variables will be likely to be more or less equally distributed among all the experimental treatments. It may sound as if this is a 'weaker' method than controlling variables, but it is simply impossible to control for all possible extraneous variables by counterbalancing subjects, settings, order and so on, either for practical reasons, or because the experimenter simply does not know which of all possible variables might be affecting subjects' behaviour. By randomizing across conditions, the assumption is that all variables, except the independent variable, will be distributed so as to make the various treatment groups comparable (Table 36).

Table 36 Methods for equalizing variables across treatments

Possible confounded variables	*Systematic controls*	*Randomization*
Maturation effects over time.	Compare the experimental group against a control group.	Allocate at random different subjects to the experimental and the control groups.
Individual differences between subjects.	Same subjects related or matched pairs designs.	Allocate at random different subjects to treatments.
Experimenter bias.	Use one experimenter for all treatments, or counterbalance experimenters for age, sex, etc.	Allocate at random different experimenters to treatments.
Order effects.	Counterbalance orders of presenting treatments.	Randomize orders of presenting treatments.
Differences in setting, instructions procedure.	Standardize as far as possible for all conditions.	

STQ (1) *State one advantage and one disadvantage of the within-group or repeated-measures design.*

(2) *Imagine an experiment designed to test memory for categorized lists of words (i.e. words that fall into categories like lion, tiger, bear, are all animals) as opposed to lists of uncategorized words. What sort of experimental design would you plan and why?*

G   Regression to the mean

Regression to the mean is a major problem in related and matched designs when the same or equivalent test is given on a second occasion. Consider an example. We give 200 people a standard test of logical reasoning for which there are two equivalent forms, or two versions of the test that we know to be equivalent. The mean score on the test is 60 of 100 possible points. We take the 25 people who score highest and the 25 who score lowest. The mean of these groups is, say 95 and 30 respectively. Then we test them again on the alternate form of the test. Now we might find that the means of the two groups are 87 and 35. On the second test the scores of these two extreme groups regressed toward the mean; the very good group scored more poorly while the very poor group had somewhat better scores. Basically it happens for the high scoring group because some people whose 'true scores' are somewhat lower than actually tested were lucky and scored higher than they should have on the test. When retested, people with extreme high scores tend to score lower, nearer their true score. The situation is reversed for the low scoring group.

This regression toward the mean is always observed under such conditions when there is less than perfect correlation between the two measures, and the more extreme the selection of scores, the greater the regression toward the mean. It also occurs in all types of measurement situations. If abnormally tall or short parents have a child, it will likely be closer to the population mean than the height of the parents. As with most statistical phenomena, regression to the mean is true of groups of observations and is probabilistic (that is, it may not occur every time). For example, a few individual subjects may regress away from the mean in the second test of mathematical reasoning, but the group tendency will be toward the mean.

How does regression toward the mean affect research where subjects have been matched on some variable? Let us assume we have an educational programme that we believe will be especially advantageous for increasing the reading scores of working-class children. This is especially important because such children's scores are typically lower than those of middle-class children, presumably due to different cultural environments. We take two groups of children, one middle and one lower class, and match them on several criteria including age, sex, and most importantly, initial reading ability. We give both groups of children the reading improvement programme and then test their reading ability after the programme. We find, much to our surprise, that the working-class children actually perform worse after the reading programme than before it, while the middle-class children improve. We conclude, of course, that the programme helped the latter children but actually hurt the former, despite the fact that it was especially designed for them.

This conclusion, even though it may seem reasonable to you, is almost surely erroneous in this case because of regression. Consider what happened when the children were matched on initial reading scores. Since the populations differed initially with working-class children lower than middle-class children, in order to match two samples it was necessary to select working-class pupils with the higher scores than the mean for their group and middle-class pupils with lower scores than their group mean. Having picked these extreme groups, we could predict because of regression to the mean that when retested, the working-class children would have poorer scores and the middle-class children would have better ones, on the average, even if the reading improvement programme had no effect at all! The exceptionally high-scoring, working-class children would tend to regress toward the mean of their group, while the low-scoring, middle-class children would regress toward the mean for their group. The same thing would have happened even if there were no programme and the children were simply retested.

The same outcome would likely have been obtained if children were matched on IQs instead of reading scores, since the two are probably positively correlated. So simply finding another matching variable may be no solution. One solution would be to match very large samples of working- and middle-class children and then split each group, giving the reading programme to one subgroup but not the other. All would be retested at the end of the one subgroup's participation in the programme. (Assignment of subjects to the subgroups should, of course, be random.) Regression to the mean would be expected in both subgroups, but the effect of the reading programme could be evaluated against the group which had no programme. Perhaps working-class children with the reading programme would show much less drop (regression to the mean) than those without, indicating that the programme really did have a positive effect.

STQ   *What do you understand by regression to the mean? In what situation might it arise? Check your response against the above material.*

18

Statistical tests for related designs

The tests which follow can be employed with any designs which use the *same* or *matched* subjects. It is possible to compare subjects' scores under two or more conditions since they came from the same subjects or matched subjects.

A The related *t*-test (parametric)

When we considered the significance of the difference between means in the previous chapter we were concerned with the means of two samples which had been drawn independently of each other from the same population.

> **STQ** *What is the name of the design in which two independent samples are used?*

Currently we have been considering the uses of other designs, the related groups or repeated measures design, and the matched pairs design. In both these designs the two sets of scores from which the means are calculated are not derived from two independent samples. As a result a somewhat different *t*-test formula has to be applied. The principle of the *t*-test for related samples is similar to that for independent samples. One compares the actual difference that has been observed between the two samples with the estimate of the difference that could be expected by chance alone, that is, the standard error of the difference. The standard error of the difference between the means for related samples is symbolized $S_{\overline{D}}$ to distinguish it from the symbol SE_{diff} (used with the independent *t*-test).

1 CALCULATION OF THE STANDARD ERROR FOR A RELATED *t*-TEST

The simplest way to calculate the standard error of the difference is known as the direct-difference method. The first step in this method is, (i) find the difference (D) between the two scores for each pair or each subject. If this difference is zero, the scores were the same for an individual under both conditions or for both members of the pair. The direction of any difference is indicated by its sign: if D is positive, then the first score is higher than the second score; if D is negative, then the second score is greater than the first score; (ii) find the sum of all the D-scores and divide by the number of pairs in order to arrive at the mean difference, $\bar{D}$. In formula form this is expressed as $\bar{D} = \Sigma D/N$. An example of this is shown in Table 37. This is a repeated-measures design but a matched-pairs calculation is exactly the same.

Table 37

Subject	Treatment 1	Treatment 2	Difference	D^2
1	6	8	-2	4
2	10	14	-4	16
3	4	2	2	4
4	15	18	-3	9
5	5	8	-3	9
			$\Sigma D - 10$	ΣD^2 42
			$\bar{D} = -2$	
$N = 5$				

The mean difference, $\bar{D}$, is the numerator for the t test for correlated samples, as shown in:

$$t = \frac{\bar{D}}{S_{\bar{D}}}$$

where: $\bar{D}$ = the mean of the difference in scores between pairs of matched observations:

$$\bar{D} = \frac{\Sigma D}{N}$$

$S_{\bar{D}}$ = the standard error of the difference between two means when observations are paired.

If you compare this with the independent t-test formula, you will notice that we have substituted $\bar{D}$ for $M_1 - M_2$ and $S_{\bar{D}}$ for SE_{diff}.

The denominator of the above formula $S_{\bar{D}}$ is calculated from the following formula:

$$S_{\bar{D}} = \sqrt{\frac{\Sigma D^2 - \frac{(\Sigma D)^2}{N}}{N(N-1)}}$$

where: ΣD^2 = sum of the squared difference scores
$\quad\quad\;\; \Sigma D$ = sum of the difference scores
$\quad\quad\;\; N$ = Number of pairs.

Thus the full formula for t when the samples are correlated is:

$$t = \frac{\bar{D}}{\sqrt{\dfrac{\Sigma D^2 - \dfrac{(\Sigma D)^2}{N}}{N(N-1)}}}$$

Continuing with the example above, the D^2 value has already been computed, so:

$$S_{\bar{D}} = \sqrt{\frac{\Sigma D^2 - \dfrac{(\Sigma D)^2}{N}}{N(N-1)}} = \sqrt{\frac{42 - \dfrac{(-10)^2}{5}}{5 \times 4}}$$

$$S_{\bar{D}} = \sqrt{1.1} = 1.05$$
$$t = \frac{\bar{D}}{S_{\bar{D}}} = \frac{-2}{1.05} = 1.90$$

When the t value has been calculated we enter as usual the t table (Appendix A p. 406) with $N - 1$ degrees of freedom, where N = the number of pairs of observations. If the calculated t equals or exceeds the tabled value, the null hypothesis that the mean difference does not differ significantly from 0 is rejected.

STQ

Subject	Before X	After Y	D	D^2
1	26	20	+ 6	36
2	17	27	−10	100
3	19	29	−10	100
4	13	33	−20	400
5	8	14	− 6	36
		$\Sigma =$	−40	672

Use the t table (Table B, Appendix A) and decide whether the null hypothesis is retained or rejected in this example at the 0.05 level.

We retain the null hypothesis since tabled t with 4 df was 2.776.

> **STQ** *An investigator is interested in assessing the effect of a film on the attitudes of students toward a certain issue. A sample of five students is administered an attitude scale before and after viewing the film. The before-and-after scores are as follows: a high score reflects positive attitudes.*
> *Perform a two-tailed test at the 0.01 level and make a statement about the null hypothesis.*

Let us now go through another worked example to make sure you know how to use the related *t*-test.

Ten subjects are presented with two lists of items. There are ten letter-digit items on one list, and ten all-digit items on the other list.

> **STQ** *The order of presenting the lists to the subjects is counter-balanced. Do you remember what we mean by counterbalancing? Why have we used the counterbalancing procedure in this instance?*

Table 38 Recall scores

Subject	Condition A letter–digit	Condition B all-digit
1	11	4
2	6	3
3	7	9
4	4	6
5	10	6
6	9	7
7	8	4
8	6	6
9	7	5
10	6	6
Means	7.4	5.6

Remember in calculating a related *t*-test, we compare each of the scores in Condition A with their corresponding scores in Condition B. We find the difference between each pair of scores and square it. The related *t*-test is able to compare pairs of scores from the same subjects, or matched subjects. This is not possible with the unrelated *t*-test, since the scores are those of *different* subjects. The degrees of freedom are found by subtracting 1 from the number of subjects because we are using only one group of subjects. You will recall that we subtracted

2 from the total number of subjects in the independent (unrelated) *t*-test because we employed two different groups of subjects.

Table 39 Results

Subjects	Condition A letter−digit	Condition B all-digit	D (A − B)	D²
1	11	4	7	49
2	6	3	3	9
3	7	9	−2	4
4	4	6	−2	4
5	10	6	4	16
6	9	7	2	4
7	8	4	4	16
8	6	6	0	0
9	7	5	2	4
10	6	6	0	0
			$\Sigma D = 18$ $\bar{D} = 1.8$	$\Sigma D^2 = 106$

(a) Find the differences D by subtracting the scores in Condition B from those in Condition A, inserting a minus sign where necessary. Total these differences then find the average difference

$$\Sigma D = 18 \qquad \bar{D} = \frac{18}{10} = 1.8$$

(b) Each difference should be squared and summed. Minus signs will, of course, disappear when squared.

$$\Sigma D^2 = 106$$

(c) Use the formula to find t

$$t = \frac{\bar{D}}{\sqrt{\dfrac{\Sigma D^2 - \dfrac{(\Sigma D)^2}{N}}{N(N-1)}}}$$

where $\bar{D}$ =   mean difference between scores in the A and B Conditions

ΣD^2 =   total of squared differences

$(\Sigma D)^2$ =   total of differences squared

N =   number of subject pairs

$$t = \sqrt{\dfrac{106 - \dfrac{18^2}{10}}{99}} \cdot 1.8 = \sqrt{\dfrac{74.6}{99}} \cdot 1.8$$

$$t = \frac{1.8}{\sqrt{0.749}} = \frac{1.8}{0.27} = 6.6$$

$$df = N - 1 = 9$$

STQ **(1)** *Find the critical values of t above from Table B, Appendix A. If the observed value of t is equal to or larger than a critical value, the null hypothesis is rejected. In our example is the observed t value smaller or larger than the critical value? Is the null hypothesis supported?*

(2) *What is the df when a matched-pairs design experiment is performed with a total of 20 subjects in all?*

(3) *In a matched-group design with the following statistics would you retain the null hypothesis using the 5% level of significance in a two-tailed test?*

$$\bar{D} = 2.10; \; S_D = 0.70; \; N \text{ in each group} = 18$$

(4) *The concept of sampling error underpins the whole subject of statistical testing. Can you explain why? Illustrate your answer by reference to two statistical tests.*

(5) *Apply a related t-test to the following data:*

Subject	Condition A	Condition B
1	20	22
2	16	15
3	21	20
4	14	17
5	17	19
6	23	20
7	12	16
8	18	18
9	20	22
10	22	24

Use the 5% level of significance (two-tailed).

Answers are to be found on p. 434.

2 COMPARISON OF THE POWER OF TESTS BASED ON INDEPEN-
DENT AND CORRELATED SAMPLES
The formula used in calculating the standard error of the difference
for related samples provides a smaller standard error than does the
formula used with independent samples. The lower standard error
results in a more sensitive test of the significance of the difference between means and increases the likelihood of rejection of the null
hypothesis when it is false. For this reason the test based on related
samples is described as being a more powerful test. In statistics, the
power of a test is defined as the probability of rejecting the null
hypothesis when it is, in fact, false.

> **STQ** *Demonstrate this smaller standard error for the related
> t-test by recalculating the example in Table 38 by the indepen-
> dent t-test as though the sets of scores came from independent
> groups. What difference do you note? Why is the standard error
> now larger?*

Hopefully recalling the material you read on why related designs are
preferable to independent designs, you will remember that error is
reduced in the former design because inter-subject variations are considerably reduced. So the experimental treatment in a related or matched design will show up much more clearly.

> **STQ** *In a t-test which of the following make it easier to reject
> the null hypothesis?*
>
> *(a)   increasing N*
> *(b)   decreasing N*
> *(c)   decreasing $\bar{D}$*
> *(d)   using a one-tailed rather than a two-tailed test?*

Answers are to be found on p. 434.

B   Sign test (non-parametric)
We use this test to examine the direction of differences in scores for a
related design when each subject or matched pairs of subjects take part
in an experiment under two experimental conditions. You will observe
that the test gives us no information about the *size* of the differences.
We do not know, for example, to what extent people in a survey may
prefer one product to another. We are right to use the test when it is impossible to know the extent or magnitude of the differences. The sign
test can be used only with nominal data.

Let us assume that we want to discover which of two television programmes has the greater appeal to ten-year-old children. We instruct ten of them to place a tick against the one they prefer and a cross against the other. If they have an equal liking for both programmes, they should place a tick against both, and if they like neither of them, a cross should be inserted against both. Because the *same* children are indicating their preferences for the two television programmes by putting ticks and crosses in the appropriate places, this must be a related-subjects design.

Table 40 Ratings of two television programmes by ten-year-old children

Subject	Television programme 1	Television programme 2	Direction of difference
1	×	✓	−
2	×	✓	−
3	×	✓	−
4	✓	×	+
5	✓	×	+
6	×	✓	−
7	×	✓	−
8	×	✓	−
9	✓	✓	0
10	×	✓	−

To discover the direction of differences between the two television programmes, place a plus sign in the fourth column when there is a tick in column two (i.e. in favour of programme 1), and a minus sign when there is a cross. If you find that your subjects indicate that they like or dislike both programmes equally, place a zero in column 4.

Do you remember what you learned earlier about the different types of hypotheses? The null hypothesis in this experiment will suppose that there will be the same number of ticks and crosses for each television programme, that is, any difference in the scores between the two conditions will be random. The experimental hypothesis will expect that there will be significantly more pluses or minuses than could occur by chance. The one-tailed hypothesis predicts that the majority of children will show a preference for one particular television programme, and if this were to be programme 2, there would be more minuses than pluses than could occur by chance. With regard to the two-tailed hypothesis, the children will prefer either of the programmes but their preference will go in either direction, in which case there will be either more pluses or more minuses.

How to calculate the sign test.

(a) Total the *less* frequently occurring sign in column 4 of Table 40. In our example this will be two pluses, so $X = 2$.

(b) How many subjects are there who do not give tied responses? There is just one subject with a tied response (Subject 9), so there are nine subjects to be counted. $N = 10 - 1 = 9$.

(c) Assuming we are to use the 0.05 level of significance (one-tailed), with $N = 9$ the critical value obtained from Table C, Appendix A will be 1.

(d) If the *observed* value of X is equal to or less than the *critical* value, we may reject the null hypothesis. In our example, the critical value = 1 and the observed value = 2. The observed value is *not* less than the critical value, so we are unable to reject the null hypothesis.

This calculation assumes that we wanted to predict the direction of the responses (a one-tailed hypothesis). If we had employed the two-tailed hypothesis instead, we should have had to double the significance level to obtain the correct level for a two-tailed hypothesis. The significance level would be $p < 0.025$, and with an N of 9 the critical value of X would be 1. As our observed value is 2, the null hypothesis would be retained.

STQ (1) *In a within-subject design experiment the DV was whether subjects were successful or unsuccessful under each condition of the IV. A score of 1 was assigned if they were successful and zero if they were not. Analyse the results below appropriately to determine whether the conditions had any effect. Treat the data as nominal and use the 5% level one-tailed.*

Subject	Condition A	Condition B
1	0	1
2	1	0
3	1	0
4	0	0
5	1	0
6	1	0
7	1	1
8	0	1
9	1	0

(2) *In a comparison of two brands of pocket calculator nine statistics professors each work out a problem on each*

machine. The problems are known to be equally equivalent in difficulty and counterbalancing was used. Perform a sign test on the data below (time in minutes to solve each problem) and come to a conclusion at the 1% level (one-tailed).

Professor	1	2	3	4	5	6	7	8	9
Brand A	9	16	12	9	7	16	14	11	13
Brand B	13	14	16	15	9	17	14	12	18

Answers are to be found on p. 434.

EXPERIMENT USING THE SIGN TEST

Because no single explanation provides an adequate account of forgetting, a number of psychologists have argued for a two-process theory of memory — short-term memory (STM) and long-term memory (LTM). This is further developed by Atkinson and Shiffrin (1971). Information enters STM for such a short period that unless a deliberate attempt is made to transfer it to LTM it will be quickly forgotten. Peterson and Peterson (1959) demonstrated this point in their classic experiment using a trigram.

We have lots of things to keep in mind at any one time. An important concept which has been studied in this connection is *storage load* (Lloyd *et al.*, 1960; Yntema and Mueser, 1960). Storage load is the number of items an individual has in his mind at the time he is asked to recall one of them. Miller (1956) has suggested that we are capable of remembering 7 (plus or minus 2) items adequately.

A student conducted an experiment to explore the effect which the number of things a person must keep track of will have on his ability to remember the present state of individual variables. It was anticipated that an increase in storage load would result in a decrease in retention.

The experiment tested the following null hypothesis: 'that an increase in storage load will result in no significant decrease in retention'.

Subjects and experimenters
The student acted as experimenter, and nine subjects were chosen to assist.

Apparatus
Two lists of words were drawn up. The first list had a storage load of two one-word items, and the second list had a storage load of five one-word items. Data sheets were employed to record the subjects' recall.

Method

A repeated measures design was used. How might the experimenter have presented his lists of one-word items to the subjects?

Results

Table 41 Number of words recalled

Storage load 2	Storage load 5
41	23
50	21
49	30
38	24
51	33
51	39
50	49
38	50
43	25

Treatment of results

A sign test was applied to the responses on this occasion.

Use the data from Table 41 and place a plus (+) if the score in the first column is higher than that in the second column, otherwise put a minus (−). Total the number of times the *less* frequent sign appears.

41	23	+	$X = 0$. $N = 9$. Look these up in Table C.
50	21	+	
49	30	+	
38	24	+	Table C value is 1
51	33	+	
51	39	+	As our observed value is less than the 0.05
50	49	+	significance level, it may be concluded that
38	50	+	there was a significant difference between
43	25	+	the two conditions.

REFERENCES

Atkinson, R. C. and Shiffrin, R. M. (1971). The control of short-term memory. *Sci. Am.*, **224**, 82–90.

Lloyd, K. E., Reid, L. S. and Feallock, J. B. (1960). Short-term retention as a function of the average number of items presented. *J. Exp. Psychol.*, **4**, 201–7.

Miller, E. A. (1956). The magical number seven, plus or minus two: some limits on our capacity for processing information. *Psychol. Rev.*, **53**, 81–97.

Peterson, L. R. and Peterson, M. J. (1959). Short-term retention of individual verbal items. *J. Exp. Psychol.*, **30**, 93−113.
Yntema, D. B. and Mueser, G. E. (1960). Remembering the present states of a number of variables. *J. Exp. Psychol.*, **60**, 18−22.

Exercise
You might like to try and repeat this experiment yourself and write it up in a report following the format explained in Chapter 13. We have deliberately not provided any discussion of results with the above experiment as we wish you to try your hand at it.

C   Wilcoxon test (non-parametric)

It is appropriate to use the Wilcoxon test for two related conditions with ordinal data when the *same* subjects perform under both conditions (repeated-measures design), or when pairs of subjects are matched on a number of variables (matched-subjects design). The Wilcoxon test is used instead of a related *t*-test if the differences between treatments can only be ranked in size, or if the data are quite skewed, or if there is clearly a difference in the variance of the two groups. The test yields more information than the sign test since it is concerned

Rating scale

1	2	3	4	5
I don't enjoy it at all	I don't enjoy it much	I enjoy it	I enjoy it a lot	I think it is great

Table 42 Ratings of two television programmes by ten-year-old children

Subject	Programme 1	Programme 2
1	1	5
2	3	4
3	2	5
4	2	5
5	4	4
6	1	5
7	3	3
8	5	4
9	3	5
10	4	2
Means	2.8	4.2

with *sizes* of differences as well as *direction* of scores.

We could employ a repeated-measures design and use the experiment described above in connection with the sign test, except that this time we might use rating scales to discover the extent of the children's choices for one or other of the television programmes.

Suppose we want to discover whether there will be a difference between ten learner-drivers who attend a recognized driving school for tuition, and ten who are taught by a member of the family at home. The two groups of adults ('tuition school' and 'home-tutored') would need to be matched on a number of variables (matched-subjects design) such as age, sex, personality, amount of tuition received, and

Table 43 Scores on a driving skills test given to adults who attend a driving school and adults who are taught at home

Pairs of subjects	Condition A driving skills tutored at home	Condition B driving skills tutored at driving school
1	2	5
2	3	4
3	3	5
4	2	5
5	4	4
6	1	5
7	3	2
8	5	4
9	3	5
10	1	4
Means	2.7	4.3

other variables which may influence the results and which should therefore be controlled. We should then need to devise a test to measure driving skills.

The Wilcoxon matched-subjects test aims to compare the results of each pair of subjects and discover whether there will be significant differences between the scores of the two groups. Subtract the scores of Condition B from those of Condition A, giving the differences as a plus or minus sign. Rank the differences in order of their absolute size; the smallest size difference is allocated a 1, the next in value is allocated a 2 etc. Add up the ranks separately for the pluses and minuses. The smaller total of ranks produces the value of T, which is consulted in the appropriate significance table.

The notion is that if there are only random differences, there ought to be about equal numbers of high and low ranks for the plus and minus differences. Should there be a large number of high ranks for

Table 44 Calculation of the value of *T*

Pairs of subjects	Condition A driving skills tutored at home	Condition B driving skills tutored at driving school	d (A −B)	Ranks of d	Smaller signed sum
1	2	5	−3	7(−)	
2	3	4	−1	2(−)	
3	3	5	−2	4.5(−)	
4	2	5	−3	7(−)	
5	4	4	0	(omit)	
6	1	5	−4	9(−)	
7	3	2	1	2(+)	+2
8	5	4	1	2(+)	+2
9	3	5	−2	4.5(−)	
10	1	4	−3	7(−)	
					T = 4
					N = 9

one sign, this would indicate that there are larger differences in one direction than could be expected by chance.

(a)　Find the difference d between the scores in Conditions A and B and give plus or minus signs. Thus, Condition A −Condition B gives the difference (d) in column 4.

(b)　Place the differences in rank order of size from the smallest (rank 1) to the largest. Ignore the signs at this stage.

(c)　Sum the ranks corresponding to the different signs. See column 5. In brackets are the signs of the ranks which correspond to the signs of the differences. Observed value of $T = 2 + 2 = 4$.

(d)　Find the total number of pairs of subjects N, but do not include any tied scores. $N = 10−1 = 9$.

(e)　Find the critical value of T for the chosen significance level ($p < 0.05$, two-tailed). If the observed value of T is *less* than or *equal* to the critical value in Table E, Appendix A, the null hypothesis can be rejected. Therefore, because our observed value of $T = 4$ is less than the critical value of 6, the null hypothesis can be rejected.

We did not predict a direction, i.e. that higher scores would be found amongst those who had been taught to drive at home or at a driving school. Thus the chosen level of significance will be that for a two-tailed hypothesis. On the other hand, if we had predicted that those who attended a driving school for tuition would perform better than those who were tutored at home, a one-tailed test of significance would be used.

STQ **(1)** *Apply the Wilcoxon test to the following data:*

Subject	Condition A	Condition B
1	100	117
2	106	110
3	104	100
4	150	138
5	110	106
6	98	107
7	120	113
8	116	122
9	125	124
10	126	121

Apply the 5% level (one-tailed)

(2) *What considerations would lead you to apply a Wilcoxon test rather than a related t-test?*

Answers are to be found on p. 435.

EXPERIMENT USING THE WILCOXON TEST
After completing an appropriate course of reading, a student decided to investigate the notion that a person's hand reaction time would be faster than his foot reaction time. This section deals with some of the main points which he included in his written report. Notice how the student allowed his idea for an experiment to develop naturally from his reading.

This *notion* about reaction time is not enough, because it is not scientifically precise. Before proceeding further he would need to state the problem in the form of a hypothesis – leading from the general to the particular. The concept of a hypothesis was discussed in Chapter 00.

Do you remember what was said about:

(a) The null hypothesis?
(b) The alternative hypothesis?

> **STQ** *Now see if you can produce a null hypothesis and an alternative hypothesis for this reaction time experiment.*

The student who conducted the reaction time experiment wrote these hypotheses; compare them to yours.

(a)   Null hypothesis: there will be no significant difference between hand reaction times and foot reaction times.

(b)   Alternative hypothesis: There will be a significant difference between hand reaction times and foot reaction times;

It would of course be perfectly legitimate to state one-tailed alternative hypotheses, *viz.*

 (i)   Hand reaction times will be significantly faster than foot reaction times.

(ii)   Hand reaction times will be significantly slower than foot reaction times.

The student went on to state that this experiment is an example of simple reaction time. Other kinds of reaction time experiments are called complex reaction times, which may involve *two* stimuli, e.g. red and green lights. In this instance there would be two kinds of responses determined beforehand, for example, a right hand response to a red light, and a left hand response to a green light.

> **STQ** *In the case of the present experiment, the experimenter looked for the dependent and independent variables. If you have forgotten about these, see Chapter 11. Can you spot which is the dependent variable, and which the independent variable in this experiment?*

You should have stated that the dependent variable is reaction time, and the independent variable in this case is the kind of response – i.e. hand or foot. We want to see if the dependent variable is affected by the independent variable.

The student's report went on to describe the environmental conditions in which the experiment was conducted. It took place on two weekday afternoons, and the conditions were normal.

> **STQ** *Why is it necessary to report on the conditions? In what ways might any one of the following factors have affected the outcome of the experiment?*

(1)	*The experiment takes place at 9 a.m.*
(2)	*The experiment is spread over 3 weeks.*
(3)	*The room temperature fluctuates from day to day.*
(4)	*There is a road drill working intermittently outside the building.*
(5)	*Some subjects present themselves for the experiment after, (i) a lecture, or (ii) a games session.*
(6)	*The type of footwear worn by the subjects.*
(7)	*The age of the subjects.*

In describing his sample, the experimenter stated that eight college students − all male − were used, and their ages ranged from 16 to 19. They were asked to take part in the experiment 'because they just happened to be available at the time'.

STQ *What kind of sample is this? Why is it necessary to pay careful attention to sampling? (see Chapter 7.)*

The apparatus was then described. It consisted of a millisecond timer, hand switch panel, light switch panel and foot pedal, a stop watch to time the intervals between trials, a data sheet to record the responses, and small pieces of paper with either 'hand' or 'foot' written on them. The latter were used to help randomize the experimental conditions. For example, some subjects would engage in the hand condition first followed by the foot condition. The remaining subjects would adopt the opposite procedure (foot − hand). Finally a screen was set up between the subject and the apparatus. Why was this precaution necessary, do you think?

STQ **(1)** *Why was it necessary to randomize the experimental conditions? How could the results of the experiment be influenced if a randomization procedure had not been employed?*

(2) *A repeated measures design was used. What does this mean, and why was it chosen in this particular instance? Can you name two other experimental designs that are employed in psychological experiments?*

At this stage, the experimenter described his method of conducting the experiment. Read it carefully and see if you can offer any criticisms, suggesting improvements where you think they are needed.

Method
The apparatus was assembled so that the experimenter sat on one side of the table behind the screen, with the millisecond timer in front of him.

The subject entered the room and was asked to select a piece of paper from the pile to determine whether he would undergo the 'hand' or 'foot' condition first. The subject then sat down facing the experimenter on the opposite side of the screen. The subject was given instructions according to whether he was to present himself first under the 'hand' condition or the 'foot' condition.

Hand instruction: please place your finger on the switch. When the light appears, press the button and keep it depressed until the light goes off. When the light is extinguished, press the switch again to reset the circuit. You will be given approximately 15 seconds between each trial to give you time to relax.

Foot instruction: please take your shoes off and place your dominant foot on the pedal. When the light appears, press your foot down and keep the pedal depressed until the light goes off, then remove your foot. You will be given approximately 15 seconds between each trial to give you time to relax.

Four trials were given before the actual experiment began. Each subject underwent ten trials under each condition, and the times in milliseconds were recorded for each subject. These are shown in Table 45 (hand) and Table 46 (foot).

Results

Table 45 Hand reaction times in milliseconds

	S_1	S_2	S_3	S_4	S_5	S_6	S_7	S_8
1	233	824	177	465	357	170	213	370
2	328	215	193	370	408	236	200	443
3	260	291	177	503	432	182	176	408
4	224	251	141	478	339	207	378	284
5	246	242	206	382	427	271	201	289
6	425	209	237	422	245	199	171	270
7	306	208	191	399	319	200	299	331
8	341	374	364	295	293	276	198	307
9	349	206	208	335	452	199	244	274
10	263	179	228	505	379	353	214	276
Mean	297.5	299.9	212.2	415.4	365.1	229.1	229.4	325.2

As they appear, Tables 45 and 46 are not very meaningful, and it is now our task to make them more intelligible in order that we may draw fairly accurate conclusions about the data. In fact, the student who conducted the experiment decided to employ a Wilcoxon test to determine whether the results were significant.

Table 46   Foot reaction times in milliseconds

	S_1	S_2	S_3	S_4	S_5	S_6	S_7	S_8
1	280	223	223	230	221	381	327	324
2	370	285	182	273	373	311	341	546
3	205	227	259	234	229	337	246	302
4	248	247	233	208	199	378	272	300
5	218	429	287	210	294	429	281	316
6	249	342	411	226	420	471	196	248
7	312	198	271	223	251	341	286	265
8	214	234	276	232	295	331	320	243
9	265	190	249	285	246	293	249	266
10	333	179	316	243	217	398	267	242
Mean	269.4	255.4	270.7	236.4	274.5	367.0	278.5	305.2

STQ   (1)   *Why did he use a Wilcoxon test? What is the parametric counterpart of the Wilcoxon test?*

(2)   *Notice that our student employed the Wilcoxon test to determine whether or not the results were significant. Explain as fully as you can what is meant by significance. (Chapter 6).*

The calculation of the Wilcoxon test, using mean scores (from Tables 45 and 46) is shown in Table 47.

Table 47

Subject	Hand condition	Foot condition	Difference (d)	Ranks (R)
1	297.5	269.4	28.1	2
2	299.9	255.4	44.5	3
3	212.2	270.7	−58.5	5
4	415.4	236.4	179.0	8
5	365.1	274.5	90.6	6
6	229.1	367.0	−137.9	7
7	229.4	278.5	−49.1	4
8	325.2	305.2	20.0	1

$T = 5 + 7 + 4 = 16$ (totals of ranks for differences with less frequent sign).

when $N = 8$ (Table E, Appendix A)
    $T = 4$

Since the observed value of T is larger than the value given in the table, there is no significant difference between the hand and foot conditions.

> **STQ** *Note that the student obtained mean scores from the data in Tables 45 and 46. Was he correct in doing so? The mean is a measure of central tendency. Name two other measures of central tendency and differentiate between them. Refer back to Chapter 2 if you must!*

The discussion of the experiment comes next. Here we try to account for the result we obtained. We ask ourselves, for example:

(1) Could we have improved on any part of the experiment to gain a better result?
(2) Was our method of sampling correct?
(3) Were the environmental conditions suitable?
(4) Was the apparatus, (a) adequate, (b) complicated, (c) noisy?
(5) Was the experimental design correct?
(6) Were the instructions, (a) clear, (b) precise, (c) intelligible to the subjects?
(7) Did the experimenter influence the subjects' performance in any way?

Now it is your turn to write a discussion for this experiment, trying to account for the result which was produced. For this purpose, use the following suggestions as a guide, and include other ideas of your own.

(1) The ages of the students in the sample.
(2) The idea of using slips of paper to randomize the experimental conditions.
(3) The finger used to depress the switch – middle? index? dominant hand?
(4) 15 seconds between each trial – too long a time or too short?
(5) The four practice trials before the experiment began. Too many or too few? Could these have affected actual performance? How?

After the discussion an attempt must be made to write a summary. In our experiment the student wrote the following summary. See if you agree with it, and decide whether you could improve it without making it too long. The summary would then be placed at the beginning of the report.

Summary
Eight subjects volunteered to take part in an experiment to investigate whether or not hand reaction time is faster then foot reaction time. Subjects were tested individually under both experimental conditions. A Wilcoxon test was applied to the results of the experiment and this

indicated that there was no significant difference between hand and foot reaction times.

Finally, the references which the student used for the background to the experiment would be included. In this instance, he used only one reference.

Gardiner, J. M. and Kaminska, Z. (1975). *First Experiments in Psychology.* (London: Methuen)

You should now attempt to write up the whole experiment for yourself, using the headings that have already been discussed in full in Chapter 13.

By now you should be ready to conduct your own experiments and write them up. A useful exercise at this stage would be to return to each experiment in the book which we have included to illustrate the various designs and statistics. Examine each one carefully, and you will notice that we have deliberately omitted some of the headings – such as 'Summary', 'Aim of Experiment and Background', 'Discussion of Results and Conclusion', etc. Using the references quoted with each experiment, and all the available data, see if you could write up fully each of these experiments if you have not done so already. Of course, the more ambitious student will want to conduct these experiments for himself and base his reports on his own data! Why not try a few experiments yourself? We have tried to encourage you to do this at the end of each experimental example so far. Learning by doing is a very sound creed. Try it!

19

Design and subject – experimenter problems

Faulty research designs

A research design is essentially a plan or strategy aimed at enabling answers to be otained to research questions. To the extent that the experiment is inappropriately conceived and therefore inappropriately designed, solutions to research questions will not be attained. Unfortunately, research is and has been conducted using designs that are inappropriate. The faulty research designs which will now be discussed briefly are examples of ones that are defective. The purpose of presenting them is to demonstrate their weakness so they can be avoided.

1 ONE-SHOT CASE-STUDY DESIGN

Look at the following piece of research and comment on its design. An institution decides to institute a training programme (*IV*). It wants to evaluate the effectiveness of the programme so on its completion, behaviour is assessed (*DV*). If the attitudes, behaviour and performance of the inmates are found to be positive then programme will be kept as a permanent feature. Diagrammatically the design looks like this:

Treatment	Response Measure
X ——————————————→ Y	

> **STQ** *Well, what do you think of this? Can you criticize the design?*

The one-shot case study design is one in which a single group of subjects or a single subject is measured on a dependent variable subsequent to the presentation of some treatment which is presumed to cause change.

For yielding scientific data, this design is of almost no scientific value. This is not to deny that case studies are of no value or that they

212

do not serve a function, but they cannot provide evidence of causal relationships. One of the basic requirements for attaining scientific evidence is that an equated comparison be included that did not receive the treatment condition. Only in this way can we attain any degree of assurance that the treatment effect, X, was actually the cause of the observed behaviour, Y. In the training programme example, the same performance *may* have been attained without the training. The point is that this design does not give any evidence of the causes of Y. Its only asset — though a valuable one — is that it can generate hypotheses about possible causal relationships which can be tested by 'good' research designs.

2 THE ONE GROUP PRE/POST-TEST DESIGN

Most researchers recognize the deficiencies in the one-shot case-study design and attempt to improve upon it, at least, by including a pretest. In evaluating a training programme some measure of improvement or success is necessary. However, it seems as though some individuals assume that all that is necessary is to include a pretest that can be compared with a post-test, the latter taken after administering some treatment condition. The design is illustrated below.

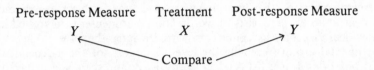

A group of subjects is measured on the dependent variable, Y, prior to administering the treatment condition. The independent variable, X, is then administered and the dependent variable, Y, is again measured. The difference between the pre- and post-test scores is taken as an indication of the effectiveness of the treatment condition. But this design only represents a small improvement over the previous one.

STQ *Can you explain why?*

There are many rival hypotheses which could explain the difference between pre- and post-test score. Other changes in the environment could be invoked such as changes in maturation, personal circumstances, regression to the mean.

The primary disadvantage of these designs is the lack of any comparison or control group by which changes due to the *IV* can be assessed over and above those brought about by other factors.

Experimental and control groups

This technique ensures that the effects of the *IV* can be determined. The control group refers to the group of subjects that does not receive the independent variable, receives a zero amount of it, or receives a value that is in some sense a standard value. The experimental group or groups refer to the groups of subjects that receive some amount of the independent variable. In a drug study, the subjects who received a placebo would represent the control group and subjects receiving the drug would represent the experimental group. In another experiment an experimenter might be interested in the effect of noise upon studying. Using a between-subjects design, one group of subjects would be exposed to loud noise for half an hour while they were studying; this is the level of interest of the independent variable. A control group would study the same material for half an hour in a quiet setting. Then both groups would be tested on the material. Any obtained difference on the test between the two groups would be attributed to the effect of noise.

The important characteristic of a control condition is that it provides a baseline against which some variable of interest can be compared. Sometimes the best baseline is no treatment, but often the best baseline requires some activity. A frequent example occurs in memory research on retroactive inhibition where a group of subjects is required to learn two different lists of words; the experimenter is interested in how learning one list interferes with learning the other. The experimental group (receiving the level of interest of the independent variable) first learns list A, then learns list B, and then is tested again on list A. The experimenter would like to show that learning list B interferes with list A. But before any conclusion of this sort can be reached, a comparison control condition is required. Merely comparing the final test of list A with the first test is insufficient, since subjects might do more poorly on the last list A test simply because they were tired or do better because they had extra practice. A control condition with no treatment would have a group learn list A, then sit around for the time it took the experimental group to learn list B, and then be tested again on list A. But this would be a poor control condition because subjects might practice or rehearse list A while they were sitting around. This would improve their final performance on the last list A test and incorrectly make the experimental group look as if list B interfered more than it really did with list A. A proper baseline condition would occupy the control group during the time the experimental group was learning list B — perhaps by having them play cards or some other 'busy work' that would prevent rehearsal.

Examples of experimental and control groups for list learning:

Experimental group	Learn list A	Learn list B	Test list A
Control group	Learn list A	Play cards	Test list A

A control group serves two functions. First, it serves as a source of comparison. The one-shot case study and the one-group before—after designs were primarily considered faulty because there was no way to tell if the treatment condition, X, caused the observed behaviour, Y. To arrive at such a conclusion you have to have a comparison group or a control group that did not receive the treatment effect. Only by including a control group – assuming all other variables are controlled – can you get any concrete indication of whether or not the treatment condition produced results different from those which would have been attained in the absence of the treatment. All variables operating on the control and experimental groups must be identical, except for the one being manipulated by the experimenter. In this way the influence of extraneous variables is held constant. In the one-group before-after design, extraneous variables such as history and maturation can creep in and serve as rival hypotheses unless a control group is included. If a control group is included, these variables will affect the performance of both the control subjects and the experimental subjects, which effectively results in having held their influence constant and thereby controlled. It is in this way that a control group also serves a control function.

	Treatment	*Response measure*
Control group	⎫	Y
	⎬ Random assignment	Compare
Experimental group	⎭ X	Y

This design, and particularly its extension, which will be discussed next, is widely used in psychology. It is effective from two standpoints. The first is the much discussed virtue of randomization which provides the needed control of extraneous variables. The second virtue is the inclusion of a control group which provides the comparability required by science.

A means for increasing the sensitivity of this design would be to match subjects on the relevant variables prior to randomly assigning them to groups.

An elaboration of this design is the pre- and post-test comparison design.

2 PRE- AND POST-TEST COMPARISON DESIGN

In this design, after random assignment into experimental and control groups plus previous matching if necessary, the experimental group receives the IV then a comparison is made. The control group receives either no *IV*, another level of *IV*, or undertakes a completely dissimilar task to prevent rehearsal.

		Pre-response measure	Treatment	Post-response measure	
Random assignment	Control group	*Y*		*Y*	Pre *Y* minus Post *Y*
	Experimental group	*Y*	*X*	*Y*	Pre *Y* and minus Post *Y*

Compare the Pre *Y* minus Post *Y* for the control group with the Pre *Y* and minus Post *Y* for the experimental group.

Practice, learning, maturation, and experimenter effects should be equally distributed in both groups while matching and random assignment have ensured initial equality of the groups.

It is of course possible to have a larger number of groups than two but the general principles are the same. For example with three levels of *IV* we would randomly assign to three experimental groups and a control group. With more than two groups a statistical technique known as analysis of variance is applied to determine if the different levels of the *IV* produce significantly different results, though we would not know between which particular means the significant differences occurred.

> **STQ** **(1)** *Write a paragraph to explain why these latter designs provide more experimental control than the first two.*
>
> **(2)** *Imagine an experiment to determine the influence of hunger on the responses given by subjects to certain stimulus words. Two-hundred subjects are deprived of food and water for 12 h. At the end of this period 85% of the responses to the stimulus words are food related and 10% thirst related. What is it reasonable to conclude?*

Answers are to be found on p. 435.

Subject—experimenter effects

1 SUBJECT BIAS

Any human experiment involves an interaction between an experimenter and a subject. Each role has specific behavioural requirements and mutual expectations, which are held by each role member. These expectations should define the behaviour that is appropriate for each member. When a person agrees to take part in an experiment he or she is making an implicit contract to play the role of the subject. Theoretically, this means that the subject will listen to the instructions and perform the tasks asked of him or her to the best of his or her ability and as truthfully as possible. In reality, such an idealistic situation does not always exist because the subject has certain perceptions of the experiment which may alter behaviour. The subject may want to comply and participate in the experiment but, because of certain perceptions and motives, may respond in several different ways. That is to say, there is an interaction between the way a person responds in an experiment and his or her motives and perception of the experiment.

A subject seldom reacts in a naive and humble way but entertains his own hypothesis about the experiment – what its purpose is and what he may reveal in it – instead of simply reacting in a naive manner. In other words, the subject is not a passive organism.

Ideally, the experimenter would like to have a naive subject who brings no preconceived notion to the laboratory. Once in the laboratory he or she should accept our instructions and be motivated to respond in as truthful a manner as possible. While such an ideal view is great and it would be wonderful if such a situation existed, it does not. The subject brings with him or her certain attitudes and predispositions which can alter his or her behaviour in the experimental task. First of all, why does a subject participate in a psychological experiment in the first place? Is it because, as we may like to think, he or she is interested in advancing science? Probably not, although the subject may be curious about the experiment and curiosity may be a motivator.

Co-operation in the psychological experiment is only infrequently a result of the subject's desire to benefit science. Instead, co-operation is attained from volunteering because subjects are curious, because they are paid to participate and they need money, they are pressured by friends or their instructor, or, as frequently occurs, compulsory participation is required by the course. Most subjects resent this requirement, and may express their pent up feelings by 'beating the researcher' in such a way that he never finds out. As you can see the subject does not enter the experiment as a *tabula rasa* but rather with a variety of positive and negative attitudes, expectations, and suspicions, any of which can distort his performance.

Laboratory experiments attempt to capture behaviour as it really exists outside the laboratory. Sometimes the laboratory setting itself, or the knowledge that an experiment is underway, may alter patterns of behaviour. Try this simple demonstration to convince yourself that such effects occur. Tell five of your friends that you are conducting an experiment for your psychology class and would like their co-operation as subjects. If they agree, ask them to undertake some ludicrous experiment. For example to stand with their eyes shut, a finger in each ear, while counting backwards from 1000. Perhaps you could think of something equally ridiculous to try. Then ask another five friends (that is if you have any left) to undertake the same behaviour without mentioning 'psychology experiment'. They will rather quickly and impolitely decline.

So there is something unusual about the ready compliance of those friends who knew they were participating in an experiment, since they were willing to co-operate for a longer period of time. Psychologists call the influence of an experimenter's expectations, or the subject's knowledge that an experiment is underway, demand characteristics. To the extent that the behaviour of research participants is controlled by demand characteristics instead of independent variables, experiments are invalid and cannot be generalized beyond the test situation.

A well-known example of a demand characteristic is the Hawthorne effect, named after the Western Electric Company plant where it was first observed. The company was interested in improving worker morale and productivity and conducted several experiments to improve the workers' environment (such as improving lighting etc.). No matter what experimental manipulation was tried, worker productivity improved. The workers knew that they were in a 'special' group and therefore tried to do their best at all times. Thus, the demand characteristics were more important in determining the workers' productivity than the experimental manipulations.

Orne (1962) has taken the position that volunteer subjects want to co-operate with the experimenter and be good subjects. To take such a position the subject attempts to identify the hypothesis of the experiment from the available demand characteristics and acts in a manner that will support the hypothesis. By demand characteristics, Orne is referring to any of the many cues available in an experiment than can serve to provide the subject knowledge as to what behaviour is desired of him or her. Orne has gone to great lengths to demonstrate that subjects reveal tremendous persistence in this 'helping' behaviour. Orne found that subjects worked for 5½ h on summing two adjacent numbers presented on sheets of paper. Each sheet of paper contained 224 additions and the subject received 2000 sheets of paper. When subjects were questioned about their perseverance, they frequently hypothesized that the experiment was concerned with endurance.

Just knowing that one is being experimented on, and consequently observed, alters behaviour regardless of one's attitudes or motivations about supporting or refuting the experimental hypothesis. Serving as a subject in an experiment is similar to being on stage or in front of a television camera. While in front of a television camera most people do not act as they normally would but produce behaviour that ranges from being silly to being stilted. Likewise, being in an experiment may generate behaviour that is more socially desirable, restrained, sub-dued, or defiant. When such a tendency is coupled with the behaviour that may be produced by attempts to use the demand characteristics of an experiment to deliberately 'co-operate' or 'outwit' the experimenter, it is easy to see how results can be produced that are inaccurate.

Complete understanding of the behaviour of Ss in the experimental context is still lacking. All we can do at this point in time is to be aware of the problem, try to mitigate any possible negative attitudes by our interpersonal behaviour and rapport, and try not to use 'forced labour'.

2 EXPERIMENTER BIAS

Another source of error arises from the potential influence of the experimenter on the outcome of the experiment. The experimenter's attributes as well as his unintentional behaviour may affect the out-come of the experiment. This type of bias is termed experimenter bias.

Experimenters are not impersonal, anonymous people, all capable of identical observation and recording. Experimenters too are human! They have attitudes, values, needs, motives, which, try as they might, they cannot stop contaminating their experiments. The experimenter firstly has a motive for choosing and carrying out the particular experiment in the first place. He has certain expectations regarding the outcome of the experiment too. This is implicit if he has carried out a sensible and critical review of previous work in the area. He would hence like to see his hypothesis confirmed. The experimenter, knowing what he does about the hypothesis and projected outcome, is likely to provide unintended verbal and non-verbal cues which may be picked up by the Ss thereby influencing their performances in the direction desired. The experimenter may therefore be one of Orne's demand characteristics.

The experimenter effect can also occur in seemingly objective ex-periments with animal subjects. Rosenthal (1966) told student experi-menters that the rats they were to test in a maze were special strains: either maze-bright or maze-dull. Actually the rats came from the same population. Nevertheless, the rats who were labelled maze-bright had fewer errors than those labelled maze-dull, and this difference was statistically reliable. The student experimenters were observed while they tested the rats and did not cheat or do anything overt to bias the results. It seems reasonable that the lucky students who got bright rats were more motivated to perform the experiment than those unfor-tunates who had to teach 'stupid' rats to go through the maze. Somehow this affected the results of the experiment, perhaps because experimenters handled the two groups of rats differently.

The best way to eliminate this kind of experimenter effect is to hide the experimental condition from the experimenter, on the premise that experimenters cannot communicate what they do not know. Such a procedure was, for instance, used in a study of the behavioural effects of air pollution. Subjects breathed either pure air or air taken from a busy roadway. The air was contained in tanks, and the experimenter did not know which tank held pure air and which tank held polluted air. The subjects' poorer performance in polluted air cannot be attributed to the experimenter's giving away the independent variable. This is an example of the double-blind technique.

Attributes of the experimenter, such as age, sex, social class, ethnic group, his warmth, dominance, need for social approval etc. will to unknown degrees also influence the Ss responses. The problem lies in the fact that these attributes have a different effect on each subject. It would be no problem if the influence of each attribute was identical for all Ss.

A further source of bias lies in the subjective interpretation of the obtained data. For example the interpretation of the same twin study data on intelligence can be subject to wide divergence of opinion, which reflects the general philosophy of life of each psychologist.

But as with subject bias it is difficult to assess accurately experimenter bias or to find ways of eliminating it. Since experiments are generally social interaction contexts all we can do at present is be aware of these sources of experimental error due to uncontrolled and possibly in some cases inherently uncontrollable variables.

Strengths and weaknesses of the experimental method

> **STQ** *What do you feel are the main strengths and weaknesses of the experimental method? When you have responded, read below.*

We believe the main strengths are precision and control. Control is achieved through sampling and design; precision through quantitative and reliable measurement. We may sometimes think that the experimental method is the sole employer of research hypotheses, the measurement of *DV*s, sampling techniques and the control of variables. This is not so. Most types of research methodology in the social sciences uses these techniques. The only unique aspect of the experimental method is the systematic manipulation of the *IV* to demonstrate a direct causal effect on a *DV*. We have tended to extol the experimental method for its virtues of control and precision but these very virtues are sources of weakness when considering the generalization of the results from a tightly-controlled laboratory experiment to real-life situations and real-life behaviour. They are often quite divorced from real life with the elimination and control of so many normally operating variables.

There is too the problem of ethics, a number of areas preclude the manipulation of variables. We cannot deliberately cause maternal deprivation or encourage the development of guilt feelings. Some would even claim that the use of people as experimental subjects is fundamentally wrong, for any attempt to arrive at laws of behaviour ignores the fact that each subject is a unique individual with his own specific experiences of the environment. Should an autonomous free agent, capable of rational thought and decision making, be manipulated at the whim of an experimenter like an inert chemical substance?

Of course the criticisms about artificiality are well justified but it would seem necessary despite them to demonstrate that a model or theory works on the criterion of predictive efficiency rather than rely purely on intuition. There is nothing wrong with the experimental method itself. The problem is how to devise ingenious experiments to investigate real-life behaviour without reducing behaviour to a trivial or artificial level. There is a continual trade-off between real life and the ability to make precise statements about predicted effects under controlled conditions.

STQ *Consider an aspect of human behaviour in which you are interested, and think how you could investigate it with an experimental treatment yet make it as real-life as possible.*

So the main advantage of experiments is control of extraneous variation. In the ideal experiment, no factors (variables) except the one being studied are permitted to influence the outcome – in the jargon of experimental psychology we say that these other factors are controlled. If, as in the ideal experiment, all factors but one (that under investigation) are held constant, we can logically conclude that any differences in outcome must be due to manipulation of that one independent variable. As the levels of the independent variable are changed, the resulting differences in the dependent variable can only occur because the independent variable changed. Putting it another way, changes in the independent variable caused the observed changes in the dependent variable. While non-experimental research techniques are limited to statements about correlation – that is, variable *A* and variable *B* are related – experiments permit statements about causation – that is, independent variable A causes dependent variable B to change.

Thus in principle, experiments lead to statements about causation.

In practice, these statements are not always true. No experiment is 100% successful in eliminating or holding constant all other sources of variation but the one being studied. However, experiments eliminate more extraneous variation than other research techniques.

Advantages and disadvantages of the experimental method

Advantages	*Disadvantages*
(1) Formulation of an experimental hypothesis which predicts a precise relationship between variables.	It is not always possible to do this particularly at the exploratory stage of a research programme.
(2) Manipulating an independent variable to show its effect on a dependent variable.	This is not suitable for situations when it is not practically or ethically possible to manipulate a variable.
(3) Collection of objective, quantitative data which can be statistically analysed to see whether it supports the experimental hypothesis	The psychologist may ignore intuitive and introspective evidence which may throw light on internal cognitive processes.
(4) Elimination of alternative explanations by controlling or randomizing confounded variables.	Control and Standardization may result in such an artificial experimental situation that the results have no bearing on real life behaviour.

REFERENCES

Orne, M. T. (1962). On the social psychology of the psychological experiment. *Am. Psychol.*, **17**, 776–83

Rosenthal, R. (1966). *Experimenter Effects in Behavioural Research.* (New York: Appleton Century Crofts)

20

Chi-square

A Rationale

The chi-square (χ^2) is a non-parametric procedure used to test hypotheses about the independence of frequency counts in various categories. For example, the data may be the proportions of smokers preferring each one of three brands of low-tar cigarettes or the proportion of people favouring a repeal of the abortion laws. Categories of responses are set up, such as Brands A, B, and C of cigarettes or Approve–Disapprove of a certain issue, and the number of individuals or events falling into each category is recorded. In such a situation one can obtain nothing more than the frequency, or number of times, that a particular category is chosen, which constitutes nominal data. With such data the only analysis possible is to determine whether the frequencies observed in the sample differ significantly from hypothesized frequencies. There are many social science variables which involve nominal data for which chi-square is a simple and appropriate means of analysis, e.g. social class levels, illness categories, age groups, sex, voting preferences, pass – fail dichotomies etc. The symbol χ is the Greek letter chi which is pronounced to rhyme with 'sky'. The distribution of chi-square is based on chance as with 't' and the various standard errors we have dealt with. Imagine you have a container holding a lot of tombola tickets of which half are even numbered, and half are odd numbered. After mixing them up well a given number of tickets are drawn out by a blindfolded person. You would expect half of the tickets to be even numbered and half to be odd numbered. This exact expectation would rarely be met; the obtained frequencies of odd and even numbers would not match the expected frequencies. Over a large number of similar draws this congruence might be achieved. This activity and principle should remind you of earlier activities with standard error and sampling (Chapter 7). So the χ^2 test provides us with the probability that any obtained frequency arose by chance (null hypothesis).

223

If many samples of equal size are randomly drawn from the container a χ^2 distribution will be formed.

$$\chi^2 = \sum \frac{(O-E)^2}{E} \text{ where}$$

O = observed frequency
E = expected frequency and
the summation is over all the categories we are measuring.

The tabled values of χ^2 can be consulted in Table F, Appendix A. It is used just like a t table. Turn to p. 413 and look it up now. The probability values along the top refer to the likelihood of the values of χ^2 listed in the columns below being reached or exceeded by chance. Our old friend df forms the left hand column.

The df value of χ^2 is different from those involved in parametric tests where df is tied closely to N. With χ^2 the df is tied to the number of categories in which frequencies are the dependent variable. We will see how to calculate df as we go along.

If the obtained value of χ^2 equals or exceeds the tabled entry then the null hypothesis of a chance association is rejected.

There are two major uses of chi square (χ^2):

(1) As a 'goodness of fit' test when it tells us how well an observed distribution fits a hypothesized or theoretical distribution.

(2) As a cross tabulation between two categories each of which can be divided into two or more sub-categories, e.g. preference for type of music (jazz, country and western, rock) against sex (male and female). The 2×2 contingency table is a special case of this and will be considered later.

But whichever of these uses χ^2 is put to the general principle remains the same. In each case one compares the observed proportions in a sample with the expected proportions and applies the χ^2 test to determine whether a difference between observed and expected proportions is likely to be a function of sampling error (non-significant) or unlikely to be a function of sampling error (significant).

> **STQ** _Since χ^2 requires categorized data at what level of measurement is its data?_

B Goodness-of-fit chi-square
As an example of the first use of the χ^2 (single sample, goodness-of-fit), let us picture a brewery which has developed three different types of beer (ale). A, B, and real ale. The brewery wants to determine

whether any one of them will be a better prospect for marketing than the others. The null hypothesis would be that among prospective customers the proportion preferring each of the beers would be equal. From among prospective customers the brewery selects a single random sample of 90 and asks each of the subjects to try the three and indicate a preference. The results are shown in Table 48.

Table 48

Brand of beer	Frequency
A	26
B	26
Real ale	38

Real ale has been chosen more often than the other two. Is this good evidence that among prospective customers from whom our sample was drawn it would be preferred? Or could the apparent preference easily be a function of sampling error? To arrive at an estimate of the probability that the observed frequency distribution is due to chance the brewer would apply the χ^2 test. The χ^2 test permits him to estimate the probability that observed frequencies differ from expected frequencies through chance alone.

In this example, his null hypothesis is that no one blend of ale would be preferred over any other. In this case, he would expect that each of the three blends would be selected by one-third of the prospective customers, giving expected frequencies of 30 : 30 : 30. If the null hypothesis is true, any departure from these frequencies would be the result of pure chance. But how far can a departure from these frequencies go before we can say that such a discrepancy would occur so infrequently on a chance basis that our observations are significantly different from those expected. Well, when χ^2 is computed it can be compared with its value at the usual levels of significance to see if it reaches or exceeds them. If it does the null hypothesis of chance variation is rejected.

STQ **(1)** *What are the two major conventional levels of significance we would employ?*

(2) *What two sets of data do we compare in a χ^2 test?*

In calculating χ^2 we need to enter our observed and expected data into a table of cells. The cells are filled with the data on the lines of the following model:

O E	where	O	=	Observed data
$(O - E)$ $(O - E)^2$		E	=	Expected data

We will now fill in the cells in Table 49.

Table 49

Blend A		Blend B		Real ale	
26	30	26	30	38	30
−4	16	−4	16	8	64

$$\chi^2 = \Sigma \frac{(O - E)^2}{E} = \frac{16}{30} + \frac{16}{30} + \frac{64}{30}$$
$$= 0.53 + 0.53 + 2.1$$
$$= 3.16$$

DEGREES OF FREEDOM IN A GOODNESS-OF-FIT χ^2

> **STQ** *Do you recall what degrees of freedom (df) represent?*

The number of observations free to vary in our example is two because once we have fixed the frequency of two categories, say blends A and B, the third has to be 38 to make the total 90. So the third category is fixed. The same principle holds true for any number of categories. The degrees of freedom in a 'goodness-of-fit' test is one less than the number of categories $(k - 1)$. In the present problem $df = 3 - 1 = 2$.

> **STQ** *If we were dealing with preferences for five brands of a product how many df would we have?*

The final step is to refer to Table F, Appendix A in order to determine whether the obtained χ^2 value is statistically significant or not. To use the table one must enter it with the appropriate degrees of freedom. In our example it is entered with 2 *df*.

The essential question one asks is: 'How often would a χ^2 of a certain value or greater occur by chance when the null hypothesis is true and there are $k - 1$ degrees of freedom?' As is true with the *t*-table and the *F*-table, if the χ^2 value one has calculated is equal to or greater than the value required for significance at a predetermined probability level for the *df*, then the null hypothesis of no real difference between the observed and expected frequencies is rejected at that level of significance. If the calculated χ^2 is smaller than the tabled value required for significance at that level, then one may not reject the null hypothesis. Table F, Appendix A tells us that with 2 *df* a χ^2 value of at least 5.99 is necessary to reject the null hypothesis at the 0.05 level. The value of χ^2 in our example is only 3.16. Since 3.16 is less than the value required for significance, the brewer cannot reject his null hypothesis. Thus, he would retain his null hypothesis and conclude that the observed frequencies do not differ significantly from the expected frequencies. The χ^2 test shows that he has insufficient evidence of a systematic preference for one type of beer over another.

At this point it is important to note the effect of the degrees of freedom upon the significance of any calculated χ^2. In Table F it can be seen that the χ^2 required for significance at any given level gets larger as the number of degrees of freedom gets larger. We saw that for 2 *df* a χ^2 of 5.99 was needed for significance at the 5% level. With 3 *df* this χ^2 value increases to 7.82, to 11.07 for 5 *df* and to 43.77 for 30 *df*. Thus it is extremely important to know the right number of degrees of freedom when attempting to interpret the significance of an obtained χ^2.

Here is another example of a goodness-of-fit χ^2. Consider the question: Are more people born in one season of the year than in another? To investigate this, we could start off by gathering some birth dates from a randomly selected sample. Let us just suppose that we now have a total of 100 birth dates, and that we have defined the seasons so that spring, summer, autumn and winter each has an equal number of days.

STQ *How many birthdays out of the 100 would you expect by chance each season, if season did not in fact have any influence?*

We would expect an even distribution. That is 25 in each season.

Now it might turn out that when we actually grouped the observed birth dates of the 100 persons they were distributed thus:

Spring	Summer	Autumn	Winter
35	28	15	22

The question now would be: Is the fact that the observed data are different from what we expected more likely due to chance or does it more likely represent actual population differences in birth rate during the different seasons?

We will now place the observed and expected data into their respective cells and calculate $(O - E)$ and $(O - E)^2$.

Table 50

Spring		Summer		Autumn		Winter	
35	25	28	25	15	25	22	25
10	100	3	9	− 10	100	− 3	9

$$\Sigma \frac{(O - E)^2}{E} = \frac{100}{25} + \frac{9}{25} + \frac{100}{25} + \frac{9}{25}$$

$$= 4 + 0.36 + 4 + 0.36$$

$$\chi^2 = 8.72$$

A relatively large χ^2 should indicate that the Es differed more from the Os than is likely by chance. As to how large a value for χ^2 is needed to reject the null hypothesis of no difference in the population, we again consult Table F, Appendix A. To enter the table we need to know the *df*.

STQ **(1)** *How many df have we in this example?*

(2) *Look up our answer of 8.72 in Table F. Is it significant at either the 0.05 or 0.01 levels?*

Our χ^2 of 8.72 with *df* = 3 is significant at the 0.05 level but not at the 0.01 level. If the result had not been significant at the 0.05 level we would have accepted the null hypothesis that the differences between the observed and expected frequencies were due solely to chance. Since the result is significant ($p < 0.05$) we can say that birthdays are significantly associated with seasons.

SPECIAL CORRECTION FOR 1 DEGREE OF FREEDOM χ^2
The sampling distribution of χ^2 as represented in Table F is a continuous theoretical frequency curve. For situations where the number of degrees of freedom is one, this continuous curve somewhat underestimates the actual probabilities. An adjustment is necessary to make the χ^2 probabilities in Table F more accurately approximate the actual probabilities of the discrete events. The appropriate adjustment is known as Yates' correction. It consists of subtracting 0.5 from the absolute difference between O and E for each category and then squaring the difference. (The absolute difference between two numbers is the difference recorded as a positive number regardless of whether that difference is actually positive or negative.) The formula for χ^2 then becomes:

$$\chi^2 = \Sigma \frac{([O - E] - 0.5)^2}{E}$$

For example if in one cell O = 60 and E = 80 then (O − E) = 20. From this would be taken 0.5 so that (O − E) is corrected to 19.5.

SUMMARY, GOODNESS-OF-FIT χ^2

Let us summarize the steps to be followed in applying the χ^2 test to a single sample with multiple categories, or, as it is called, a χ^2 test for goodness of fit.

(1) The first step is to set up categories for responses that are mutually exclusive and exhaustive of all possible responses.

(2) Next, expected frequencies are proposed for each of the categories either on the basis of a theoretical model or on the basis of whatever information one may already have available.

(3) A random sample of subjects is drawn and their responses recorded in the appropriate categories. This provides us with the obtained frequencies which we will compare with the theoretical or expected chance frequencies.

(4) The null hypothesis, which states that no actual difference exists between the observed and expected frequencies, is assumed. The χ^2 is calculated. If the number of degrees of freedom is one, Yates' correction is applied in the calculation.

(5) At a predetermined level of significance, the calculated χ^2 is compared with the tabled value for the appropriate degrees of freedom ($k - 1$). If the calculated χ^2 is equal to or greater than the tabled value, then the null hypothesis of no difference can be rejected. The investigator may conclude that the difference between the observed and expected frequencies is significant at the predetermined level and is unlikely to be due to chance factors. If the calculated χ^2 is smaller than the tabled value, the null hypothesis cannot be rejected; that is, the null hypothesis is retained and it is concluded that any difference between the observed and expected distributions is not significant and therefore could easily be due to chance.

STQ **(1)** *A random sample of residents in a local authority were asked, 'Should the local council economize by cutting down the number of hours the town swimming pool is open?' The results were:*

Agree	Disagree	Indifferent
12	24	12

(a) *What is the null hypothesis?*

(b) *What is the expected value for each category under the null hypothesis?*

(c) What is the value of χ^2?
(d) What are the degrees of freedom?
(e) Is the value significant at the 0.05 level?
(f) What conclusion would be reached?

(2) *An investigator studying sex stereotypes in basic reading texts finds that one has 16 episodes in which Joe plays the role of leader and four in which Jane plays the role of leader. Could these proportions be a function of chance?*

(3) *A sample of 300 voters was asked which of those candidates they planned to vote for with the following results:*

Candidate	Frequency
Smith	50
Jones	200
Brown	50

Test the null hypothesis that, there is no difference in preference for any of the candidates. Is there a significant difference between the observed and expected frequencies?

Answers are to be found on p. 435.

C χ^2 Test of the independence of categorical variables (cross classification)

We have just seen how to deal with categories divided on the basis of a single variable. However, another widely used application of the χ^2 procedure involves its use with data that are in the form of paired observations on two variables. That is, a sample of subjects is classified into categories on two variables and the question concerns the presence or absence of a relationship between the variables. For example, one might ask: Is there a relationship between the socioeconomic background of a child and his preference among extra-curricular activities at school? Is there a difference in the extent of reported drug use among adolescents coming from different socio-economic backgrounds? The independence or the association of these variables can be determined by means of the χ^2 test.

When data of these types are gathered, they are recorded in what is called a contingency table. The paired responses are categorized into cells organized by rows and columns. Let us consider whether there is an association between family size and religious persuasion. Table 51 shows the observed data from our survey.

Table 51

	One child	*Two children*	*Three or more children*
Jew	20	16	8
Protestant	40	22	10
Roman Catholic	12	36	42

STQ *What is the null hypothesis for this relationship?*

We hypothesized that there was no significant relationship between religious persuasion and the size of family.

It is now necessary to determine the expected frequency values for each of the cells in the contingency table. When the χ^2 procedure is applied to a contingency table to test for independence of the row and column variables, there is no a priori basis for hypothesizing the expected frequency distribution as there was in the χ^2 goodness-of-fit test. The expected frequencies in each cell are derived from the data themselves. These expected cell frequencies are those one would expect to get if the two variables were completely independent of each other and are derived from the row and column totals. To obtain the expected frequency we must first find the row totals and column total and grand total. This is shown in Table 52. The expected frequency

Table 52

	One child	*Two children*	*Three or more children*	*Row totals*	*Grand total*
Jew	20 a	16 b	8	44	
Protestant	40	22	10	72	
Roman Catholic	12	36	42	90	
Column totals	72	74	60		206

for each cell is calculated by multiplying the row total for that cell by the column total for that cell and then dividing by the grand total.

$$\text{Expected for cell 'a'} = \frac{44 \times 72}{206} = 15.4$$

$$\text{Expected for cell 'b'} = \frac{44 \times 74}{206} = 15.8$$

Now you work out the rest.

The expected frequencies have all been placed in the respective cells

(Table 52). So now we must complete each cell by adding in $(O - E)$ and $(O - E)^2$. This has been done for you (Table 53).

Table 53

	One child		Two children		Three or more children		Row totals	Grand total
Jew	20	15.4	16	15.8	8	12.8	44	
	4.6	21.1	0.2	0.04	4.8	23.0		
Protestant	40	25.2	22	25.9	10	21.0	72	
	14.8	219	3.9	15.2	11	121		
Roman Catholic	12	31.5	36	32.3	42	26.2	90	
	19.5	380.2	3.7	13.7	13.8	190.4		
Column totals	72		74		60			206

$$\chi^2 = \Sigma\frac{(O - E)^2}{E} = \frac{21.1}{15.4} + \frac{0.04}{15.8} + \cdots \frac{190.4}{26.2}$$

$$\chi^2 = 1.37 + 0.002 + 1.8 + 8.7 + 0.59 + 5.8 + 12.1 + 0.42 + 7.27 = 38.05$$

DEGREES OF FREEDOM FOR CONTINGENCY TABLE

Recall that in any statistic the degrees of freedom are the number of values that are free to vary. The general rule is that the degrees of freedom for a contingency table equal the number of rows minus one multiplied by the number of columns minus one:

$$df = (\text{rows} - 1)(\text{columns} - 1)$$

In our example with three rows and three columns we have $(3 - 1)(3 - 1) = 4$ *df*.

STQ (1) *If we had had a 3 × 4 table the df would have been how many?*

(2) *Look up in Table F, Appendix A the intersection of 4 df and 0.05 level of significance. Is our value of χ^2 significant at the 0.05 level? Is it significant at the 0.01 level as well?*

(3) *Make a statement concerning the null hypothesis of this study.*

Since our computed χ^2 far exceeds the critical tabled values of 9.488 (0.05 level) and 13.277 (0.01 level) we are well justified in claiming that there is a significant association between family size and religious persuasion in our sample. We reject the null hypothesis that there is only a chance relationship, i.e. that both categories are independent.

Let us consider another example: A pollster has drawn a random sample of 200 individuals whom he asked to indicate their political preference: Conservative, Labour or Liberal, and also whether they approve or disapprove of private education. Thus one has a single random sample classified on two different nominal variables: political preference and approval – disapproval of private education. The frequency data are tabulated and placed in the appropriate cells of the table. The pollster wants to know whether the proportions of Conservative, Labour and Liberals who favour private education differ significantly, indicating a relationship between political preference and attitude towards private education. Since the data are in the form

Table 54

	Approve	Disapprove	Row totals	Grand total
Conservative	50	10	60	
Labour	8	60	68	
Liberal	20	20	40	
Column totals	78	90		168

of frequencies in categories, the χ^2 test is the appropriate statistical procedure to use in analysing the data.

The null hypothesis to be tested in such cases will state that the variables are independent or unrelated; that is, knowledge of one variable tells us nothing about the other variable. In our example the null hypothesis would be: 'There is no significant relationship between political preference and attitude towards private education. This null hypothesis will be retained if the χ^2 value is found to be not statistically significant. If the obtained χ^2 is statistically significant, the null hypothesis of indpendence is rejected. One would therefore conclude that the two variables are associated and dependent and that knowledge of one would tell us something about the other.

Table 54 is a contingency table showing the results of the poll. The observed frequencies were obtained by asking the subjects their political preference and how they felt about private education. Note that the cells are arranged in rows according to political preference and in columns according to attitude toward private education. This creates six cells plus marginal totals for the rows and columns.

STQ *Do you remember how to calculate the expected frequency in a contingency table. Refer back to p. 231 if in difficulty. Now calculate the expected frequencies for each cell.*

The expected frequencies have been entered into Table 55 already as have the row, column and grand totals. The expected values for each cell are found by multiplying the row total by the column total for that cell and dividing the answer by the grand total. For example the expected frequency for the Conservative Approve cell is $(60 \times 78)/168$; similarly the expected frequency for Labour Disapprove is $(68 \times 90)/168$ and so on. The expected frequencies have already been entered into Table 55 but below you will see how they were calculated:

$$\text{Cell a} \qquad E = \frac{60 \times 78}{168} = 27.9$$

$$\text{Cell b} \qquad E = \frac{60 \times 90}{168} = 32.1$$

$$\text{Cell c} \qquad E = \frac{68 \times 78}{168} = 31.6$$

$$\text{Cell d} \qquad E = \frac{68 \times 90}{168} = 36.4$$

$$\text{Cell e} \qquad E = \frac{40 \times 78}{168} = 18.6$$

$$\text{Cell f} \qquad E = \frac{40 \times 90}{168} = 21.4$$

$$\text{Expected frequency} = \frac{\text{(row total) (column total)}}{\text{grand total}}$$

We can now calculate $(O - E)$ and $(O - E)^2$ for each cell. These too have been included already in Table 55.

Table 55

	Approve		Disapprove		Row totals	Grand total
Conservative	50	27.9	10	32.1	60	
	a		b			
	22.1	488.4	22.1	488.4		
Labour	8	31.6	60	36.4	68	
	c		d			
	23.6	557	23.6	557		
Liberal	20	18.6	20	21.4	40	
	e		f			
	1.4	1.96	1.4	1.96		
Column total	78		90			168

$$\chi^2 = \Sigma\frac{(O - E)^2}{E} = \frac{488.4}{27.9} + \frac{488.4}{32.1} + \frac{557}{31.6} + \frac{557}{36.4} + \frac{1.96}{18.6} + \frac{1.96}{21.4} =$$

$$\chi^2 = 17.5 + 15.21 + 17.62 + 15.30 + 0.1 + 0.09 = 65.82$$

Now we must determine whether our χ^2 value of 65.82 is significant. For this we need to know the *df* also.

STQ (1) *How do we calculate df for a contingency table? How many df have we in our example above?*

(2) *With $\chi^2 = 65.82$ and 2 df is the result significant? Use Table F, Appendix A to find out. Make a statement about the null hypothesis of the example after you have checked on the result in Table F.*

Entering Table F with 2 *df* we find that the value of χ^2 required for significance at the 5% level is 5.99 and at the 1% level is 9.21. The obtained χ^2 value of 65.82 is therefore highly significant. The pollster can reject the null hypothesis of independence. In other words, he would conclude that there is a relationship between the variables of political preference and attitude towards private education. Whether the respondent approves of the plan seems to be in part dependent upon his political preference. Thus, when the pollster rejects the null hypothesis of independence, he accepts the alternate hypothesis of dependence. Or, if one had stated the null hypothesis in the form of no difference between supporters of various political parties in their attitudes, then this hypothesis of no difference would have been rejected. Rather, one would conclude that Conservatives, Labour and Liberals do differ significantly in their approval of private education.

D 2 × 2 Contingency table
One of the most common uses of the χ^2 test of the independence of categorical variables is with the 2 × 2 contingency table, in which there are two variables each divided into two categories. Let us imagine our categories are, (i) smoker/non-smoker, and (ii) death through lung cancer/death not through lung cancer. The χ^2 table would be as Table 56.

STQ *It is up to you now to work out E, (O − E) and (O − E)². Does Yates' correction mean anything to you? When you have done all this calculate χ^2 and check for significance at the 0.05* *and 0.01 levels. How many degrees of freedom are you to use? What is your conclusion about the results in terms of the null hypothesis? A completed table and interpretation of results will be found below for the cowardly.*

Table 56

	Smoker	Non-smoker	Row totals	Grand total
Lung-cancer death	120	18	138	
Death through other causes	20	98	118	
Column totals	140	116		256

Table 57

	Smoker		Non-smoker		Row totals	Grand total
Lung-cancer death	120	75.5 44.5 1936	18	62.53 44.5 1936	138	
Death through other causes	20	64.53 44.5 1936	98	53.5 44.5 1936	118	
Column totals	140		116			256

χ^2 = 122.78
df = 1 (always in a 2 × 2 table!)
(Did you remember to use Yates' correction!)

The result is extremely significant well beyond the 0.01 level. Hence the null hypothesis that there is only a chance association between smoking and lung-cancer death is rejected for this sample. The two categories are not independent of each other for the sample considered.

SUMMARY OF χ^2 TEST OF INDEPENDENCE (CONTINGENCY TABLES)

(1) The null hypothesis states that the two variables are independent of each other; that is, knowledge of an individual's classification on one variable would indicate nothing of his classification on the other variable.

(2) A random sample is drawn and the subjects classified on two or more variables.

(3) A contingency table is set up with the variables indicated in the rows and columns of the table.

(4) The observed frequencies are recorded in the proper cells and the marginal totals determined.

(5) The expected frequencies are derived from the observed data themselves. The sum of the expected frequencies will equal the sum of the observed frequencies.

(6) Since the data consist of frequencies in categories, the χ^2 test of independence is the appropriate statistical test. The calculated χ^2 value is compared with the tabled value at a predetermined level of significance and with (rows − 1) (columns − 1) degrees of freedom. In a 2 × 2 table where the number of degrees of freedom is one, Yates' correction should be used in calculating χ^2.

(7) If the calculated χ^2 value equals or exceeds the tabled value, the finding is significant and the null hypothesis of independence is rejected; one concludes that the two variables are dependent or related at the given level of significance. If the calculated χ^2 value is smaller than the tabled value, the null hypothesis of independence may not be rejected; one retains the null hypothesis and concludes that there is not sufficient evidence of relationship between two variables.

E Restrictions in the use of the χ^2
(1) It is important to remember that χ^2 is most appropriate for the analysis of data that are classified as frequency of occurrence within categories (nominal data). When the data are ordinal or interval other tests of significance are usually preferred. It must be used on frequencies only, not on percentages.

(2) When nominal data are arranged into categories for a χ^2 analysis, these categories must be mutually exclusive categories, which means that each response can be classified only once. This is true because a fundamental assumption in the use of the χ^2 test is that each observation or frequency is independent of all others. Thus one could not obtain several responses or observations from the same individual and classify each as if it were independent of the others. If this is done, the same individual is placed in several categories, which inflates the size of N, and may lead to the rejection of the null hypothesis when it should not be rejected.

(3)   Another restriction in the use of the χ^2 test is that when there are multiple categories, larger samples are needed. If N is small and consequently the expected frequency in any cell is small, the sample statistic may not approximate the theoretical χ^2 distribution very closely. A rule-of-thumb which one may follow is that in a χ^2 analysis with 1 *df*, the expected frequency in all cells should at least equal or be greater than 5. When the number of degrees of freedom is greater than one, the expected frequency should be equal to or greater than 5 in at least 80% of the cells. If the data do not meet these restrictions, a useful (or a possible) remedy is to combine some of the categories so that the expected frequencies will be raised to an acceptable size. However, there must be some logical basis for the combination of categories, otherwise one is not justified in combining them and should not proceed with a χ^2 analysis.

(4)   Basically, the χ^2 test decides whether it is likely that the observed frequencies in two or more categories occurred by chance if all frequencies were the result of independent random sampling in the same population. Therefore, being sensitive to difference but not direction of difference, it is inherently two-tailed.

STQ   (1)   *Which of the following values of χ^2 is least likely to have occurred by chance?*

(a) χ^2 =   6.55   *df* = 1
(b) χ^2 = 10.50   *df* = 2
(c) χ^2 =   8.75   *df* = 3
(d) χ^2 = 12.31   *df* = 4
(e) χ^2 = 14.79   *df* = 6

   (2)   Four large department stores report the following incidences of shoplifting over a two-week period: 50, 81, 27, and 42. Perform a χ^2 test and decide whether a significant difference exists among the stores, using $p = 0.05$

_____ = χ^2

_____ = *Critical value of χ^2*

   (3)   Let us assume you are interested in the relationship between parental smoking (i.e. one or both parents smoke or neither parent smokes) and whether their children smoke when they become adults. In order to test your view you randomly select 200 adults between the ages of twenty-one and thirty and assess whether they smoke and whether their parents smoked when they were children. One variable is whether the parents

---

smoked; the second is whether the subject smokes. The hypothetical results for this experiment are presented below. Do a χ^2 test to determine whether the variables are related.

	Subject	
	Smokes	Does not smoke
One or both parents smoked	70	40
Neither parent smoked	37	53

(4) In an investigation of the relationship between attendance at college and average grade over a whole course, the following table of data was obtained:

	Grade				
Attendance	A	B	C	D	E
100% attendance	5	5	5	5	1
90–99% attendance	5	10	5	5	2
75–89% attendance	5	5	10	6	4
<75% attendance	0	3	8	9	2

What type of association between grade and frequency of attendance does the table display?

(a) strong positive
(b) weak positive
(c) no association
(d) weak negative
(e) strong negative

(5) Use the appropriate statistic and determine whether there is a significant relationship between attendance and grade in the table above.

(6) A random sample of employees was classified as shopfloor, supervisory, secretarial and management. They were asked if they would favour joining a union. The results were as follows:

	Shopfloor	Supervisory	Secretarial	Management
Yes	30	26	20	4
No	10	14	20	36

Are these response differences significant?

> **(7)**   *A sample of children were classified into those who took paper rounds out every evening and those who did not. Teacher was then asked to indicate which children had failed to hand in homework at least once during the last month.*
>
> | | Failure to hand in homework | Homework always handed in |
> |----------------|:---------------------------:|:-------------------------:|
> | Paper round | 12 | 8 |
> | No paper round | 6 | 19 |
>
> *Is this difference statistically significant?*
>
> **(8)**   *A sample of husbands and wives were asked their preference on car size and the results came out thus:*
>
> | | Small | Medium | Large |
> |----------|:-----:|:------:|:-----:|
> | Husbands | 20 | 30 | 10 |
> | Wives | 10 | 20 | 30 |
>
> *Is there an association between car size preference and the husband/wife roles?*

Answers on page 435.

EXPERIMENT EMPLOYING χ^2

The aim of the experiment was to test the null hypothesis that male drivers of private cars are not significantly different from female drivers in their response to stopping at a zebra crossing for a person waiting to cross.

The student who conducted this experiment used the references listed at the end of the experiment.

Subjects and experimenters

The subjects were private car drivers excluding 'L' drivers; 135 male and 133 female subjects were observed and there were 12 experimenters.

Method

Experimenters observed six zebra crossings at 11 a.m. and 3 p.m. on one day for half an hour each time. It was noted whether or not a driver stopped when requested to do so by a pedestrian waiting to cross. The frequency responses are recorded in Table 58.

Results

Table 58 Stopping behaviour of male and female car drivers

	Male	*Female*	*Total*
Stop	A 69	B 85	154
Non-stop	C 66	D 48	114
Total	135	133	268

Expected frequencies:

$$\text{Cell A: E} = 154 \times 135 \div 268 = 77.6$$
$$\text{Cell B: E} = 154 \times 133 \div 268 = 76.4$$
$$\text{Cell C: E} = 114 \times 135 \div 268 = 57.4$$
$$\text{Cell D: E} = 114 \times 133 \div 268 = 56.6$$

$(O - E)$: $(O - E - \frac{1}{2})$:

Cell A	$=$ -8.6	-8.1
Cell B	$=$ 8.6	8.1
Cell C	$=$ 8.6	8.1
Cell D	$=$ -8.6	-8.1

$(O - E - \frac{1}{2})^2$: $\dfrac{(O - E - \frac{1}{2})^2}{E}$:

Cell A: 8.1^2 = 65.61	$65.61 \div 77.6$ =	0.85
Cell B: 8.1^2 = 65.61	$65.61 \div 76.4$ =	0.86
Cell C: 8.1^2 = 65.61	$65.61 \div 57.4$ =	1.14
Cell D: 8.1^2 = 65.61	$65.61 \div 56.6$ =	1.16

$$\chi^2 = 0.85 + 0.86 + 1.14 + 1.16 = 4.01$$
$$df = 1$$

STQ *Using Table F, Appendix A and the 5% level of significance what may be concluded from this result?*

Exercise

Now you might like to try and repeat this experiment or a modification of it (say car drivers versus bus drivers, or car drivers with passengers versus car drivers without passengers etc). Read the references so that your report commences with a succinct review leading into your hypothesis. Conclude your report with a discussion of your results relating them where possible to previous literature and/or theory.

REFERENCES

Dean, D. G. and Valdes, D. M. (1963). *Experiment in Sociology.* (Appleton-Century-Crofts)

Divesta, F. J. (1958). Susceptibility to pressures toward uniformity of behaviour in social situations: a study of task, motivational and personality factors in conformity behaviour. *Syracuse University*

Kagan, J. and Moss, J. A. (1960). The stability of positive and dependent behaviour from childhood through adulthood.. *Child Devel.*, **31**, 577–591

Maccoby, E. (1966). *The Development of Sex Differences.* (Stanford University Press)

21

Correlation

A Introduction

You will already be familiar with the above word but we wonder if you have asked yourself 'Why not just *relation*? Why *correlation?*' Our dictionary defines 'Correlation' as:

> the mutual relation of two or more things; the act or process of showing the existence of a relationship between things.

You may note that the relationship is mutual or reciprocating and that we do not include in our concept of correlation any idea at all of the one thing being the cause and the other thing being the effect. We play safe. We merely say that we have discovered that two things are connected. Now it may well be that one thing is a cause of another but correlation does not delve thus far down on its own.

In principle, correlation is different from any of the inferential statistics you have so far studied on the course (chi square, or *t*-tests etc) because these techniques compare groups as groups, and not the individuals who compose them. Ask yourself 'What happens to the individual in chi square?' We throw him into a cell with a number of others and forget all about the individual. (Indeed we like large numbers in chi square cells in case the expected frequency is less than 5!) In *t*-tests we do not analyse the individual but only the performance of the group to which we have allocated him. *t*-Tests cannot function with only one individual making up a 'group' – we need at least two subjects and prefer far more than two.

Basically, however, all these techniques are 'difference' testings.

> Are the persons in Group A (as a group) better than those in Group B at doing something or other, etc?

We are using the razor of difference to settle a question. But in relationship testing we are examining the strength of a connection between two characteristics both belonging to the same individual, or at least two variables with a common basis to them. You will see this concept of correlation more clearly, however, after you have examined the computation technique in the following pages.

Many variables or events in nature are related to each other. As the sun sets the temperature decreases; as children increase in age their size of vocabulary also increases; persons bright in one academic area tend to be bright in other areas. These relationships are called correlations. If the river rises when it rains then the two events are said to have a positive correlation, i.e. when an increase in one variable coincides with an increase in another there exists the positive correlation. There is a negative correlation between altitude and air pressure, as an increase in altitude brings with it a decrease in pressure. In children there is a negative correlation between age and bed-wetting. A negative correlation thus occurs when an increase in one variable coincides with a decrease in another.

I have no doubt that most of you have tried to play the piano at some time. The movement of the hands over the keys also illustrates correlation. Imagine you are practising the scale of C major and both hands are commencing on C, an octave apart, to travel up the keyboard in unison. This is a positive correlation between the movements of the hands (or scores). If both my hands stay in the same position on the keyboard this is not a correlation since there is no movement (or scores) to calculate. Correlation is here a measure of mutual movement up and down a scale of scores.

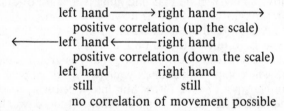

left hand ⟶ right hand ⟶
positive correlation (up the scale)
⟵ left hand ⟵ right hand
positive correlation (down the scale)
left hand   right hand
still   still
no correlation of movement possible

If you commence both hands on the same note and play the scale simultaneously in different directions, the right hand going up as the left hand travels down then there is a negative correlation.

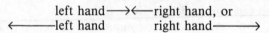

left hand ⟶⟵ right hand, or
⟵ left hand   right hand ⟶

When I play notes at random the movements of my hands on the keyboard bear no systematic relationship in direction with each other; then it is a zero correlation. But when the hands sometimes go in a systematic relationship with each other then there is calculated a modest correlation, negative or positive as the case may be. Now that we have some glimpse of what correlation is concerned with we will desert our piano practice and turn to drawing graphs.

B The correlation coefficient

The main equipment of any investigation of relationship between variables is that we should have observations arising from the same source. We can thus examine the extent to which high scores on one test are accompanied by high scores on the other test, and similarly how low scores on one test are accompanied by low scores on the other test. Every additional pair of scores provides us with more information about the extent of their relationship. Obviously if we were looking at scores obtained from different groups of children we would have no information of this kind. We could only make comparisons between overall performance among the two groups on the two tests. We would have no means of telling how performance on the two tests is related.

Given that we have data from one sample of children on two variables such as locus of control and self esteem, how can we describe the extent of their relationship? The simplest method is to plot the two sets of scores against one another in the form of a graph or scattergram. Let us consider a number of possibilities represented by Figures 27–31. Notice that each point on these graphs represents a child's score on the two variables.

In Figures 27 and 28 all the points lie on a straight line. Each score is perfectly predictable from every other score because any change in one variable is accompanied by a proportional change in the other variable. In the first case Figure 27 increases in one variable are accompanied by proportional increases in the other variable. We call this perfect positive correlation.

A numerical index called the coefficient of correlation expresses the degree or magnitude of the relationship. The numerical index $+1.0$ is the highest possible value that the correlation coefficient assumes and it indicates perfect relationship between the variables. A perfect positive relationship $(+1)$ indicates a direct relationship where each individual is as high or as low on one variable as he is on the other. In other words, each subject has the same z score on X as his z score on Y. In a perfect correlation all the dots in the scattergram can be connected with a single straight line (Figure 27). An example of a perfect positive relationship would be the heights of subjects measured in inches and the heights of these subjects measured in centimeters.

In the second case (Figure 28) increases in one variable are accompanied by proportional decreases in the other variable. We call this a perfect negative correlation. A correlation coefficient of -1.0 indicates this perfect negative relationship. This means that the two variables bear an inverse relationship to each other so that the highest z score on one variable is associated with the lowest z score on the other, and so forth. An example of a perfect negative relationship is

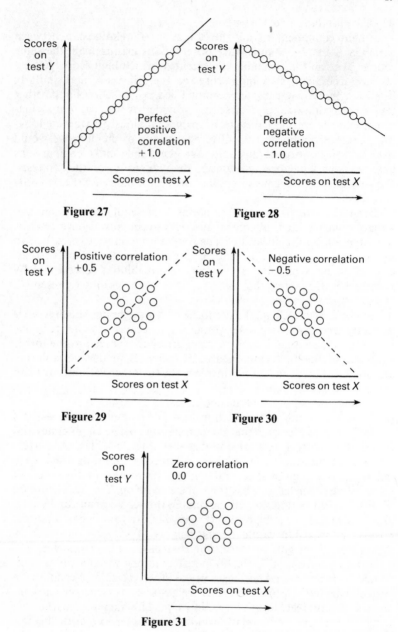

Figure 27

Figure 28

Figure 29

Figure 30

Figure 31

Figures 27–31 Scattergrams depicting various degrees of correlation

that between the volume of a gas and the pressure applied when temperature is held constant. As pressure increases the volume of the gas decreases. Perfect correlations both positive and negative are not generally found among educational, social and psychological variables.

Since perfect positive and negative correlations are unlikely to be met with in our studies the sort of picture we are most likely to find is that of Figures 29, 30 and 31. In Figures 29 and 30 the points are scattered about a straight line in a roughly elliptical shape. Although there is a tendency for pairs of scores to go together, the prediction of one score from another is no longer perfect. We describe the first diagram as showing positive correlation and the second diagram as showing negative correlation. Now finally look at Figure 31. In Figure 31 we have the situation where there is no discernible relation between the two sets of scores.

As a positive relationship between variables becomes less close, the correlation coefficient assumes a value smaller than 1.0. Students with high intelligence tend to make high grades, but there are exceptions because of several factors other than intelligence that affect school marks. Although still positive the correlation coefficient between these two variables is less than 1.0. Other variables may show a negative relationship that is less than perfect; in such cases the correlation coefficient would have a negative sign but between 0 and −1.0. A negative relationship would be expected between the number of truancies among boys and their scholastic performance, but the relationship again would certainly not be perfect. When there is no relationship between the variables, the coefficient is 0.0.

Thus a coefficient of correlation indicates both the direction and the strength of relationship between two variables. The direction of relationship is indicated by the sign of the coefficient (+ or −) and the strength of relationship is represented by the absolute size of the coefficient, that is, how far the coefficient is from 0 and how near it is to +1.0 or −1.0. Figures 27−31 provide us with the broad framework in terms of which the concept of correlation can be examined. The following is a rough but useful guide to the degree of relationship indicated by the size of the coefficients.

0.90−1.00	Very high correlation: very strong relationship.
0.70−0.90	High correlation: marked relationship.
0.40−0.70	Moderate correlation: substantial relationship.
0.20−0.40	Low correlation: a definite relationship but a small one.
less than 0.20	A slight correlation: relationship so small as to be negligible.

Be careful never to confuse negative correlation with zero correlation. The latter simply means no correlation or relationship whatever between two sets of data, whereas a negative correlation is a definite relationship, the strength of which is indicated by its size. It is absolutely necessary to place the algebraic sign (+ or −) before the numerical value of the correlation as the interpretation of the correlation is affected by its positive or negative condition.

A correlation of −1.00 is as strong as a correlation of +1.00, for the strength of a correlation is directly related to its numerical size and not to whether it is positive or negative. For example a correlation of −0.75 indicates a stronger or closer relationship than one of +0.65. A correlation coefficient is not a direct measure of the percentage of relationship between two variables. One cannot say that a correlation of 0.90 is three times as close as a relationship of +0.30, but merely that it indicates a much higher degree of relationship.

The correlation coefficient is a simple arithmetic figure which will indicate the extent to which two variables are correlated. It is a pure number that has no connection with the units in which the variables are measured. Correlations are usually expressed to two and often three places of decimals. There are a number of different correlation coefficients which can be calculated to express the strength of the relationship between two variables. The interpretation of each one rests on a particular set of assumptions which we make about the nature of the data we are dealing with. All correlation coefficients, however, share in common the property that they have limits within the range between −1 and +1.

C The calculation of the Pearson correlation coefficient

While inspection of a scattergram furnishes some visual impression of the relationship between two sets of measures for a given group, a numerical index indicating precisely the degree of relationship is much more helpful. Several correlation indices have been developed. The most widely used is an index which is employed when both variables are expressed as interval data. The use of this procedure for measuring relationships was first proposed by an English statistician, Karl Pearson. It is called the Pearson product − moment correlation coefficient. The rationale of the Pearson coefficient is most clearly shown through the concept of covariance.

1 THE CALCULATION OF A CORRELATION VIA COVARIANCE

We think of correlation as the degree to which variation in one variable corresponds to or is related to variation in another, and this leads to the idea of covariation. Now one way of 'measuring' covariation is to look at the variation in the value of each variable in terms of the differences of each value from its appropriate arithmetic mean. For each pair of values we can take $(X - M_x)$ and $(Y - M_y)$ and compare each pair of differences. This is essentially what is accomplished by a statistical measure known as the covariance — it multiplies the two differences for each point or observation, and sums the resulting 'cross-products'. The sum is then divided by the number of observations; this is necessary since the resulting statistic would otherwise depend on the number of observations rather than the degree of relationship expressed by the sum of the cross-products. The covariance, Cov, can then be written as:

$$\text{Cov} = \frac{\Sigma(X-M_x)\,(Y-M_y)}{N}$$

where N is the number of observations, M_x is the mean of the X variable and M_y is the mean of the Y variable. How does this help? As we shall see, the covariance does fulfil some of the desirable criteria for a correlation coefficient. It will have a value of zero when there is no linear relationship; it will take positive and negative values in situations where the data show evidence of corresponding to a positive or negative linear trend and covariance will increase or decrease as the strength of the relationship, or tendency to perfect linearity, increases or decreases.

Figure 32 shows a scatter diagram divided into four quadrants by axes drawn through the mean of the X variable and the mean of the Y variable. Taking quadrant I first, for any point falling in this quadrant such as (X_1, Y_1) any value Y such as Y_1, will be larger than its mean M_y so that (Y_1-M_y) is positive, any X value such as X_1 will be larger than its mean M_x, and (X_1-M_x) is positive. Thus, the product $(X-M_x)\,(Y-M_y)$ is a product of two positive quantities and so will be positive. The contribution to covariance of any pair of values in quadrant 1 such as (X_1, Y_1) will thus be positive. Similarly, the contribution to covariance of any point which falls in quadrant III will be positive because $(X-M_x)$ will be negative and also (Y_1-M_y) will be negative; the resulting product of two negative quantities will be positive. For any point which falls in quadrant II (Y_1-M_y) will be positive, (X_1-M_x) will be negative; the product of two such quantities will be negative and so will their contribution to covariance. For points falling in quadrant IV (Y_1-M_y) will be negative and (X_1-M_x) will be positive, so their product will be negative and their contribution to covariance will be negative. Figure 32 summarizes these relationships between the part of the scatter diagram in which a data point falls and whether, as a consequence, its contribution to covariance is positive or negative.

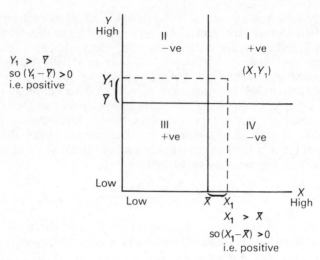

Figure 32 Positive and negative areas in a scatter graph

Thus, the cross-products contributing to covariance will vary depending upon where in the scatter diagram each point falls. As a result, different scatters will have different values of covariance.

This is what we showed earlier in Figures 27–31 with the scattergrams. For example in Figure 30 most of the points lie in the negative quadrants while in Figure 31 there is equality between all four quadrants.

But while covariance helps to explain the principle behind the correlation, it is of limited value as a measure of relationship. To begin with, its value depends on the types of units being used. Consider a set of data showing the incomes and ages of a number of individuals; with annual income and age in years we can calculate the covariance as a measure of relationship. If we changed the data to weekly income and age in years, the covariance would be much smaller; the value of the covariance changes, not because the underlying relationship between income and age has changed but simply because the numerical value of annual income is larger than the value of weekly income. In addition, the covariance has no set upper or lower values which we can use to judge the strength of a relationship.

A statistic is needed which will overcome these problems and it is given by a simple adaptation of the covariance. It is a standardization procedure. All that is done is to divide the covariance (Cov) by the product of the two standard deviations. The effect is that the resulting statistic has all the desirable characteristics of the covariance, plus the added advantages that it is unaffected by the units used and will never exceed a maximum value of $+1$ or a minimum value of -1. A value of $+1$ will be attained in the case of a perfect positive linear relationship and -1 in the case of a perfect negative linear relationship. This statistic is Pearson's product–moment correlation coefficient and is represented by r. Thus

$$r \;=\; \frac{\mathrm{Cov}}{\sigma_x \sigma_y} \;=\; \frac{\dfrac{\Sigma(X-M_x)\,(Y-M_y)}{N}}{\sigma_x \sigma_y}$$

Since it does not matter mathematically whether we divide by N first or by $\sigma_x \sigma_y$ first in the above formula we can switch the formula round and eventually form an easier formula to calculate. Here is the denominator switch:

$$r \;=\; \frac{\Sigma(X-M_x) \times (Y-M_y)}{\dfrac{\sigma_x \;\times\; \sigma_y}{N}}$$

We met z scores in an earlier chapter (Chapter 3) and if you recall the z-score formula you can now see it staring you in the face above, ($z = X-M_x)/\sigma_x$. So we can now reduce our formula further.

$$r \;=\; \frac{\Sigma(zX \times zY)}{N}$$

This is Pearson's Product–Moment Correlation for interval data.

2 THE PEARSON PRODUCT–MOMENT CORRELATION COEFFICIENT
The formula runs as follows:

The correlation coefficient ('r' for short) = The z score of each person's X performance multiplied by his z score for his Y performance. This joint-score (or cross-product score or correlated score) is taken for each individual in the group, then all are added together, and finally averaged by dividing by the number of people in the group. In mathematical language it is:

$$r_{xy} \;=\; \frac{\Sigma(zX \times zY)}{N}$$

Example 1

Original mark	List of z scores for X	Products of z scores of X and Y	List of z scores of Y	Original mark
X	zX	zX × zY	zY	Y
16	1.5	2.25	1.5	16
14	1.0	1.00	1.0	14
12	0.5	0.25	0.5	12
10	0	0	0	10
8	−0.5	0.25	−0.5	8
6	−1.0	1.00	−1.0	6
4	−1.5	2.25	−1.5	4
M = 10	Sum of products = 7.00			M = 10
σ = 4	Average product = $\frac{7.00}{7.00}$ r_{xy} = + 1.00			σ = 4

Now, as you can see, the scores for test X and those for test Y varied systematically to the highest degree, that is, each person did precisely as well or as badly, on Y as on X, and so the 'r' coefficient came out as + 1.0 (the highest possible). With this degree of correlation one could have predicted a subject's score on X from his score on Y and saved oneself the trouble of testing him on X, or vice versa.

Let us look closely at the middle column in the above example – the products of zX scores and zY scores. Some people score a lot in this column and some score little – one subject scores zero. In other words these subjects are each contributing quite different amounts to the sum of the cross-products, that is to the numerator in the formula (which was $\Sigma(zX \times zY)$). Why should they so differ in their contributions when they all duplicate exactly their score on X and Y? Each person did precisely as well or as badly. The reason is seen in their z score on X or on Y. Those people who had large z scores, that is, those people who were most different from their average colleagues, and who were consistently different (on Y as well as on X) contributed a high XY score in the middle column. (If you bet that you can pick the winner in both horse races you should be promised more winnings than if you bet only that you can pick the winner in one race, quite divorced from your ability to do so in any other). In placing 'a doubles' bet with the bookmaker (and I hope you never will for it is a tricky thing to pull off) you are claiming the ability to judge horse variations systematically. Next, let us look at the average man in the street – the scorer on the mean, here equalling 10. Now he contributes nothing to the pool because he does not vary one way or another, neither negatively or positively, so he contributes zero, even though he is consistent in his non-variance. He is a little like the two hands on the piano keyboard which never move up or down the keyboard.

In real life one rarely finds a group where everyone duplicates his score exactly and Example 2 is one of a modest or moderate correlation ($r = +0.46$). While this z score interpretation facilitates our understanding of the concept of correlation, the definitional formula using z scores is not recommended for computational purposes, especially if the number of cases is large. It is too laborious and time-consuming, because each score in the pair of measures must be converted to a z score which, of course, requires prior computation of the mean and standard deviation of each distribution.

Example 2

Mark	z Scores	Product of z scores	z Scores	Mark
X	zX	zX zY	zY	Y
16	1.5	0.75	0.5	12
14	1.0	−0.50	−0.5	8
12	0.5	0.75	1.5	16
10	0	0	1.0	14
8	−0.5	0.75	−1.5	4
6	−1.0	0	0	10
4	−1.5	1.50	−1.0	6

$M = 10$ Sum of $zX\ zY = 3.75 - 0.50$ $M = 10$
$\sigma = 4$ $= 3.25$ $\sigma = 4$

Average product $= \dfrac{3.25}{7} \backsimeq +0.46 = r$

Other formulas have been derived from the basic definitional formula. One of the most convenient allows us to work directly with the original raw scores without the necessity of finding the means and standard deviations.

$$r_{xy} = \frac{N\Sigma XY - (\Sigma X)(\Sigma Y)}{\sqrt{[N\Sigma X^2 - (\Sigma X)^2][N\Sigma Y^2 - (\Sigma Y)^2]}}$$

where:
ΣY	=	sum of the raw X scores
ΣY	=	sum of the raw Y scores
ΣXY	=	sum of the products of each X times each Y
ΣX^2	=	sum of the squares of each X score
ΣY^2	=	sum of the squares of each Y score
$(\Sigma X)^2$	=	the square of the total sum of X scores
$(\Sigma Y)^2$	=	the square of the total sum of Y scores
N	=	the number of paired scores

Table 58 illustrates the computation of the correlation coefficient using this raw score formula.

Table 58 Computation of the correlation coefficient using raw scores

X	Y	XY	X^2	Y^2
8	6	48	64	36
20	14	280	400	196
26	10	260	676	100
17	8	136	289	64
14	2	28	196	4
Σ 85	40	752	1625	400

$$
\begin{array}{ll}
\Sigma X = 85 & \Sigma Y = 40 \\
\Sigma XY = 752 & \Sigma X^2 = 1625 \\
\Sigma Y^2 = 400 & (\Sigma X)^2 = 7225 \\
(\Sigma Y)^2 = 1600 & N = 5
\end{array}
$$

$$
r_{xy} = \frac{5 \times 752 - (85 \times 40)}{\sqrt{[5 \times 1625 - 7225][5 \times 400 - 1600]}}
$$

$$
= \frac{3760 - 3400}{\sqrt{900 \times 400}}
$$

$$
= \frac{360}{\sqrt{360\,000}} = \frac{360}{600}
$$

$$
r_{xy} = +0.60
$$

D Rank order correlation (Spearman)

This correlation is typically used when there are only a few cases (or subjects) involved and the data are ranked or can be ranked. There is no assumption that ranks are based on equal-interval measures, or that there is any measurement involved. The ranks are merely an indication that this person is first in this attribute or test, this person second, and so on. This correlation is usually designated as '*rho*' to distinguish it from Pearson's '*r*',

> **STQ** *What level of measurement is rho used on?*

The formula for '*rho*' is:

$$rho = 1 - \frac{6\Sigma d^2}{N(N^2-1)}$$

where d is the difference between ranks for each pair of observations, and N is the number of pairs of observations. For example if a subject is ranked first on one measure but only fifth on another $d = 1 - 5 = 4$ and $d^2 = 16$.

Rank order correlation has the same range as outlined earlier *viz.* it ranges from $+1$ to -1. It is very simple to use but always remember to convert data into rank order. It also demonstrates very clearly the effect of changes in covariation between the two sets of data. Look at the three following examples.

(i)

X	Y	d	d²
1	1	—	—
2	2	—	—
3	3	—	—
4	4	—	—
5	5	—	—
			$\Sigma 0$

$$rho = 1 - \frac{6 \times 0}{5 \times 24} = 1 - 0 = +1$$

i.e. perfect agreement in ranks

(ii)

X	Y	d	d²
1	5	−4	16
2	4	−2	4
3	3	0	0
4	2	2	4
5	1	4	16
			$\Sigma 40$

$$rho = 1 - \frac{6 \times 40}{5 \times 24} = 1 - \frac{240}{120}$$
$$= 1 - 2 = -1$$

i.e. perfect inverse relationship.

(iii)

X	Y	d	d^2
1	1	0	0
3	2	1	1
5	3	2	4
4	4	0	0
2	5	−3	9
			14

$$rho = 1 - \frac{6 \times 14}{5 \times 24} = 1 - \frac{84}{120}$$

$$= 1 - 0.7 = + 0.3$$

i.e. a low positive relationship.

> **STQ** *Now you try switching the ranks around and notice how the correlation changes. The combination of the resulting r with the visual impression of the rankings will bring home to you, if you do not fully comprehend already, what correlation implies.*

Here is a research example. We hypothesized that there would be a relationship between the order (or sequence) in which students signed up for a psychological experiment and their scores on an experimental task. Table 59 shows a hypothetical set of scores, designed to test this hypothesis.

Table 59 Rank order correlation example

(a) Sign-up order	(b) Score on experimental task	(c) Rank order on experimental task	(d) d (c−a)	(e) d^2
1	20	1	0	0
2	24	3	1	1
3	23	2	1	1
4	25	4	0	0
5	29	7.5	2.5	6.25
6	28	6	0	0
7	30	9	2	4
8	32	10	2	4
9	27	5	4	16
10	29	7.5	2.5	6.25
				$\Sigma = 38.5$

The order in which the students register for the experiment (column (a)) serves as one set of rankings. The test scores need to be ranked, however. The lowest score will be assigned the rank of 1, the next lowest a score of 2, etc., as has been done in column (c) of the data. Where two or more subjects have the same score the rank is calculated by averaging the ranks those subjects cover. In our example above two candidates obtained 29. They were in seventh equal position, i.e. covering ranks 7 and 8. Hence they are both ranked as 7.5.

Column (d) is the difference between the rankings in column (a) and (c) irrespective of + or − signs, since squaring them in column (e) eliminates the negative numbers.

Using the sum of column (e), the rank-order correlation can be determined as follows:

$$rho = 1 - \frac{6 \times 38.5}{10 \times 99} = 1 - \frac{231.0}{990}$$
$$= 1 - 0.23 = +0.77$$

i.e. there is a strong relationship between the two rankings. A further example is shown in Table 60.

Table 60 The scores of thirteen boys on two variables − verbal fluency and desired age of leaving school

Boy	Desired school leaving age X	Verbal fluency Y	Rank X	Rank Y	d	d^2
1	15	6	9	6.5	2.5	6.25
2	16	8	4.5	3.5	1	1
3	15	10	9	1	8	64
4	15	4	9	11	2	4
5	17	7	2.5	5	2.5	6.25
6	15	8	9	3.5	5.5	30.25
7	15	6	9	6.5	2.5	6.25
8	18	5	1	8.5	7.5	56.25
9	15	4	9	11	2	4
10	15	9	9	2	7	49
11	16	4	4.5	11	6.5	42.25
12	17	5	2.5	8.5	6	36
13	14	2	13	13	0	0
						$\Sigma d^2 = 305.5$

You can see from the columns X and Y again how we deal with the problem of 'tied ranks'. On verbal fluency Y for example, two boys obtained a score of 8. These scores take up the ranks 3 and 4 in the class, and so that all ranks $1-13$ will finally be taken up we assign the average of these two ranks to each boy, i.e. 3.5. Similarly seven boys had the score of 15 on the desired age of leaving school variable. These take up the ranks of $6-12$ in the class so we assign the average rank of

9 to each of them. Having converted each boy's score into a rank we subtract one rank from another (ignoring the sign) to give the values in Table 60 column (d). We then square each of the d values and add them together (Σd^2). We can now substitute values into our formula for *rho*

$$rho = 1 - \frac{6 \times 305.5}{13 \times 168}$$
$$= +0.16$$

This suggests barely any relation between these two variables in this sample of boys. That is to say 'verbal fluency' and 'desired age of leaving school' show only a small positive correlation with each other.

While *rho* is only suitable for ranked (or ordinal) data, you will have realized from the above example that interval data can be used provided it is first ranked. However, *rho* will always provide a lower estimate of correlation than r because the data is degraded, i.e. *rho* throws away information in changing interval data into ranks.

EXPERIMENT USING SPEARMAN'S RANK ORDER CORRELATION
A student had become interested in experimental aesthetics and had read extracts from the references concluding this section.

Aim of experiment and background
Relevant information was extracted from the reference and this form- ed the research background for the experiment. At the end of this sec- tion the student stated his aim: to determine whether there would be a relationship between perceived complexity and degree of interesting- ness in visual material. For this purpose it was considered that irregular objects and objects which contain more stimulus elements are thought to be more complex than regular objects or objects which have fewer stimulus elements.

> **STQ**   *Could you convert this into a null hypothesis?*

Conditions
The experiment took place in a classroom situation.

Subjects and experiments
There were ten subjects, these being equal numbers of males and females. All subjects were students studying for a psychology examin- ation.

> **STQ**   *What kind of sample was this?*

Apparatus

The apparatus consisted of twelve cards (shown at the end of the experiment as Figure 33). Each card had a letter of the alphabet on the reverse side (i.e. A—L).

Method

The cards were randomized by shuffling and then placed in a pile. The subject entered the room and sat down at a table. He was given the pile of cards and then instructed to look carefully at them, arranging them in order of complexity with the most complex card on the top of the pile. The same procedure was adopted for the 'interestingness' condition.

STQ *How would you word these instructions? Start off by saying: 'I would like you to take these cards . . .'.*

When each subject had completed the experiment, the experimenter recorded the rank for each card. The data for every subject were combined and a final ranking for each card was obtained in both conditions. This is shown in the Results section below.

Results

Table 61 Responses in complexity condition

Rank	Subjects									
	1	2	3	4	5	6	7	8	9	10
1	K	D	K	K	A	K	K	K	D	D
2	A	A	D	D	K	D	A	A	A	K
3	D	K	A	A	D	I	D	I	K	A
4	I	H	I	I	B	A	I	D	G	I
5	G	G	G	L	I	F	G	G	J	B
6	J	I	B	G	H	G	B	J	F	J
7	B	J	L	H	F	H	F	H	B	G
8	F	F	F	J	I	L	L	F	H	L
9	H	C	J	F	G	B	H	B	I	H
10	C	E	H	B	C	J	J	L	L	F
11	E	L	C	C	L	C	C	E	C	C
12	L	B	E	E	E	E	E	C	E	E

To obtain the final ranking for each card, the sum of ranks for each letter in turn was calculated. For instance, take the letter 'A' in Table 1. It is ranked first on one occasion, second on five occasions etc. So we have:

$$1/2\ 2\ 2\ 2\ 2/3\ 3\ 3/4 = 24$$

You will notice that this total appears opposite the letter 'A' in Table 63. The experimenter completed Table 63 for all the letters. See if you agree with his results. He then ranked these totals.

Table 62 Responses in 'interestingness' condition

Rank	Subjects									
	1	2	3	4	5	6	7	8	9	10
1	A	I	I	A	A	D	E	K	K	B
2	K	A	A	L	J	A	D	A	A	I
3	D	K	D	K	I	K	A	I	D	D
4	H	G	K	H	D	I	K	H	G	L
5	L	H	G	F	E	H	I	J	J	A
6	I	J	F	I	C	G	H	G	I	K
7	E	F	H	C	K	L	B	D	F	F
8	F	D	J	D	F	B	F	E	H	J
9	G	C	C	E	B	F	J	C	B	H
10	J	E	E	B	G	J	C	L	C	G
11	B	B	L	J	H	C	G	F	L	E
12	C	L	B	G	L	E	L	B	E	C

STQ *Work out the final rankings for each of the cards in the 'interesting' condition in the same way. Do yours agree with those in Table 64?*

Table 63 Rank order of cards in complexity condition

Card	Total	Rank
A	24	3
B	75	6.5
C	107	11
D	22	2
E	116	12
F	76	8.5
G	57	5
H	76	8.5
I	46	4
J	75	6.5
K	16	1
L	90	10

Table 64 Rank order of cards in 'interestingness' condition

Card	Total	Rank
A	21	1
B	90	11
C	95	12
D	42	4
E	85	9
F	76	7
G	77	8
H	63	5
I	37	3
J	74	6
K	34	2
L	86	10

TREATMENT OF RESULTS

The experimenter applied the Spearman rank order correlation procedure to the results:

X Comp.	Y Int.	d Diff.	d^2 Diff. squared
3	1	2	4
6.5	11	4.5	20.25
11	12	1	1
2	4	2	4
12	9	3	9
8.5	7	1.5	2.25
5	8	3	9
8.5	5	3.5	12.25
4	3	1	1
6.5	6	0.5	0.25
1	2	1	1
10	10	0	0
			$\Sigma d^2 = 64$

$$p = 1 - \frac{6 \times \Sigma d^2}{N(N^2 - 1)}$$

$$p = 1 - \frac{6 \times 64}{12 \times 143} = \frac{384}{17.6}$$

$$p = +0.78$$

Now it is your turn to carry out this experiment and write it up in report form. Read as many of the references below as you can then write a review of them as the major part of the background section. You will need to conclude your report with a discussion of your results.

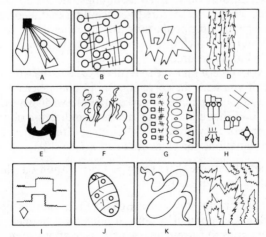

Figure 33 Stimulus cards

REFERENCES

Berlyne, D. E. (1971). *'Aesthetics and Psychobiology'* (New York: Appleton Century Croft)

Berlyne, D. E. (1972). Reinforcement values of visual patters through concurrent performance. *J. Exp. Anal. Behav.* **18**, 281–285

Berlyne, D. E. and Boudewijns, W. J. (1971). Hedonic effects of uniformity in variety. *Can. J. Psychol.*, **25**, 195–206

Berlyne, D. E., Ogilvie, J. C. and Parham, L. C. C. (1968). The dimensionality of visual complexity, interestingness and pleasingness. *Can. J. Psychol.*, **22**, 376–387

E   Statistical significance of correlation coefficients

> **STQ**   *You have met statistical significance several times now. Can you state what we mean by statistical significance?*

We take it to mean that a statistic has occurred at a chance probability level which is so low as to suggest that the result is due to the experimental manipulation.

Let us imagine that you have followed the tortuous path of correlation without getting lost and are now the proud owner of a shiny new correlation coefficient of $r = +0.69$ between extraversion and social popularity – at least among the 50 students you managed to test at your school or college. Wonderful, but then what?

You have demonstrated a correlation that pertains to 50 people, 50 pairs of observations, only. Even assuming that the 50 chosen were typical people, can we feel secure in concluding that a correlation between extraversion and popularity exists in general? If only because you are well inured to such questions by this time, you will allow that we cannot feel at all secure.

After all, you did not manage to test everyone in the world; it is conceivable that if you had, the correlation might have been 0. Accidents do happen, and the 50 people observed might have displayed their correlation as a long-shot coincidence, not as an indication of any general rule. In other words, you have a choice: you must pick one of the following explanations for your obtained *r*.

(a)   It happened because there really is a correlation out there, and it showed up in your sample.

(b)   There really is not any general overall relationship between extraversion and popularity, but accidents do happen, especially when one tries to formulate a general rule about some 50 million people (with more to follow!) on the basis of only 50.

Can we ever conclude that our obtained (sample) r does reflect a population correlation?

An affirmative answer, which we would certainly enjoy having, depends upon two factors, (a) the size of the correlation coefficient obtained in the sample, and (b) the size of the sample. We must also (as always) be able to assume, with some good reason, that the sample is a random one.

The need for these two factors should be clear. If a correlation coefficient is small, it could be merely an accident of sampling, and such an accident will be relatively likely if the sample is small. If either the correlation coefficient or the sample is very large, the probability of such an accident is reduced.

In line with this principle we need to interpret any correlation coefficients we obtain. What we must ask is could a correlation of the size we have obtained come from this sample even if the population correlation coefficient were zero? Our r of course is a statistic and is our only estimate of the population r. We would expect that random samples of the population would produce a range of r values because of sampling error. This is the same argument we used when discussing the significance of mean differences using the t test, and when considering standard error. Our r is thus only one of many possible estimates. Theoretically all these r values derived from random samples of the same population will distribute themselves 'normally' round the mean of 0. If this argument is still a closed book to you consider the result of drawing 30 pairs of numbers from a random number table. The r should be zero or close to it, but if we do this task many times on occasions an r that is quite high will emerge by chance. Coefficients of correlation, as well as means and differences, have to be weighed in the balance by stacking them up against their standard errors. Fortunately, this is easy to do since tables of r values for different levels of significance and for different size samples are given in most statistics texts as in this book (Table I Appendix A). Thus, with r values it is not necessary to compute and use the standard error of an r. The reasoning behind the tables has to be understood, however. For *rho* use Table H Appendix A.

The statistical significance of r depends on sample size (i.e. N). For example, in order to be statistically significant, a coefficient of correlation computed between 30 pairs of measures has to be approximately 0.36 to be significant at the 0.05 level and approximately 0.46 at the 0.01 level. With about 100 pairs of measures the problem is less acute (the law of large numbers again). To carry the 0.05 day, an r of about 0.20 is sufficient; to carry the 0.01 day, an r of about 0.25 does it. If r values are less than these levels, they are considered to be not significant.

By using very large samples even a low r or rho becomes significant. Many of the correlations between personality factors and academic performance are in the order of 0.2 and 0.3. This means that they predict only up to 9% of the common variance. However, such correlations are significant because samples have often been numbered in thousands, e.g. Entwistle (1972).

Now in any population of X and Y scores, there is always some degree of relationship between X and Y, even if the relationship is 0. And for every population correlation coefficient, there will be a range of sample correlation coefficients, which will fall into a sampling distribution. The shape of this distribution is approximately normal only when the population correlation coefficient is 0. When the population coefficient is other than 0, the sampling distribution is skewed. Usually though, it is the null hypothesis that $r = 0$ that we would like to reject. So, for any obtained sample value of r, we can ask, 'Assuming that population $r = 0$, what is the probability that this sample r came from the sampling distribution?' If the probability is too small, less than 5% or 1%, we reject the null hypothesis and adopt instead the hypothesis that the population itself contains a correlation between X and Y. Table I Appendix A shows that the critical value of r, whether for the 1% or 5% level, is related to the size of sample. It is not possible to interpret any correlation coefficient unless the value of n is known.

Compare your obtained value of r with the proper critical value in the table; if the obtained coefficient equals or exceeds the tabled value, the null hypothesis may be rejected at the level of risk chosen. We will do this for your hypothetical result, in which $n = 50$ and $r = +0.69$. We find in Table I that a relationship that strong (or stronger) will occur less than 1% of the time if H_0 is true, the critical value of r being 0.361; far less than ours of 0.69. So you can generalize that extraversion and popularity are related – to some unknown extent – in the population. It is not possible, however, to use this procedure to infer the strength of the population correlation; you can merely infer its existence (always with not-quite-absolute certainty).

As well as discerning whether an obtained correlation is significant or not it is possible to define the strength of a relationship in a more precise way. The square of the correlation coefficient between X and Y gives the proportion of variance in Y which is predictable from variance in X. Similary $1 - r_{xy}^2$ gives the proportion of variance in Y which is not predictable from variance in X. Another way of expressing this is to say that we can 'partition' the variance of Y into two component parts – that predictable from X and that not predictable from X.

Now let us bring the algebra to life by looking at a few examples.

Let us imagine that we found a correlation of $+0.73$ between WISC scores and EPV scores. This means that $(0.73)^2 = 0.53$, or 53% of the variance in the WISC scores is predictable from the variance in the EPV scores. Similarly if we find an estimated correlation of $+0.16$ between desired age for leaving school and verbal fluency. This means that if we designate the former variable as dependent and the latter variable as independent, only $(+0.16)^2 = 0.03$ or 3% of the variance in desired age of leaving school is predicted from verbal fluency.

You can now see that we can use the product moment correlation coefficient r to interpret the strength of relationship between two variables in a much more precise way. We·can define the strength of relationship as the proportion of variance in one variable which is predictable from variance in the other. We can go further and say now that a correlation of 0.71 is twice as strong as a correlation of 0.50 in the sense that the former correlation predicts twice the amount of the variance in a dependent variable than is predictable by the latter.

The variance interpretation of correlation emphasizes the point that even with strongly correlated measures a substantial amount of variance in the dependent variable remains unaccounted for. It is as well to bear this in mind when looking at correlations reported in research. Many researchers set their sights at finding statistically significant correlations which simply means that the correlation is unlikely to have occurred by chance. When they come to draw causal inferences from their findings, however, the amount of variance they have actually explained by a significant correlation is very small indeed.

Take for example Entwistle's correlations between a number of personality characteristics and academic performance in higher education (Entwistle, 1972). The two largest correlations are -0.41 for 'neuroticism' among women students in polytechnics and 0.39 for A-level grades among female students at colleges of education. It is notable that in the former case only $(0.41)^2 = 17\%$ of the variance in academic performance is explained by neuroticism and in the latter case 15%. Yet such correlations are significant because N is large. Personality factors are here explaining only a small part of the variance in academic performance.

Of course there is a difference between statistically significant results and psychologically significant ones. By 'psychologically significant' is meant results that substantially increase our understanding of, and our ability to account for, individual differences. Since in Entwistle's study only 17% of the variance in achievement is accounted for by neuroticism, we have not made a great deal of progress. Despite its significance at the 5% level, i.e. such relationships would arise by chance in only 5% of samples. It has been said that it is inappropriate to bother with *r*s of 0.10, 0.20, and 0.30. With *r*s of about 0.10 or less, this point is well taken. But with *r*s of about 0.30, the point is not well taken. If an *r* of 0.30 is statistically significant, it may help the investigator later to find an important relationship – if he can clear up, say, his measurement problems. That is, he might, by dropping a statistically significant *r* of 0.30, be losing a valuable lead for theory and subsequent research.

An example may help to drive this point home. Sears, Maccoby, and Levin (1957) in their large study of child-rearing practices, report a large number of relations, some of them in coefficient of correlation form. Most of these *r* values are quite small, sometimes so small that one wonders whether they are 'psychologically significant'. Sears and his colleagues were measuring very complex variables and their measures were relatively crude (but not inept – quite the contrary). They report, for instance, the correlation between an accepting, tolerant attitude toward the child's dependent behaviour and being warm toward the child: 0.37. This *r* is not high, true. But since it is based presumably on an *N* of 379, it is statistically significant. Also, it reflects, very probably, an important relation. Other significant, but low, relations reported are between tolerant attitude toward dependent behaviour and gentleness in toilet training (0.30); low physical punishment (0.30); high in esteem for self (0.39); and high in esteem for husband (0.32). Such relations, though low, are the makings of important research findings and theory building.

Rokeach (1960) reports a number of important relations, among which the following are interesting because they were computed from samples with very low numbers in each sample. The correlation between Dogmatism and Opinionation (interpreting these terms with their usual meanings will not be too misleading for the present purpose) is 0.66. Since $n = 13$, this is significant at the 0.05 level but not quite significant at the 0.01 level. The correlation between Authoritarianism and Ethnocentrism is 0.46. But since $n = 10$, this *r* is not significant at the 0.05 level. These examples illustrate two points. One, tests of the significance of *r* values are essential to adequate interpretation of computed relations. Two, working with samples that are too small can be dangerous. Small samples yield relatively large standard errors.

F   Problems and errors in interpreting a correlation coefficient

There are a number of problems and likely errors which must be avoided if the interpretation of the correlation is to be meaningful. When interpreting a correlation coefficient one should always consider the nature of the population in which the two variables were observed. The correlation coefficient observed between two variables will vary from one population to another because, (a) the basic relationship is different in different populations, or (b) the variability in the populations differs, or (c) the correlation of the two variables is influenced by their relationship with a third variable. We will examine these three issues more closely.

(a) The inherent relationship of variables may differ from population to population. Among humans between the ages of 10 and 16 physical prowess and chronological age are highly correlated. Among humans between the ages of 20 and 26 these two variables are not correlated. Among children the variables mental age and chronological age are positively correlated, among the middle-aged there is no correlation between these two variables: among the elderly they are somewhat negatively correlated.

(b) When a population is heterogeneous in the variables of concern we expect to observe a higher correlation than when a population is homogeneous in these variables. For example, in a general population of male college students we expect a positive correlation between height and success in basketball because the taller boys will tend to do better at the game. In a professional basketball team we would not expect such a relationship. The members of a professional team are all tall and all very good at the game. In a group that is very homogeneous we would not observe the correlation that exists in the population at large. A test of manual dexterity may be highly correlated with machinist skills in the general population but among veteran machinists we would find little correlation between the two variables as the veteran machinists are all highly skilled at their trade. This restriction in the sample is termed attenuation. A sample of university students would provide a very attenuated sample of IQ since they would all tend to have well above average IQs. A correlation of their IQs with their academic performance would produce a low positive correlation. Yet throughout the whole population there is a high correlation since the whole range of IQ and performance levels are being employed.

(c) We may find a correlation between two variables not because there is an intrinsic relationship between these variables but because they are both related to a third variable. We may note rather frequently in Britain the high positive correlation between the wearing of raincoats and the raising of umbrellas. One obviously does not cause the other; the cause is a third variable – inclement weather. This leads on to a fourth problem hinted at in the introduction, that of falling into the seductive trap of assigning causality, i.e. that one variable causes the other.

(d) Causality. Examine these persuasive communications:

   (i)   'Buy an Apex Typewriter. Studies have proved that a relationship exists between typewriter use and essay marks. Get a typewriter now, and improve your marks.'
   (ii) 'The most desirable and sought-after men and women use "The Magic Look" electric hairbrush. It's the easy way to keep hair looking great. Buy a "Magic Look" here and become more popular.'
   (iii) 'Brown, your grades were failing at Christmas. Now I don't think you've been applying yourself, have you? The most successful students study at least nine hours a day. Now, if you apply yourself to your studies, I'm sure you will do much better by the end of the school year!'

Can you detect the flaws in these arguments? In each case, there may be an undisputed fact of the relationships implied. Typewritten essays do tend to get better grades. Electric hairbrushes may be used most by the most popular people. Successful students often do study long hours. The flaws are not in the facts, but in the inferences of causation. Mere correlation does not imply causation. Good students may be the ones who buy most of the typewriters, but they would do well anyway. People who are very popular (for whatever reasons) may have more preoccupation with their appearance, and maybe more to lose; popularity is more likely to be an indirect cause of use of electric hairbrushes than an effect of it. The failing student may be stupid, or badly taught, or in the wrong kind of school, rather then lazy; a lot of study is done by bright students, but study is not the only requirement for good grades.

   Illegitimate inferences of causation are often very subtle; they also become socially important when, for example, a high correlation is noted between poverty and delinquency of behaviour. If the conclusion is drawn that poor people naturally tend toward delinquency (and it often has been drawn), the mere existence of the correlation does not support that conclusion. Many other possible explanations besides poverty could be found for delinquent behaviour.

When there is a high correlation between two variables it is possible to predict the values of one variable from those of the other. If there is a high positive correlation between seaside drownings and the sale of theatre tickets for the Pier Pavilion we can predict that if ticket sales increase, so too will the number of drowning accidents. But while we can predict the likely occurrence of one event from another event we cannot say that one event is the cause of the other. This statement cannot be over-emphasized, so easy is it to assume that two correlated conditions are causally related. Look back at our seaside drama. It is fairly obvious that drownings do not increase the sale of tickets nor vice versa (unless the acts are so poor the patrons prefer to commit suicide by throwing themselves into the sea!). A third variable, such as holiday activities, heat waves encouraging more seaside trips etc. are behind the relationship.

(e) A final source of erroneous thinking about correlations lies in the fact that since correlations are only a mathematical index and therefore can be calculated between any two sets of data, it is apparent that some very high correlations, while mathematically correct, are in reality meaningless. It is easy to calculate correlations between trade statistics and survey data in which, for example, there may be a very high positive correlation between the increase in church attendance and the increase in attendance at 'blue film' cinemas in an area of rapid population growth over the last ten years, or between the increase in the import of bananas and increase in the divorce rate over a twenty-year period, but it would take an unusual theory (or a rather warped mind) to relate either of these two in a causal manner!

An important point emerges from the foregoing. Anyone who knows how can go through the motions of determining correlation coefficients and getting arithmetically correct results. However, it need not follow that such results have any meaning, or the meaning imputed to them. Besides knowing the mathematical drill, the user (and consumer-critic) of statistics must know when (and when not) to use statistical procedures. Mathematical ability is not a substitute for wisdom.

STQ **(1)** *Write true or false for the following statements.*

(a) *A coefficient of correlation indicates both the direction and the extent of relationship between two variables.*

 (b) *The sign of the coefficient indicates the extent of relationship.*
 (c) *The direction of the relationship is indicated by the absolute size of the coefficient.*
 (d) *The extent of relationship is dependent on the sign of the correlation coefficient.*

  (2) *Which one of the following best describes the relationship between X and Y shown in the scattergram below?*

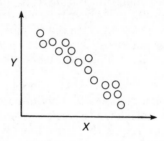

 (a) *high positive correlation*
 (b) *zero correlation*
 (c) *low negative correlation*
 (d) *high negative correlation*
 (e) *low positive correlation*

  (3) *Would you expect the correlation between the following variables to be, (i) positive, (ii) negative, (iii) near zero?*

 (a) *The IQs of siblings.*
 (b) *The chronological age and height in primary school children.*
 (c) *Chronological age and IQ.*
 (d) *Grades in chemistry and art.*
 (e) *Extent of fatigue and performance on a speed test.*
 (f) *Horsepower of car and miles per gallon.*

  (4) *Which correlation coefficient represents the strongest relationship between two variables?*

 (a) *0.0*
 (b) *−0.80*
 (c) *+0.60*

---

(5) *A researcher reported the correlation coefficient between two variables to be 1.55. How would you interpret this finding?*

(6) *Listed below is a pair of test scores. Use the Pearson formula to compute the correlation.*

Test A	Test B
4	7
3	8
5	2
7	5
6	4
9	10
7	5
6	3

(7) *Find rho for the following:*

Score A	Score B
12	6
10	9
2	8
7	2
40	12
8	5

(8) *In an investigation to discover whether the pretty girls are the ones who get the best marks at college, a panel of judges rank order the female students for attractiveness, and continuous assessment marks were obtained. What statistical test should be used to analyse the data?*

Answers are to be found on p. 435.

REFERENCES

Entwistle, N. J. (1972). Personality and academic attainment. *Br. J. Educ. Psychol.* **42,** 137–51

Rokeach, M. (1960). *The Open and Closed Mind.* (New York: Basic Books)

Sears, R., Maccaby, E. and Levin, H. (1957). *Patterns of Child Rearing.* (Evanston: Row Petersen)

22

One-way analysis of variance

A Introduction
We introduced the *t*-test in Chapter 15 as a technique for testing the significance of the difference between means of two random samples.

STQ *Can you remember the basic idea behind the t test?*

Hopefully you have remembered that the *t*-test is a critical ratio to evaluate whether an observed difference between means is greater than that to be expected on the basis of random error. Often we are concerned with more than two samples, groups, or levels of the *IV*. The appropriate technique with three or more levels is analysis of variance (ANOVA).

ANOVA is not just another statistic; it is a method or an approach to data analysis. Modern statistical methods culminate in ANOVA and factor analysis.

In ANOVA the approach is conceptually similar to the *t*-test, although the method differs. The method of analysis of variance uses variances entirely, instead of using actual differences and standard errors, even though the actual difference to standard error ratio reasoning is behind the method. Two variances are always pitted against each other. One variance, that presumably due to the experimental (independent) variable or variables is pitted against another variance, that presumably due to error or randomness. This is a case, again, of information versus error, or, as information theorists say, information versus noise.

In a typical one-way analysis of variance, subjects are randomly assigned to a number of experimental groups, with a different level of the *IV* applied to each group. A measure of the *DV* is obtained for every member of each group and from these measures the means of each group are calculated. If the manipulation of the *IV* has had no differential effect on the *DV* then the sample means should be approximately the same. The experimental treatment has had no effect; this is the null hypothesis. ANOVA is simply a test of the null hypothesis which states that samples are independent random samples drawn from the same population.

By now you are well aware that even in the absence of any effect from the *IV* there will be some random fluctuation in sample means. If the *IV* has had any effect then the variation will be significantly greater than that to be expected from random fluctuation and only if this can be shown to be so can the null hypothesis be rejected.

B Variance. What is it?

The variance of a set of scores has important uses in data analysis. It is most simple to see it as describing the amount of variation in a set of scores. Much of data analysis is concerned with analysing such variation with a view to finding out why it has occurred. 'Why do some children do well at school and others badly?' for example. We often want to know whether variation in such a variable as locus of control can be attributed to variation in another variable such as age, or whether the two are unrelated. And we define this variation in terms of variances. We state our research problem as one of determining how much variance in locus of control can be attributed to variance in age.

The variance is a measure of the dispersion of the set of scores. It tells us how much the scores are spread out. If a group of subjects is very heterogeneous in degree of authoritarianism, then the variance of their authoritarianism scores will be large compared with the variance of a group that is homogeneous in degree of authoritarianism. The variance, then, is a measure of the spread of the scores; it is a description of the extent to which the scores differ from each other. To measure this, it is convenient to have a reference point. The mean is that reference point. Once we know the mean we can find the difference between each raw score and the mean, and then add up all these difference scores. (We did this in Chapter 2)

However, the sum of the deviations from the mean is not a suitable measure of variability (i.e. the extent to which scores differ or fluctuate) because it will always be zero; the sum of the positive deviations is always equal to the sum of the negative deviations. The problem could be 'solved' by ignoring the minus sign and adding all the deviations regardless of sign. Although this procedure would yield a measure of variability, there are statistical and practical reasons for not using such an index.

> **STQ** *You have already met one statistic which is used to measure the variability of scores round the mean. What is it called and what is the basis by which it is calculated? Look back to Chapter 2 if you are not sure.*

This statistic is of course the standard deviation, which is the square root of the sum of the squared deviation of scores from the mean. It takes the mean as the reference point and provides an index of the average variation of scores above and below that point. The variance is an index of variability based on the same principle. It is the sum of the squared deviations from the mean divided by N (for a population). If we are dealing with samples, we take into account as usual, the degrees of freedom available, and divide by $N-1$ to obtain an unbiased estimate of the population variance.

Here is the basic variance formula:

$$\text{Variance} = \frac{\Sigma(X-M)^2}{N-1}$$

> **STQ** *From the previous paragraph and a close inspection of the formula you will have realized that there is a close relationship between variance and σ. Can you state in words or as a formula what the relationship is?*

We hope you will have deduced that variance $= \sigma^2$, or looking at it the other way round that $\sigma = \sqrt{\text{variance}}$. In future variance will be symbolized as MS, since this cryptic message stands for mean sum of squared deviations (or mean sum of squares). Another symbol you need is SS. This has no wartime connotations though you may be feeling rather bellicose towards the authors as you struggle with these terms. SS stands for sum of squared deviations (or sum of squares). If we now rewrite the variance formula in these new terms their meaning should be clearer. Here goes:

$$MS = \frac{SS}{N-1} = \frac{\Sigma(X-M)^2}{N-1} = \text{variance}$$

> **STQ** *Just to recap and see if you are following these symbols can you explain,*
>
> *(a)   What SS represents?*
> *(b)   What MS means*
> *(c)   Why variance $= \Sigma(X-M)^2/N-1$ is the same as $MS = SS/N-1$*

C   Sample variance and population variance

1   SAMPLE VARIANCE

We have emphasized on several occasions and demonstrated through coin tossing and random number selection that if we have a population and take two samples at random from it, it is highly unlikely that the mean of Sample 1 will be exactly the same as mean of Sample 2. Furthermore, neither of these means will be the same as the population mean. Similarly the variance of Sample 1 will differ from that of Sample 2, and both will differ from the population variance.

But we do know something about how much these sample statistics differ from each other. Suppose we have a population with a mean IQ of 100 and a variance of 225 (15^2). If we were to take all possible samples, each of 200 people, from this population and calculate the mean of each one, we should find that they follow a normal distribution (called the sampling distribution of the mean.) You will recall that this sampling distribution has a standard deviation much smaller than that of the distribution of raw scores.

> **STQ**   *What do we call the standard deviation of the sampling distribution of the mean? Check your answer with the information in Chapter 15.*

The sampling variance is the variance computed from a sample. Theoretically the variances of a large number of random samples drawn from the same population is normally distributed around the true population variance. The standard error of this distribution can be computed and this permits us to evaluate our sample variance, just as we did with standard error and sample means in Chapter 8.

2   POPULATION VARIANCE

Population variance is the variance of all the scores in a defined population. As we have seen all the population scores are usually not available and we have to make do with estimating parameters of the population from sampling statistics.

In studying standard error and the standard error of the difference we demonstrated the above points repeatedly. What is important to grasp is that random sample means will vary randomly because of individual variations within the groups and that in deciding on significance of results we must be as certain as we can that variation in means due to the effect of the *IV* is far greater than that expected from chance variation. We have emphasized this point before in terms of the *t*-test and the critical ratio. However, there is a restriction in the number of groups that can be compared on a *t*-test. Two groups is the maximum so if more than two levels of *IV* are involved ANOVA is the procedure to be applied, not a *t*-test.

D Systematic and error variance

Another way to classify variance is to divide it into systematic and error variance.

(a) Systematic variance is the variation in scores due to known and/or unknown influences that 'cause' the scores to lean in one direction more than another. Any natural or man-made influences that 'cause' events to happen in a certain predictable way are systematic influences. The achievement test scores of the children in a wealthy suburban school will tend to be systematically higher than the achievement test scores of the children in a city slum area school. Coaching or practice may systematically influence performance in any skill. 'Fair' dice will turn up all the numbers 1 to 6 equally often. Loaded dice, on the other hand, lean in one direction systematically: certain numbers will turn up more often than other numbers. Similarly, marked cards and crooked roulette wheels show systematic variance.

There are many causes of systematic variance. The scientist seeks to separate those in which he is interested from those in which he is not interested. And he must also separate from his systematic variances, as we shall see, variance that is random, i.e. error variance. Indeed, research may narrowly and technically be defined as the controlled study of variances.

In any experiment or study, the independent variable (or variables) is a source of systematic variance – at least it should be. The researcher 'wants' the experimental groups to differ systematically. He usually seeks to maximize such variance while controlling or minimizing other sources of variance, both systematic and error.

(b) Error variance; it is probably safe to say that the most pervasive kind of variance in research is error variance. Error variance is the fluctuation or varying of measures due to chance. Error variance is random variance. It is the variation in measures due to the usually small and self-compensating fluctuations of measures – now here, now there; now up, now down. The sampling variance discussed earlier in the chapter, for example, is random or error variance. Many events and occurrences cannot be explained. Much variance eludes identification and control. This is error variance – at least as long as identification and control elude us.

While seemingly strange and even a bit bizarre, this mode of reasoning is useful, provided we remember that some of the error variance of today may not be the error variance of tomorrow. Suppose that we perform an experiment on teaching methods in which we assign pupils to three groups at random. After we finish the experiment, we study the differences between the three groups to see if the methods have had an effect. We know that the scores will always show minor fluctuations, now plus a point or two or three, now minus a point or two or three, which we can probably never control. Something or other makes these scores fluctuate in this fashion. According to the view under discussion, they do not just fluctuate for no reason, there is probably no 'absolute randomness'. Assuming determinism, there must be some cause or causes for the fluctuations. True, we can learn some of them and possibly control them. When we do this, however, we have systematic variance.

We find out, for instance, that sex 'causes' the scores to fluctuate, since boys and girls are mixed in the experimental groups. (We are, of course, talking figuratively here. Obviously sex does not make scores fluctuate.) So we do the experiment and control sex by using, say, only boys. The scores still fluctuate, though to a somewhat lesser extent. We remove another presumed cause of the perturbations: social class. The scores still fluctuate, though to a still lesser extent. We carry on removing such sources of variance. We are controlling systematic variance. We are also gradually identifying and controlling more and more unknown variance.

Now note that before we controlled or removed these systematic variances, before we 'knew' about them, we would have to label all such variance as error variance – partly through ignorance, partly through inability to do anything about such variance. We could go on and on doing this and still there would be variance left over. Finally we give in; we 'know' no more; we have done all we can. There will still be variance. A practical definition of error variance, then, would be: error variance is the variance left over in a set of measures after all known sources of systematic variance have been removed from the measures.

E   Apportionment of variance
The point is that the results of any experiment consist of a whole range of different scores. Some of these differences in scores will be due to the experimenter's manipulation of one or more independent variables. But a lot of the differences in scores will be due to all the other irrelevant variables which are influencing subjects' behaviour. For example, some of the differences in solution times of anagrams

278 *Experimental psychology*

will be due to whether the words are short or long, frequent or infrequent. But the times will also be affected by many other factors, moments of distraction, some people being generally quicker than others, being avid crossword puzzlers and so on. ANOVA enables us to estimate how much of all the differences in scores are due to the independent variables and how much are due to all the other randomly distributed irrelevant variables. The essential thing to grasp about ANOVA is that it enables you to discover what proportion of the total variability (i.e. all the differences in scores) is due to the predicted effects of the independent variables and what proportion is due to all the other irrelevant variables.

Let us take as an example an experiment in which recall scores for lists of nonsense syllables for psychology students are compared with recall scores for lists of nonsense items for sociology students. The recall scores for ten subjects in each of the two groups come out as shown in Table 64.

Table 64 Number of items correctly recalled (out of 10)

Condition 1 psychology students	Condition 2 sociology students
10	2
5	1
6	3
7	4
9	4
8	5
7	2
5	5
6	3
5	4

First let us look at what the total variability in scores would look like. We can do this by plotting a histogram as shown in Figure 34. The histogram shows the number of items correctly recalled along the bot-

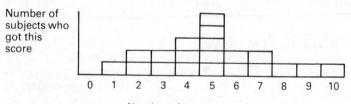

Number of subjects who got this score

0 1 2 3 4 5 6 7 8 9 10

Number of items correctly recalled

Figure 34

tom, i.e. all possible scores from 0 items correct to ten items correct, and the number of subjects who got that score up the vertical axis (each square representing a person). We have used all 20 subjects regardless of which experimental condition they were in. The resulting histogram shows the total distribution of the recall scores. This distribution of scores represents the total variability of the scores.

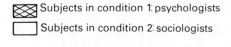

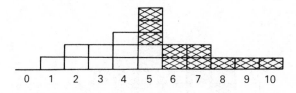

Number of items correctly recalled

Figure 35

This histogram represents the total variability in the scores of all the subjects, but, of course, what we are interested in is the differences between the recall scores of subjects in the different conditions. If we use different shadings for the two groups (shaded for condition 1 and plain for condition 2), we get a histogram like that shown in Figure 35. Check that this represents the same recall scores as those shown in Table 64 and Figure 34.

STQ

(a) How many subjects in condition 1 scored 5 items?
(b) How many subjects in condition 2 scored 5 items?
(c) Did the subjects in condition 1 or in condition 2 recall more items correctly?
(d) Can you work out the mean scores (i.e. average scores) for correct items in each condition?
Hint: It is easiest to do this by looking back to Table 64 adding up the number of items correct for the ten subjects in each condition, and dividing by 10.
(e) What is the difference between the mean scores for condition 1 and condition 2?

As you would expect from the recall scores in Table 64 and Figure 35 the psychology subjects had considerably higher mean recall scores than the sociology subjects. Another way of putting it is to say that a large proportion (indeed nearly all) of the total variability (i.e. differences in subjects' scores) was due to the predicted effects of manipulating the independent variable of academic subjects studied.

In most cases, of course, there would not be such a clear-cut division between the scores in the two groups. Much more usual would be to find a histogram like that in Figure 36.

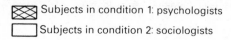

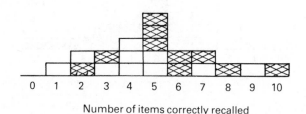

Number of items correctly recalled

Figure 36

STQ

(a) *What are the mean scores of items correct for condition 1 and condition 2? (This time you will have to read off the scores for each group from Table 64.)*

(b) *What is the difference between the mean scores for the two conditions?*

(c) *How many subjects on condition 2 had a higher recall score than at least one person in condition 1?*

In Figure 36 some scores for psychologists are quite low (e.g. three items correct) and some scores for sociologists are quite high (e.g. seven items correct). There are, of course, still some differences in scores due to the experimental conditions, since scores for psychologists are on average higher than those for sociologists (a difference in mean scores of 1.3 items). However, there must also have been a certain amount of variability which had nothing to do with the effects of the academic subject variable. Something else must have been causing the relatively low scores for some and the relatively high scores on nonsense items.

The distinction between the two sets of scores in Figures 35 and 36 can be described as follows. In Figure 35 a large proportion of the total variability in scores is due to differences in scores between the experimental conditions. In Figure 36 a smaller proportion of the total variability in scores is due to differences in scores between the experimental conditions.

This notion of proportions of variability is central to ANOVA. The whole idea is to estimate the proportion of total variability which is due to the predicted effects of the experimental conditions (i.e. caused by manipulation of the independent variable) and the proportion which is due to all other irrelevant variables. This can be expressed in the following way:

total variability =
variability due to independent variables + variability due to all other variables.

F Variance ratios
As we have stressed so often before, the aim of all statistical tests is to decide whether the predicted effects of the experimental conditions are really significant or whether the experimental results are due to random or chance variations. In terms of the variability 'equation' shown above, the larger the proportion of total variability in scores which is due to the independent variables, the more likely it is that differences between conditions are significant. If, on the other hand, only a small proportion of the total variability in scores is due to the independent variables, then such differences are likely to be small and perhaps simply due to random chance variability. Now we are back with the problem of deciding how great a proportion of the total variability must be due to the experimental conditions to allow an experimenter to claim that his result is significantly due to the predicted effects of the independent variable.

The first step is to express the proportions of variability as a ratio. This is done in order to compare the amount of variability due to the independent variable against the amount of variability due to all other variables (known as error because it is due to variables not controlled by the experimenter).

$$\frac{\text{variability due to independent variables}}{\text{variability due to all other variables (error)}}$$

The higher this ratio, the greater will be the proportion of variability due to the independent variables and less to other variables. The value of this ratio is used to determine whether the differences in scores are significantly due to the predicted effects of the experimental hypothesis.

Since variance is simply a statistical measure of variability, variability can be replaced by the term variance in the above ratio. Therefore, the total amount of variance reflects the total variability in scores. The amount of variance due to an independent variable reflects the variability in scores due to the independent variable. The amount of variance due to all other variables reflects the amount of variability due to all other variables (i.e. error variance):

STQ *Can you now formulate the ratio above in terms of variance?*

You might have formulated the following:

$$\frac{\text{variance due to independent variables}}{\text{variance due to all other variables (error)}}$$

or using the symbols provided on p. 274.

$$\frac{MS \text{ due to } IV}{MS \text{ due to all other variables (error)}}$$

As before, the higher the ratio, the greater is the amount of variance due to the independent variable. So what we want to be able to assess is how high this ratio must be to allow us to say that the experimental results are significant, rather than due to random variability (error) as stated by a null hypothesis.

You will remember that the way we assessed significance was to see how likely it was that our experimental results were due to chance. If there was very small chance probability (1% or 5%), then we were prepared to reject the null hypothesis that the result was due to chance, and to accept instead the alternative experimental hypothesis that it was due to the predicted effects of the independent variable.

In exactly the same way, what we want to know is what are the probabilities of getting the particular variance ratio found in the experiment on a random chance basis. In fact, there is just such a statistical distribution, giving the probabilities of obtaining all possible variance ratios randomly by chance. By looking up this table of chance probabilities you can see how likely it is that the particular variance ratio found in your experiment occurred by chance. On this basis, if this chance probability is very low, i.e. less than 5% ($p < 0.05$) or 1% ($p < 0.01$), you can reject the null hypothesis and accept that the differences in mean scores between experimental conditions support your experimental hypothesis.

Such variance ratios are known as *F* ratios named in honour of Ronald Fisher, and they form the basis for calculating significance using analysis of variance. You can probably see by now that the reason this statistical technique is called analysis of variance is because it provides a method for calculating, from the scores in an experiment, the amounts of variance due to all the possible sources of variability in the experiment. If you think about it, what we have been doing is apportioning, or analysing, the total amount of variance in the experimental scores into constituent parts, that is, into (1) the variance due to the independent variables, and (2) variance due to all other variables. The *F* ratio between these two variances represents the proportion of variance that is due to the predicted effects of the independent variables, as opposed to the error variance due to all other randomly distributed variables.

This has been a long haul. A brief recapitulation of the main points may be useful. Any set of measures has a total variance. If the measures from which this variance is computed have been derived from the responses of human beings, then there will always be at least two sources of variance. One will be due to systematic sources of variation like individual differences of the subjects whose characteristics or accomplishments have been measured and differences between the groups or subgroups involved in research. The other will be due to chance or random error, fluctuations of measures that cannot be accounted for. Sources of systematic variance tend to bias scores in one direction or another. This is reflected in differences in means, of course. If sex is a systematic source of variance in a study of school achievement, for instance, then the sex variable will tend to act in such a manner that the achievement scores of girls will tend to be higher than those of boys. Sources of random error, on the other hand, tend to make measures fluctuate now this way, now that way. Random errors are self-compensating; they tend to balance each other out.

ANOVA enables us to calculate from the scores in an experiment the proportion of the total variance which is due to the independent variables and the proportion due to all other variables (error variance). The *F* ratio compares the proportion of variance due to independent variables with the error variance as follows:

$$F = \frac{\text{variance due to independent variables}}{\text{error variance (due to other variables)}}$$

The higher the *F* ratio for a particular experiment, the higher is the proportion of variance due to the predicted effects of the independent variables. The lower the *F* ratio, the higher is the proportion of variance due to random error, i.e. to a random distribution of irrelevant variables, as stated by the null hypothesis.

The statistical tables associated with ANOVA give the probabilities of obtaining high or low F ratios by chance. In general, for a given number of experimental conditions and subjects, the higher the F ratio, the lower the probability that it was a chance result.

G   Between-groups and within-group variance

The MS due to the IV is often termed between-groups variance or MS_b. The MS due to error is termed the within-group variance or MS_w. Since these are the two estimates of variance required for the F ratio we must look at them more closely.

1 BETWEEN-GROUPS VARIANCE (MS_b)

The type of systematic variance most important in research is between-groups or experimental variance. Between-groups or experimental variance, as the name indicates, is the variance that reflects systematic differences between groups.

Between-groups variance and experimental variance are fundamentally the same. Both arise from differences between groups. Between-groups variance is a term that covers all cases of systematic differences between groups, experimental or non-experimental. Experimental variance is usually associated with the variance engendered by active manipulation of independent variables by experimenters.

Here is a simple example of between-groups – in this case experimental – variance. Suppose an investigator tests the relative efficacies of three different methods of learning nonsense syllables. After teaching three groups of four children each he computes the means of the groups. Suppose that they are 30, 25 and 17. Each raw score is then converted to the mean of the group and its squared deviation from the overall mean of 24 is calculated. The easiest way to do this is to treat the three means as scores and multiply the squared deviation of the group mean from the overall mean by the number of cases in the group, as below. This variance between groups is an index of the variability of the three group means, or the variability of the three groups taken as wholes.

In the experiment just described, presumably the methods tend to 'bias' the scores one way or another. This is, of course, the experimenter's purpose: he wants method A, say, to increase all the recall scores of an experimental group. He may believe that method B will have no effect and that method C will have a depressing effect. If he is correct, the recall scores under method A should all tend to go up,

	Group means	$X - M$	$(X-M)^2N$		
	30	6	36×4	=	144
	25	1	1×4	=	4
	17	-7	49×4	=	196
ΣX:	72				
M:	24				
$\Sigma(X-M)^2$:					344

$$MS_b = \frac{344}{3-1} = 172.00$$

whereas under method C they should all tend to go down. Thus the scores of the groups, as wholes – and, of course, their means – differ systematically. Methods of learning is an active variable, a variable deliberately manipulated by the experimenter with the conscious intent to 'bias' the scores differentially. Thus any experimenter-manipulated variables are intimately associated with systematic variance.

The basic idea behind the famous 'classical design' of scientific research, in which experimental and control groups are used, is that, through careful control and manipulation, the experimental group's outcome measures (also called 'criterion measures') are made to vary systematically, to all go up or down together, while the control group's measures are ordinarily held at the same level. The variance, of course, is between the two groups, that is, the two groups are made to differ.

The greater the differences between groups, the more an independent variable or variables can be presumed to have operated. If there is no or little difference between groups, on the other hand, then the presumption must be that an independent variable or variables have not operated, that their effects are too weak to be noticed, or that their influences have cancelled each other out. We judge the effects of independent variables that have been manipulated, then, by between-groups variance.

To illustrate the principle again take the example of anxiety and its relationship to school achievement. It is possible to manipulate anxiety by having two experimental groups and inducing anxiety in one and not in the other. This can be done by giving each group the same test with different instructions. We tell the members of one group that their grades depend wholly on the test. We tell the members of the other group that the test does not matter particularly, that its outcome will not affect grades. If there is an observed difference between the means then we may have systematically induced variance into the experiment through the manipulation of levels of anxiety.

2   WITHIN-GROUP VARIANCE (MS_w)

We compute the within-group variance, essentially, by computing the variance of each group separately and then averaging the two (or more) variances; this estimate of error is unaffected by the differences between the means. Thus, if nothing else is causing the scores to vary, it is reasonable to consider the within-group variance as a measure of chance fluctuations of sampling error. If this is so, then we can stack up the variance due to the experimental effect, the between-groups variance, against this measure of chance error, the within-group variance. The only question is: how is the within-group variance computed?

Remember that the variance of a population of means can be estimated with the standard variance of the mean (the standard error squared). One way to compute the within-group variance is to compute the standard variance of each of the groups and then average them for all of the groups. This should yield an estimate of error that can be used to evaluate the variance of the means of the groups. The reasoning here is basic. To evaluate the differences between the means, it is necessary to refer to a theoretical population of means that would be obtained from the random sampling of groups of scores. If the sampling has been random and nothing else has operated – that is, there have been no experimental manipulations and no other systematic influences have been at work – then it possible to estimate the variance of the means of the population of means using the standard variance of the means (SE_m^2). Each group provides such an estimate. These estimates will vary to some extent among themselves. We can pool them by averaging to form an overall estimate of the variance of the population means.

If an experimental manipulation has been influential, then it should show up in differences between means above and beyond the differences that would arise by chance alone. And the between-groups variance should show the influence by becoming greater than could be expected by chance. Just as we can use MS_b then, as a measure of experimental influence, equally we can use MS_w as a measure of chance variation. Therefore, we have almost reached the end of a rather long but profitable journey: we can evaluate the between-groups variance, MS_b, against the within-groups variance, MS_w. Or information, experimental information, can be weighed against error or chance. To explain these sources of variance, let us imagine a lecturer is keen to find out whether reinforcing comments written on student essays in addition to a mark is more effective in improving a subsequent essay then merely writing a mark on.

STQ   *What are the IV and DV in this example?*

The *IV* has two levels (conditions) and they are 'reinforcement plus mark', and 'mark only'. The *DV* is the mark gained on the subsequent essay.

The lecturer assigns ten students at random to two groups and assigns levels at random, then gives a written assignment and follows the procedure indicated. A week later a similar assignment is given and the papers are marked. The scores are as follows:

	Reinforcement	Mark only
	5	3
	4	5
	6	1
	7	4
	3	2
M:	5	3

The means are different; they vary. Thus there is between-groups variance. Computing it just as we did with an earlier example, we get:

		$(X-M)$	$(X-M)^2 N$
	5	1	1×5
	3	-1	1×5
M:	4		
$\Sigma(X-M)^2$:			10.00

$$MS_b = \frac{10.00}{1} = 10.00$$

We simply treat the two means as though they were individual scores, and go ahead with an ordinary variance calculation. The between-groups variance, MS_b is, then, 10.00.

If we put the ten scores in a column and calculate the variance, we obtain:

	X	$(X-M)$	$(X-M)^2$
	5	1.0	1.0
	4	0.0	0.0
	6	2.0	4.0
	7	3.0	9.0
	3	-1.0	1.0
	3	-1.0	1.0
	5	1.0	1.0

Table Continued

	X	$(X-M)$	$(X-M)^2$
	1	−3.0	9.0
	4	0.0	0.0
	2	−2.0	4.0
M:	4.0		
$\Sigma(X-M)^2$:			30.00

$$MS_t = \frac{30.00}{9} = 3.33$$

This is the total variance or MS_t. $MS_t = 3.33$ contains all sources of variation in the scores. We already know that one of these is the between-groups variance $MS_b = 10.00$. Let us compute still another variance. We do this by computing the variance of the reinforcement group alone and the variance of the grade-only group alone and then averaging the two:

	X	$(X-M)$	$(X-M)^2$	X	$(X-M)$	$(X-M)^2$
	5	0	0	3	0	0
	4	−1	1	5	2	4
	6	1	1	1	2	4
	7	2	4	4	1	1
	3	−2	4	2	−1	1
ΣX:	25			15		
M:	5			3		
$\Sigma(X-M)^2$:			10			10

$$MS_w = \frac{10}{4} = 2.5 \qquad MS_w = \frac{10}{4} = 2.5$$

The variance of both is 2.5. The average of these two is 2.5. Since each of these variances was computed separately and then averaged, we call the average variance computed from them the 'within-group variance'. We label this variance MS_w meaning within variance, or within-group variance. Thus $MS_w = 2.5$.

The total of all sources of variance is formed from between-group variance (the effect of the *IV*) plus within-group variance (random error). In our experiment then the different *IV* conditions produced a component of variance, as did uncontrolled idiosyncratic variations between the individuals composing the two groups. This latter within-groups variance is the error variance because we cannot isolate and identify its sources.

(A useful check in the calculations is that the $SS_t = SS_b + SS_w$. In the above example we find then that $30 = 10 + 20$.)

STQ *Explain the source of the variation measured by:*

(a) The total sum of squares.
(b) The between-groups sum of squares.
(c) The within-group sum of squares.

H   An example of ANOVA

Now that the basic concepts have been presented, let us look at an experiment and take it right through to the stage of supporting or refuting of the null hypothesis. We wish to test the effects of three rates of presentation on recall of nonsense syllables. The three rates of presentation of the nonsense syllables will form three levels of *IV*. The *DV* is the number recalled. The results are tabulated below (Table 65). This is a between-groups design with five Ss per group.

Table 65

	Rate of presentation		
	Group A *level 1*	*Group B* *level 2*	*Group C* *level 3*
Recall	5	3	2
Scores	4	5	1
	3	2	1
	4	4	2
	4	1	4
Total	20	15	10
Mean	4	3	2

The question is now how do we decide on the basis of this evidence whether there is a real difference caused by presentation rate? We know that we would not obtain identical performances, even if the rate of presentation had been the same for each group, because of sampling error. What we need to know is whether our obtained differences are large enough to suggest that there are significant differences in recall scores caused by difference levels of the *IV*. The way in which we answer this question is not to compare the scores themselves, because they are only samples. We do not know how typical they are, or whether another set of samples might have produced equal scores for all three methods. What we do know is how much samples from a single population vary from each other (i.e. we can work out the sampling distribution of the mean.)

STQ *Can you formulate the hypotheses for this experiment?*

We formulated two hypotheses, *viz:*

(a) That there is no significant difference in the recall of nonsense syllables between the rates of presentation (null hypothesis).
(b) That there is a significant difference (alternate hypothesis).

Because we know how samples from the population vary, we can consider hypothesis (a) in more detail. We can decide how likely it is to be true; if we find that we can reject it, then we can accept the alternate hypothesis by default. This, as you know by now, is the usual method of hypothesis testing. So our reasoning proceeds as follows:

(a) Make the assumption that there is no significant difference between the rates of presentation.
(b) On this assumption, each of the sets of results is a random sample from the same population.
(c) Because of this, any of these results, singly or in some combination, can be used to estimate the population variance.
(d) If the estimates do not tally sufficiently well, then our initial assumption must be invalid; therefore there must be differences between the presentation rates after all. If the estimates do tally, then our initial assumption of 'no real difference' stands.

This is the essence of analysis of variance. There are many different ways of carrying out step (c), depending on how the groups were chosen to begin with, but the essential principles are the same.

1 THE ESTIMATES OF POPULATION VARIANCE

The testing of our null hypothesis above is then based on comparing estimates of the population variance. The two estimates used are, (i) the within-group variance (MS_w), and (ii) the between-group variance (MS_b).

(a) Within-group variance (or MS_w)

The variability in performance within each group provides an estimate, so there are as many estimates as there are groups. We need only one estimate based on fluctuations of scores within groups, so we take an average of the sample variances as the best within-group estimate of population variance. This within-group estimate only reflects chance fluctuation because all subjects within a group are subject to the same conditions.

(b) Between-groups variance (or MS_b)

If the null hypothesis is true, the group means can be regarded as a distribution of sample means from the same population. This distribution of sample means can be used to obtain another estimate of population variance. Because this second estimate is based on group means it is a between-groups estimate of population variance. The first estimate of population variance (MS_w) is influenced by fluctuations within each group, and the second, the MS_b which is based on differences between means, is influenced by differences between groups (between means). In fact the between-group variance reflects chance variation plus any effect of the *IV*. If the *IV* has had any effect the between-groups variance should be larger than the within-group variance. If only chance is operating (i.e. the *IV* has no effect) the two estimates of the population variance should be approximately the same.

2 THE RATIONALE OF ANALYSIS OF VARIANCE (ANOVA)

It should be apparent that ANOVA involves obtaining two independent estimates of the population variance, *viz* within-group and between-groups estimates so that a comparison can be made between them to assess the effects of the manipulation of the *IV* which should reveal itself in the between-groups variance.

The between-groups estimate should be larger than the within-group estimate if there is a treatment effect. If the independent variable does not have an effect, then the group means can be considered samples means, which are estimates of the same population mean. However, when it does have an effect the group means will not all be estimates of the same mean because the independent variable will result in an increase or decrease in one or more of the group means. In short, there should be greater fluctuations between the group means when the independent variable has an effect than when it does not. But there is no reason to expect within-group fluctuations to increase if the independent variable has an effect, since every member of a group receives the same level of *IV* and hence only the same random fluctuations in score round the group mean will occur even if the means differ between themselves.

In sum, the crux of the analysis of variance test is to compare the between-groups and within-group estimates of population variance. If the two estimates are about the same, there is no reason to reject the null hypothesis. If the between-groups estimate is considerably larger than the within-group estimate, then the null hypothesis can be rejected. To conclude that the independent variable has an effect, the within-group fluctuations must be smaller than the between-groups fluctuations (Figure 37).

The major problem in ANOVA is to organize the data into a proper layout. Once this is done not even a formula is needed to get you working properly. There are two layouts required. The first is a layout of the raw data as in Table 66, with a further eight columns for data derived from the raw data. This blank table will gradually be

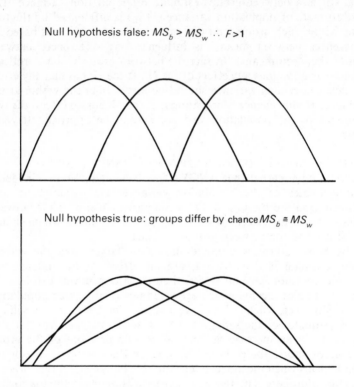

Null hypothesis false: $MS_b > MS_w$ $\therefore$ $F > 1$

Null hypothesis true: groups differ by chance $MS_b \cong MS_w$

Figure 37

completed until it looks like Table 67. We will do this shortly. The second layout is a summary table (Table 68) which again we will gradually fill in as we proceed, until we reach the conclusion of the calculation (Table 69).

We can now start the calculations necessary to fill our raw-data layout table. We will sequence the tasks; you may wish to do these tasks too as you go through them by writing in pencil the various calculations, in the blank table. At the end you can compare your results with ours in completed table. If you are not to carry out the calculations, follow the tasks by referring to Table 67.

Table 66 Example of commencing layout for ANOVA

(1)		*Finding the total sum of squares*		*Finding the sum of squares within groups*			*Finding the sum of squares between groups*		
		(2)	(3)	(4)	(5)	(6)	(7)	(8)	(9)
	Scores	Deviation of scores from grand mean	Squared deviation from grand mean	Group mean	Deviation of scores from group mean	Squared deviation from group mean	Deviation of group mean from grand mean	Squared deviation	Squared deviation weighted according n, size of group
Group I	5								
	4								
	3								
	4								
	4								
$\Sigma =$									
$M =$									
Group II	3								
	5								
	2								
	4								
	1								
$\Sigma =$									
$M =$									
Group III	2								
	1								
	1								
	2								
	4								
$\Sigma =$									
$M =$									
Sum of all scores $=$									
Grand mean $=$									

(a) Calculate ΣX and M for each group separately and write in at the relevant place.

(b) Calculate the sum of all the scores and the mean of all the scores (grand mean) and write in at the bottom of column 1.

(c) Find the SS_t by summing all the squared deviations of all scores from the grand mean (columns 2 and 3).

Table 67 Recall data for groups using three different presentation rates

| | Finding the total sum of squares | | | Finding the sum of squares within groups | | | Finding the sum of squares between groups | | |
	(1) Scores	(2) Deviation of scores from grand mean of 3	(3) Squared deviation from grand mean	(4) Group mean	(5) Deviation of scores from group mean	(6) Squared deviation from group mean	(7) Deviation of group mean from grand of 3	(8) Squared deviation	(9) Squared deviation weighted according n, size of group
Group A	5	2	4	4	1	1	1	1	5
	4	1	1		0	0			(5 × 1)
	3	0	0		−1	1			
	4	1	1		0	0			
	4	1	1		0	0			
	$\Sigma = 20$				$\Sigma = 0$	2			
	$M = 4$								
Group B	3	0	0	3	0	0	0	0	0
	5	2	4		2	4			(5 × 0)
	2	−1	1		−1	1			
	4	1	1		1	1			
	1	−2	4		−2	4			
	$\Sigma = 15$				$\Sigma = 0$	10			
	$M = 3$								
Group C	2	−1	1	2	0	0	−1	1	5
	1	−2	4		−1	1			(5 × 1)
	1	−2	4		−1	1			
	2	−1	1		0	0			
	4	1	1		2	4			
	$\Sigma = 5$				$\Sigma = 0$	6	$\Sigma = 0$		
	$M = 2$								
Sum of all scores = 45	$\Sigma = 0$	$SS_t = 28$			$SS_w = 18$				$SS_b = 10$
Grand mean = 3									

(d) Calculate the SS_w by finding for each group separately the sum of the squared deviations of scores in that group from that group's mean. This provides an SS_w for each group. These are added to find the overall SS_w (columns 4, 5 and 6), i.e. SS of group 1 + SS of group 2 + SS of group 3.

(e) Calculate the SS_b by determining the deviation of each group mean from the grand mean. This in each case is squared and multiplied by the number of scores in the group. The sum of these squared deviations weighted according to the size of group is the SS_b (columns 7, 8 and 9).

Now compare your table (Table 66) if you have been filling it in with ours (Table 67). We can now turn to the summary table.

The first thing we must have is df values. Total df equals $N-1$ (where N is the total number of scores in the experiment). The number of degrees of freedom between cells (experimental groups) is the number of such groups (or cells) minus one. There are two ways of finding the within-cell df: since df_t must equal $df_b + df_w$, we could merely subtract df_b from the total and use the remainder. Or else we could take the total number of scores, N, and subtract the number of groups since 1 df is lost for each. Since there are three groups, 3 df are lost. Hence, $df_w = N-C$ (where C denotes the number of groups).

> **STQ** *In our experiment write down in the blank summary table (Table 68) (in pencil perhaps) df_t, df_b and df_w. Then compare your answer to the data in Table 69.*

Table 68 Summary table

Source of variance	df	SS	MS	F
Between				
Within				
Total				

The next step is to transfer the various sum of squares from the data Table 67 (p. 294) to the summary table. You might like to write them in in Table 68. At last we are ready to calculate the *MS*.

> **STQ** *Can you go ahead and do this? Do you remember what the MS is?*

We have completed the *MS* entries in our summary Table 69. Do you recall that $MS = SS/df$.

The final task to complete our summary table is the calculation of *F*. The *F* statistic is:

$$\frac{\text{between group variance estimate}}{\text{within group variance estimate}} \quad \text{or} \quad \frac{MS_b}{MS_w}$$

In our example therefore $F = 5/1.5 = 3.33$.

Table 69   Summary table

Source of variance	df	SS	MS	F
Between	2	10	5	3.33
Within	12	18	1.5	
Total	14	28		

How do we interpret this F of 3.33?

Whenever we calculate an F ratio we are faced with our two mutually exclusive possibilities or hypotheses. The first possibility reads as follows:

Null hypothesis – The two samples have been drawn from the same population. Any apparent differences have been caused by trivial factors such as sampling fluctuations.

The second possibility reads as follows:

Alternate hypothesis – The observed difference between the two variance estimates is due to a real effect. The samples can be said to be drawn from two different populations.

Fisher's F tables (Appendix A, Table B) are used to interpret the F statistic and enable us to decide between the two hypotheses. The tables make one simple assumption, that the two samples are drawn from the same population. Under these circumstances, we expect the F ratio to equal one but from time to time it could be much higher or lower depending upon random fluctuations in sampling.

STQ   *Can you explain why we expect the F ratio to equal 1 on the basis of the null hypothesis?*

The F tables are easy to use. There is one table for each of the main significance levels (5%, 1%). The 5% tables gives us those extreme values of F which we expect to obtain on approximately 5% of occasions even when the null hypothesis is true, i.e. even when the difference in variance estimates is due to trivial random factors. The 1% tables gives us that value of F which is exceeded on at least 1% of occasions even when there is no real difference between the groups.

In order to locate the critical F ratio for different sizes of samples, we use the degrees of freedom associated with each sample. In our case, we had $2 df$ for MS_b and 12 df were associated with MS_w. The degrees of freedom for the MS_b is given along the top of the table, and this determines the column we are to use. The row to be used is determined by the degrees of freedom associated with the MS_w.

The following shorthand symbols refer to the degrees of freedom:

v_1 symbolizes the degrees of freedom associated with the MS_b
v_2 symbolizes the degrees of freedom associated with the MS_w

We write the F ratio thus:

$$F_{v1,\ v2} = \frac{MS_b}{MS_w}$$

In our example:

$$F_{2,12} = \frac{5}{1.5} = 3.33$$

We should now consult the F tables for 2 and 12 degrees of freedom to find which values of F need to be exceeded to be significant at the different percentage levels. Consulting the tables for $F_{2,\ 12}$:

$$5\% \text{ level } F = 3.88$$
$$1\% \text{ level } F = 6.93$$

Our obtained F value of 3.33 is smaller than all of these. Accordingly, we described the result as statistically non-significant and, consequently, we retain the null hypothesis and reject the hypothesis that the rates of presentation significantly influenced recall scores. Our F was too small and suggested no experimental effect. F must equal or exceed the tabled value to be significant and lead to a rejection of the null hypothesis. Analysis of variance tests for the presence of differences in means in a total set of data; it is not designed nor is it able to answer questions about differences between particular means. A significant F ratio indicates only that there are statistically significant differences among the groups contributing to the total set of data but it does not indicate where the significance lies.

ASSUMPTIONS UNDERLYING ANALYSIS OF VARIANCE
One-way analysis of variance is used to test the significance of the differences in means when only one independent variable has been manipulated. In the examples in this chapter there was only one *IV*. There are three assumptions involved in one-way analysis of variance. These are:

(a) That the variables investigated are normally distributed in the population from which the samples are drawn.
(b) That the variances in the populations from which the samples are drawn are also equal (homogeneity of variance).
(c) That all Ss are randomly drawn from the population.

In practice few experiments satisfy all the above criteria but it has been found that provided the departures from normality and homogeneity of variance are not too great, the validity of the F test is not seriously threatened. This is particularly true if group Ns are equal.

STQ (1) *As the difference between groups decreases, the F ratio:*

(a)   decreases
(b)   increases
(c)   stays the same
(d)   cannot tell since it depends on the specific situation.

(2) *Which of the following is influenced by the observed differences between the groups?*

(a) MS_w
(b) MS_b
(c) ΣN
(d)   df

(3) *Variance between groups is presumably due to:*

(a)   individual differences
(b)   error
(c)   random factors beyond the control of the researcher
(d)   experimental manipulation.

(4) *The variance estimate derived from the variance of group means around the grand mean is called the:*

(a) MS_w
(b) MS_b
(c)   F ratio
(d) SE_m

(5) *If experimental manipulation has no effect on the dependent variable this will:*

(a)   decrease the variance between group means
(b)   decrease the total variance
(c)   increase the variance between group means
(d)   increase the variance derived from the variation of scores within each group.

(6) *A sum of squares divided by its degrees of freedom is called:*

(a)   population mean
(b)   F ratio
(c)   sample mean
(d)   MS

(7) *The null hypothesis in ANOVA states that:*

(a) *the F ratio is less than 1*
(b) *the group means differ only as a function of chance*
(c) $\dfrac{MS_b}{MS_w} = 0$
(d) *none of the above.*

(8) *Which of the following is the null hypothesis to be tested by analysis of variance?*

(a) $M_1 = M_2 = M_3$
(b) $SS_1 = SS_2 = SS_3$
(c) $SS_{b1} = SS_{b2} = SS_{b3}$
(d) *none of the above.*

(9) *Complete this summary table for the analysis of variance.*

Source of variation	df	SS	MS	F
Between groups	2			
Within groups		650		
Total	99	800		

(a) *What is the between-groups SS?*
(b) *What is the within-group df?*
(c) *What is MS_b?*
(d) *What is MS_w?*
(e) *What is the F ratio?*
(f) *Is the F significant at the 0.01 level?*

(10) *Complete the following summary table:*

Source	df	SS	MS	F
Between groups	2	40		
Within groups	117			
Total		374		

(11)
(a) *What ratio is used to test hypotheses in ANOVA?*
(b) *What happens to the F ratio as the difference between the groups increases?*

(12) *When a sum of squares is divided by its degrees of freedom, an unbiased estimate of the population variance is obtained. What is this estimate of the population variance called?*

(13)   *Under which of the following conditions would the null hypothesis be rejected?*

(a)   When the MS_w is about the same as the MS_b.
(b)   When the MS_b is much larger than the MS_w.
(c)   When the MS_b is much smaller than the MS_w.

(14)   *Complete this summary table for the analysis of variance and check for significance at the 0.05 level.*

Source of variation	df	SS	MS	F
Between groups	—	60	—	—
Within groups	56	—	—	—
Total	59	450		

(15)   *Forty students were randomly divided into four groups, each group receiving a different method of instruction in speed reading. The four groups, which did not differ initially in reading speed, were tested at the end of the course on a speed reading test. The following data were obtained:*

Group I	Group II	Group III	Group IV
11	10	15	14
9	10	13	11
6	10	12	8
7	10	10	7
6	6	7	6
5	6	6	4
3	5	6	3
2	5	5	2
2	5	3	1
1	5	2	1

Use analysis of variance to determine whether the treatment means differ significantly.

Answers are to be found on p. 435.

23

Statistical tests

A Comparison between parametric and non-parametric tests
The function of both kinds of test is identical. In both cases
an experimenter uses the tests to discover the probability that the
results of his experiment occurred randomly by chance. On the basis
of this he can decide whether the chance probability is low enough to
warrant rejecting the null hypothesis and accepting the experimental
hypothesis.

ASSUMPTIONS FOR PARAMETRIC TESTS
(a) Levels of measurement
The first issue is that of level of measurement. You will remember that
when you used the sign test, you simply allocated the differences between experimental conditions according to whether they go in one
direction (+) or in the other direction (−). The level at which the sign
test handles these differences is at the nominal level of measurement,
i.e. allocating them to the categories of plus or minus.

But if you are using the Wilcoxon test, then you not only allocate
the differences in scores to one direction or the other, but you can take
into account the size of the score differences by rank ordering these
from the smallest to the largest differences. So the Wilcoxon test
handles the score differences at an ordinal level of measurement by
putting them into a rank order.

However, with parametric tests like the *t* test we need experimental
data that can be treated as numbers with equal intervals. So
parametric tests handle interval or ratio data, and should be restricted
to 'naturally' numerical measures such as IQ scores, recall scores, and
reaction times. However, psychologists often resort to allotting
numbers to all sorts of scales and then assuming they are equal interval scales, e.g. attitude scales, thereby allowing parametric procedures
to be applied.

(b)   Distribution of scores
A second factor influencing the choice between parametric and non-parametric tests is the distribution of data. For a parametric test data should be normally distributed or closely so. Extremely unsymmetrical distributions should not be the basis for parametric testing.

(c)   Homogeneity of variance
The final assumption about the experimental data if you are going to use parametric tests is that the amount of random, or error, variance should be equally distributed among the different experimental conditions. This goes back to the idea that all the variability due to variables which cannot be controlled should be equally distributed among experimental conditions by randomization. The formal term for this is homogeneity of variance; the word homogeneity simply indicates sameness, i.e. that there should not be significantly different amounts of variance in the different conditions of the *IV*.

The normal procedure is for the experimenters to check for these three assumptions before using a parametric test. The point is that, if these theoretical assumptions are not met, then the percentage probability you look for in a statistical table may not be the correct one. However, some statisticians have claimed that parametric tests are in fact relatively robust. This means that it is unlikely that the percentage probability will be very inaccurate unless your data do not meet the assumptions at all, i.e. are not on an interval scale and/or are distributed in a very unsymmetrical fashion.

Summary
Assumptions about experimental data for parametric tests.

(1)   The first assumption is that the experimental scores are measured on at least an interval scale.
(2)   The second assumption is that the experimental scores are normally distributed.
(3)   The third assumption is that there is homogeneity of variance between scores in the experimental conditions.

WHY USE PARAMETRIC TESTS?
By this time you may be wondering why, if all these complicated assumptions have to be met, you should ever use parametric tests at all. After all, non-parametric tests seem to give perfectly good estimates of the chance probabilities of obtaining experimental results. One major consideration needs to be taken into account — power.

THE POWER OF STATISTICAL TESTS

The best way to introduce the notion of 'power' is to think about the difference between the sign test and the Wilcoxon test. The Wilcoxon test was described as being more 'sensitive' because it makes more use of the experimental data. Instead of looking only at the direction of differences, as with the sign test, the Wilcoxon also takes into account the size of the differences in scores in either direction.

The term 'power' refers to the sensitivity of a test, the extent to which it is likely to pick up any significant differences in scores which actually exist in the data. In this sense the Wilcoxon is a more powerful test than the sign test, because you are more likely to find a significant difference.

In the same way that the Wilcoxon test is considered to be more sensitive, or powerful, than the sign test because it takes into account more aspects of the data, so parametric tests are considered to be more powerful because they not only take into account just the rank order of scores but are also able to calculate variances. It has been argued, therefore, that parametric tests are more powerful than non-parametric tests at picking up significant differences.

However, there has been a lot of argument about this question of the relative power of tests among statisticians. Not all of them agree that parametric tests are much more powerful than non-parametric tests, and moreover rank-ordering methods and equations for non-parametric tests are equally quicker and easier to compute.

Summary
When to use parametric and non-parametric tests

Disadvantages	*Advantages*

Non-parametric tests

(1) Because non-parametric tests only look at the effects of single variables in isolation, they ignore a lot of the complexity of human behaviour.	(1) They can be used for investigating the effects of single variables, and when your experimental data do not meet the three assumptions.
(2) Because they make use of rank ordering rather than exact calculations of variance, they may have slightly less power, in that they are less likely to pick up significant differences.	(2) They are particularly useful when measurement is at only a nominal or ordinal level.
	(3) Most of the calculations are extremely easy and quick.

Disadvantages	Advantages

Parametric tests

(1) The experimental data have to meet the three assumptions of interval measurement, normal distribution, and homogeneity of variance.

(2) The mathematical calculations are somewhat more complicated.

(1) They enable you to analyse interactions between two or more variables.

(2) They may be more 'powerful' at picking up significant differences.

Choosing statistical tests

1 TYPE OF HYPOTHESIS

We saw in Chapter 9 that hypotheses in psychological research are very often tested from estimates of population differences on some variable, for example, whether children who attend pre-school play groups differ from children who did not attend play groups in social development on entry to infant school. But it was also pointed out that sometimes a hypothesis can state explicitly that one variable, say perceptual rigidity, is associated with another variability, say anxiety, among children. In general terms therefore we can distinguish two types of hypothesis in psychological research:

(a) Difference hypotheses (between populations).

(b) Hypotheses of association (or correlation) between variables in a population.

The tests of statistical significance we apply to each type of hypothesis are different. In the case of different hypotheses we employ a test of significance of the difference between two or more values of a statistic. On the other hand in testing a hypothesis of association we apply a test of statistical significance to a single measure of the association between the variables.

2 TYPE OF EXPERIMENTAL DESIGN

(a) Using same subjects for different experimental conditions (within-subjects, related design) *or*

(b) Using different subjects for different experimental conditions but making sure that the people in each condition are matched on some relevant criterion (matched-pairs design which can be treated statistically as if it were a related design).

(c) Using different, non-matched subjects for each experimental condition (between-subjects, independent groups, unrelated design).

There are different statistical tests which should be used for related and unrelated designs.

3 LEVELS OF DATA

The data may be nominal, ordinal, interval or ratio. The level obtained influences the choice of test.

4 STATISTICAL ASSUMPTIONS

However, any statistical test is valid only under certain conditions. In applying a test we generally have to assume that these conditions are satisfied. Hence we refer to the assumptions of a particular test.

The most common types of assumptions are:

(a) Assumptions about characteristics of the population distribution from which samples are drawn; for example we make the assumption that the population distribution is normal.

(b) Assumptions about observations of individuals comprising a sample; for example the assumption that observations are random and independent − the inclusion of any one individual in the sample does not affect the chances of any other individual being included in the sample.

In research the best tests are those tests whereby we are least likely to make errors in our decision to accept or reject a null hypothesis. These tests involve a number of important assumptions. For example the small sample t and F tests assume:

(a) That the underlying population distribution(s) is normal.
(b) That observations are independent.
(c) That populations have equal variances.

t and F tests may usefully be employed when the actual characteristics of available data depart to some degree from the above conditions. But you should always bear in mind that extreme departures from these conditions might invalidate a t or F test.

Tests which are appropriate for categorical data such as χ^2 or data in the form of ranks such as the rank-order correlation *rho* in general involve fewer assumptions than t or F tests. Many such tests do not specify conditions about the shape or character of the distribution of the population from which samples are **drawn**. Such tests are called distribution free, or non-parametric.

In using distribution-free tests we do **not test** hypotheses involving

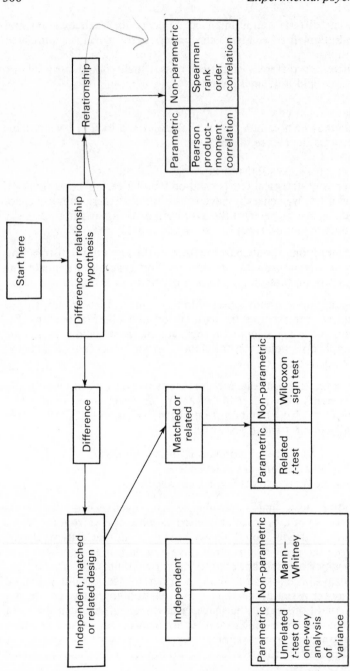

Figure 38 Choosing your test

specific values of population parameters. This eliminates hypotheses involving values of M, σ or other descriptive parameters of population distributions. Hence the term non-parametric is also used to describe such tests.

Although distribution-free tests involve fewer assumptions than parametric tests such as t or F tests, and hence may be more widely applicable, they are nevertheless in general far less powerful than parametric tests. We are less likely to reject a false null hypothesis with a non-parametric or distribution-free test than we are with a parametric test.

In testing statistical hypotheses where more than one test seems appropriate we should choose the most powerful of the available tests. It is defined as the probability of rejecting a false null hypothesis. As has been stated, parametric tests are more powerful than non-parametric tests.

To conclude therefore, in evaluating techniques of statistical analysis you determine:

(a) Whether the statistics employed are appropriate for the type of data available.
(b) Whether the test employed is appropriate for the type of hypothesis being tested.
(c) Whether the test employed is suitable for the design.
(d) Whether the assumptions involved in the test are realistic.
(e) Whether the test of statistical significance is valid.

Finally you must consider whether alternative methods of analysis might have been appropriate, or whether a number of different methods might be usefully employed.

Figure 38 is a guide to the selection of the correct statistical test.

24

Factor analysis

This chapter aims to present a simple explanation of what factor analysis is so that an understanding of the vitally important factor analytic approaches to personality (*Cattell; Eysenck*) and to intelligence and creativity (*Spearman; Vernon; Thurstone; Guilford*) is more readily possible. No mathematical or computational demands are made on the reader in this chapter.

A The aim of factor analysis

The aim of factor analysis is simplification, to make order out of chaos, to identify basic underlying factors which explain in a parsimonious way a larger number of other related variables. Think of the doctor's task when called to your bedside. He notes a number of related variables such as raised temperature, rapid heart beat, muscular pain, and so on. Such clusters of symptoms which appear together in a consistent fashion (a syndrome) are underlain by a particular illness, perhaps in this case influenza. While medical diagnosis is not as easy as this, it does illustrate the fact that a factor is a way of explaining the simultaneous occurrence of other variables. The major cause of car breakdowns seem to relate to problems either with the battery, alternator, condenser, distributor, or with the carburettor, choke, fuel pump and fuel line. These eight elements can be grouped into two factors – those of fuel feed problems and those of electrical problems. A final example of a commonsense factor or underlying common element is seen when we note the great similarity between length of arm, length of leg and body height in each individual. The common element or factor is that of linear size. A factor then is the outcome of discovering a group of variables having a characteristic in common. It shows how variables are grouped. This commonness is revealed by the nature of the correlations between the variables.

A commonsense or intuitive interpretation of the fact that two measures vary together as reflected by a strong correlation coefficient, is that they share something in common. If scores on an anxiety scale correlate strongly with scores on a hypochondriasis scale but show virtually no correlation with scores on a transfer of training task, this suggests that the performances on the anxiety and hypochondriasis scales were quite similar and shared something in common, i.e. were underlain by some common factor. Such a common factor was not evident in the anxiety–transfer of training relationship. This is a reasonable interpretation and the correlation coefficient (or strictly r^2) may be statistically interpreted as the proportion of variance that is common to the two measures. Refer back to p. 265 if you have forgotten this point.

STQ *If two measures correlate $+0.8$ what proportion of the variance in scores on one is predicted by performance in the other?*

---

r^2 Is a measure of the common variance of the two variables correlated: i.e. how much of the variability in one variable is common to the other or can be predicted by the other.

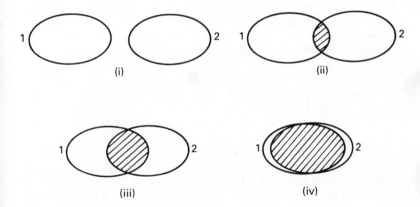

Figure 39 Common variance of two variables

In the four situations below (Figure 39) for the two variables 1 and 2:

(a) Corresponds to no correlation ($r = 0$: no common variance).
(b) Corresponds to a small correlation ($r = 0.3$ say: 9% common variance).

(c)   Corresponds to a high correlation ($r = 0.6$ say: 36% common variance).

(d)   Corresponds to a very high correlation ($r = 1$): approaching 100% common variance).

If the variability in scores on one variable is also reflected in the variability in scores on another, then there must be a high r between them since they are measuring mainly the same variability and hence mainly the same common factor.

Factor analysis is a technique that extends and generalizes this approach, so that a large number of intercorrelations can be analysed in which complex interactions between variables or tests would be impossible to discern by eye. By employing factor analysis the whole matrix of correlations can be analysed to find out how much of the variation in performance on all the tests can be accounted for by one or more factors. It is a powerful mathematical technique for unravelling complex patterns of relationships.

The factor analyst aims to describe a welter of confusing information in terms of a small number of factors, without losing too much of the information in the process. There are two main areas in psychology in which factor analysis is vital. The first involves the factor analysis of personality, and the second is concerned with factor-analytic studies of intelligence. In the first case the 'welter of confusing information' consists of all the different ways in which personality can be described, and factor analysis attempts to reduce these to a manageable number while still preserving most of the individual variations involved. The aim is to describe an individual's personality in terms of such variables as his degree of extraversion, his level of self-confidence, how gregarious he is, how anxious he is, and so on. The number of fine distinctions we can make between people is considerable, but the aim of factor analysis is to find a simple set of personality factors that will pick up most of these differences.

In the second area, the factor-analytic study of intelligence, there is again an overwhelming mass of data to be made sense of. This time it consists of performances on innumerable tests, all purporting to measure aspects of intelligence. The aim is to attribute this bewildering array of scores to a small number of factors: verbal ability, spatial ability and general intelligence, among others. A related area is the issue of whether intelligence and creativity are two independent characteristics, or whether they are related to each other. The trouble with factor analytic approaches is that data of this kind can be simplified or reduced to their essentials in more than one way. In the two main areas we are concerned with there is considerable controversy as to which of two particular methods is 'better'. There is no consensus of opinion, in either case, as to which is better in any absolute sense – indeed, perhaps the most fruitful response to both controversies is to say that sometimes one approach and sometimes the other is the most useful in a given situation. The nature of these controversies should become clearer as you read the subsequent material on the different subject areas.

B Elementary linkage analysis

But before you read further you will probably find it helpful to carry out some simple analysis of a correlation matrix (Table 70) yourself.

Table 70 Hypothetical matrix (or table) of intercorrelations between five tests

	A	B	C	D	E
A		0.08	0.08	0.04	0.68
B	0.08		0.86	0.69	0.10
C	0.08	0.86		0.76	0.20
D	0.04	0.69	0.76		0.14
E	0.68	0.10	0.20	0.14	

A and E are tests of intelligence; B, C and D are tests of creativity.

Elementary linkage analysis is not strictly the same as factor analysis, but it bears a strong relationship to it. It is a technique that involves you in no calculation at all, but carrying out such an analysis should provide you with insights into what factor analysis is all about.

The object of elementary linkage analysis is to link one variable to another, when the first variable has a higher correlation with the second variable (i.e. is more similar to it) than with any other variable. These two variables form the nucleus of a 'cluster', to which other variables are added in turn, on the same principle. In this way we hope to isolate clusters of similar variables. The statistical techniques of factor analysis are in fact considerably more sophisticated than these procedures; nevertheless, there is a strong analogy between the two. Below you are given a step-by-step explanation of elementary linkage analysis.

Steps of an elementary linkage analysis

Step 1: Draw a circle round the highest correlation in each column of the matrix.

	A	*B*	*C*	*D*	*E*
A		0.08	0.08	0.04	(0.68)
B	0.08		(0.86)	0.69	0.10
C	0.08	(0.86)		(0.76)	0.20
D	0.04	0.69	0.76		0.14
E	(0.68)	0.10	0.20	0.14	

Step 2: Find the highest pair of correlations in the matrix and draw a line through them. (By doing this you are identifying the most closely related pair(s) of variables.)
Then write down the names (letters) of the most closely linked tests. (If there are two pairs of correlations equally high, write down either pair.)

	A	*B*	*C*	*D*	*E*
A		0.08	0.08	0.04	(0.68)
B	0.08		(0.86)	0.69	0.10
C	0.08	(0.86)		(0.76)	0.20
D	0.04	0.69	0.76		0.14
E	(0.68)	0.10	0.20	0.14	

B───────────────C

Step 3: Read across the rows B and C and draw a line through all circled entries. Write down the tests which these entries link to your first pair. (By doing this you are finding those additional variables which are more closely linked to your initial variables (B and C, here) than to any others.)

D is a 'first cousin' linked to C, so we can represent the cluster as in the diagram above. (In this case there is only one first cousin: there may, of course, be several.)

Step 4: Read across the rows of these first cousins, drawing a line through any circled entries and writing down the tests which are thus linked to those already extracted. (Now you are looking for further variables which fit in better with the ones you have already selected than with any others.)

There are no 'second cousins' to link to D, since there are no circled entries in D's row.

Step 5: Repeat this procedure with the 'second cousins', third cousins, etc., until there are no more circled entries in the rows. The first cluster is now produced.

The first cluster consists of tests B, C, and D.

Step 6: Repeat the procedure from step 2 onwards, starting with the highest circled entry in the matrix without a line through it. Continue this repetition until all tests are separated into clusters.

	A	*B*	*C*	*D*	*E*
A		0.08	0.08	0.04	(0.68)
B	0.08		(0.86)	0.69	0.10
C	0.08	(0.86)		(0.76)	0.20
D	0.04	0.69	0.76		0.14
E	(0.68)	0.10	0.20	0.14	

A————————E

There are no first and later cousins: this matrix is now analysed into clusters:

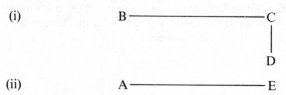

(i)   B ─────────────── C
                                                       |
                                                       D

(ii)   A ─────────────── E

Step 7: Identify the clusters by the character of the tests linked together.

The first cluster contains the three creativity tests and the second the two intelligence tests. We can therefore identify the first cluster as 'creativity', and the second as 'intelligence'.

The matrix can then be restructured so as to place those tests which form a cluster adjacent to each other. If the elementary linkage analysis has produced clear clusters then the higher correlations will tend to appear closely 'together' in groups, instead of being scattered throughout the body of the matrix. Is this so?

We can draw around the two clusters and show this more closely (Table 71).

Table 71

	A	*E*	*B*	*C*	*D*
A		0.68	0.08	0.08	0.04
E	0.68		0.10	0.20	0.14
B	0.08	0.10		0.86	0.69
C	0.08	0.20	0.86		0.76
D	0.04	0.14	0.69	0.76	

We have succeeded in reducing the five variables, of measurable aspects of behaviour, into two clusters – one of three variables and the other of two. Each cluster contains aspects of behaviour which are similar, so each cluster can be thought of as analogous to the psychologist's factors. But it must be stressd that, in spite of the analogy, there are essential theoretical differences between the clusters produced by elementary linkage analysis and the factors produced by factor analysis; these theoretical differences are not, however, critical for our discussion.

C A geometrical approach

Now that you have had the opportunity to do something akin to factor analysis for yourself, you should find the following material easier to follow than you would otherwise have done.

First of all we shall consider how the problems can be represented diagrammatically, because diagrams may help you to understand what is involved. The factor analyst's raw data consists of a set of measurements – personality measures, ability tests, attitudes or individual test items and so on – and a correlation coefficient between every pair of these measurements. We can represent each of these measures by a line, usually called a vector, pointing in a definite direction. Two measures which are highly correlated will be represented by lines pointing in very similar directions, so that they have a small angle between them as in Figure 40(a). Two measures which have a low correlation, however, will have an angle between them that is close to a right angle, as in Figure 40(b).

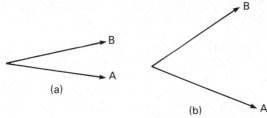

Figure 40 Geometric representation of correlation between two variables

So the correlation between two variables can be expressed geometrically. Each variable or test can be represented as a straight line (or vector), the cosine of the angle between the two lines is equal to the correlation coefficient between them (see Figure 41).

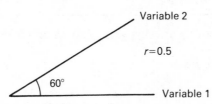

Figure 41 Relationship between cosine of angle and correlation coefficient

Where the correlation is 0.0 (or cosine = 90) then the angle between the two variables is a right angle since cosine $90° = 0$. Two variables at right angles to each other are known as orthogonal and represent a zero correlation (Figure 42).

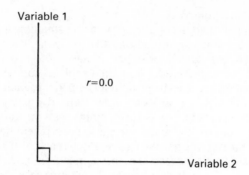

Variable 1

$r=0.0$

Variable 2

Figure 42   Orthogonal variables

A correlation of 1.0 would produce a cosine of 0, i.e. the vectors representing the variables would be the same line.

Now we have this representational technique, we can consider the situation where we have a considerable number of vectors – the situation which factor analysis is concerned with.

Generally speaking, we shall not be able to draw a simple diagram even if we have only ten vectors, let alone 50 or a 100; not even a three-dimensional model would be able to do this accurately. Just consider the simple case of three tests, *X, Y* and *Z*. The correlations between these tests are such that, if they are represented diagrammatically:

the angle between *X* and *Y* must be 50°
the angle between *Y* and *Z* must be 20°
the angle between *X* and *Z* must be 35°

STQ   *You might like to try and draw a diagram on a piece of paper in which all these conditions are satisfied, before reading on. Did you manage it?*

Suppose we began by drawing vectors for *X* and *Y* as in Figure 43.

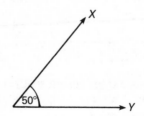

Figure 43   Vectors *X* and *Y*

Can we now fit Z on to this diagram so that the angle between Y and Z is $20°$ and the angle between X and Z is $35°$? Since the angle between B and C is $20°$, there are only two possible positions for C if we insist on remaining in two dimensions, that is, on a flat surface. They are illustrated in Figures 44 and 45.

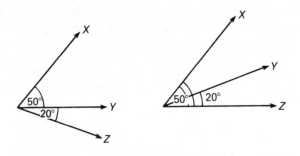

Figure 44   **Figure 45**

In neither diagram is the angle between X and Z the angle of $35°$, as we wanted; in the first diagram it is $70°$ and in the second it is $30°$.

Thus to represent correctly the relationships between even these three tests, we need to go into three dimensions. But we can still discuss the essential points in factor analysis in terms of two- or three-dimensional situations – as long as we remember that we are most unlikely to be able to confine ourselves to three dimensions in an actual problem, which makes geometrical treatment impossible. With more than three variables we are into the heady world of hyperspace.

In this geometrical model of factor analysis we are concerned with expressing economically these intercorrelations. This is similar to resolving vectors in physics. A vector becomes a line of reference to which the variables, related by the cosine of the angle between them, can be attached. The best analogy for you to use during the rest of this section is that of a half-open umbrella, in which the radiating spokes are the tests or variables with particular angles between them to represent their intercorrelations, while the handle is used as the reference vector or factor.

D Factor-analytic studies of personality

Consider the following adjectives, all of which describe aspects of personality: shy, quiet, aloof, withdrawn, gregarious, outgoing, sociable.

There are subtle distinctions between the first four of these, but nevertheless there is likely to be a tendency for them to be used to describe the same individual. That is, an individual whom one person describes as shy may very well be described as quiet, aloof or withdrawn by other persons, or by the same person on a different occasion. In any sample of people there are likely to be fairly high correlations between the use of these adjectives to describe individuals in the sample. Conversely, people described as shy and withdrawn are very unlikely to be described as gregarious or sociable. There will probably be a substantial negative correlation between the use of the last three adjectives in the list and the first four.

Now we can represent this diagrammatically, as was discussed in the previous paragraphs. We can represent adjectives which are highly correlated as lines with a small angle between them, as in Figure 46.

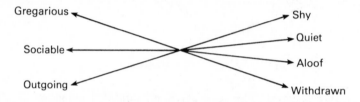

Figure 46   Correlations between adjectives

Adjectives which are more or less opposite in meaning, so that there is a large negative correlation between them, will point more or less in opposite directions. Figure 46 represents the kind of situation we might well find in a given sample of people. Acutally, it is unlikely that we should be able to represent even this small number of correlations absolutely accurately in a two-dimensional diagram such as this, but we shall assume that we can do this because it makes the argument easier to illustrate. Now look at Figure 47, which is Figure 46 with an addition.

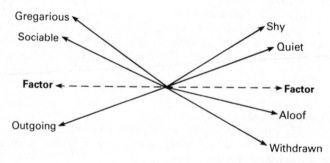

Figure 47   'People-orientated' factor

This particular group of adjectives could be represented fairly well by just one 'factor' which, without much loss of detail, we might call 'people-orientated'. We should say that each of the seven adjectives has a high loading on the factor, which we might equally well call 'gregariousness/aloofness', using representative adjectives from either extreme.

This was the kind of exercise carried out by Cattell, who extended it to all the adjectives he could find describing personality. We could add a second cluster of adjectives to Figure 46 – say, fastidious conscientious, careless – producing Figure 48. (The correlations represented in Figure 48 should not be taken as representing the 'real' situation accurately: the figure is only designed to illustrate the issues that concern personality factor analysts.) In Figure 48 the 'conscien-

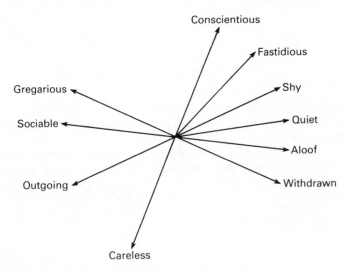

Figure 48 Two clusters of adjectives

tious, fastidious, careless' cluster bears moderate to low correlations with the original 'shy, quiet, gregarious, outgoing' cluster. We can simplify Figure 48, just as we simplified Figure 46, by regarding each cluster as representing a single factor (or personality dimension). But this can be done in more than one way, and it is at this point that factor analysts disagree as to method. There are two broad techniques.

In method 1 the analyst insists that the factors must be independent of each other. The 'best' possible factors are drawn that fulfil this condition, illustrated in Figure 49. They are called independent or

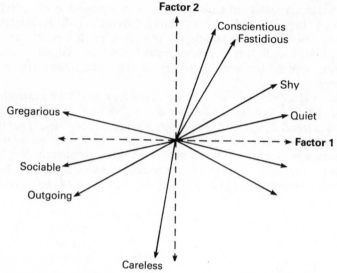

Figure 49 Orthogonal Factors

orthogonal factors, and are at right angles to each other. This method
is often termed an unrotated solution and for many factor analysts is
an interim one.

The unrotated solution often provides a factor 1 which has large
loadings on every test and subsequent smaller factors which possess

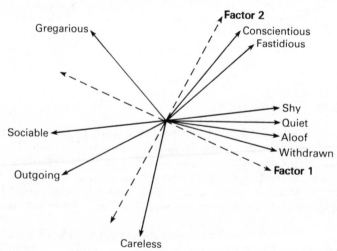

Figure 50 Rotated factors (oblique)

negative as well as positive loadings. This sort of unrotated solution was the sort that led to concept of *g*, a large general intellectual factor.

The problem with unrotated solutions is that the negative loadings on some of the factors proves difficult to interpret. The next state of the factor-analysis process is to rotate the interim solution to a psychologically acceptable final solution. The rotation is the rotation of the axes to ensure that negative loadings are removed. Look at Figure 50.

Method 2 is illustrated in Figure 50. Each cluster of tests is taken to represent a factor, and each factor is the 'best' line through the cluster, as in Figure 50. The important point to notice about these two factors is that they are correlated with each other because they are no longer at right angles. You will remember that it is only when factors are at right angles to each other that the correlation between them is zero. In method 2 the factors produced are therefore not independent of each other – they are oblique, in Cattell's terminology. The factor axes have been rotated each through a different number of degrees.

These two methods raise an issue which constantly occurs in discussions of factor analysis. Should we insist on orthogonal factors? The advantages of orthogonal factors, as in Figure 49, are:

(a) They are much easier to handle mathematically.
(b) Even with slightly different tests, similar factors tend to be produced, so that we have a fairly stable description of personality which is relatively independent of the actual tests used.

The main advantage of oblique factors is that each factor is very closely related to one cluster of tests and only marginally related to all the others.

Which we prefer, orthogonal or oblique, depends, then, upon what we want. If we want a fairly stable description in terms of independent factors which we are not particularly anxious to measure in a pure form, then we can opt for orthogonality. If, on the other hand, we want to measure the factors fairly accurately using a single test for each factor, we can opt for obliqueness. Cattell opts for a system of sixteen oblique personality factors, while Eysenck opts for a system of two orthogonal factors, extraversion/introversion and neuroticism/stability. This particular controversy has further ramifications, for oblique factors are correlated with each other and can thus be factor analysed themselves, giving second-order factors.

SECOND-ORDER AND HIGHER-ORDER FACTORS
Because Cattell's sixteen personality factors are oblique, and so have some correlation with each other, it is possible next to take the sixteen factors as initial vectors and subject them to the same kind of factor-

analytic procedure as was done at the first stage. This has been done and, interestingly enough, the two most important second-order factors produced are very akin to Eysenck's two main factors. The procedure can be extended still further by factor analysing the second-order factors, so producing third-order factors, which can in their turn be analysed . . .! There are only two factors left at the fourth stage, so the procedure, fortunately, terminates!

E   Factor-analytic studies of intelligence

Similar problems arise when considering intelligence. The controversy between group-factor analysis and multiple-factor analysis concerns once more the issues of orthogonality and the degree to which a factor can be represented by a single test; the two are often mutually exclusive in practice.

Tests of intelligence are, almost invariably, positively correlated with each other. Represented diagrammatically, the situation looks rather like Figure 51. The angle between each pair of vectors is acute, even between the extremes of test W and test Z indicating positive correlations between each pair. Again, you should remember that in reality it would be very unlikely that we could represent the correlations in a two-dimensional diagram, nor yet in a three-dimensional model (which would look rather like a half-open umbrella), but the essential points are still the same.

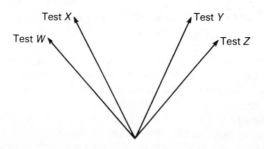

Figure 51   Correlations between intelligence tests

The question, then, is how to reduce such data to a limited number of factors. One approach, the British hierarchical approach, which is often known as the group-factor method, is as follows. All the tests in Figure 51 tend to point towards the top of the page rather than the bottom; some of them point to the right and some to the left, but they all point up the page rather than down. Therefore, take as the first factor one pointing in this direction, as in Figure 52. In the three-

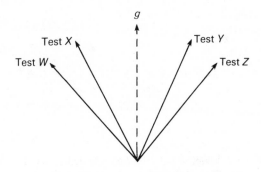

Figure 52

dimensional situation, where the vectors representing the tests are the spokes of a half-open umbrella, this factor will correspond to the umbrella's handle. It will probably be the most important factor, as it has substantial positive correlations with all the tests. It is called *g*, standing for 'general intelligence'.

The next step will probably be best understood if you continue to think in terms of the umbrella, where *g* is the vertical handle and the other four tests are spokes sloping at various angles to it. Each of these tests also has a definite horizontal direction, which may be east, west, north, south or anywhere between these. Suppose these make the pattern shown in Figure 53.

Figure 53

It is repeatedly found in such studies that the tests fall into two distinguishable groups, more or less independent of each other, so that two independent (or orthogonal) factors can be used to describe the situation fairly accurately, as in Figure 54.

These factors are always identified with this approach to extracting factors and are usually known as *v.ed* (verbal−educational factor) and *km* (mechanical−spatial factor). Thus we have so far a description of intelligence in terms of three factors: *g*, which is general intelligence, and the more specific factors of verbal and spatial ability. Such a description would be adequate for many purposes. It can be

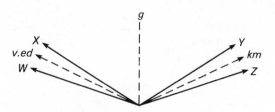

Figure 54

represented as a hierarchy with g at the head, as the factor which enters into every test, and then $v.ed$ and km, which enter into one or other of the groups of tests (see Figure 55).

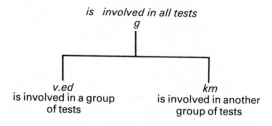

Figure 55

Now a completely different way of reducing the same set of data to a limited number of components aims to follow a similar procedure to that used by Cattell, namely, to identify clusters of highly correlated tests and take each cluster to represent a factor. Such factors are usually not orthogonal, but oblique. Figure 56 is a repeat of Figure 51, representing the same set of tests as we analysed before. This time

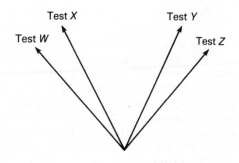

Figure 56

we look for clusters of related tests, which in our diagram would be *W* and *X* as one cluster and *Y* and *Z* as another. Factors would be like those illustrated in Figure 57.

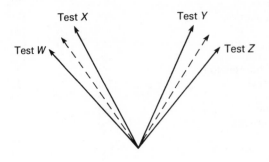

Figure 57

In fact, Thurstone identified eight such clusters; these were: verbal ability, perceptual speed, inductive reasoning, number, rote memory, deductive reasoning, word fluency and spatial ability. The arguments about these two different approaches are very similar to those discussed in connection with the personality material, namely: the hierarchical approach (producing orthogonal factors) gives a stable description of intelligence in terms of independent factors (in order of importance, also). It is stable in the sense that, even when a group of people is different and the intelligence tests are different a similar factor pattern is usually found.

The multiple-factor approach produces oblique factors, each of which can be estimated from single tests. Each factor is of more or less equal importance, but the factor structure is less than in the hierarchical, group-factor approach.

F   Interpreting a factor-analysis table
The principal outcome of a factor analysis is a table of factor loadings. Table 72 shows such a table resulting from a factor analysis of the performance of a sizeable group of students on thirteen psychological tests. (The boxes round sets of figures would not normally be there.)

All the figures in the body of the table should be preceded by a decimal point, i.e. 0.10, 0.25, 0.71, 0.57 etc. These are usually omitted for ease of presentation. The figures have also been rounded to two decimal places for the same reason.

Table 72

Test		Factors			
		I	*II*	*III*	h^2
1	Raven's matrices	10	25	71	57
2	Cubes	10	09	43	20
3	Paper form board	14	01	60	38
4	AH5 spatial	19	12	52	32
5	General information	70	32	24	66
6	AH5 verbal	72	21	30	65
7	Antonyms	78	24	24	72
8	Synonyms	56	29	37	54
9	Word meaning	79	20	23	72
10	Uses	12	76	−10	60
11	Consequences	11	65	16	46
12	Circles	−08	70	21	55
13	Product imp.	07	62	27	46
Contribution of factor		2.67	2.29	1.87	6.83

Table 72 shows:

(a) The battery of tests that was used together with brief descriptive labels. There were thirteen of these tests all of which were given to the same group of subjects.

(b) Three factors labelled I, II and III. These factors show, in their respective columns, the factor loadings, i.e. such numbers as 0.71, 0.43, 0.60, etc., for the first three tests in factor III. These factor loadings look like correlation coefficients and in essence this is what they are.

(c) Certain figures down the right-hand side headed h^2. These figures refer to the commonality of each test, a term we shall return to. The maximum value which can appear in this column is 1.00. The figures (all less than 1.00) show how much of the total test (*viz* how much of 1.00) has been accounted for by the three factors I, II and III taken together. In each case part of the test is not accounted for.

(d) Certain figures at the foot of each column described as 'Contribution of factor'. These figures show the size and hence, in some degree, the importance of each factor.

(e) A figure, *viz* 6.83, in the bottom right-hand corner, which is the sum of the column and also the sum of the row against which it appears.

We have also drawn in certain lines. These boxes contain all the big loadings. For the moment 'big' means greater than 0.40. A rearrangement of the order in which the tests are presented in the table (which is a completely arbitrary matter; each person can list his tests in whatever order best suits his purpose) has brought the boxed factor loadings together as far as possible.

With any necessary shuffling of test order this table is the manner in which the research worker would be presented with his results. These results would ordinarily come to him from the computer. He would then locate his groupings by shuffling the test order or as we have in this case with our boxes. He would see, as we do,

(a)   A grouping of tests 5, 6, 7, 8 and 9 in factor I as revealed by the high loadings.
(b)   A grouping of tests 10, 11, 12 and 13 in factor II.
(c)   A grouping of tests 1, 2, 3 and 4 in factor III.

The results in Table 72 are only a mathematical answer to our investigation of the factors underlying the original inter-correlations. We want to go further. We need to interpret our factors. This takes us to the psychological level of explanation. It has nothing to do with statistics but a lot to do with the insight, knowledge and subjective judgement of the researcher. The factors are identified essentially by looking at the variables on which they load strongly and then naming them subjectively on that basis. Our factors appear to be as follows:

(a)   Factor I is heavily loaded on verbal tests so let us call it the verbal factor.
(b)   Factor 2 is heavily loaded on tests that purport to measure creativity so let us call it the creativity factor.
(c)   Factor 3 is loaded on tests that index spatial/non-verbal ability so let us name it the spatial factor.

Of course other workers might have given these factors different names. Can you propose any? We juggled around with a number of alternatives. For example factor 1 could well have been labelled 'convergent thinking' and factor 2 'divergent thinking'. But whatever names we finally agree on they are based on:

(a)   Seeing what tests are substantially involved in each.
(b)   Seeing what tests are largely absent from each.

The figures at the foot of each column in Table 72 (2.47, 2.29, and 1.87) are the contribution of the factor to the total variance. They have been obtained by squaring and adding the loadings in each column. If the column of factor loadings for any one factor were to read

1, 1, 1, 1 etc., then the total contribution of this particular factor would be 13, the same number as the number of tests in the battery in this particular example. This is the highest value that is theoretically possible. Clearly if such a figure arose for a factor this factor would have completely accounted for performance in the test battery and nothing would be left for any further factors to explain. Such a situation has never been known to occur.

These three factors taken together contribute 6.83 to the total variance. This figure is around 52% of 13; hence the three factors account for only 52% of the total variance (the total battery performance) and we shall need to enquire later what has happened to the other 48%.

A test such as test 12 is largely a factor II test. It has very small elements of factor I and factor III in its make-up. Such loadings as appear in factors I and III for this test are sufficiently small to be disregarded, i.e. they can be considered as zero loadings for practical purposes. One is the more encouraged to do this since we know that error is always present in any experiment and we have learnt to ascribe small figures (e.g. small differences between means; small correlations, etc.) as being indistinguishable from error. Similar conclusions can be drawn about other tests.

Just as only a proportion of the total test battery has been accounted for by the three factors (52%), so only a proportion of each test has been accounted for by the three factors. These proportions are the figures entered in the column headed h^2. They have been obtained by squaring and adding the factor loadings in each row. In the case of test 7 as also for test 9 a substantial proportion (72%) of the individual test variance has been accounted for. For test 4 only can be described as being due to the operation of the three underlying factors. Such figures are referred to as the commonalities of a test. They show how much of each test is accounted for by the operation of the common factors (in this case three). The question of what is happening to the balance of the test in each case remains to be answered!

The above features are explicit in the table. Another important matter is implicit. The factor loadings are essentially correlation coefficients showing the correlations between each of the tests and the factor. The thirteen tests can be seen as the real tests (with all the imperfections and errors that go with real things) and each factor can be regarded as a hypothetically perfect test. When the research worker seeks to identify each factor, he is identifying a hypothetically perfect test with which each real test is correlated. The correlation will be imperfect ($r < 1$) since one of the two variables involved in each case is real and therefore imperfect. Thus factor I is imagined to be a perfect measure of verbal ability. Real test 6 is a very fair but still imperfect measure of this; it correlates 0.72 with pure verbal ability. Real test 9 (verbal meaning) is marginally better ($r = 0.79$). Real test 2 is virtually useless as a test of verbal ability ($r = 0.10$) and so on. This thinking backwards and forwards between the tests and the factors and the factors and the tests is what gives insight into and hence definition of each factor and insight into and understanding of the nature of each test.

G Problems of factor analysis

(a) Although it may seem reasonable to interpret these statistical factors as fundamental psychological qualities, they do not emerge conveniently labelled as intelligence or extraversion etc. The factors are simply evidence of co-variation between several variables and their common properties. The big jump from the mathematical answer to the psychological quality always requires careful justification. There is a superficial aura of objectivity about a complex mathematic technique employing computers yet this objectivity is less than one might think when the assumption is made that a psychological quality is proved. The naming of the factor(s) is quite subjective with the research worker reviewing the types of tests or test items that load heavily on a particular factor so that he can produce a name for the factor that will subsume all those individual variables.

(b) No method of analysis can analyse what is not there. The analysis is only as good as the input of data. The initial choice of tests by the research worker will control the sort of factor structure that emerges.

(c) Finally, factor analysis cannot conclusively demonstrate that a particular set of factors is the true one, since whatever scheme is put forward it is perfectly permissible for another research worker to substitute an alternative and mathematically correct equivalent though quite different in structure and assigned nomenclature. Different factor analytic methods will produce such alternative answers, in fact an infinite number of mathematically equivalent answers. This accounts for much of the apparent disagreement about the structures of ability and personality.

25

Reliability and validity

Introduction
One day, sometime in the future, one of your children may come running in from school eagerly reporting to you that he got 80 in a test on arithmetic problems and 115 on an IQ test. As a parent you may initially be quite proud and satisfied but as a psychologist your training will start to make you ponder on that information.

> **STQ** *Given these two test scores and no other information, what further questions would you pose?*

The questions we would ask ourselves ran along these lines:

(1) What do such scores imply?
(2) What further information do I need to interpret them?
(3) What level of performance did the rest of the class generate?
(4) Are the results an accurate reflection of my child's ability?
(5) Which specific tests were they?
(6) Were the tests proper measures of what they claimed to be?

Some of the statistical information required to pursue questions (1) to (3) above has been considered earlier in this book.

> **STQ** *What statistical information would you seek to respond to questions (1), (2) and (3)? Refer to Chapter 3 if you are not sure.*

The use of z scores (standardized scores) in addition to information about *M* and *σ* of the distributions will answer queries (1) and (3).

The answers to questions (4) and to (6) will be the focus of this chapter. What you want to know is if your child took the examinations again would he get the same scores of 80 and 115, or different scores, i.e. how reliable, consistent and accurate is the test. The other questions involve the problem of discerning whether a test is measuring what it claims it is, i.e. is the arithmetic problem solving test a valid measure of that or is it simply measuring the four basic rules of mechanical arithmetic $(+, -, \div, \times)$? Again is the IQ test measuring verbal, non-verbal, spatial aptitude or some global intellectual ability? The concepts of reliability and validity are central to test and score interpretation.

A Reliability

Synonyms for reliability are: dependability, stability, consistency, predictability, accuracy. A reliable person, for instance, is one whose behaviour is consistent, dependable, and predictable – what he will do tomorrow and next week will be consistent with what he does today and what he did last week. An unreliable person, on the other hand, is one whose behaviour is much more variable. More important, he is unpredictably variable. Sometimes he does this, sometimes that. He lacks stability. The first person is stable; the latter is inconsistent.

So it is with psychological and social science measurements; they are more or less variable from occasion to occasion. They are stable and relatively predictable or they are unstable and relatively unpredictable; they are consistent or not consistent. If they are reliable, we can depend upon them. If they are unreliable, we cannot depend upon them.

It is possible to approach the definition of reliability in three ways:

(a) One approach is epitomized by the question, 'Is the score which I have just obtained for student X the same score I would obtain if I tested him tomorrow and the next day and the next day?' A reliability coefficient, computed in a certain manner, reflects whether the obtained scores is a stable indication of the student's performance on this particular test. This question implies a definition of reliability in stability, dependability, and predictability terms. It is the definition most often given in elementary discussions of the subject.

(b) The second approach asks, 'Is this test score, which I have just obtained on student X, an accurate indication of his "real" ability?' The reliability coefficient may be used to estimate the accuracy with which student X's 'true score' has been approximated on the test he has just taken. This is an accuracy definition, which really asks whether measurements are accurate. Compared to the first definition, it is further removed from common sense and intuition, but it is also more fundamental. These two approaches or definitions can be summarized in the words stability and accuracy. However, the accuracy definition implies the stability definition.

(c) The third and final approach which helps to solve the theoretical and practical problems also implies the previous two approaches. This approach asks, 'How much error is there in this measuring instrument?'

STQ *When we considered ANOVA (Chapter 22) we said that variability in scores stemmed from two sources. Can you recall these two sources? (p. 281)*

The two sources are, (i) experimental variability induced by real differences between individuals in the ability to perform on the test, and (ii) error variability which is a combination of error from two other sources:

(a) Random fluctuation. Subtle variations in individual performance from day to day.

(b) Systematic or constant error. This is the result of one or more confounding variables which always push scores up or always push scores down, e.g. practice effect.

The amount of error in a score is a measure of the unreliability of the score. The less error the more reliable the score since it represents more closely the 'true' performance level of the subject.

Errors of measurement are assumed to be all random error. They are the sum or product of a number of causes: the ordinary random or chance elements present in all measures due to unknown causes, to temporary or momentary fatigue, to fortuitous conditions at a particular time that temporarily affect the object measured or the measuring instrument, to fluctuations of memory or mood, and other factors that are temporary and shifting. To the extent that errors or measurement are present in a measuring instrument, to this extent the instrument is unreliable. In other words, reliability can be defined as the relative absence of errors of measurement in a measuring instrument; reliability is associated, then, with random or chance error. Error and reliability are opposite sides of the same coin. The more error the less stable and less accurate the measurement. We will be looking at this inverse relationship in more detail later on. But now through our three approaches above we can recognize that reliability is the accuracy, stability, and relative lack of error in a measuring instrument.

A homely example of reliability will further clarify the concept for those still in a fog. Suppose we wished to compare the accuracy of two crossbows. One is an antique, well used and a bit sloppy in its action. The other is a modern weapon made by an expert. Both pieces are solidly fixed in granite bases, aimed and zeroed in by a sharpshooter. Equal numbers of darts are fired with each. The target on the left of Figure 58 represents the pattern of shots produced by the older weapon.

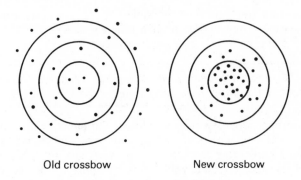

Old crossbow   New crossbow

Figure 58   Targets to illustrate concept of reliability

Observe that the shots are considerably scattered. Now observe that the pattern of shots on the target of the right is more closely packed. The shots are closely clustered around the bull's-eye. It is obvious that if we computed measures of variability, say a standard deviation, or a variance from the two-shot patterns, the antique bow would have a much larger measure of variability than the newer bow. These measures can be considered reliability indices. The smaller variability measure of the new one indicates much less error, and thus much greater accuracy, stability and predictability. The new bow is reliable; the old bow is unreliable.

Similarly, psychological and educational measurements have greater and lesser reliabilities. A measuring instrument, say a personality scale, is given to a group of children – usually only once. Our goal, of course, is a multiple one: we seek to hit the 'true' score of each child. To the extent that we miss the 'true' scores, to this extent our measuring instrument, our test, is unreliable.

THE THEORY OF RELIABILITY
A study of the theory of reliability takes us back to the analysis of sources of variance, as we hinted earlier. Every set of measures must have variance. Consider an examination candidate who is unsuccessful and who has to repeat the examination a year later. This time he would sit a different paper set supposedly to examine a similar group of candidates who have followed the same course. The two papers will be different since there are many more topics to be covered by the examination than there are questions, and therefore not all topics can appear in any one paper. Over many years there are a large number of possible papers which could be set on a particular syllabus, each one of which is intended to serve the same purpose.

Let us now suppose that the candidate continues to be unsuccessful and has to sit (in theory) all possible papers. What sort of results might we expect him to obtain? It is unlikely that he would have the same score every time.

> **STQ**   *Can you list some of the reasons why the candidate would not receive the same score every time?*

Just to mention a few we thought of: the papers will vary in the accuracy with which their sample of the course matches the candidate's knowledge – a paper may be very easy for the candidate, or very hard; the candidate will vary in his approach on the different occasions; the conditions under which he sits the examinations will vary; the examiners will vary in their marking standards.

> **STQ**   *If we plotted every total score of this candidate can you deduce what the distribution would look like? (Remember what sort of 'error' you are dealing with.)*

In general the distribution would be normal since the candidate is just as likely to obtain a mark higher than his 'real worth' as to obtain a mark lower than it. (The words 'real worth' are used here to represent the idea of the candidate's underlying real level of achievement.) This random error arises from two main sources then.

(a)   Instrument-centred errors resulting from ambiguities in test questions and directions and also from the fact that we test only a sample rather than a total universe of information and skills.

(b)   Errors resulting from temporal fluctuations in the individual examinee – variations from one testing occasion to another in his attitudes, speed of working, and other factors.

The M of this normal distribution of an infinite number of testings would be the best available estimate of the candidates level of performance. Hence, we can term this M his 'true score' so that each score from a single testing is equal to this 'true score' plus 'error'. (This 'plus' is not algebraic since error can decrease a score!)

This situation is unrealistic, and any particular candidate will never actually take many similar examination papers. But it is very convenient to define the true score of a candidate as being the average of the scores which he would obtain if able to sit a very large number of similar (or 'parallel') examination papers. This definition of true score forms the basis of a simple mathematical model (presented below) which is generally known as the 'classical test-theory model'.

The measurement of a candidate's underlying level of achievement will be blurred by other influences, such as have been mentioned before. These give rise to the error 'score' component in the observed score. Thus, for any candidate three scores need to be considered, the true score, the observed score, and the error score. A simple equation can be written which links these three scores. Observed score = true score + error score, or more simply,

$$X_{\text{ob}} = X_t + X_e$$

Where X_{ob} = observed score, X_t = true score, X_e = error score.

The error score may of course be positive or negative, depending on whether a candidate 'overscores' or 'underscores' with reference to his true ability. The smaller the error score, the closer the observed score approximates to the true score and the greater the reliability. We can define the reliability of any set of measurements as the proportion of their variance which is true variance, in other words the ratio of true variance to observed variance. When the true variance is equal to the observed variance, i.e. when there is no error variance, this ratio has a value of +1.0. This is the 'perfect reliability' value,

$$\frac{X_t}{X_{ob}} = 1 \text{ or } r_{tt} = +1.0 \ (r_{tt} \text{ symbolizes reliability})$$

When there is no true variance present, i.e. when the observed variance is entirely error, the ratio has a value of zero. This is the 'nil reliability' value, $r_{tt} = 0$

viz
$$X_{\text{ob}} = X_t + X_e$$
$$X_{ob} = 0 + X_e$$
$$\frac{X_t}{X_{ob}} (0) = 0$$

or conversely
$$\frac{X_e}{X_{ob}} = 1$$

(i.e. entirely error variance)

Similarly it can be shown that the total variance in obtained scores for a group of examinees would equal the sum of the 'true variance' and the error variance.

$$\sigma_{ob}^2 = \sigma_t^2 + \sigma_e^2$$

This equation is the key to the test theory of reliability.

If the equation is divided through on each side by the total or observed variance σ_{ob}^2, the following equation is the result:

$$1 = \frac{\sigma_t^2}{\sigma_{ob}^2} + \frac{\sigma_e^2}{\sigma_{ob}^2}$$

This equation indicates that the ratio of the true-score variance to the total variance plus the ratio of the error variance to the total variance equals 1. The proportions of the total variance represented by the true scores and by the error scores sum to 1. The ratio of the true-score variance to the total variance, or that proportion of the variance in the obtained scores which may be attributed to the true scores, forms the basic definition of reliability.

By substituting r_{tt} (the symbol for the reliability of a test) for σ_t^2/σ_{ob}^2, it can be seen that the equation may be stated: reliability equals 1 minus the error variance divided by the obtained variance.

$$r_{tt} = 1 - \frac{\sigma_e^2}{\sigma_{ob}^2} \text{ (definition of reliability)}$$

The proportion of the total variance which is true-score variance may be obtained by simply subtracting the proportion of the variance which is error from 1. The two basic theoretical equations for the reliability coefficient are:

(i)
$$r_{tt} = \frac{\sigma_t^2}{\sigma_{ob}^2} \text{ or } \frac{\text{true variance}}{\text{observed variance}}$$

(ii)
$$r_{tt} = 1 - \frac{\sigma_e^2}{\sigma_{ob}^2} \text{ or } 1 - \frac{\text{spread of error scores}}{\text{spread of test scores}}$$

Reliability is defined, so to speak, through error: the more error, the greater the unreliability; the less error, the greater the reliability. Practically speaking, this means that if we can estimate the error variance in any measure we can also estimate the measure's reliability. This brings us to two equivalent definitions of reliability:

(a) Reliability is the proportion of the 'true' variance to the total obtained variance of the data yielded by a measuring instrument.

(b) Reliability is the proportion of error variance to the total obtained variance of the data yielded by a measuring intrument subtracted from 1.00, the index 1.00 indicating perfect reliability.

TEST-THEORY ASSUMPTIONS

There are two basic assumptions in test theory. These assumptions are related to the nature of the true scores and the way in which true scores and error scores are combined. The first assumption is that the true score is a measure of a stable and continuing characteristic. It is necessary to assume that the student's performance on the test has not been simply a chance indication of a momentary preference, but rather that it is an indication of a stable ability or trait.

The second assumption is that the error component of a score is a randomly determined variable. That is, each test score reflects not only a student's true ability, but also some degree of error or incorrect assessment of the student's ability. This second assumption indicates that the amount of error associated with any particular score is a matter of chance. The assumption that errors are randomly associated with scores implies that there is no correlation between the obtained scores and the error scores. A student with a high score on a test should be just as likely to have a large error associated with his score (either positive or negative) as the person with the worst score.

METHODS OF DETERMINING RELIABILITY
Up to this point the discussion has been concerned with theory. There is no way we can ever measure X_t or σ_t^2. The σ_e^2 of course is the standard error squared of the distribution of all possible scores produced by a subject on an infinite number of testings. This too is inconceivable to achieve. Hence, to estimate the reliability of a test or a set of scores we must employ other procedures. There are three methods for computing reliability coefficients. These are based on the principle that two test scores may be obtained or derived for a set of students on a particular test. The two sets of scores are correlated to determine the reliability of the test, i.e., to determine the amount of variance in the test scores which may be attributed to true differences among individuals. Reliability coefficients are thus correlation coefficients between two sets of scores. The methods used in computing reliability estimates are:

(a) Test−retest method
(b) Alternate forms method
(c) Split-half method
(d) Internal consistency method

(a) Test−retest method
When reliability is measured by the test−retest method, a coefficient of stability is obtained. This reliability coefficient measures error variance due to temporal variations in characteristics of the examinee, as well as variation in conditions of test administration. Some of this temporal instability in test scores is due to variations from one testing occasion to another in the examinee's general characteristics, such as in his health or emotional tension; part of it is due to variations in their reactions to the specific test.

The test−retest reliability of a test is simply expressed as the correlations between the scores from two administrations of the same test to the same students. There is no standard duration of time which should separate the two administrations. However, a minimum of one day and perhaps a maximum of one year are boundaries generally considered acceptable for test−retest reliability estimates. In general a 2−3 month period is best.

> **STQ** *Why does a 2−3 month lapse of time between test and retest seem the optimum? What would you see as the problems stemming from (a) too short a time lapse and (b) too long a time lapse?*

If the period is too short the subjects may remember the answers they gave on the first occasion so spuriously increasing the consistency of scores. On the other hand, boredom, decreased motivation etc. may influence the second testing thus reducing the congruence of results between the two occasions of testing.

If the period is too long, maturational factors, e.g. learning, experience, age, will influence changes of score on the second occasion and cause an under-estimation of the reliability.

It is difficult to state any general rule concerning an appropriate period of intervening time for all tests. If the test is designed to measure a relatively stable trait or characteristic and the individual is not subjected during the intervening time to experiences which may, in some way, affect the particular characteristic involved, then the intervening period can be relatively long. However, when measuring a trait which is influenced by the individual's intervening experiences, the time should be shorter, but not short enough to allow memory or practice effects to inflate artificially the relationship between performance on the two administrations. Thus an appropriate period of intervening time can be decided upon only in the context of the situation.

Since the rationale of the test − retest method implies that the same level of cognitive, intellectual, motivational and personality variables are demonstrated on each occasion so that any changes are due to the instability of test itself, changes which occur within the subjects during the interval between test and retest are the largest source of error in the test−retest reliability estimate. The subject must always be a 'different' person for the sole fact of having taken the test on the first occasion.

> **STQ** *If the correlation between the scores from two occasions of testing was + 1.0, what does this imply for reliability and error?*

If you recall your studies of the correlation coefficient, you should realize that $r = +1.0$ would imply perfect reliability with no measurement error evident.

STQ *If reliability is less than + 1.0 what does this imply?*

As the test – retest correlation declines from unity we are measuring the effects of increasing random error.

STQ *For each of the following indicate whether they would contribute to true score or error score variance when a test – retest method is employed.*

(a) Noise in the next room on the first test.
(b) Reading ability.
(c) Broken pencil during retest.
(d) Headache on both occasions.
(e) Knowledge of a specific fact prior to the first test.
(f) Knowledge of a specific answer that was missed on the first test.

(b) Alternate- (or equivalent-) forms method
Because both general ability and specific knowledge may change differentially among students from test to retest, a second method of estimating reliability has been proposed; namely the alternate forms method. Standardized tests may have two or more equivalent forms that have been designed to be comparable in content, length, difficulty level, and variance e.g. Eysenck's Personality Inventory. When two equivalent forms (say forms A and B) are administered to students on the same occasion, these are correlated and a coefficient of equivalence is obtained, which measures the consistency of examinee performance from one specific sampling of test content to another. This method does not take into account temporal fluctuations in examinee performance.

This procedure has two advantages over the previous method. First, one need not be as concerned about memory and practice effect, since the two forms of the test are composed of different items. Secondly, a more accurate estimate of reliability is likely to be obtained because the estimate is based on a larger sampling of the universe of test items. However, these advantages are gained at the price of further time and effort involved in the construction of the instrument itself. It is obviously more difficult to construct two forms of a test than to construct just one. In addition, there are problems of ensuring that the forms are indeed equivalent. If they are not, the estimate of the reliability of either form is likely to be too low, since non-equivalency will tend to lower the correlation between the two tests.

What are the criteria of equivalency that must be observed? One of them is obviously item content; a second is the difficulty of the items; and a third is the discriminatory power of the items, i.e. the power of an item to discriminate between those who do well on the total test and those who do poorly. The general procedure for constructing equivalent test forms involves the following steps:

(1) Development of a universe of test items which represents the kinds of knowledge, abilities, skills, attitudes, interests, etc., that the test is to measure.

(2) Categorization of test items according to specific item types, content areas, difficulty levels, and levels of discriminatory power, in order to achieve subgroups of items which are relatively homogeneous with respect to these factors.

(3) Selection of items from within each of these subcategories, basing the number selected upon the relative emphasis accorded the particular content involved and upon the purpose of the test.

(4) Random subdivision of the items selected into two groups, one group to comprise one form of the test and the other group to comprise the second form.

Although the construction of equivalent test forms is difficult even for an experienced test maker, careful adherence to the procedure suggested above should produce reasonably satisfactory results.

In some situations, the equivalent-forms method is not at all feasible, but for testing achievement of cognitive abilities, it is generally possible to develop equivalent forms without undue difficulty. Most publishers of achievement and intelligence tests for example, publish two or more forms of most of their tests. In certain non-cognitive areas, however, the universe of test items is somewhat limited, and it is often difficult to construct equivalent forms. This is particularly true in measuring personality characteristics, attitudes, interests etc.

This alternate-form method better estimates the true-score differences in the general abilities of the students because the same items do not appear on both tests. However, the estimate is still influenced by temporary factors in the environment, by the test administration, and temporary conditions of the students, such as boredom or fatigue. It cannot be assumed that these factors will be present on both administrations of the test, and therefore they contribute to the error variance and reduce the estimated reliability of the tests. Because of these conditions, however, the alternate forms method is often used, since these factors influence the actual use of tests. In summary, the alternate forms procedure for computing a reliability coefficient assumes as true-score variance differences in scores attributable to general and lasting characteristics of the students and includes as error variance that difference attributable to specific skills with specific items on the two-test forms.

(c) Split-half method

The third form of reliability estimate is known as the split-half method, or perhaps more accurately, the internal-consistency estimate of reliability. The split-half method is based on the proposition that many of the temporary factors which influence the test — retest and alternate forms methods of estimating reliability could be eliminated if a reliability coefficient could be determined from the scores of a single administration of a test. It was therefore hypothesized that two scores could be obtained simply by splitting the test into halves. The scores obtained on the first half of the test could be correlated with scores on the second half of the test.

> **STQ** *Can you think why splitting a test into a first half and a second half would not be a good way of splitting the test for a split-half reliability estimate?*

The major problems with that sort of split is that, (i) different types of items with different difficulty levels may occur in each half, (ii) some subjects may run out of time and not finish the second half, (iii) boredom may set in on the second half.

Hence a commonly accepted way of splitting a test into two halves is to divide it into odd-numbered items and even-numbered items. If the test is constructed so that adjacent items tend to be similar in difficulty level, discriminatory power, and content, this is not an unreasonable procedure. However, one might ask what difference in the computed coefficient there would have been if the test had been split in some other way. A test of 20 items, for example, may be divided into two equal parts in exactly 184 756 different ways. Unless the 20 items are exactly equivalent (which, incidentally, would give us a rather silly test), there would probably be some variation in the reliability estimates obtained by splitting the test in so many different ways. In spite of this difficulty, the split-half reliability coefficient based on the odd—even split still provides the test constructor with useful information. One should use caution, however, in the interpretation of coefficients based on the split-half procedure.

Another method is to correlate the scores obtained during equal length odd- and even-numbered time intervals (first period, second period, third period etc.) into which the total testing time might be divided. But even under these more refined conditions, error scores will manifest themselves. For example, performance on individual items may be influenced by such temporary factors as attention to the item, interest, or guessing. The latter is often found to be an important factor when the test is quite difficult. In summary, although the split-half procedure avoids some of the error factors associated with test–retest and alternate-forms methods, it still has limitations based on the method by which the items are divided. A further problem exists.

When a test is divided into two parts and the scores are correlated, the result is a correlation between scores on tests that have only one-half as many items as were originally administered. The Spearman–Brown formula is used to estimate the reliability of the test in its original length. The general formula for the reliability of a test n times as long as the given test is:

$$r_{tt} = \frac{nr_{tt}}{1 + (n-1)\, r_{tt}}$$

In this formula n is the ratio of the length of the desired test to the length of the present test (length is defined as number of test items), and r_{tt} is the already obtained reliability. If the correlation between the scores on the odd items and the scores on the even items were 0.50, this correlation based on ten item pairs would be substituted into the Spearman–Brown formula as follows:

$$r_{tt} = \frac{(2)\,(0.50)}{1 + (2-1)\,(0.50)} = \frac{1.0}{1.5} = 0.67$$

The value 2 has been substituted for n because it was necessary to determine the reliability of the test twice as long as the two 10-item half tests used to obtain the original reliability coefficient. The formula indicates that the split-half reliability of the 20-item test is 0.67.

It is important to remember that any time the split-half method of reliability estimate is utilized, the Spearman – Brown formula must be applied to the correlation coefficient in order to obtain a reliability estimate which is appropriate for the total test length.

STQ *The split half reliability of a 50-item test is 0.79. What is its corrected reliability?*

(d) Internal consistency method

Another form of reliability measure which is commonly used is one developed by Kuder and Richardson (1937), the internal consistency method. The derivations of several formulas for estimating the reliability of a test that had been administered only once was stimulated by the problems, already described, which are inherent in the use of the split-half method of estimating reliability. As we have seen there are a number of ways in which a test may be split in order to compute 'half-test' scores, which then enter into the computation of a correlation coefficient. For each split, a different reliability coefficient might be obtained. Kuder and Richardson formulated measures of reliability that used item statistics, as opposed to part or total scores, as the basic unit of measurement. The result is a reliability estimate which is equivalent to the average of all possible split-half coefficients.

The simplest Kuder–Richardson formula is Formula 21 (often referred to as K–R 21). With this, reliability coefficients can be computed fairly easily, just on the basis of M, the number of test items and σ. The K–R 21 formula is:

$$r_{\text{K-R 21}} = \frac{N}{N-1}\left(1 - \frac{M(N-M)}{N(\sigma^2)}\right)$$

For example on a self-concept scale, where n is 100, the mean is 78, and the σ is approximately 10, the computation is as follows:

$$r_{\text{K-R 21}} = \frac{100}{99}\left(1 - \frac{78 \times 22}{100 \times (10^2)}\right)$$

$$= 1.01\left(1 - \frac{1716}{10000}\right) = 1.01\,(1 - 0.17)$$

$$= 1.01\,(0.83) = 0.84$$

This method, like the equivalent-forms method, takes into account variance due to the specificity of the tests and fails to measure temporal instability in test performance of students. It measures the consistency of performance on each test item.

There is a basic assumption underlying the application of the Kuder–Richardson formulas which states that the test for which the reliability is to be determined is essentially a unifactor test; i.e. all the items in the test are measuring the same characteristic of the individual. Seldom is one measuring a single factor with a test, and to this extent almost all tests are composed of items which measure more than one characteristic. The greater the diversity of test items, in terms of the skills required to determine the correct answers, the lower the correlations of the performance on the various test items. This decrease in the inter-item correlations reduces the obtained internal-consistency reliability estimate. An additional assumption is that the test items are scored 1 for correct responses and 0 for incorrect responses, and the total score is the sum of the number of items correct.

The split-half method of estimating test reliability is inappropriate with a speeded test. The same is true for the Kuder–Richardson formulas. Because a test is speeded, it will cause the inter-item correlations to be artificially inflated, and therefore give a biased estimate of the reliability.

REVIEW OF METHODS

Other things being equal, finally the investigator will choose the test with the highest quoted reliability. A test with a reliability of +0.90 is surely better than one with a reliability of +0.80!

But pause a moment! Things should not always be taken at face value, including reliability coefficients. The quoted values need interpretation, in terms of the method chosen to estimate reliability data, in terms of the situation in which the particular data were gained, and in terms of the sources of error they control (or do not control).

An interesting way of differentiating between these kinds of reliabilities is to note some of the causes of error variance in observed scores. These causes can crudely be grouped into four categories.

(a) Error variance associated with the measuring procedure itself (e.g. an elastic ruler produces poor measures!)

(b) Error variance associated with the subjects (children develop; attitudes change, etc.).

(c) Error variance associated with the conditions under which the measurement occurs (e.g. different administrators may present tests differently).

(d) Error variance associated with the marking (different markers have different standards).

STQ *Complete Table 73, indicating where the appropriate error variance will be present. The 'Alternate form' column has been completed for you. Table 73 has been completed in Table 73(a).*

Clearly we cannot always be certain that no error variance will be present. For example even if an immediate test – retest method is used, it is possible that error variance associated with the subjects will still be present, since they may be a little more tired on the retest. But it is

Table 73

	Type of reliability coefficient			
Source of error variance	Test–retest immediate	Test–retest delayed	Alternate form	Split half
The procedure			Yes	
The subject			No	
The conditions			No	
The marking			Yes	

Table 73(a)   Completed Table 73

	Type of reliability coefficient			
Source of error variance	Test–retest immediate	Test–retest delayed	Alternate form	Split half
The procedure	Yes	Yes	Yes	No
The subject	No	Yes	No	No
The conditions	No	Yes	No	No
The marking	Yes	Yes	Yes	Yes

unlikely to be as great as the error variance associated with the subjects if a delayed test – retest method is used, with a long time interval between retests. And the longer the interval, the lower will be the reliability figures obtained. So the important point is not the exact specification of the source of error variance. The point is that a reliability quoted by a test constructor must be interpreted according to the method used to calculate it.

STQ   (1)   *What sort of reliability method is used when:*

(a)   Different forms of the same test are administered.
(b)   One test is administered on two separate occasions.

   (2)   *To which sort of variance (true or error) does knowledge of a specific item of information contribute with:*

(a)   Test–retest method.
(b)   Alternate forms method.

> **(3)** *On how many administrations of a test are internal-consistency reliability estimates based?*
>
> **(4)** *In the split-half technique why are the various ways of splitting a test in half not all equally acceptable?*
>
> **(5)** *Why does the split-half technique not indicate the stability of obtained scores?*

FACTORS THAT INFLUENCE TEST RELIABILITY

A number of factors may influence the reliability of any test. These factors can be grouped in the following three categories:

(1) Factors dealing with the nature of the test items and the test itself.
(2) The nature of the subjects who are being tested.
(3) Factors related to the administration of the test.

The three basic methods for computing a reliability coefficient that have been presented often lead to differing estimates of the reliability of the test scores. The various conditions which can influence the outcome of the computation of a reliability coefficient further emphasize the notion that no test has a single reliability coefficient.

(a) Length of test

One of the major factors which will affect the reliability of any test is the length of that test. On an intuitive basis, one can see that as the number of items in any particular test is increased, the chance factors which might enter into a score are greatly reduced or balanced out. For example, performance on a three-item, multiple-choice test could be greatly influenced by various chance factors which might influence student responses. However, if the three-item test were lengthened to 30 or 40 items, the error sources would have a greater tendency to cancel each other out, and a better estimate of the true scores of the students would be achieved.

In addition, it can also be assumed that, as a test is lengthened, the test maker is providing a more adequate sample of items which measure the trait in question; i.e., the students will have a greater opportunity to display their ability over a wider range of items which tap the ability being measured.

You may already have noted that increasing the length of the test increases its reliability. This assumption is inherent in the use of the Spearman–Brown formula. Although this formula is used most often in the computation of the split-half reliability coefficient, it may also be used to compute the increased reliability due to tripling or adding ten times as many items to a test.

The Spearman–Brown formula may also be used to determine the number of items which must be added to an already existing test in order to increase its reliability to some desired level. However, a law of diminishing returns sets in so that as reliability increases it requires a tremendous extension in length to improve reliability a little. For example if a test with a reliability coefficient of only 0.82 is doubled in length, the estimated reliability coefficient of the longer test would be 0.90; if it were tripled in length, the estimated reliability coefficient would be 0.93.

(c) Restrictions in group performance
This refers to the range of ability or spread of scores within the group on which r_{tt} is computed. For example, the reliability coefficients for intelligence tests, computed on all comprehensive-school groups, tend to be higher than those computed on sixth-form groups, which show much less dispersion with respect to IQ.

(d) Methods of estimating reliability
Methods that take into account both stability and equivalence will tend to give lower coefficients than the other methods because all major types of error variance are included. The Kuder–Richardson method will tend to yield lower coefficients than the split-halves method because the former reflects test homogeneity, as reflected in all inter-item relationships, rather than merely the consistency of scores on two halves of a subdivided test.

With any method involving two testing occasions, the longer the interval of time between two test administrations, the lower the coefficient will tend to be.

(e) Objectivity of scoring
Another major factor affecting reliability of measurement is subjectivity of judgement. We tend to get low reliability coefficients for rating scales, essay examinations, projective tests etc. Objective tests produce high reliabilities.

EXPERIMENT TO ILLUSTRATE TEST–RETEST RELIABILITY
Tests, questionnaires, rating scales etc., need to be reliable and valid. A useful American scale to measure locus of control in children is the Nowicki and Strickland Locus of Control Scale. The authors tested the scale for reliability and found correlations ranging from 0.63 to 0.71 according to the grade levels of the children. Would the scale be more or less reliable when administered to British children?

A student decided to conduct a test–retest reliability study on this scale amongst a sample of 14-year-old children. Before doing so he read the relevant literature which is listed at the end of the experiment.

Subjects and experimenters
Subjects were 35 boys and girls aged 14 years, selected randomly from classes in a comprehensive school. One psychology student acted as experimenter.

Apparatus
A set of the Nowicki—Strickland Locus of Control Scales and Response sheets.

Method
Subjects were brought together in the school hall and each was given a locus of control scale and a response sheet. The following instructions were read out aloud by the experimenter:
'Read each of the 40 statements carefully and then I want you to mark each statement in the following way. If the statement describes how you usually feel, put a tick under the 'yes' column. If the statement does not describe how you usually feel, put a tick under the 'No' column. Please tick only one column for each of the 40 items. This is not a test and there are no right or wrong answers. Your response will be treated in confidence. Any questions? Then begin now.'
At the end of the session the subjects were thanked for their help and were asked if they would be willing to return in 6 weeks time to repeat the same procedure. The subjects response sheets were collected and scored according to the instructions in the manual. The same procedure was carried out six weeks later and the responses obtained from the two sessions are tabled in the Results (Table 75).

Results *Responses to the Nowicki—Strickland Locus of Control Scale*

Table 75 Test—retest data

S	Responses		S	Responses	
	First session	Second session		First session	Second session
1	18	18	19	17	20
2	22	14	20	22	21
3	6	10	21	14	8
4	12	10	22	14	16
5	17	10	23	19	21

Table 75 Continued

	Responses				Responses	
S	*First session*	*Second session*		S	*First session*	*Second session*
6	15	18		24	9	17
7	20	18		25	12	9
8	9	8		26	13	15
9	9	7		27	13	20
10	15	18		28	11	12
11	20	18		29	17	12
12	20	15		30	14	17
13	14	14		31	14	11
14	20	20		32	15	14
15	17	18		33	16	12
16	13	8		34	20	16
17	19	17		35	18	18
18	19	18				

Treatment of results

STQ *The Pearson product moment correlation procedure was adopted. Why?*

X	Y	X^2	Y^2	XY
18	18	324	324	324
22	14	484	196	308
6	10	36	100	60
12	10	144	100	120
17	10	289	100	170
15	18	225	324	270
20	18	400	324	360
9	8	81	64	72
9	7	81	49	63
15	18	225	324	270
20	18	400	324	360
20	15	400	225	300
14	14	196	196	196
20	20	400	400	400
17	18	289	324	306
13	8	169	64	104
19	17	361	289	323
19	18	361	324	342

Table Continued

X	Y	X²	Y²	XY
17	20	289	400	340
22	21	484	441	462
14	8	196	64	112
14	16	196	256	224
19	21	361	441	399
9	17	81	289	153
12	9	144	81	108
13	15	169	225	195
13	20	169	400	260
11	12	121	144	132
17	12	289	144	204
14	17	196	289	238
14	11	196	121	154
15	14	225	196	210
16	12	256	144	192
20	16	400	256	320
18	18	324	324	324
$\Sigma X = 543$	$\Sigma Y = 518$	$\Sigma X^2 = 8961$	$\Sigma Y^2 = 8266$	$\Sigma XY = 8375$

$$r = \frac{N\Sigma XY - (\Sigma X)(\Sigma Y)}{\sqrt{[N\Sigma X^2 - (\Sigma X)^2][N\Sigma Y^2 - (\Sigma Y)^2]}}$$

$$= \frac{35 \times 8375 - (543 \times 518)}{\sqrt{[(35 \times 8961) - 543^2][(35 \times 8266) - 518^2]}}$$

$$= \frac{293\,125 - 281\,274}{\sqrt{[313\,615 - 294\,849][289\,310 - 268\,324]}}$$

$$r = \underline{+\ 0.60}$$

> **STQ** *Write notes evaluating this scale in terms of its reliability as shown above.*

Exercise
Carry out a test−retest, or alternate forms or internal consistency reliability as appropriate on a test of your choice, and write it up as an experimental report.

REFERENCES
James, W. H. (1957). Internal vs External Control of Reinforcement as a Basic Variable in Learning Theory. Unpublished doctoral dissertation. Ohio State University.
Nowicki, S. and Strickland, B. R. (1972). A locus of control for children. *J. Consult. Clin. Psychol.* (In press)
Phares, E. J. (1963). Changes in Expectancy in Skill and Chance Situations. Unpublished doctoral dissertation. Ohio State University.
Rotter, J. B. (1954). *Social Learning and Clinical Psychology.* (New York: Prentice Hall)

STANDARD ERROR OF MEASUREMENT
The major methods of estimating the reliability of a test have been presented. There is one additional concept which is important in any discussion of reliability − namely, the standard error of measurement (SE_{meas}). It is a necessary statistic for interpreting the value of a reliability coefficient. We noted early in this chapter that a series of scores obtained by an individual on repeated administration of a single test will approximate to a normal distribution. The spread of this distribution is another way of conceptualizing the reliability of the test. The smaller the spread, the greater the fidelity with which any one observed score can be taken to represent the individual's true score. We use the standard deviation of this distribution as the index of its spread. This standard deviation of the error distribution is known as the standard error of measurement, or SE_{meas}.
The formula is:

$$SE_{meas} = \sigma\sqrt{1 - r_{tt}}$$

where σ is the standard deviation of the test scores and r_{tt} is the reliability coefficient of the test.

The interpretation of the standard error of measurement is similar to that of the standard deviation of a set of test scores. It may be stated, with a probability of 0.68, that a student's obtained score does not deviate from his true score by more than plus or minus one standard error of measurement. The probability is 0.95 for $X_{ob} \pm 2SE_{meas}$ and $0.99+$ for $X_{ob} \pm 3SE_{meas}$. This interpretation of the SE_{meas} is predicated upon the assumption that errors in measurement are equally distributed throughout the range of test scores. Research has suggested that the computed SE_{meas} for a test might be interpreted as an average value across the score range. If a subject obtains a score of 110 on a standardized intelligence test which has a $M = 100$, $\sigma = 15$ and $r_{tt} = 0.96$, what are the IQ limits within which 95% of the scores from an infinite number of testing of this subject would lie? Here we need to know the SE_{meas} since $2 \times SE_{meas}$ will define the 95% limits. Substituting in we obtain,

$$
\begin{aligned}
SE_{meas} &= 15\sqrt{1-0.96} \\
&= 15\sqrt{0.04} \\
&= 15 \times 0.2 \\
SE_{meas} &= 3
\end{aligned}
$$

i.e. the IQ scores he would obtain from an infinite number of testings would have a $\sigma = 3$. The 95% limits are therefore 2×3 IQ points above and below the only real score we know he has. So the range of error using the 95% confidence limits are 114 ± 6 ($108 - 120$). This range is quite revealing for it shows that even with a highly reliable test there is still quite a considerable band of error round an obtained score. If the reliability is lower this range increases. For example, with an r_{tt} of 0.75 and $\sigma = 15$, the 95% limits are ± 15 marks on each side of the obtained score. The limiting cases are when $r_{tt} = 0$ and $r_{tt} = 1$. In the former case SE_{meas} is the same as the σ of the scores; in the latter case SE_{meas} is zero, for there is no error.

STQ **(1)** *Calculate the 95% and 99% score ranges for the following:*

(a) *Raw score 114, $\sigma = 10$, $r_{tt} = 0.91$,*
(b) *Raw score 62, $\sigma = 5$, $r_{tt} = 0.84$.*

   (2) *To have confidence in an obtained score would you want a small or a large SE_{meas}? Justify your answer.*

SUMMARY

It would seem appropriate to summarize this long section on reliability at this point. A person's test score summarizes data on his performance on a sampling of tasks or test items. The concept of reliability is concerned with the consistency and accuracy of measurement, or the extent to which an individual's scores vary from one sample to another of the same type of behaviour.

If the same test is readministered on two different occasions, we obtain data on variance in scores due to temporal variations in the examinees. If two forms of a test are administered on the same occasion, we obtain data on variance in scores due to specificity of the samplings of test items.

Split-half and internal-consistency methods do not tell us anything about the temporal stability of the measures.

The reliability of a test, or the consistency of student scores from one test sample to another, depend largely on the length of the test, the homogeneity of the universe sampled, and the objectivity of test scoring.

Although reliability coefficients are most useful in assessing the comparative reliability of different tests, the standard error is more valuable in the interpretation of test scores for individuals.

Table 74 Relative merits of reliability assessment methods

Reliability method	Advantages	Disadvantages
Test–retest	Holds items constant. Requires only one scale.	Subject may recall specific items. Motivation may be reduced by having to retake test. Maturation and learning may have altered the subject in the time lapse. Some subjects may not turn up for retest.
Equivalent (alternate) forms	Effects of time interval removed. Loss of subjects on second test unlikely.	Two parallel forms needed. No measure of temporal stability.
Split half and internal consistency.	Only one scale required. Effects of time interval removed. Effects of recall removed. No loss of subjects.	No measure of temporal stability. Needs the application of Spearman–Brown formula. Not suitable for a timed test.

B Validity

The subject of validity is complex, controversial, and peculiarly important in psychological research. Here perhaps more than anywhere else, the nature of reality is questioned. It is possible to study reliability without inquiring into the meaning of the variables. It is not possible to study validity, however, without sooner or later inquiring into the nature and meaning of one's variables.

A test which was perfectly reliable would seem to be quite valuable, but the test user would also raise the questions: 'How valid is it? Does the test measure what I want it to measure?' A perfectly reliable test may not measure anything of value, and it may not correlate with any other test score. Validity information gives some indication of how well a test measures a given area, under certain circumstances and with a given group. It is for this reason that any one test may have many types of validity, and a unique validity for each circumstance and group tested.

THE DIFFERENCE BETWEEN RELIABILITY AND VALIDITY

Initially many students confuse these two terms. Let us imagine that the quality control department of a factory that manufactured one-foot, wooden, school rulers went on strike and some rulers were retailed which were inaccurate. The inaccuracy lay in the fact that each inch division was slightly longer than one inch; each was $1^1/_{12}$ inch long. Hence when we thought we were drawing a line twelve-inches long we were in fact drawing a line thirteen inches long ($1^1/_{12} \times 12$).

STQ *Is this ruler, (i) reliable, (ii) valid?*

Surprising as it may seem the ruler is quite reliable, for it produces consistent results even though the measurements are not what we think they are. Every time we draw what we assume to be a line twelve-inches long, we produce a line thirteen-inches long consistently. The ruler produces a reliable measurement *but it is not a valid measure of twelve-inches.* It is a valid measure of thirteen inches, but since we bought it on the presumption that it measured twelve inches it cannot be measuring what it purports to measure. Similarly test instruments can be very reliable, producing consistent results from occasion to occasion, but may not be valid as measures of what they set out to measure. On the other hand if an instrument is unreliable it cannot be valid.

Perhaps the most important consideration in judging the adequacy of a test or scale is its validity. This concept relates to the question, 'What does the test measure?' The importance of this question would seem obvious; yet the testing and measurement literature contains many examples of tests being used without proper consideration of their validity for the user's purpose. This lack of attention to test validity may seem somewhat surprising, since most tests are clearly labelled with a title intended to indicate quite specifically what is measured. But one of the first steps in evaluating a new test is to disregard the title, which may represent only what the test author had hoped to measure. A test of reading comprehension may, in fact, measure only a general intelligence factor. A test of achievement may be an equally good measure of general test-taking ability, particularly if the items are poorly constructed. It is important, therefore, that the test user be able to judge for himself whether a test is valid for his purposes.

The definition of validity has changed somewhat since the concept was first used in measurement. Some years ago textbooks on measurement defined validity in terms of the extent to which a test measured what it purported to measure. This idea was not unreasonable in view of the manner in which tests were constructed and validated. The test maker usually decided in advance what he wished to measure, constructed a test he thought measured it, and then proceeded to demonstrate how well 'it' was in fact measured by the test. The possibility that a scale of neuroticism might measure something else, such as a response set, or the ability to see through the test and give a favourable impression, was seldom considered.

TYPES OF VALIDITY

Five types of validity can be distinguished: predictive, concurrent, content, and construct. Each of these will be examined briefly, though we put the greatest emphasis on construct validity, since it is probably the most important form of validity from the scientific research point of view.

(a) Content validity

Content validity is most appropriately considered in connection with achievement testing. An achievement test has content validity if it represents faithfully the objectives of a given instructional sequence and reflects the emphasis accorded these objectives as the instruction was carried out. It is assumed, of course, that the teacher did, in fact, follow a plan based upon specific objectives during the course of his teaching and that the test was based upon that plan. A test in algebra would have low-content validity for measuring achievement in history. A test in long division would have low-content validity if administered to infant-school pupils. When students criticize a test as not fairly representing the actual content of the course, they are in reality remarking about the test's content validity.

Content validity then is the representativeness or sampling adequacy of the content – the substance, the matter, the topics – of a measuring instrument. Content validation is guided by the question: Is the substance or content of this measure representative of the content or the universe of content of the property being measured?

Ordinarily, and unfortunately, it is not possible to draw random samples of items from a universe of content. Such universes of content exist only theoretically. True, it is possible and desirable to assemble large collections of items, especially in the achievement area, and to draw random samples from such collections for testing purposes. But the content validity of such collections, no matter how large and how 'good' the items, is always in question.

Content validity is most often determined on the basis of expert judgement. The test analyst examines carefully an outline of the content and objectives of the unit for which the test was designed. He then prepares an outline based on the test itself, indicating the content represented and the kinds of knowledge and abilities which the examinee must possess in order to answer the items correctly. The two outlines are compared and discrepancies between them noted. The overall judgement concerning content validity is based on the extent of agreement between the test and the instructional plan.

One can ensure that a test has adequate content validity by adhering carefully to a course outline or plan as one constructs the test. Such an outline then becomes a blueprint for the construction itself.

It should be pointed out that an achievement test may have adequate content validity at a given time for a particular class and teacher but may not be equally valid for testing another group taught by a different teacher at a different time. A criticism of commercially published, standardized tests is that they sometimes do not fairly test the achievement of pupils in 'my' classes; i.e., they do not have satisfactory content validity in some situations. This criticism suggests one of the cautions which must be kept in mind in interpreting the scores on such tests and one which might well apply to the teacher's own tests if they are not made up especially for the groups to be tested. It should not be inferred that the results of standardized tests are useless; they actually form an important part of the body of necessary information about pupils. Neither should one infer that teacher-made tests should be used only once and then discarded. One should, however, keep in mind that the content validity of a test is not necessarily a fixed and changeless characteristic. It must be examined anew whenever the test is used with a different group or when the testing situation is altered.

(b) Predictive validity

Predictive validity involves the wish to predict, by means of test or examination results, subjects' success on some other criterion. The extent to which an examination meets this need is a measure of its predictive validity. An example of such a situation was the use of eleven-plus examinations; it was desired to select those pupils from the primary schools who would do well at grammar schools. The correlation between performance on the eleven-plus test and performance at grammar school is a measure of the predictive validity of the eleven-plus tests. Note the contrast to the assessment of content validity, which often rests on a subjective assessment of the extent to which a test fits a required blueprint. Note also that the only way to tell whether a particular test reaches an acceptable level of predictive validity is to wait until the results of basing a selection procedure on that examination are known. Predictive validity is vitally important for vocational selection techniques, because a person responsible for the selection of students likely to succeed in a given job, college, or curriculum is concerned with test scores as aids in doing a better job of selection. Counsellors also use tests as predictors, but usually in placement rather than selection decisions, and helping the student to predict from test data whenever scores on aptitude and interest tests are interpreted in terms of probable chances of succeeding in different colleges or in different vocations.

Primary-school teachers use reading readiness and intelligence tests as predictors when they use them as aids in grouping children. Predictive validity cannot be judged by an examination of a test's content. It can only be assessed by comparing a later performance (perhaps several years later) with the original test scores. This later performance, which is to be predicted, is often termed the criterion performance and may be a rather crude one such as successfully completing an apprenticeship, achieving an acceptable short-hand rate, making at least a 'C average' on a course, or developing a particular neurotic or psychiatric symptom. We rarely require the prediction of a precise score.

It is usually possible to express predictive validity in terms of the correlation coefficient between the predicted status and the criterion. Such a coefficient is called a validity coefficient. Suppose, for example, that a college admissions officer predicts the status (either passed or failed) at the end of the first year for each of 100 first-year college students using information available to him at the beginning of the year. He then observes their actual status at the end of the year and determines the extent of agreement between his predictions and the observed status. The extent of the agreement may be expressed in the form of the coefficient of predictive validity for the method of prediction used. If he used a single test for his predictions, then this coefficient may be regarded as a measure of the predictive validity of that test.

Many criteria are unfortunately very remote in time. For example to discern whether O-level results have any predictive validity for university degree classification would necessitate a wait of at least six years. Even 'success on the job' is difficult to define operationally when trying to validate job selection tests. For example, should one consider income, or self-ratings of ability, or happiness in one's profession, or supervisor's ratings, or perhaps some combination of a number of these individual criteria?

Although there is no simple answer to the problem of how best to choose a criterion measure, a few suggestions might be given:

(a) One should be sure that performance on the criterion measure is a result of the same individual characteristics and external environmental conditions which affected performance on the test one is attempting to validate.

(b) The criterion measure should be reliable; that is, it should be stable or consistent from day to day or time to time. Obviously it is very difficult to predict something that fluctuates markedly over short periods of time.

(c) In choosing a criterion measure, one should consider such factors as the time and the expense required to obtain the measure.

What is a satisfactory correlation between predictor and criterion measure? Must the correlation be close to 1.00 before a predictive measure is of any practical use, or is the information provided by a test which correlates only 0.3 with the criterion of sufficient help to warrant its use? The answer to this question is complex, because it depends upon the purpose for which the predictive measure is being employed. In some cases, a correlation of 0.3 could result in a substantial saving in time and money, particularly if no other predictive information were available. But in most situations in education and psychology, one should not be satisified unless the coefficient is about 0.7 or higher. It should be emphasized, however, that no general evaluative rule can be given and that the predictive validity of a test must always be judged in relation to its intended purpose.

The basic procedure for obtaining the predictive validity of a test is:

(a) To administer the test to a group of students or prospective employees.

(b) Follow them up and obtain data for each person on some criterion measure of his later success.

(c)   Compute a coefficient of correlation between individual's test scores and their criterion scores, which may represent success in college, in a specific training programme, or on the job. Such a coefficient of correlation may be called a predictive validity coefficient.

We can interpret predictive validity coefficients in terms of the standard error of estimate of predicted scores. The formula for standard error of estimate for predicted criterion scores is as follows:

$$SE_{criterion\ scores} = SD_{predictor}\sqrt{1 - r^2}$$

where r is the predictive validity coefficient.

When we use this method of interpretation with typical validity coefficients (which usually range in size from 0.3 to 0.6), it seems that most predictor tests make little contribution to our accuracy of prediction. As an illustration, we will compute the standard error of estimate for a fairly high validity coefficient of 0.60 between an aptitude test and some criterion of success in a training programme.

If the SD were 10 in both we would obtain the following standard errors of estimate:

If $r = 0.60$

$$SE_{criterion\ scores} = 10\sqrt{1 - (0.60)^2} = 10\sqrt{1 - 0.36}$$
$$= 10\sqrt{0.64} = 10\ (0.8) = 8.0$$

If $r = 0$

$$SE_{criterion\ scores} = 10\sqrt{1 - 0} = 10\sqrt{(1.0)} = 10.0$$

In other words, if we based our predictions on a test that had a validity coefficient of 0.60, rather than on one with no predictive validity, we would have reduced our standard error of estimate from 10 points to 8 points, or only 20%.

The formula for index of forecasting efficiency, which is based on this type of comparison, gives us a value of 20%. In other words, we reduce our error of prediction by only 20% when the validity coefficient is 0.60. Since we realize that predictive validity coefficients are seldom this high, the contribution of test scores to the prediction process seems very unpromising. This is often the case because the criterion is usually a subjective estimate of on-the-job performance (training programme) or a clinical diagnosis (personality, abnormality) etc.

> **STQ** *Which of the following requires a test with predictive validity:*
>
> *(a) A mental patient is given a personality test prior to discharge.*
> *(b) A student requires an estimate of success before commencing training.*
> *(c) A teacher wishes to assess what her history class has learned.*

(c) Concurrent validity

Concurrent and predictive validity are very much alike. They differ only in the time dimension. For example, if we developed a neuroticism scale we would require an answer to the question, 'Will a high scorer on this test become a neurotic at some time in the future?' for predictive validity but an answer to the question, 'Is this high scorer a neurotic now?' for concurrent validity. Predictive and concurrent validity are both characterized by prediction to an outside criterion and by checking a measuring instrument, either now or in the future, against some outcome, A test predicts a certain kind of outcome, or it predicts some present or future state of affairs. In a sense, then, all tests are predictive. Aptitude tests predict future achievement; achievement tests predict present and future achievement; and intelligence tests predict the present and future ability to learn and to solve problems.

Since concurrent validity coefficients, in which we relate test scores to present performance, can be obtained with less expense and delay than predictive validity coefficients (involving future performance), many aptitude-test manuals present concurrent validity data only. But high concurrent validity is no guide to high predictive validity.

The concurrent validity of a test must be considered when one is using the test to distinguish between two or more groups of individuals whose status at the time of testing is different. An example of a test originally developed to have high concurrent validity for a specific purpose is the Minnesota Multiphasic Personality Inventory, better known as the MMPI. The MMPI has been used as a screening device for identifying persons who, at the time of testing, have a personality disorder which requires treatment. A preliminary form of this instrument was administered to a group of hospitalized mental patients and also to their normal visitors. Items of the test were then carefully analysed to identify those which distinguished clearly between the two groups – i.e. patients and visitors. These items were then administered to other groups of patients and visitors, and on the basis of their responses (and without knowledge of their actual status), these individuals were classified as either patients or visitors. A comparison of test-based categorization and actual status provided a measure of the concurrent validity of the test. Concurrent validity is thus always expressed in terms of the relationship between test performance and an accepted contemporary criterion. The correlation coefficient provides a quantitive measure of this relationship.

Concurrent validity may also be a relevant concern in the evaluation of achievement tests. In everyday classroom experiences, there frequently are appropriate contemporary criteria with which achievement test performance should be compared. A pupil who performs well in a spelling test, for example, may be expected to exhibit his spelling skill in such tasks as writing compositions, finding spelling errors in his own work, and performing in classroom spelling games. The score on a test of reading comprehension should be related to teacher observations of the pupil's skill in classroom recitation or of his work in small reading groups. Test performance in arithmetic computation should be related to computational skill exhibited in other subject areas such as science or geography. The failure to find such relationships between test performance and contemporary behavioural criteria may indicate, (i) that the criteria themselves are not acceptable, (ii) that the same behaviours are not being assessed by the test and the criteria, or (iii) that the test itself has low concurrent validity. The latter conclusion should be drawn only after the first two have been carefully examined and discounted.

STQ **(1)** *What is the purpose of a criterion in concurrent and predictive validity?*

(2) *Criticize the following criteria:*

(a) *Ratings by pupils as an index of teaching ability.*
(b) *Number of accidents a car driver has per year as an index of driver competence.*
(c) *Number of church services attended per year as an index of Christian belief.*

(d) Construct validity
A 'construct' is a quality which has been suggested to explain aspects of human behaviour. Thus we find it helpful to use hypothetical constructs such as 'intelligence', 'sensitivity', 'self-concept' etc. to explain behaviour, although we cannot observe the constructs themselves. Some tests are intended to measure such constructs. How, for example, can we be sure that a test of 'sensitivity' is measuring this con-

struct? We cannot specify the content to everyone's satisfaction; we may not intend to use the test for prediction; there may well be no other such test which we can use concurrently with our test.

We must validate our test through a variety of kinds of indirect evidence. For example, the items must be internally consistent, i.e. show good agreement one with another, for if not, they are measuring different qualities. We could collect careful ratings of the construct from teachers and determine how well our test correlated with the ratings. We should expect reasonable correlations with tests measuring in related areas. The techniques of factor analysis (see Chapter 24) would help us decide whether our test was assessing an underlying quality common to all measures and ratings in the area. The following passage from Cronbach (1969, p. 200) should make this situation clear and the use of construct validity:

> The person making the first mental test was in the position of the hunter going into the woods to find an animal no one has ever seen. Everyone is sure the beast exists, for he has been raiding the poultry coops, but no one can describe him. Since the forest contains many animals, the hunter is going to find a variety of tracks. The only way he can decide which one to follow is by using some preconception, however vague, about the nature of his quarry. If he seeks a large flat-footed creature he is more likely to bring back that sort of carcass. If he goes in convinced that the damage was done by a pack of small rodents, his bag will probably consist of whatever unlucky rodents show their heads.

Binet (the first researcher really concerned with the measurement of intelligence) was in just this position. He knew there must be something like intelligence, since its everyday effects could be seen, but he could not describe what he wished to measure as it had never been isolated. Some workers, then and now, have objected to this circular and tentative approach whereby mental ability can be defined only after the test has been made. Tests are much easier to interpret if the items conform perfectly to a definition laid down in advance.

The process of construct validation is the same as that by which scientific theories are developed. A researcher will note that previous evidence may suggest that construct X accounts for performance in test Y. He then hypothesises that if that is so construct X should also influence performance in certain other scales or demonstrate itself in certain observable behaviours. An experiment is performed, deductions are tested. The construct may then be accepted as part of a theory, or a theory may have to be modified.

Thus, by using construct validity in correlating the results of several tests which had not been previously validated, a closer approach to the construct of say intelligence and the construction of an intelligence test is made. Of course, in specific instances with only two tests say, a correlation between the results on the tests could simply imply that they were both measuring the same thing to a certain degree, and not what they were both measuring. The inclusion of more and more tests of various types helps us to see that over these many tests the only common element remaining is a general mental ability.

So in designing a test to measure a construct (e.g. ego strength; intelligence; neuroticism) we are concerned with all types of evidence that make the interpretation of test scores more meaningful, that help us to understand what the scores signify. Construct validity is an analysis of the meaning of test scores in terms of psychological concepts. Let us take an example. We might attempt to study the construct of social withdrawal. Some persons who rank high on this 'construct' may actually appear unsociable; others may engage in some social activities but reveal and experience more emotional stress in doing so, e.g. talk very little to others; blush on being talked to. Hence, scores in any test of social withdrawal would not be consistently associated with, or highly correlated with, any single criterion. However, we might be able to make several hypotheses about ways in which individuals who are socially retiring would differ from those who are not – with respect to types of occupations pursued, leadership or followership roles assumed, symptoms of emotional stress when engaged in social activities, or behaviour in experimental situations that allow opportunities to measure suggestibility, initiative in a leaderless group discussion, and other factors presumably related to the construct. When correlations between the test and all these other criteria are analysed by factor analytic techniques one hopes that a major common factor will emerge, which theoretically is the underlying social withdrawal factor. We elaborated on the role of factor analysis as a systematic procedure for studying the inter-relationship between tests or test items in Chapter 24.

If a construct is to be useful in promoting the understanding of individual behaviour, then it should be possible to demonstrate statistically its relationship to that behaviour and to other traits possessed by the individual. Therefore, a great deal of attention is given to the relationships between the test score and a number of other factors which one would rationally expect to be related to it. Evidence of a test's construct validity may be provided by, (i) its high correlations with other tests, which are accepted measures of the same construct, and (ii) its low correlations with other tests which are accepted measures of other constructs. Insofar as these relationships can be demonstrated, particularly by factor analysis, the construct validity of the test is supported. If such relationships cannot be demonstrated, then one must conclude either that the test is not valid for measuring the construct involved or that the rationale for predicting the relationships was in some sense faulty. A large common factor revealed by factor analysis is taken as evidence that performance on a set of measures reflects the proposed hypothetical construct. Thus the test has construct validity.

Scientifically speaking, construct validity is one of the most significant advances of modern measurement theory and practice. It is a significant advance because it unites psychometric notions with scientifically theoretical notions. Construct validity really gets down to the question of what is actually being measured.

One can see that construct validation and empirical scientific inquiry are closely allied. It is not simply a question of validating a test. One must try to validate the theory behind the test. There are three parts to construct validation: suggesting what constructs possibly account for test performance, deriving hypotheses from the theory involving the construct, and testing the hypotheses empirically.

The significant point about construct validity, that which sets it apart from other types of validity, is its preoccupation with theory, theoretical constructs and scientific empirical inquiry involving the testing of hypothesized relations. Construct validation in measurement contrasts sharply with empirical approaches that define the validity of a measure purely by its success in predicting a criterion. For example, a purely empirical tester might say that a test is valid if it efficiently distinguishes individuals high and low in a trait. Why the test succeeds in separating the subsets of a group is of no great concern. It is enough that it does. But is it enough?

(e) Face validity

The primary types of validity which you will encounter are content, predictive, concurrent, and construct. However, there are several other types with which you should be familiar. For example, in certain circumstances, one may be concerned with the question: 'Does the test appear, from examination of the items, to measure what one wishes to measure?' Or 'Does the test appear to test what the name of the test implies?'

This is usually the concern of the layman who knows little or nothing about measurement, validity, or reliability. Public relations personnel often require 'high face validity' for popular tests which they use in testing programmes for industry, the military, and schools. However, it is difficult, if not impossible, to measure a validity of this type. The high face validity will hopefully motivate the subjects to tackle the test in a workman-like way. If the naive subjects looked at a test and started thinking that the items were ridiculous and seemed (to them) unrelated to the aim of the test then motivation would be considerably reduced. Up to a few years ago we often chuckled when we read abusive letters in national newspapers from parents asking how on earth some particular quoted question could ever measure IQ. Obviously face validity had failed in instances like this, yet the items probably had high construct, predictive and concurrent validity.

Face validity can also serve other functions. When one wishes to test for mental illness, it would be better to give a test with low face validity, e.g. projective techniques, so that the naive remain naive. Tests must be disguised where faking expected answers or faking bad answers could have serious consequences. Face validity is important in the field of attitude measurement. With attitude scales there may be large differences between what a scale looks as though it is measuring (face validity) and what it is in fact measuring (explored through concurrent validity with respect to other attitude scales, or construct validity). Accepting the face validity of an attitude scale is a dangerous process due to a possible ambiguity in the interpretation of the items used in the scale. It is possible to hide the true aim of a test or scale and at the same time increase its face validity by including a lot of filler items that are not going to be marked. In this way a false face validity is created; subjects believe it is measuring one thing when in fact it is measuring another!

> **STQ** *In what situations might you find it desirable to have low face validity in an assessment instrument?*

There is a relationship between reliability and validity. An unreliable test cannot be very valid, since the more unreliability the more error variance in the scores. This error component cannot in any way correlate with a criterion. The validity of a test cannot exceed the square root of the r_{tt}., i.e. the validity coefficient r_{tc}. (c represents the criterion) cannot exceed $\sqrt{r_{tt}}$.

Summary

Validity is a fundamental and crucially important concern in any type of measurement. A test does not have validity in general, but only in terms of its use for specific purposes and with specific groups. Hence, the subject of validity is the most complex one in the entire field of measurement.

The term 'validity' refers to the value of a test as a basis for making judgements about examinees. For a test to be valid, it must measure 'something' consistently (or with reliability), and that 'something' must be either a representative sample of the behaviour we wish to judge, or it must have demonstrated relevance to that behaviour.

If we wish to know how individuals perform at present with respect to certain skills and knowledges, we try to devise a test which samples those skills and knowledges. If the behaviour to be measured can be exactly defined, content validity can be attained by including in the test a random sampling of the complete list of spelling words, multiplication facts, or some other defined universe. Whenever the skills or knowledges to be sampled cannot be accurately defined and randomly sampled, human judgement must enter into the selection of learnings to be tested. Our concern is with the representativeness of the test sample in terms of the universe about which we wish to make inferences.

Concurrent validity is the relationship of individuals' test scores to their results on some measure of contemporary criterion behaviour external to our test. The concurrent validity of a group intelligence test might be studied by determining the relationship between students' scores on that test and their scores on an individual intelligence test, for which it was designed to be an economical substitute.

There are many situations in school and industrial work in which one wishes to predict a person's future performance in a subject, curriculum, school, or job. The predictive validity of a test cannot be adequately judged without following up a group of examinees to see how well they achieve on such criteria as job performance or average marks in specific college curricula. Predictive validity coefficients between test scores and appropriate criterion scores must be obtained.

When a test presumes to measure the degree to which individuals possess some trait or construct, evidence concerning its construct validity must be obtained. Tests that claim to measure the same trait frequently show low intercorrelations (e.g. self-concept scales), hence we cannot assume that test names accurately describe what is being measured. In research studies or in situations in which we wish to describe individuals as the basis for inferences regarding several decisions, we prefer to measure relatively pure traits which have meaning in terms of psychological concepts and which enable us to make inferences concerning correlated behaviours.

In studying the construct validity of a test which presumes to measure a relatively pure trait, several criteria must be used. For example, many hypotheses can be made concerning the differences in test and non-test behaviour between groups of high-scoring and low-scoring students on a specific intelligence test. If correlations were obtained between scores on that test and several other variables, psychological theory would predict high correlations with some variables and low or negative correlations with other variables. Confirmation of the hypotheses based on theory would provide evidence for the construct validity of the test.

Factor analysis is used to study the extent to which tests measure unitary, independent dimensions, and also to help in interpreting the major sources of variation in test scores. Face validity is an attempt to improve test motivation and/or disguise the real nature of the assessment.

STQ **(1)** *A child achieves a score of 90 on each of five tests of academic ability. Standard deviations and reliability coefficients for each test are supplied below. Which of tests A, B, C, D or E probably represents the child's 'true' score on the ability the test measures with greatest fidelity?*

Test	σ_t	r_{tt}
A	10	0.84
B	25	0.91
C	10	0.96
D	20	0.96
E	25	0.99

(2) *Which one of the following properties of a test would be taken as evidence of its reliability and not its validity?*

(a) *The scores obtained by children on two successive administrations of the test were correlated 0.95.*

(b) *The even numbered questions on the test were found to yield a substantially higher mean score than the odd numbered questions.*

(c) *Scores on the test correlated highly with scores on another test designed to measure the same ability.*

(d) *Scores on the test at the beginning of the school year predicted scores on the final examination.*

(3) *Using the reliability information set out below which one of the following tests would you select as being most reliable?*

Test	Reliability estimate
A	0.96 (split half)
B	0.96 (parallel form delayed)
C	0.96 (parallel form immediate)
D	0.96 (test – retest immediate)

(4) *Explain the meaning of the expression $X_o = X_t + X_e$ and discuss the assumptions of test theory.*

(5) *List the three major types of reliability coefficients and indicate uses and precautions associated with each.*

(6) *Describe the usefulness in reporting the standard error of measurement as well as the reliability for a test.*

(7) *Discuss the question, 'How reliable should a test be?'*

Answers to questions 1−3 are to be found on p. 436.

26

Attitude measurement

A   Introduction

The study and measurement of attitudes forms a central focus of social psychology. Attitudes are evaluated beliefs which predispose the individual to respond in a preferential way. That is, attitudes are predispositions to react positively or negatively to some social object. Most definitions of attitudes suggest there are three major components, the cognitive, affective and behavioural components. The cognitive component involves what a person believes is so whether true or not; the affective component is the feelings about the attitude object which influences its evaluation; the behavioural component reflects the actual behaviour of the individual though this is rather an unreliable indication of an attitude, e.g. LaPière's (1934) study of ethnic attitudes.

Attitude scales involve the application of standardized questionnaires to enable individuals to be placed on a dimension indicating degree of favourability towards the object in question. The assignment to a position on the dimension is based on the individual's agreement or disagreement with a number of statements relevant to the attitude object. Psychologists have generated many hundreds of scales indexing attitudes to a wide range of objects. A valuable collection of scales can be perused in Shaw and Wright (1968).

Despite the existence of many reliable and valid published attitude scales, the researcher often finds that he wishes to assess attitudes to a specific social object for which no scales exist or for which scales produced and validated in another culture are not appropriate in our context. The construction of attitude scales is not difficult but there are a number of differing methods of construction, of response mode and of score interpretation. These various approaches will be considered shortly.

The individual items or statements in an attitude scale are usually not of interest in themselves; the interest is usually located in the total score or sub-scores. In effect any set of items works as well as any other set of items provided they elicit the same final score i.e. are equally reliable and valid. An attitude scale usually consists of statements, i.e. the belief component of the theoretical attitude. These statements could all be preceded by 'I believe that . . .'. Some or all depending on the particular method adopted are rated on a 3, 5, 7 (or even more) – point scale. This rating provides an index of the emotive value or affective component of each statement. Of course the third element of an attitude, the behavioural act, is not assessed. This behavioural component may not be congruent with the expressed attitude as measured on the questionnaire since other factors, e.g. social convention, social constraints, expectation etc. may prevent the act which should follow being performed. For example, a person who rates high on negative attitudes to other ethnic groups may not display such prejudice in his overt behaviour because of fear of the law, consideration of what others would think, etc.

B Methods of attitude scale construction

The following section briefly outlines the major types of attitude scales and their construction. A more thorough and detailed account can be consulted in Edwards (1957).

In some scales the items form a graduation of such a nature that the individual agrees with only one or two, which correspond to his position on the dimension being measured, and disagrees with statements on either side of those he has selected. Such scales, in which a person's response localizes his position, are sometimes called differential scales. In other scales, the individual indicates his agreement or disagreement with each item, and his total score is found by adding the subscores assigned to his responses to all the separate items; such scales are sometimes called summated scales. Still others are set up in such a way that the items form a cumulative series; theoretically, an individual whose attitude is at a certain point on the dimension being measured will answer favourably all the items on one side of that point and answer unfavourably all those on the other side.

1 DIFFERENTIAL SCALES (THURSTONE TYPE)

(a) Their construction

Differential scales for the measurement of attitudes are closely associated with the name of L. L. Thurstone. The methods he devised represent attempts to facilitate interval scale measurement.

> **STQ** *Write down now what you remember an interval scale to be, then check your answer with the material in Chapter 12.*

Such a scale enables one to compare differences or changes in attitude, since the difference between a score of 3 and a score of 7 is equivalent to the difference between a score of 6 and a score of 10 and to the difference between any other two that are four points apart.

A differential scale consists of a number of items whose position on the scale has been determined by some kind of ranking or rating operation performed by judges. Thurstone (1929) used various methods of securing judgements of scale position. The most common are the method of paired comparisons and the method of equal-appearing intervals. It is beyond the scope of this volume to give details of these procedures; we shall only present in broad outline the method of equal-appearing intervals, which is the most commonly used.

In selecting the items for the scale and assigning values to them, the following procedure is used. A large number of statements (which express various degrees of positive and negative feeling toward some institution or group) are obtained, each statement reproduced on a card or slip of paper. Then, a large number of judges independently sort these slips according to their position on an eleven-point continuum (ranging from 'extremely favourable' through 'neutral' to 'extremely unfavourable'). The judges do not give their personal reactions to the statements but arrange them on a continuum of intensity of positive and negative feeling.

Items that are assigned a variety of values by the judges are eliminated as ambiguous or as unrelated to the attitude being judged. Only those statements that show relatively low interjudge variability are retained. From among these statements, there would be selected 15–25 statements that were fairly evenly spaced, with respect to median rating they had been given by the judges on the attitude continuum. For example, on an eleven-point scale, items might be selected with median intensity values of 0, 0.5, 1.0, 1.5, and the like, up to 11. The median rating is termed the scale value.

Once the statements have been selected, they are arranged in random order on the printed form. The student then marks those statements with which he agrees; and his score is the median intensity value of statements he has marked. Scales of the Thurstone type have been constructed for attitudes toward church, war, censorship, capital punishment, and many other institutions and issues, as well as for attitudes toward a number of ethnic groups. The scales are quickly administered and easily scored. The method of scaling is objective and reliable because many independent judgements are used. It is often possible to construct duplicate forms of the scale from items not used on the original form. The following examples are from a Thurstone type scale, with scale values attached.

1.1   I know that God hears and responds to prayer.
10.7 Prayer is a demonstration of ignorance.
6.9   Church leaders have too little understanding of life's practical problems.
2.6   Missionary work affords opportunity to engage in unselfish activity.

The scale values, of course, are not shown on the questionnaire, and the items are usually arranged in random order rather than in order of their scale value. The mean of the scale values of the items the individual checks is interpreted as indicating his position on a scale of favourable – unfavourable attitude toward the object. It seems reasonable to assume that the subject will choose statements on either side of, but close to, his true position. So an average scale value will be a good estimate of this position.

Theoretically, if a Thurstone-type scale is completely reliable and if the scale is measuring a single attitude rather than a complex of attitudes, an individual should check only items that are immediately contiguous in scale value. If the responses of an individual scatter widely over non-contiguous items, his attitude score is not likely to have the same meaning as a score with little scatter. The scattered responses may indicate that the subject has no attitude or that his attitude is not organized in the manner assumed by the scale. There is no *a priori* reason to expect that all people have attitudes toward the same things or that attitudinal dimensions are the same for all.

(b)   Criticisms of Thurstone-type differential scales
Several objections have been raised against the Thurstone-type scale.

(a)   Many have objected to the amount of work involved in constructing it. Undoubtedly, the procedure is cumbersome. However, the amount of time and labour involved in constructing a scale by the method of equal-appearing intervals is not substantially different from that involved in constructing a summated scale. In any case, it is doubtful that simple methods for the rigorous construction of scales will ever be developed. The precise measurement of attitudes is perhaps a vain hope.

(b)   Since an individual's score is the mean of the scale values of the several items he checks, essentially different attitudinal patterns may be expressed by the same score. Dudycha (1943), after six years' use of the Peterson test of attitude toward war with college students, reported that the average student, instead of checking only two or three contiguous items, covered more than a third of the scale; some students endorsed statements ranging from those placed at the 'strongly favourable' end of the scale to statements at the 'strongly opposed' end. (One must, of course, consider the possibility that such students had no clear attitude toward war and that it was therefore inappropriate to try to measure their attitude by any technique.) Dudycha questioned the meaning to be given to a mean derived from such a range of responses. However, the criticism that identical scores do not necessarily indicate identical patterns of response is not unique to the Thurstone-type scale; it applies at least as strongly, as we shall see, to summated scales.

(c) Do the attitudes and backgrounds of the judges affect the position of the various items on the scale? This obviously is a matter that is open to experimental inquiry. A number of early studies supported the view that the scale values assigned did not depend on the attitude of the judges. For example (Hinckley, 1932) found a correlation of 0.98 between the scale positions assigned to 114 items measuring prejudice toward Negroes by a group of Southern white students in the United States who were prejudiced against Negroes and those assigned by a group of unprejudiced Northern students.

But a subsequent study by Kelley *et al.* (1955), using twenty of the Hinckley items, found marked differences between the scale values assigned to items by white and by Negro judges, with the statements fairly evenly distributed from 'favourable' to 'unfavourable' by the white judges, but bunched at the two ends of the continuum by the Negro judges. Granneberg (1955), in constructing a scale of attitudes toward religion, found not only that a religious group and a non-religious group differed significantly in the scale values they assigned to items, but that judges of superior and of low intelligence differed, and that there was an interaction between attitude and intelligence which affected the scale position to which items were assigned.

Such findings, of course, cast serious doubt on the meaning of the scale positions and the distances between them. It should be noted, however, that even those studies that found marked differences between groups of judges in the absolute scale values they assigned to items found high agreement in the rank order in which judges with differing attitudes arranged the items along the favourable – unfavourable continuum. Thus, although the assumption that Thurstone-type scales are true interval scales seems dubious, it is still possible for them to constitute reasonably statisfactory ordinal scales; that is, they provide a basis for saying that one individual is more favourable or less favourable than another. If in practice individuals agreed with only a few continuous items, so that a given score had a clear meaning, the Thurstone methods would provide highly satisfactory ordinal scales. But, as noted above, individuals may agree with items quite widely spaced on the scale, and in such cases the mean or even the median of the items checked may not provide a meaningful basis for ranking the individual in relation to others.

(d)   An obvious criticism of Thurstone's scales is that the subjects normally endorse only a small number of items and the score for a particular subject will be based on only the small number of statements he endorses. For this reason Thurstone's scales need to be longer than Likert's scales to obtain the same reliability.

(e)   Thurstone, on the assumption that scales constructed by this method were true interval scales, advocated the use of statistics appropriate to interval scales – the mean and the standard deviation. Other investigators, operating on the more cautious assumption that the intervals are not truly equal, have favoured the use of the median as appropriate to ordinal scales.

2 SUMMATED SCALES (LIKERT TYPE)
(a)   Construction
A summated scale, like a differential scale, consists of a series of items to which the subject is asked to react. However, no attempt is made to find items that will be distributed evenly over a scale of favourableness – unfavourableness (or whatever dimension is to be measured). Only items that seem to be either definitely favourable or definitely unfavourable to the object are used, not neutral or 'slightly' favourable or unfavourable items. Rather than checking only those statements with which he agrees, the respondent indicates his agreement or disagreement with each item. Each response is given a numerical score indicating its favourableness or unfavourableness; often, favourable responses are scored plus, unfavourable responses, minus. The algebraic summation of the scores of the individual's responses to all the separate items gives his total score, which is interpreted as representing his position on a scale of favourable – unfavourable attitude toward the object. The rationale for using such total scores as a basis for placing individuals on a scale seems to be as follows. The probability of agreeing with any one of a series of favourable items about an object, or of disagreeing with any unfavourable item, varies directly with the degree of favourableness of an individual's attitude. Thus, one could expect an individual with a favourable attitude to respond favourably to many items (that is, to agree with many items favourable to the object and to disagree with

many unfavourable ones); an ambivalent individual with an unfavourable attitude to respond unfavourably to many items.

The type of summated scale most frequently used in the study of attitudes follows the pattern devised by Likert (1932) and is referred to as a Likert-type scale. In such a scale, the subjects are asked to respond to each item in terms of several degrees of agreement or disagreement; for example, (i) strongly approve, (ii) approve, (iii) undecided, (iv) disapprove, (v) strongly disapprove. The first step in the Likert method is also the collection of a large number of statements expressing various degrees of positive and negative feelings about an object, institution or class of persons. The selection of items for the attitude scale, however, does not involve the use of judges; rather, the selection is based on the results of administering the items to a representative group of subjects. Each item is rated by subjects taking the attitude scale on a five-point continuum from 'strongly approve' to 'strongly disapprove'. The total score is the sum of all the item scores. The responses to the various items are scored in such a way that a response indicative of the most favourable attitude is given the highest score. It makes no difference whether 5 is high and 1 is low or vice-versa. The important thing is that the responses be scored consistently in terms of the attitudinal direction they indicate. Whether 'approve' or 'disapprove' is the favourable response to an item depends, of course, upon the content and wording of the item. The responses are analysed to determine which of the items discriminate most clearly between the high scorers and the low scorers on the total scale. For example, the responses of those subjects whose total scores are in the upper quarter and the responses of those in the lower quarter may be analysed in order to determine for each item the extent to which the responses of these criterion groups differ. Items that do not show a substantial correlation with the total score, or that do not elicit different responses from those who score high and those who score low on the total test, are eliminated to ensure that the questionnaire is 'internally consistent' – that is, that every item is related to the same general attitude.

(b) Example items of a Likert scale
We are interested in your feelings about the following statements. Read each statement carefully and decide how you feel about it. *Please* respond to each item whether or not you have had direct experience with a Trade Union.

If you strongly agree, encircle SA
If you agree, encircle A
If you are undecided or uncertain, encircle ?

If you disagree, encircle D
If you strongly disagree, encircle SD

(a) Trade Unions hold back progress   SA A ? D SD
(b) I regard my union subscription as a good
     investment   SA A ? D SD
(c) The closed shop should be abolished   SA A ? D SD

(c) Advantage of Likert method
The Likert-type scale, like the Thurstone scale, has been used widely in studies of social attitude etc. It has several advantages over the Thurstone scale.

The advantages of the Likert method include, (i) greater ease of preparation, (ii) the fact that the method is based entirely on empirical data regarding subjects' responses rather than subjective opinions of judges, (iii) the fact that this method produces more homogeneous scales and increases the probability that a unitary attitude is being measured; and therefore that validity (construct and concurrent) and reliability are reasonably high, (iv) the scales provide more information about the subject's attitudes, since an intensity reaction is given to each of many items.

The Thurstone and Likert-type scales for the same institution or group tend to yield results that agree or intercorrelate highly. Reliability coefficients for such scales tend to be in the 0.80s and are highly satisfactory for group comparisons.

(d) Disadvantages of Likert scales
(a) The Likert-type scale does not claim to be more than an ordinal scale; that is, it makes possible the ranking of individuals in terms of the favourableness of their attitude toward a given object, but it does not provide a basis for saying how much more favourable one is than another, nor for measuring the amount of change after some experience. Whether it constitutes a disadvantage of the Likert scale in comparison with the Thurstone scale depends on one's judgement of whether Thurstone scales really meet the criteria for interval scales.

(b) The total score of an individual has little clear meaning, since many patterns of response to the various items may produce the same score. We have already noted that Thurstone-type scales are also subject to this criticism, but it applies even more strongly to the Likert scales since they provide a greater number of response possibilites.

The fact that different patterns of response may lead to identical scores on either a Thurstone or a Likert scale is not necessarily as serious a drawback as it may at first appear. Some of the differences in response patterns leading to a given score may be attributable to random variations in response. Others may arise because specific items involve not only the attitude being measured but also extraneous issues that may affect the responses. Thus some of the differences in response patterns leading to the same score may be thought of as error from the point of view of the attitude being measured, rather than as true differences in attitude that are being obscured by identical scores. The fact that the scale contains a number of items means that these variations on individual items unrelated to the attitude being measured may cancel each other out.

3 CUMULATIVE SCALES (GUTTMAN TYPE)
(a) Construction
In evaluating both Likert's and Thurstone's methods we pointed out that subjects can obtain the same score by different combinations of responses, and that individual inconsistencies in response could often be quite marked.

The basic model used by Guttman (1947) differed from the other approaches. It assumed that all probabilities of a positive response were either zero or one, that is, the subject was certain to endorse an item or certain not to. The procedure for constructing a scale of this kind is to develop statements which will produce this pattern of responses from the subjects. Departures from this ideal pattern should be few in number, and are interpreted as careless omissions or endorsements which do not reflect the subject's 'true' attitude.

The method of analysing responses in order to form a Guttman scale is referred to as scalogram analysis. For scalogram analysis, a complete record of all response patterns is required. Subjects are grouped and ordered according to the number of positive responses. In Table 75 a perfect set of response patterns is displayed, with + indicating agreement and − disagreement.

Table 75   A perfect Guttman scale pattern

Subject groups	*Statements*				
	1	2	3	4	5
Group 5	+	+	+	+	+
Group 4	+	+	+	+	−
Group 3	+	+	+	−	−
Group 2	+	+	−	−	−
Group 1	+	−	−	−	−
Group 0	−	−	−	−	−

From Table 75 it is clear that knowledge of the group to which a subject belongs also involves knowledge of which statements he endorses and which ones he does not. Perfect sets of response patterns of this kind are very rare in practice. Theoretically there are 32 possible response patterns to five statements having only two alternative responses, 'agree' or 'disagree'. While an accidental omission or an unintended endorsement may lead to one of the six scale patterns, it is more likely to lead to a non-scale pattern and so indicate an error. The proportion of detected error responses should be small, less than 10% of all responses being the usually accepted criterion. A coefficient of reproducibility was proposed by Guttman (1947) as a measure of scalability of responses.

$$\text{Coefficient of reproducibility} = 1 - \frac{\text{number of non-scale responses}}{\text{total number of responses}}$$

In evaluation of a set of response patterns the frequency with which a particular non-scale pattern occurs should be noted. If this frequency is relatively large, the statements cannot be thought of as forming a single scale, even though the coefficient of reproducibility is greater than 0.90.

So in a cumulative scale the items are related to one another in such a way that ideally, an individual who replies favourably to item 2 also replies favourably to item 1; one who replies favourably to item 3 also replies favourably to items 1 and 2 etc. Thus, all individuals who answer a given item favourably should have higher scores on the total scale than the individuals who answer that item unfavourably. The individual's score is computed by counting the number of items he answers favourably. This score places him on the scale of favourable – unfavourable attitude provided by the relationship of the items to one another. The whole aim of this approach is the production of a unidimensional scale. The pattern of responses reveals this unidimensionality, through the criterion of reproducibility.

The important thing about the pattern of responses is that, if it holds, a given score on a particular series of items always has the same meaning; knowing an individual's score makes it possible to tell, without consulting his questionnaire, exactly which items he endorsed. Consider, for example, the following items, with which respondents are asked either to agree or to disagree.

(a)   Sikhs should be forced to wear crash helmets for their own safety when riding motorcycles.
(b)   Coloured immigrants should accept the laws and customs of the host country.
(c)   Coloured immigrants should not be allowed to enter the country.

If these items were found to form a perfect cumulative scale, we would know, for example, that all individuals with a score of 2 on the scale support statements (a) and (b). A person with a score of 1 would only be supporting statement (a).

In practice, perfect cumulative, or unidimensional, scales are rarely or never found in social research, but approximations to them can often be developed. Sometimes the items as they appear in the scale are arranged in order of favourableness; sometimes they are randomly arranged. Ordinarily, no attempt is made to determine whether the intervals between items are equal; thus, in practice, cumulative scales are ordinal scales. Examples of Guttman-type scales are the Social Distance Scale (Bogardus 1925) and the Self-Esteem Scale (Rosenberg 1965).

(b) Criticism

The Guttman technique is a method of determining whether a set of items forms a unidimensional scale; as a number of writers have pointed out, it offers little guidance for selecting items that are likely to form such a scale. It is sometimes assumed that unidimensionality is a property of a measuring instrument, rather than of the patterning of an attitude among a given group of individuals. For one group, a number of items may be arranged unidimensionally in a given order; for another group, the same items may fall into a different order; for still another group, they may not form a unidimensional pattern at all. The experiences of different groups can lead to different patternings of items.

4 SEMANTIC DIFFERENTIAL

This is an extremely flexible technique rather than a particular scale. It was originally developed (Osgood *et al.* 1951) to measure the meaning systems of individuals, essentially connotative meaning. It has become a very economic method of assessing attitudes to *n* objects within the ambit of one instrument. Basically the method involves sets of polar adjectives, e.g. good−bad, happy−sad, reliable−unreliable, listed down every page. Each page is headed with a stimulus word or phrase. The pairs of adjectives are listed as endpoints of a continuum divided into an uneven number, usually 5 or 7, of response gradations. Subjects are requested to consider the stimulus in terms of each of the scales, and place a check-mark in one of the divisions on the continuum to indicate the relative applicability of the polar terms. Warr and Knapper (1968) provide a comprehensive review of this technique in person perception. Factor analysis has generally revealed three distinct orthogonal factors, *viz* evaluation, potency and activity, of which the evaluative is the dominant one. This led Osgood to believe that the attitudinal variable in human thinking is primary. Consequently, Osgood claimed that the semantic differential could be employed as an attitude-measuring device provided scales loaded only on the evaluative dimension were used. The reliability and validity of the semantic differential is well documented, (e.g. Warr and Knapper, 1968). Scales which are loaded on the evaluative dimension are, for instance: good−bad, successful−unsuccessful, beautiful−ugly, cruel− kind, clean−dirty, wise−foolish, honest−dishonest, happy−sad, nice−awful.

However, Burns (1976) reviews various investigations which reveal that scales weighted heavily on the evaluative dimension for one concept may not be strongly evaluative when applied to another concept. It would seem necessary for a factor analysis to be undertaken to ensure that presumed evaluative scales actually do index the evaluative dimension when referring to a particular attitude object. The marker scale 'good − bad' which is consistently evaluative will help identify the other evaluative scales. The meaning of a scale may vary considerably depending on the concept being judged.

A typical layout and instructions for the semantic differential techniques is a follows:

The purpose of this study is to measure the *meanings* which certain concepts have for you. This is done by having you judge them against a set of descriptive scales which consist of adjectives and their opposites. You are asked to make your judgements on the basis of what these things mean *to you*. On each page of this booklet, you will find a different concept to be judged and beneath it a set of scales. You are asked to rate the concept on each of the scales in order.

Here is how you are to use the scales:

If you feel that the concept at the top of the page is *very closely related* to one end of the scale, you should place your check-mark as follows:

fair :__X__: :____: :____: :____: :____: :____: :____: unfair

OR

fair :____: :____: :____: :____: :____: :____: :__X__: unfair

If you feel that the concept is *quite closely related* to one or the other end of the scale (but not extremely), you should place your check-mark as follows:

weak :____: :__X__: :____: :____: :____: :____: :____: strong

OR

weak :____: :____: :____: :____: :____: :__X__: :____: strong

If the concept seems only *slightly related* to one side as opposed to the other (but is not really neutral), then you should place your check-mark thus:

active :____: :____: :__X__: :____: :____: :____: :____: passive

OR

active :____: :____: :____: :____: :__X__: :____: :____: passive

The direction towards which you check, of course, depends upon which of the two ends of the scale seems most characteristic of the concept you're judging.

If you consider the concept to be *neutral* on the scale, both sides of the scale equally associated with the concept, or if the scale is completely irrelevant, unrelated to the concept, then you should place your check-mark in the middle space, thus:

safe :___: :___: :___: :___: : X___ :___: :___: :___: dangerous

IMPORTANT:

(1) Place your check-mark in the middle of the spaces not at the boundaries.
(2) Be sure you check every scale for every concept, *do not omit any.*
(3) Never put more than one check-mark on a single scale.
(4) Do not look back and forth through the items. Do not try to remember how you checked similar items earlier in the test. *Make each item a separate and independent judgement.*
(5) Work fairly quickly through the items.
(6) Do not worry or puzzle over individual items. It is your first impressions, the immediate 'feelings' about the items that is wanted. On the other hand, do not be careless, for it is your true impression that is wanted.

Concept — Myself

good :___: :___: :___: :___: : X :___: :___: :___: :___: bad

rigid :___: :___: :___: :___: :___: :___: : X :___: flexible

independent :___: : X :___: :___: :___: :___: :___: :___: submissive

democratic : X :___: :___: :___: :___: :___: :___: :___: authoritarian

disorganised :___: :___: :___: :___: :___: :___: : X : organised

co-operative :___: :___: : X :___: :___: :___: :___: :___: unco-operative

non-conforming :___: :___: :___: :___: : X :___: :___: :___: conforming

etc

The particular scales included are those the investigator wishes to include — usually on the grounds of relevance to the attitude under investigation — though, as has been already argued, factorial validity for the evaluative dimension is the ultimate criterion. In using the semantic differential in self-concept or attitudes to self studies the following concepts would be particularly useful to employ:

Myself as I am.
Myself as I would like to be.
Myself as others see me.
Myself as a student (or husband, father etc.).

To prevent the acquiescence response, set-scale polarity is reversed for pairs in random order, and for these the scoring on the 1—7 range is reversed. For individuals a total score reflecting level of self-evaluation can be obtained on the dubious assumption — as with most other intruments — that all items are equal in their contribution. With groups such totals would be averaged or an average response could be computed for each scale. The semantic-differential technique appears appropriate for use with children of twelve years of age and upwards.

5 THE RELIABILITY AND VALIDITY OF ATTITUDE SCALES

(a) The reliability-of-attitude scales is usually assessed via the test—retest method, or where occasionally there are two parallel forms of the scale an alternate form reliability can be obtained.

STQ (1) *What do you understand by the test—retest method. Refer back to Chapter 25 if in difficulty.*

  (2) *Why should a split-half reliability not be used?*

It would be impossible to split a Likert attitude scale into two comparable halves. It would be feasible but difficult in a Thurstone scale provided items of the same scale value were included in each half. This would be akin to parallel forms of the scale.

Measures of internal consistency are possible with Likert scales by correlating item score to total score, the general principle being that item score should be congruent with total score. An item that is not may well be measuring some other attitude.

(b) The validity-of-attitude scales is often checked by concurrent validity using known criterion groups, i.e. sets of individuals who are known in advance to hold different attitudes to the relevant object. For example random samples of Labour Party and Conservative party members could act as criterion groups for the concurrent validation of an attitude scale towards nationalization. If the scale differentiated statistically significantly between these two groups then it could be said to have concurrent validity.

STQ *What criterion would you select to check the concurrent validity of, (i) an attitude towards the wearing of seat-belts scale, and (ii) an attitude scale towards fox-hunting?*

Predictive validity is also possible by selecting some criterion in the future such as voting behaviour. Content validity can be gauged by requesting judges to indicate whether the items are relevant to the assessment of that particular attitude. Finally, of course, construct validity using factor analysis of the inter-correlations of item responses will demonstrate homogeneity or heterogeneity of Likert and Semantic Differential Scales. Many attitude scales are multi-factorial or multi-dimensional in that they do not measure one unitary attitude, but groups of items each measure different dimensions of the attitude. Guttman's approach was an attempt to produce unidimensional scales. Face validity can cause problems. In order to ensure motivation, the statements are often fairly obviously related to the attitude object in question. In fact it is extremely difficult to disguise the purpose of the scale in most cases. However, because the manifest content of the statements usually makes clear the nature of the dimension being studied, it is possible for the individual, deliberately or unconsciously, to bias his results in the direction he thinks will best suit his own purposes. With attitude scales it is often possible for the subject to bias his results to any extent in either direction.

6 GENERAL CRITICISMS

The chief criticism that might be levelled at all attitude scales is concerned with the indirectness of measurement, that is, verbal statements are used as a basis for inferences about 'real' attitudes. Moreover, attitude scales are easily faked. Although administering the scales anonymously may increase the validity of results, anonymity makes it difficult to correlate the findings with related data about the individuals unless such data are obtained at the same time. It seems that we must limit our inferences from attitude-scale scores, recognizing that such scores merely summarize the verbalized attitudes that the subjects are willing to express in a specific test situation. The student will recognize the difficulty of studying the concurrent validity of verbal attitude scales by studying their relationship with behavioural criteria. Persons with the same attitude will manifest different behaviours.

Such attitude scales are self-report measures and they suffer from the same problems as all other self-report techniques. What a subject is willing to reveal about himself would seem to depend on such factors as willingness to co-operate, social expectancy, feelings of personal adequacy, feelings of freedom from threat, dishonesty, carelessness, ulterior motivation, interpretation of verbal stimuli, etc. The study of human emotions, feelings and values about objects in the environment is clouded by those very same variables.

Response sets too, such as acquiescence (the tendency to agree with items irrespective of their content) and social desirability (the tendency to agree to statements which social consensus it is believed would indicate are socially desirable and reject those that are socially undesirable) fog the data derived from attitude scales. The best way of eliminating acquiescence is to randomly order positive and negative items to prevent a subject ticking madly away down the same column.

References

Bogardus, E. S. (1925). Measuring social distances. *J. Appl. Sociol.*, **9**, 299−308

Burns, R. B. (1976). The concept-scale interaction problem. *Educ. Stud.*, **2**, 121−7

Dudycha, G. (1943). A critical examination of the measurement of attitude. *J. Soc. Psychol.*, **39**, 846−60

Edwards, A. L. (1957). *Techniques of Attitude Scale Construction.* (New York: Appleton-Century-Crofts)

Granneberg, R. T. (1955). The influence of individual attitude and attitude-intelligence interaction on scale values of attitude items. *Am. Psychol.*, **10**, 330−1

Guttman, L. (1947). The Cornell technique for scale and intensity values. *Educ. Psychol. Meas.*, **7**, 247−80

Hinckley, E. D. (1932). The influence of individual opinion on construction of an attitude scale. *J. Soc. Psychol.*, **3**, 283−96

Kelley, H. H. *et al.* (1955). The influence of judges' attitude in three methods of attitude scaling. *J. Soc. Psychol.*, **42**, 147−58

La Pière, R. T. (1934). Attitudes versus actions. *Social Forces,* **14**, 230−7

Likert, R. (1932). A technique for the measurement of attitudes. *Arch. Psychol. No. 140*

Osgood, C. E. *et al.* (1957). *The Measurement of Meaning.* (University of Illinois Press)

Rosenberg, M. (1965). *Society and the Adolescent Self Image.* (University of Princetown Press)

Shaw, M. and Wright, J. (1968). *Scales for the Measurement of Attitudes.* (New York: McGraw Hill)

Thurstone, L. L. (1929). *The Measurement of Attitude.* (University of Chicago)

Warr, P. and Knapper, C. (1968). *Perception of People and Events.* (London: Wiley)

27

Non-experimental methods

We have concentrated on the experimental method of investigation in this text but students should not believe that this is the only acceptable method in the social sciences. We will now have a brief look at several other methods which possess their own particular merits. As you read this chapter try to compare the relative advantages of the experimental method, observational techniques in field work, and survey techniques using interviews and questionnaires.

A Surveys

1 MAJOR FORMS OF SURVEY

(a) The descriptive survey aims to estimate as precisely as possible the attributes of a population, e.g. its demographic composition, its attitude to abortion, its religious beliefs, voting intentions, its child-rearing practices.

(b) The explanatory survey seeks to establish cause and effect relationships but without experimental manipulation, e.g. the effects on employee motivation of bonus schemes, the effects of social climate on adolescent values. Sometimes, of course, both descriptive and explanatory studies can be carried out in the same enquiry.

For descriptive surveys, representative sampling of the population is as crucial as in the experiment, since without representation estimates of population, statistics will be inaccurate. In explanatory studies, control is crucial, for failure to anticipate the necessity to control potentially confounding variables may invalidate the findings. All the problems inherent in the obtaining of reliable and valid measures are equally as important in surveys as in the experimental method.

Statistical control can be effected in the design strategy. It involves being able to separate out the effects of the *IV* from other variables. If, for example, we wished to survey levels of attainment in schools of different sizes, we would have to try and eradicate the effect of 'neighbourhood' on attainment by selecting different sized schools all in the same type of neighbourhood or by representing every school-size category in each type of neighbourhood. Hypotheses are generated in explanatory surveys to state the expected relationships between the variables.

The chief characteristics of the survey are:

(a) It requires a sample of respondents to reply to a number of standard questions under comparable conditions.
(b) It may be administered by an interviewer or by sending the respondent a form for self-completion.
(c) The respondents represent a defined population. If less than 100% of the defined population are sampled then a sample survey has been conducted; a 100% survey is a census.
(d) The results of the sample survey can be generalized to the defined population.
(e) The use of standard questions enables comparisons of individuals to be made.

Survey methods include both interviews and questionnaires, the latter being a self-administered interview with no interviewer present to interpret the questionnaire for the respondent. The interview is a particular form of verbal interaction in which the interviewer attempts to elicit information, opinions, or belief from another. It can be highly standardized with a schedule of questions which must be asked in the same order, with the same wording and even the same voice tone to ensure each subject is responding to the same instrument. In less-standardized interviews the interviewer adopts a more passive role giving only enough direction to stimulate a respondent to cover the area of interest in depth while having freedom of expression. But the choice of method is affected by the following considerations, amongst others:

(a) Nature of population, e.g. age, reading or writing skills, wide geographical dispersal or localized.
(b) Nature of information sought, e.g. sensitive, emotive, boring.
(c) Complexity and length of questionnaires/interviews.
(d) Financial and other resources, e.g. time.

The aim is to select an approach that will generate reliable and valid data from a high proportion of the sample within a reasonable time period at minimum cost.

An interviewer-administered survey is more accurate and obtains more returns than a postal self-completion survey. Interviewers are essential if the survey is on a sensitive or difficult area or if respondents are not likely to be sufficiently competent in filling in the questionnaire.

Face-to-face interviewing may be essential where, (a) the population is inexperienced in filling in forms or poorly motivated to respond, (b) the information required is complicated or highly sensitive, and (c) the schedule is an open one, requiring, as the Newson's research did, individualized phrasing of questions in response to the respondent's answers. The least expensive method, self-administered postal questionnaires, would be the obvious one to adopt if the opposite conditions held, especially if the population was highly scattered geographically. The Newson and Newson (1967) survey dictated the method.

> It must be borne in mind always that basically and in essence our aim is to create a climate in which the ordinary mother's ability to talk about her own child is freed from ordinary constraints: so that, first by stimulating her with questions which are relevant and meaningful to her situation, and second by being totally receptive and responsive to whatever she may say, the conversation becomes extraordinarily highly charged with information while retaining its natural feel. The means to this end are tape recorder, schedule of questions, pencil and trained interviewer. (Newson and Newson (1967) p. 33)

The advantage of the survey is that it can elicit information from a respondent that covers a long period of time in a few minutes, and with comparable information for a number of respondents can go beyond description to looking for patterns in data. But the attempt to produce comparable information by standard questions can lead to the obscuring of subtle differences. Simplification of behaviour is the price paid to find patterns and regularities in behaviour by standard measures.

Interview schedules and questionnaires should be tried out in 'pilot studies' to remove ambiguity, test adequacy of response categories, and all the working involved in the administration.

2 OPEN-ENDED AND CLOSED QUESTIONS

The former leaves the respondent free to answer in a relatively unrestricted manner. A closed question restricts response-choice by forcing the respondent to respond to fixed categories or alternatives. Open-ended questions appear most appropriate when:

(a) We want to find out the respondent's level of information.
(b) The issue may lie outside the respondent's experience, where closed questions might force a blind choice in order not to appear ignorant.

Closed questions are useful when:

(a) There are limited frames of reference from which the respondent can answer.
(b) Within the range of possible answers there are clearly defined choice points.

But closed questions do demand little effort or motivation to answer and do not require the respondent to evaluate his experiences. On the other hand open questions produce such a wide range of material that analysis becomes difficult.

Easy introductory questions should be given at the beginning of a survey, e.g. age, occupation, marital status. Complex and/or emotional questions come later with some easier questions at the end to allow the dissipation of tension.

STQ   *What do you infer as the merits and demerits of*

(a)   The highly standardized interview?
(b)   The 'unstructured' interview?

---

3 TYPES OF SURVEY

Some surveys involve multiple or repeated contact. 'Before and after' studies come into this category where there is an attempt to establish the effect of some event on the experimental group which has occurred between the two phases of the survey, e.g. the effect of a television commercial on the use of car seat-belts.

There are two basic approaches in collecting survey data from large samples. The first of these is the cross-sectional approach. As the name implies, the method involves taking a cross-section of the population, selecting, for example, a particular age group, and measuring the value of one or more variables, such as height, reading ability, etc. These data can then be used to calculate norms for that particular age group. Cross-sections of other age groups can then be taken and the changes in norms from one cross-section to another can be used as an estimate of the development occurring between one age and another.

However, there are often difficulties in interpreting cross-sectional data. For one thing, there may be changes from year to year in the variable being studied. For example, if one were interested in using a cross-sectional approach to examine the development of number skills between the ages of four and six, one might assess these skills in two samples of a hundred children at each of the two ages. It might then be found that the norms showed advances in some skills, no difference in others, and decrements in the rest between the two age groups. However, the actual sample of four-year-old children might, if followed up after two years, turn out to be much better in all skills than the original six-year-olds in the sample. The reason for this could be that environmental conditions relevant to the development of those number skills had changed during this period, though there are other equally likely explanations.

The cross-sectional method is most often used to produce developmental norms for different ages, thus allowing one to assess whether a particular child is ahead of or behind the norm, which is often an important diagnostic question. However, by concentrating on averages, this approach tells us very little about individual patterns of development, and may indeed give a false picture of growth. If some children develop very quickly between the ages of four and five, and others very slowly, this will be obscured in the cross-sectional data. The impression would be that all develop at a steady rate.

The final difficulty with a cross-sectional approach is that chronological age is by no means equivalent in terms of physical development for every individual. There are considerable differences in developmental status between children who are ostensibly the same 'age'.

The alternative approach for studying large samples of individuals is a longitudinal study. This avoids the pitfalls outlined above, by collecting observations and measurements through repeated contact with the same individuals over a period of years. By collecting information in this way, one can interpret an individual's status in terms of his own past growth, and pick up many of the variations and individual differences in developmental progress.

A good example of a longitudinal approach is the National Child Development Study (Davie, Butler, and Goldstein, 1972) which followed up nearly 16 000 children from their birth, during one week in March 1958, for 11 years. A population followed up in this way in a longitudinal study is commonly called a cohort. The data from this particular study have been used to assess, for example, the long-term effects of the mother working on children's attainment.

Although it is a much more valuable way of studying development, the longitudinal approach is extremely time-consuming, organizationally complex and slow in producing results. Some indication of the difficulty of maintaining large-scale longitudinal surveys is given by the fact that only four British studies with samples of more than 1000 are recorded. Particular care must be used in selecting the sample, because any initial errors are likely to have an increasing influence on the results as the study progresses. The study becomes increasingly difficult as the years go by, because families move and have to be followed up, and changes in research personnel may introduce error into the data collection. There is also a common tendency for the sample to become biased towards those who are more co-operative in informing the investigators of changes of address, and in addition bias can occur because, for example, different social-class groups may be affected by differential illness and death rates.

Douglas (1976), who followed through a sample of children born in one week in 1947 to their late-twenties, spells out some of the particular advantages of longitudinal studies.

(a)   Information is more accurate or more complete if collected during the course of a longitudinal survey.

(a)   In cohort studies no duplication of information occurs, whereas in cross-sectional studies the same type of background information has to be collected on each occasion. This increases the interviewing costs.

(c)   The omission of even a single variable, later found to be important, from a cross-sectional study is a disaster, whereas it is usually possible in a cohort study to fill the gap, even if only partially, in a subsequent interview.

(d)   A cohort study allows the accumulation of a much larger number of variables extending over a much wider area of knowledge than would be possible in a cross-sectional study because the collection can be spread over many interviews. Moreover, information may be obtained at the most appropriate time: for example, information on job entry may be obtained when it occurs even if this varies from one member of the sample to another.

(e)   Starting with a birth cohort removes later problems of sampling and allows the extensive use of subsamples. It also eases problems of reliability of information affected, as it is so easily, by retrospective distortion.

(f)   Longitudinal studies are free of the major obstacles to causal analysis, namely the reinterpretation of remembered information so that it conforms with conventional views of causation. It also provides the means to assess the direction of effect. (Douglas, 1976)

On the debit side, longitudinal surveys:

(a)   Produce their results slowly.
(b)   Are costly and need staffing over a long time period.

4 RELIABILITY AND VALIDITY

Many of the criticisms of questionnaires and interview schedules hinge on the reliability and validity of poorly designed questions.

STQ   *See if you can recall what is meant by 'reliability' and 'validity' (Chapter 25).*

We need questions which will measure consistently, and appropriately, what we wish to measure and accurate communication between interviewer and respondent lies behind this. Three components of the communication process in particular influence reliability and validity. These are language, conceptual level of questions and frame of reference.

(a) Language
This involves a compromise between stating an information-getting question and employing a shared researcher — respondent vocabulary which still conveys the exact meaning without being too difficult or over-simplified.

(b) Conceptual level
This is very much related to language above (a). But even if the respondent shares a common vocabulary with the researcher, they may not share the cognitive organization necessary. The respondent may not order his feelings or beliefs in the same way as the researcher.

(c) Frame of reference
This links to both of the above points. Most words can be interpreted from different points of view. For example 'work' may evoke different conceptions. Ask a housewife is she did any work last week and she might say not, regarding work as something done for pay.

Other factors influencing the reliability and validity of subject's responses involve his personality, and where interviewers are concerned, the interaction of both of their personalities and social attributes. The sex, age, dress, race, social class, and attractiveness of the interviewer are all known to influence the responses to and rapport with the interviewers.

Just as a respondent's motivation to supply information is affected by the interviewer so, too, care needs to be taken with the presentation of the questionnaire. It is its own salesman.

The characteristics that make for good interviewers seem to be the same as those Rogers emphasizes in client centred therapy, i.e. empathy, warmth and unconditional acceptance.

Surveys are open to memory and viewpoint biases which affect reliability and validity, for many issues surveyed often involve hypothesized long-term effects which rely extensively on retrospective accounts subject to memory distortion, e.g. early child-rearing practices.

Self-reporting in interview or on questionnaires is affected by the willingness of the subject to co-operate, social expectancy, the subject's feelings of freedom from threat, degree of self-knowledge, understanding of the question and the availability of adequate symbols for expression.

In the survey method, whether by interview or questionnaire, heavy reliance is placed on the subject's verbal report, i.e. what he is willing and able to reveal about himself.

The impersonal standardized nature of the questionnaire does ensure some uniformity from one measurement situation to another. Yet even here, questions are capable of slight variations in interpretations by different subjects. But the interview, no matter how well trained the interviewers are, is never exactly the same from one interview to the next, for each is an interaction of different personalities.

Questionnaires do give respondents a greater confidence in their anonymity and therefore facilitate freer expression. But questionnaires are limited to those capable of filling them out. Mailed questionnaires have a poor response rate, usually less than 50% returned. Those who do return them tend to be biased toward the more literate, interested middle-class.

The interview is more flexible than the questionnaire, for if in the former a subject misinterprets a question or requires clarification this can be remedied. But there is little that can be done if that occurs with the latter technique.

As in any other method, the survey requires a decision to be made as to what the research population and sample will be. The task is to identify a population that will provide all the information needed for a particular research problem. The Newson and Newson (1963) survey in Nottingham, although confined to that city, adequately reflected the whole range of child-rearing practices and attitudes to child rearing that they wished to investigate.

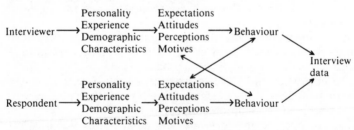

Figure 60   Interviewer–respondent interaction

The stages in planning a survey would be:

(a) Assessing constraints and resources.
(b) Structuring the problem – research hypothesis (explanatory survey).
(c) Specifying population and sample.

(d)   Method of data collection – choice and design.
(e)   Pilot study.
(f)   Main data collection.
(g)   Data processing and analysis.
(h)   Report writing.

These stages are not as clear cut as this in practice, with decisions being mutually dependent.
   The strength of the survey method would appear to be that:

(a)   It is often the only way to obtain information about a subject's past life.
(b)   It is one of the few techniques available to provide information on beliefs, attitudes and motives.
(c)   It can be used on all normal human populations except young children.
(d)   It is an efficient way of collecting data in large amounts at low cost in a short period of time.
(e)   Structured surveys are amenable to statistical analysis.

STQ   (1)   *Briefly outline the relative merits of the longitudinal and cross-sectional survey methods.*

   (2)   *What do you perceive to be the major factors which may lower reliability and validity indices in, (i) an interview, (ii) a questionnaire?*

If you need help on these re-read the preceding pages.

Fieldwork and observation
This method originated in the early twentieth century with anthropology during the studies of primitive and simple societies in Africa, the Americas and the Pacific.
   Fieldwork was the observation and study of a culture in its natural habitat. This method of observation of natural social processes is no longer confined to anthropology nor to simple societies. It is often termed 'Ethnography' now and is employed in the detailed study of small, well-defined groups within a complex society. Groups which involve face-to-face social interaction in which social positions are far from the modern settings for ethnographic investigations, e.g. a study of factory workers' responses to piece-work payment. In this area there is an unsupported belief by management that all workers want to maximize earnings. Yet workers tend to have outputs which vary little from one person to another.

One researcher (Roy, 1952) showed that this was because groups of workers develop norms about productivity, rules which other workers would fall into line with. Roy used fieldwork in that he became a factory worker and studied his fellow workers norms, beliefs and behaviour in secret. To do this he employed a technique called participant observation in which the observer shares in the group activities, accepted as one of the group. Another well-known study employing participant observation in a field work setting is Whyte's (1955) study of values and culture in an adolescent street gang.

The field study has as its major merit the fact that it is naturalistic, studying individuals and groups in their natural settings with regard to how behaviour and meanings depend on interaction with others. A participant observer involved in the group's life is in a better position to understand the complexities and subtleties of behaviour and its meaning than the social scientist applying standardized questionnaires or creating artificial and restrictive laboratory situations.

On the debit side, fieldwork is time consuming and laborious. The observer needs to be accepted as a 'natural' part of the setting or else his presence will influence what he observes.

Another problem is that we never know how typical or representative the individuals and group studied are of other groups. Finally there is the reliability of the observations and their analysis.

STQ *Can you think of reasons why field-work observations and their analysis may not be reliable?*

The selection of what is, and what is not, significant has to be made so that the former is recorded. Different observers of the group behaviour may record subtly different aspects and furthermore may interpret the same behaviour in different ways. In fieldwork, research design refers to the decisions that have to be taken over the whole course of the fieldwork. There is an orientation to research which is different from the experimental and survey styles in that there is:

(a)   An aim to understand behaviour from the point of view of the behaving person. The social world is socially constructed therefore we have actors and actions rather than subjects and behaviour. Action is seen as purposive and meaningful from the perspective of the actor.

(b)   An emphasis on process in that interpretation is not fixed and actors are always in a state of becoming. Social meaning and interpretation derive from the process of interaction. We cannot on this view merely measure input and output (IV and DV), we must study how these are perceived and interpreted.

(c) A commitment to study behaviour in natural settings not 'artificial' ones. Furthermore, there is no manipulation and control but an attempt to minimize the observer's impact so that the observations are based on normal social events and processes. There is a parallel here with ethologists who insist on the observation of animal behaviour in the wild and argue against any extrapolation from captive animals.

The emphasis in fieldwork is less concerned with theory testing as in experimental work than with the generation and development of theories. The approach is inductive not deductive. The danger of the deductive approach is that the experimenter will tend to impose his structure of the world. The inductive approach will generate theory and hypothesis out of the observations as the fieldwork proceeds. Fieldwork starts by the field worker collecting data to try out a range of possible ideas and lines of enquiry guided only by broad research interests. After this initial phase, significant persons, behaviours and events emerge, so that research problems become more refined and focused. Working hypotheses can now be formuated and then tested. The guiding principle at the outset is that of a naive observer, who does not take things on trust. There is an avoidance of sharpening problems into specific hypotheses until considerable exploratory investigation has occurred. One major early problem in fieldwork is the selection of a research setting which is typical so that results can be generalized. But it is often difficult to know if a selected field-work setting is typical.

1 OBSERVATION

We are all involved in observation every day. I observe that it is raining outside; I observe cars stopping at the traffic lights, and so on. Observation is a pervasive human activity, but to make it a scientific activity too:

(1) It must be planned systematically.
(2) It must be recorded systematically.
(3) It must be related at some stage to theory and hypothesis.
(4) It must be subject to reliability and validity checks.

The great asset of observation is that it is possible to record behaviour as it occurs. All too often survey data can depend entirely on retrospective or anticipatory reports of behaviour, these reports being made in a context remote from the real situation yet influenced by the 'demand characteristics' and 'experimenter effects' of the interview situation.

Another valuable role of observation lies in investigations with subjects such as infants or animals who obviously cannot provide verbal reports of feelings or behaviour. For example Spitz and Wolf (1946) observed babies in nurseries and came to the conclusion that maternal deprivation may lead to severe depression and social withdrawal. Hebb and Thomson (1954) report observations on the social behaviour of animals. But in addition to a subject's ability to respond to a survey there is also the question of his willingness to report. Some people do resent being interviewed or filling in forms. They may lie, give socially acceptable answers, use defence mechanisms etc. Although observation cannot overcome all resistance to research, it is less demanding on active co-operation by the subjects. Agreed, people who know they are being observed may deliberately try to alter habits which is probably more difficult than the distortion of memory in surveys.

Observation does have its limitations. It is impossible to record or observe everything and we may have to wait a considerable time before the event we want occurs, e.g. observation of human behaviour in an earthquake disaster. Other events are rarely open to observation, e.g. sexual acts, death, suicide etc.

Observation may serve a variety of purposes. It may be used in an exploratory way to obtain insights that serve as the bases of hypotheses for later experimental studies. It may be used as an ancillary aid in the interpretation of data derived by other techniques. Observational procedures may range from use-application of detailed observation schedules to completely unstructured approaches. The observer himself may be part of the group (participant observation) with his presence either known or unknown, or be an extra group observer. The style of participation/non-participation, secrecy/known presence, depends on the purpose of the study. For example the social behaviour of young children at play may be observed through a one-way window; some therapists may act as participant observers in a therapy group.

But whatever the purpose of the study, your decisions have to be made:

(1) What should be observed?
(2) How should observations be recorded?
(3) How can reliability and validity be attained?
(4) What relationship should exist between observer and observed?

2 UNSTRUCTURED OBSERVATION
Unstructured observation often takes the form of participant observation, and is often used in exploratory investigations. This means that what the observer feels is important to observe may change as he goes

along. Such changes are not to be criticized; they mark the optimal use of unstructured observation. This change in what is observed is often a focussing down onto a narrower range of more central events and behaviours. Usually four major elements are observed:

(1) The participants — who they are and their social relationships with each other — role behaviour.
(2) The setting — its effect on the restriction or encouragement of various behaviours.
(3) The purpose — why are the participants in the setting? What formal or informal goals are being pursued?
(4) Behaviour — what do the participants do? What are the objectives, effects and intensities of the behaviour? How typical is it?

The recording of observations in the participant role is difficult. The best time to record is of course immediately but it would often disturb the proceedings or arouse suspicions. So the records must be written up as soon as possible after the observation. It is impossible to check the reliability of the record for once the event has passed there can be no action replay as on television. The best solution is, if possible, to use two or more observers who can compare notes and check bias. But if reliability can be improved this way, it does little for the validity of interpreting the data, for all the observers are likely to have a common cultural background and training. A middle class observer may perceive the good natured horse play between members of an adolescent street gang as overt aggression. The participant observer will also have difficulty in maintaining objectivity as relationships develop between himself and the other group members.

In some situations secret observation is the only means possible. For example Festinger *et al.* (1956) joined a sect predicting the end of the world by posing as converts. Sherif and Sherif (1953) observed gang activities of boys in a summer camp by working as labourers in the camp grounds.

3 STRUCTURED OBSERVATION
Much of what has been said about unstructured observation also applies to structured observation. The major difference is that in the latter the observer knows beforehand the behaviour relevant to his research purposes, and can thus generate a specific plan for collecting and recording the observations. An observational instrument or schedule is usually created which contain observer-defined categories for which tallies of observations are made.

Structured observation usually measures four elements:

(1) Form. This is the behaviour in its various pre-designated categories as specified in the schedule. e.g. giving an order.

(2) Duration. This simply is the length of time the specified behaviour lasts.
(3) Frequency. This refers to the number of times any specified behaviour occurs in a given time period.
(4) Antecedent and consequent behaviours. These refer to the preceding and succeeding behaviours or events.

Structured observation provides greater reliability than recall or unstructured observation since there is more control and precision involved with the observer knowing what he is to observe and inferential demands placed on him. For example it is easier to note anxiety through eye blink rates say than to infer it through simply watching several interacting subjects for anything that, one might feel, is suggestive of current anxiety. Structured observational schedules are adaptable to many different research settings.

Typical examples of observation schedules are Bales' (1950) Schedule for recording group interaction and Flanders' (1970) Interaction Analysis Categories for observing teacher–pupil–classroom interaction. The main problem is that the use of such standard frames of reference limits what is observed and recorded. Subtleties are lost and other behaviours go unrecorded. Observers have to master the codes that are used to record the observations. Reliability in recording can be quite high when observers are well trained. The measure of reliability often taken is inter-observer reliability in which a high concentration will be found between two observers viewing the same events if they code them in the same way on most occasions.

> **STQ** *If two observers produced a low positive correlation between their coded observations, what might this imply?*

The greatest source of unreliability is the constant error introduced by the observer because of distortion of his perceptions by his own needs and values. Training and practice can help to overcome this in some people, but not in all, and constant biases by two observers in the same direction cannot be detected by inter-observer reliability coefficients.

> **STQ** *Can you explain why?*

The non-participant observer faces the same problems as the participant observer in establishing relations with those whom he is observing. Such observers usually try to create the impression of a neutral, psychologically invisible person.

The problem with structured observation is that categories are usually not refined enough to allow an observer to be absolutely clear in every case where to allocate an observation and there may not be sufficient categories. For example the Bales' system does not permit much discrimination in terms of the intensity of verbal interaction, and Flanders' system does not allow any discrimination between silence and chaos, nor does it consider non-verbal behaviour.

4 PARTICIPANT AND NON-PARTICIPANT OBSERVATION

A further problem lies in the presence of a non-participant observer. He is often conspicuous since our society possesses no norms for relationships with non-members who are present. The behaviour of the group may be changed in unknown ways by his presence.

Exercise

Take either Bales' (1950) system or Flanders' (1970) system and try them out if you can find a co-operative group. Make a critical evaluation of the system you use. Participant observation need not be less systematic than structured observation. The source of bias is different in each. Participant observation biases stem from the interactional nature of the observer's role whereas structured observation leads to bias arising from the imposed coding system.

Participant observation material can be coded after the event, but its initial openness is a strong point in the study of social situations where little is known beforehand. It also provides data over a long period of time for many variables, whereas structured observation can only be used on a few variables over a short period of time. The field worker is not constrained by an initial hypothesis but can reformulate the problem as he proceeds. If he starts off on the wrong track he can modify his plans, and follow a more promising line.

A danger in participant observation is that the investigator will 'go native'. He must always remain conscious of the roles he is playing, and be able to detach himself from the situation. It is a tightrope between being accepted yet not allowing this new perspective to interfere with his own analytic perspective.

The earliest form of unstructured observation was the baby biography, a diary-type account of the behaviour of an individual child. All or any behaviour was noted. These anecdotal accounts were usually the product of an interested close relative. Rarely was any attempts made to separate recordings of observable behaviour from interpretation of that behaviour. Motives and characteristics were imputed to the child which perhaps were more a reflection of the observer's own needs, wishes and feelings. However such diaries did provide some normative information on the appearance of various developmental behaviour, e.g. walking. Clearly, though, there was no random sampling and observer bias was potent.

An important way of improving an unstructured observation is by quantifying observational data through time sampling. By defining categories of behaviour then it is possible to count the number of times a behaviour occurs in a fixed time period. If we wished to study nervous habits in children we might define biting on nails, twisting the hair, pulling at ear, sucking the thumb, as the main indicators. Then observing the child for say 20 5-minute periods in a free play situation at school we can tally the frequency of each type of nervous mannerism. The reliability of the behaviour can be established by correlating the simultaneous observations of two observers.

Exercise

Observe a young child and record in long hand everything you observe in his behaviour during a 5–10 min period. Choose a time when the youngster is playing by himself to simplify the observations. When you have done this answer the following questions.

(1) To what extent do you feel you were able to record *all* of the behaviour? What might you have missed?
(2) Do you feel you were biased towards observing only certain features?
(3) Did you concentrate on motor activity, or verbal activity?
(4) What did you learn about the child's behaviour that you did not know before?
(5) Do you feel that observing the child altered his behaviour in any way? How? Could you have avoided it?
(6) Did you interpret his behaviour from your point of view?

Exercise

Repeat the above exercise with a different child. Use two observers simultaneously. Compare the two records at the end.

(1) To what extent were the two observers looking at the same type of behaviour? Was one observer recording more general behaviour than the other?
(2) How might we increase inter-observer agreement?
(3) Was there any behaviour which was interpreted differently by each observer?

STQ *What do you regard as the relative merits of, (i) structured and unstructured observation, (ii) participant and nonparticipant observation?*

C COMPARISON OF INVESTIGATION METHODS

(a) The main difference between the methods has to do with hypotheses. Each method must employ hypotheses as these are the guiding framework of the investigation. They determine the selection of data, relevant to the investigation. But the formulation of the hypotheses may take place at different points in the various methods. In an experiment the hypothesis is clearly and precisely stated in advance of the research. In a survey a hypothesis is necessary in the drawing up of an inteview schedule or questionnaire though both schedule and hypothesis will probably be revised and refined as a result of pilot studies. The ethographic or field work method reveals considerable fluidity in the way a hypothesis is progressively delineated during the fieldwork and analysis stages. There is a gradual narrowing of the focus as information comes to light and is analysed.

(b) A further difference lies in the role of the investigator. No investigator can avoid interacting with participants. The experimental method requires the investigator to be actively involved, allocating conditions and treatments of the *IV* to the subjects, controlling and standardizing other variables and even establishing deceptive circumstances, e.g. Milgram (1974). In surveys, however, there is an attempt to adopt a 'neutral' role so as not to affect the responses given. In fieldwork the role chosen which might vary from participant observation to outside observer depends on the context being studied.

(c) All the styles of investigation can involve ethical problems and often do. We must always rule out the allocation of potentially harmful treatments, e.g. actual physical or psychological abuse, the giving of drugs with noxious effects. Even the intrusion of an interviewer or observer into people's privacy can be potentially damaging to some subjects.

The recruitment of subjects can cause ethical dilemmas. The use of compulsion or remuneration would not generally create the kind of motivation required yet the use of volunteers can bias the results since volunteers may not be a representative sample of the population. The need to stress the confidentiality and anonymity of individual responses in all types of investigation can never be emphasized enough.

A final ethical problem involves the use of deception even if it is only temporary. This does not solely occur in experimental situations. A field worker may function as a secret participant in a group who are unaware of their real role. The interviewer might 'trick' respondents by asking about their opinions of 'non-existent' issues.

Some researchers have argued for an ethical code that would forbid some dubious practices under any circumstances. Other researchers would prefer to leave such decisions to the conscience of the particular investigator. Ultimately the decision is a trade-off between ethical commitment and the likely value of the findings of the investigation.

This has been a very brief introduction to other methods of investigation to show you that the experimental method, the focus of this book, is not the only approach, nor is it always appropriate.

REFERENCES

Bales, R. F. (1950). *Interaction Process Analysis.* (Reading, Mass: Addison-Wesley)

Davie, R., Butler, N. and Goldstein, H. (1972). *From Birth to Seven. 2nd Report of the National Child Development Study.* (London: Longman)

Douglas, J. B. W. (1976). The use and abuse of national cohorts. In Shipman, M. (ed.) *The Organization and Impact of Social Research.* (London: Routledge)

Festinger, L. (1956). *When Prophecy Fails.* (University of Minnesota)

Flanders, N. (1970). *Analysing Teaching Behaviour.* (Reading, Mass: Addison-Wesley)

Hebb, D. O. and Thompson, W. (1954). The social significance of animal studies. In Lindzey, G. (ed.) *Handbook of Social Psychology* Vol 1. (Reading, Mass: Addison-Wesley)

Milgram, S. (1974). *Obedience to Authority.* (New York: Harper Row)

Newson, J. and Newson, E. (1963). *Infant Care in an Urban Community.* (London: Allen & Unwin)

Newson, J. and Newson, E. (1976). Parental roles and social contexts. In Shipman, M. (ed.) *The Organization and Impact of Social Research.* (London: Routledge)

Roy, D. (1952). Quota restriction and gold-bricking in a machine shop. *Amer. J. Sociol.* **57**, 427–42

Sherif, M. and Sherif, C. (1953). *Groups in Harmony and Tension.* (New York: Harper)

Spitz, R. and Wolf, K. (1946). Anaclitic Depression. The Psychoanalytic Study of the Child Vol 2

Whyte, W. F. (1955). *Street Corner Society.* (University of Chicago Press)

Appendix A

Statistical Tables

Tables B to I tell us the probability of obtaining the results of our investigations if they are randomly distributed on a chance basis. Remember that there is always a specific probability (no matter how small) of each experimental result being a chance result.

The purpose of using these statistical tables is to find out whether your differences or relationships are significantly bigger than would be expected if scores were randomly distributed.

Table A *Areas under the normal curve*

z	0 z	0 z	z	0 z	0 z	z	0 z	0 z
0.00	.0000	.5000	0.55	.2088	.2912	1.10	.3643	.1357
0.01	.0040	.4960	0.56	.2123	.2877	1.11	.3665	.1335
0.02	.0080	.4920	0.57	.2157	.2843	1.12	.3686	.1314
0.03	.0120	.4880	0.58	.2190	.2810	1.13	.3708	.1292
0.04	.0160	.4840	0.59	.2224	.2776	1.14	.3729	.1271
0.05	.0199	.4801	0.60	.2257	.2743	1.15	.3749	.1251
0.06	.0239	.4761	0.61	.2291	.2709	1.16	.3770	.1230
0.07	.0279	.4721	0.62	.2324	.2676	1.17	.3790	.1210
0.08	.0319	.4681	0.63	.2357	.2643	1.18	.3810	.1190
0.09	.0359	.4641	0.64	.2389	.2611	1.19	.3830	.1170
0.10	.0398	.4602	0.65	.2422	.2578	1.20	.3849	.1151
0.11	.0438	.4562	0.66	.2454	.2546	1.21	.3869	.1131
0.12	.0478	.4522	0.67	.2486	.2514	1.22	.3888	.1112
0.13	.0517	.4483	0.68	.2517	.2483	1.23	.3907	.1093
0.14	.0557	.4443	0.69	.2549	.2451	1.24	.3925	.1075
0.15	.0596	.4404	0.70	.2580	.2420	1.25	.3944	.1056
0.16	.0636	.4364	0.71	.2611	.2389	1.26	.3962	.1038
0.17	.0675	.4325	0.72	.2642	.2358	1.27	.3980	.1020
0.18	.0714	.4286	0.73	.2673	.2327	1.28	.3997	.1003
0.19	.0753	.4247	0.74	.2704	.2296	1.29	.4015	.0985
0.20	.0793	.4207	0.75	.2734	.2266	1.30	.4032	.0968
0.21	.0832	.4168	0.76	.2764	.2236	1.31	.4049	.0951
0.22	.0871	.4129	0.77	.2794	.2206	1.32	.4066	.0934
0.23	.0910	.4090	0.78	.2823	.2177	1.33	.4082	.0918
0.24	.0948	.4052	0.79	.2852	.2148	1.34	.4099	.0901
0.25	.0987	.4013	0.80	.2881	.2119	1.35	.4115	.0885
0.26	.1026	.3974	0.81	.2910	.2090	1.36	.4131	.0869
0.27	.1064	.3936	0.82	.2939	.2061	1.37	.4147	.0853
0.28	.1103	.3897	0.83	.2967	.2033	1.38	.4162	.0838
0.29	.1141	.3859	0.84	.2995	.2005	1.39	.4177	.0823
0.30	.1179	.3821	0.85	.3023	.1977	1.40	.4192	.0808
0.31	.1217	.3783	0.86	.3051	.1949	1.41	.4207	.0793
0.32	.1255	.3745	0.87	.3078	.1922	1.42	.4222	.0778
0.33	.1293	.3707	0.88	.3106	.1894	1.43	.4236	.0764
0.34	.1331	.3669	0.89	.3133	.1867	1.44	.4251	.0749
0.35	.1368	.3632	0.90	.3159	.1841	1.45	.4265	.0735
0.36	.1406	.3594	0.91	.3186	.1814	1.46	.4279	.0721
0.37	.1443	.3557	0.92	.3212	.1788	1.47	.4292	.0708
0.38	.1480	.3520	0.93	.3238	.1762	1.48	.4306	.0694
0.39	.1517	.3483	0.94	.3264	.1736	1.49	.4319	.0681
0.40	.1554	.3446	0.95	.3289	.1711	1.50	.4332	.0668
0.41	.1591	.3409	0.96	.3315	.1685	1.51	.4345	.0655
0.42	.1628	.3372	0.97	.3340	.1660	1.52	.4357	.0643
0.43	.1664	.3336	0.98	.3365	.1635	1.53	.4370	.0630
0.44	.1700	.3300	0.99	.3389	.1611	1.54	.4382	.0618
0.45	.1736	.3264	1.00	.3413	.1587	1.55	.4394	.0606
0.46	.1772	.3228	1.01	.3438	.1562	1.56	.4406	.0594
0.47	.1808	.3192	1.02	.3461	.1539	1.57	.4418	.0582
0.48	.1844	.3156	1.03	.3485	.1515	1.58	.4429	.0571
0.49	.1879	.3121	1.04	.3508	.1492	1.59	.4441	.0559
0.50	.1915	.3085	1.05	.3531	.1469	1.60	.4452	.0548
0.51	.1950	.3050	1.06	.3554	.1446	1.61	.4463	.0537
0.52	.1985	.3015	1.07	.3577	.1423	1.62	.4474	.0526
0.53	.2019	.2981	1.08	.3599	.1401	1.63	.4484	.0516
0.54	.2054	.2946	1.09	.3621	.1379	1.64	.4495	.0505

The table shows the area of the shaded portions relative to the area of the whole distribution. The shaded areas pertain only to the upper half of the distribution. To find the area between $-z$ and $+z$, or beyond $-z$ and $+z$, double the figures given in the table.

Table A (cont)

1	2	3	1	2	3	1	2	3
z	0 z	0 z	z	0 z	0 z	z	0 z	0 z
1.65	.4505	.0495	2.22	.4868	.0132	2.79	.4974	.0026
1.66	.4515	.0485	2.23	.4871	.0129	2.80	.4974	.0026
1.67	.4525	.0475	2.24	.4875	.0125	2.81	.4975	.0025
1.68	.4535	.0465	2.25	.4878	.0122	2.82	.4976	.0024
1.69	.4545	.0455	2.26	.4881	.0119	2.83	.4977	.0023
1.70	.4554	.0446	2.27	.4884	.0116	2.84	.4977	.0023
1.71	.4564	.0436	2.28	.4887	.0113	2.85	.4978	.0022
1.72	.4573	.0427	2.29	.4890	.0110	2.86	.4979	.0021
1.73	.4582	.0418	2.30	.4893	.0107	2.87	.4979	.0021
1.74	.4591	.0409	2.31	.4896	.0104	2.88	.4980	.0020
1.75	.4599	.0401	2.32	.4898	.0102	2.89	.4981	.0019
1.76	.4608	.0392	2.33	.4901	.0099	2.90	.4981	.0019
1.77	.4616	.0384	2.34	.4904	.0096	2.91	.4982	.0018
1.78	.4625	.0375	2.35	.4906	.0094	2.92	.4982	.0018
1.79	.4633	.0367	2.36	.4909	.0091	2.93	.4983	.0017
1.80	.4641	.0359	2.37	.4911	.0089	2.94	.4984	.0016
1.81	.4649	.0351	2.38	.4913	.0087	2.95	.4984	.0016
1.82	.4656	.0344	2.39	.4916	.0084	2.96	.4985	.0015
1.83	.4664	.0336	2.40	.4918	.0082	2.97	.4985	.0015
1.84	.4671	.0329	2.41	.4920	.0080	2.98	.4986	.0014
1.85	.4678	.0322	2.42	.4922	.0078	2.99	.4986	.0014
1.86	.4686	.0314	2.43	.4925	.0075	3.00	.4987	.0013
1.87	.4693	.0307	2.44	.4927	.0073	3.01	.4987	.0013
1.88	.4699	.0301	2.45	.4929	.0071	3.02	.4987	.0013
1.89	.4706	.0294	2.46	.4931	.0069	3.03	.4988	.0012
1.90	.4713	.0287	2.47	.4932	.0068	3.04	.4988	.0012
1.91	.4719	.0281	2.48	.4934	.0066	3.05	.4989	.0011
1.92	.4726	.0274	2.49	.4936	.0064	3.06	.4989	.0011
1.93	.4732	.0268	2.50	.4938	.0062	3.07	.4989	.0011
1.94	.4738	.0262	2.51	.4940	.0060	3.08	.4990	.0010
1.95	.4744	.0256	2.52	.4941	.0059	3.09	.4990	.0010
1.96	.4750	.0250	2.53	.4943	.0057	3.10	.4990	.0010
1.97	.4756	.0244	2.54	.4945	.0055	3.11	.4991	.0009
1.98	.4761	.0239	2.55	.4946	.0054	3.12	.4991	.0009
1.99	.4767	.0233	2.56	.4948	.0052	3.13	.4991	.0009
2.00	.4772	.0228	2.57	.4949	.0051	3.14	.4992	.0008
2.01	.4778	.0222	2.58	.4951	.0049	3.15	.4992	.0008
2.02	.4783	.0217	2.59	.4952	.0048	3.16	.4992	.0008
2.03	.4788	.0212	2.60	.4953	.0047	3.17	.4992	.0008
2.04	.4793	.0207	2.61	.4955	.0045	3.18	.4993	.0007
2.05	.4798	.0202	2.62	.4956	.0044	3.19	.4993	.0007
2.06	.4803	.0197	2.63	.4957	.0043	3.20	.4993	.0007
2.07	.4808	.0192	2.64	.4959	.0041	3.21	.4993	.0007
2.08	.4812	.0188	2.65	.4960	.0040	3.22	.4994	.0006
2.09	.4817	.0183	2.66	.4961	.0039	3.23	.4994	.0006
2.10	.4821	.0179	2.67	.4962	.0038	3.24	.4994	.0006
2.11	.4826	.0174	2.68	.4963	.0037	3.25	.4994	.0006
2.12	.4830	.0170	2.69	.4964	.0036	3.30	.4995	.0005
2.13	.4834	.0166	2.70	.4965	.0035	3.35	.4996	.0004
2.14	.4838	.0162	2.71	.4966	.0034	3.40	.4997	.0003
2.15	.4842	.0158	2.72	.4967	.0033	3.45	.4997	.0003
2.16	.4846	.0154	2.73	.4968	.0032	3.50	.4998	.0002
2.17	.4850	.0150	2.74	.4969	.0031	3.60	.4998	.0002
2.18	.4854	.0146	2.75	.4970	.0030	3.70	.4999	.0001
2.19	.4857	.0143	2.76	.4971	.0029	3.80	.4999	.0001
2.20	.4861	.0139	2.77	.4972	.0028	3.90	.49995	.00005
2.21	.4864	.0136	2.78	.4973	.0027	4.00	.49997	.00003

SOURCE: Richard P. Runyon and Audrey Haber, *Fundamentals of Behavioral Statistics,* Second Edition (1971), Reading, Mass.: Addison-Wesley Publishing Co. Artwork from Robert B. McCall, *Fundamental Statistics for Psychology,* Second Edition (1975), New York: Harcourt Brace Jovanovich, Inc.

Experimental psychology

Table B Critical values of *t*

df	Level of significance for one-tailed test					
	0.10	0.05	0.025	0.01	0.005	0.0005
	Level of significance for two-tailed test					
	0.20	0.10	0.05	0.02	0.01	0.001
1	3.078	6.134	12.706	31.821	63.657	636.619
2	1.886	2.920	4.303	6.965	9.925	31.598
3	1.638	2.353	3.182	4.541	5.841	12.941
4	1.533	2.132	2.776	3.747	4.604	8.610
5	1.476	2.015	2.571	3.365	4.032	6.859
6	1.440	1.943	2.447	3.143	3.707	5.959
7	1.415	1.895	2.365	2.998	3.499	5.405
8	1.397	1.860	2.306	2.896	3.355	5.041
9	1.383	1.833	2.262	2.821	3.250	4.781
10	1.372	1.812	2.228	2.764	3.169	4.587
11	1.363	1.796	2.201	2.718	3.106	4.437
12	1.356	1.782	2.179	2.681	3.055	4.318
13	1.350	1.771	2.160	2.650	3.012	4.221
14	1.345	1.761	2.145	2.624	2.977	4.140
15	1.341	1.753	2.131	2.602	2.974	4.073
16	1.337	1.746	2.120	2.583	2.921	4.015
17	1.333	1.740	2.110	2.567	2.898	3.965
18	1.330	1.734	2.101	2.552	2.878	3.922
19	1.328	1.729	2.093	2.539	2.861	3.883
20	1.325	1.725	2.086	2.528	2.845	3.850
21	1.323	1.721	2.080	2.518	2.831	3.819
22	1.321	1.717	2.074	2.508	2.819	3.792
23	1.319	1.714	2.069	2.500	2.807	3.767
24	1.318	1.711	2.064	2.492	2.797	3.745
25	1.316	1.708	2.060	2.485	2.787	3.725
26	1.315	1.706	2.056	2.479	2.779	3.707
27	1.314	1.703	2.052	2.473	2.771	3.690
28	1.313	1.701	2.048	2.467	2.763	3.674
29	1.311	1.699	2.045	2.462	2.756	3.659
30	1.310	1.697	2.042	2.457	2.750	3.646
40	1.303	1.684	2.021	2.423	2.704	3.551
60	1.296	1.671	2.000	2.390	2.660	3.460
120	1.289	1.658	1.980	2.358	2.617	3.373
∞	1.282	1.645	1.960	2.326	2.576	3.291

SOURCE: R. Fisher. *Statistical Methods for Research Workers.* 14th edn. Hafner Press. Adelaide 1970.

NB When there is no exact *df* use the next lowest number, except for very large *df*s (well over 120), when you can use the infinity row.

Table C Sign test

Critical values of X (the number of cases with the less frequent sign) for a one-tailed test*. N is the total number of subjects, or matched pairs of subjects minus ties.

	Level of significance				Level of significance		
N	0.05	0.025	0.01	N	0.05	0.025	0.01
5	0	—	—	16	4	3	2
6	0	0	—	17	4	4	3
7	0	0	0	18	5	4	3
8	1	0	0	19	5	4	4
9	1	1	0	20	5	5	4
10	1	1	0	21	6	5	4
11	2	1	1	22	6	5	5
12	2	2	1	23	7	6	5
13	3	2	1	24	7	6	5
14	3	2	2	25	7	7	6
15	3	3	2				

SOURCE: S. Miller, *Experimental Design and Statistics,* Methuen 1975;

*For a two-tailed test the significance levels should be multiplied by 2.

Table D (1) Critical values of the Mann–Whitney U for a one-tailed test at 0.005: two-tailed test at 0.01

n_2										n_1										
	1	2	3	4	5	6	7	8	9	10	11	12	13	14	15	16	17	18	19	20
1	–	–	–	–	–	–	–	–	–	–	–	–	–	–	–	–	–	–	–	–
2	–	–	–	–	–	–	–	–	–	–	–	–	–	–	–	–	–	–	0	0
3	–	–	–	–	–	–	–	–	0	0	0	1	1	1	2	2	2	2	3	3
4	–	–	–	–	–	0	0	1	1	2	2	3	3	4	5	5	6	6	7	8
5	–	–	–	–	0	1	1	2	3	4	5	6	7	7	8	9	10	11	12	13
6	–	–	–	0	1	2	3	4	5	6	7	9	10	11	12	13	15	16	17	18
7	–	–	–	0	1	3	4	6	7	9	10	12	13	15	16	18	19	21	22	24
8	–	–	–	1	2	4	6	7	9	11	13	15	17	18	20	22	24	26	28	30
9	–	–	0	1	3	5	7	9	11	13	16	18	20	22	24	27	29	31	33	36
10	–	–	0	2	4	6	9	11	13	16	18	21	24	26	29	31	34	37	39	42
11	–	–	0	2	5	7	10	13	16	18	21	24	27	30	33	36	39	42	45	48
12	–	–	1	3	6	9	12	15	18	21	24	27	31	34	37	41	44	47	51	54
13	–	–	1	3	7	10	13	17	20	24	27	31	34	38	42	45	49	53	56	60
14	–	–	1	4	7	11	15	18	22	26	30	34	38	42	46	50	54	58	63	67
15	–	–	2	5	8	12	16	20	24	29	33	37	42	46	51	55	60	64	69	73
16	–	–	2	5	9	13	18	22	27	31	36	41	45	50	55	60	65	70	74	79
17	–	–	2	6	10	15	19	24	29	34	39	44	49	54	60	65	70	75	81	86
18	–	–	2	6	11	16	21	26	31	37	42	47	53	58	64	70	75	81	87	92
19	–	0	3	7	12	17	22	28	33	39	45	51	56	63	69	74	81	87	93	99
20	–	0	3	8	13	18	24	30	36	42	48	54	60	67	73	79	86	92	99	105

Table D (2) Mann−Whitney U: one-tailed test at 0.01; two-tailed test at 0.02

n_2	n_1																			
	1	*2*	*3*	*4*	*5*	*6*	*7*	*8*	*9*	*10*	*11*	*12*	*13*	*14*	*15*	*16*	*17*	*18*	*19*	*20*
1	−	−	−	−	−	−	−	−	−	−	−	−	−	−	−	−	−	−	−	−
2	−	−	−	−	−	−	−	−	−	−	−	−	−	0	0	0	0	0	1	1
3	−	−	−	−	−	−	−	0	0	1	1	1	2	2	2	3	3	4	4	5
4	−	−	−	−	0	1	1	2	3	3	4	5	5	6	7	7	8	9	9	10
5	−	−	−	0	1	2	3	4	5	6	7	8	9	10	11	12	13	14	15	16
6	−	−	−	1	2	3	4	6	7	8	9	11	12	13	15	16	18	19	20	22
7	−	−	0	1	3	4	6	7	9	11	12	14	16	17	19	21	23	24	26	28
8	−	−	0	2	4	6	7	9	11	13	15	17	20	22	24	26	28	30	32	34
9	−	−	1	3	5	7	9	11	14	16	18	21	23	26	28	31	33	36	38	40
10	−	−	1	3	6	8	11	13	16	19	22	24	27	30	33	36	38	41	44	47
11	−	−	1	4	7	9	12	15	18	22	25	28	31	34	37	41	44	47	50	53
12	−	−	2	5	8	11	14	17	21	24	28	31	35	38	42	46	49	53	56	60
13	−	0	2	5	9	12	16	20	23	27	31	35	39	43	47	51	55	59	63	67
14	−	0	2	6	10	13	17	22	26	30	34	38	43	47	51	56	60	65	69	73
15	−	0	3	7	11	15	19	24	28	33	37	42	47	51	56	61	66	70	75	80
16	−	0	3	7	12	16	21	26	31	36	41	46	51	56	61	66	71	76	82	87
17	−	0	4	8	13	18	23	28	33	38	44	49	55	60	66	71	77	82	88	93
18	−	0	4	9	14	19	24	30	36	41	47	53	59	65	70	76	82	88	94	100
19	−	1	4	9	15	20	26	32	38	44	50	56	63	69	75	82	88	94	101	107
20	−	1	5	10	16	22	28	34	40	47	53	60	67	73	80	87	93	100	107	114

Table D (3) Mann–Whitney U: one-tailed test at 0.025; two-tailed test at 0.05

n_2	n_1																			
	1	*2*	*3*	*4*	*5*	*6*	*7*	*8*	*9*	*10*	*11*	*12*	*13*	*14*	*15*	*16*	*17*	*18*	*19*	*20*
1	—	—	—	—	—	—	—	—	—	—	—	—	—	—	—	—	—	—	—	—
2	—	—	—	—	—	—	—	0	0	0	0	1	1	1	1	1	2	2	2	2
3	—	—	—	—	0	1	1	2	2	3	3	4	4	5	5	6	6	7	7	8
4	—	—	—	0	1	2	3	4	4	5	6	7	8	9	10	11	11	12	13	13
5	—	—	0	1	2	3	5	6	7	8	9	11	12	13	14	15	17	18	19	20
6	—	—	1	2	3	5	6	8	10	11	13	14	16	17	19	21	22	24	25	27
7	—	—	1	3	5	6	8	10	12	14	16	18	20	22	24	26	28	30	32	34
8	—	0	2	4	6	8	10	13	15	17	19	22	24	26	29	31	34	36	38	41
9	—	0	2	4	7	10	12	15	17	20	23	26	28	31	34	37	39	42	45	48
10	—	0	3	5	8	11	14	17	20	23	26	29	33	36	39	42	45	48	52	55
11	—	0	3	6	9	13	16	19	23	26	30	33	37	40	44	47	51	55	58	62
12	—	1	4	7	11	14	18	22	26	29	33	37	41	45	49	53	57	61	65	69
13	—	1	4	8	12	16	20	24	28	33	37	41	45	50	54	59	63	67	72	76
14	—	1	5	9	13	17	22	26	31	36	40	45	50	55	59	64	67	74	78	83
15	—	1	5	10	14	19	24	29	34	39	44	49	54	59	64	70	75	80	85	90
16	—	1	6	11	15	21	26	31	37	42	47	53	59	64	70	75	81	86	92	98
17	—	2	6	11	17	22	28	34	39	45	51	57	63	67	75	81	87	93	99	105
18	—	2	7	12	18	24	30	36	42	48	55	61	67	74	80	86	93	99	106	112
19	—	2	7	13	19	25	32	38	45	52	58	65	72	78	85	92	99	106	113	119
20	—	2	8	13	20	27	34	41	48	55	62	69	76	83	90	98	105	112	119	127

Table D (4) Mann−Whitney U: one-tailed test at 0.05; two-tailed test at 0.10

n_2	1	2	3	4	5	6	7	8	9	10	11	12	13	14	15	16	17	18	19	20
1	−	−	−	−	−	−	−	−	−	−	−	−	−	−	−	−	−	−	−	−
2	−	−	−	−	0	0	0	1	1	1	1	2	2	2	3	3	3	4	4	4
3	−	−	0	0	1	2	2	3	3	4	5	5	6	7	7	8	9	9	10	11
4	−	−	0	1	2	3	4	5	6	7	8	9	10	11	12	14	15	16	17	18
5	−	0	1	2	4	5	6	8	9	11	12	13	15	16	18	19	20	22	23	25
6	−	0	2	3	5	7	8	10	12	14	16	17	19	21	23	25	26	28	30	32
7	−	0	2	4	6	8	11	13	15	17	19	21	24	26	28	30	33	35	37	39
8	−	1	3	5	8	10	13	15	18	20	23	26	28	31	33	36	39	41	44	47
9	−	1	3	6	9	12	15	18	21	24	27	30	33	36	39	42	45	48	51	54
10	−	1	4	7	11	14	17	20	24	27	31	34	37	41	44	48	51	55	58	62
11	−	1	5	8	12	16	19	23	27	31	34	38	42	46	50	54	57	61	65	69
12	−	2	5	9	13	17	21	26	30	34	38	42	47	51	55	60	64	68	72	77
13	−	2	6	10	15	19	24	28	33	37	42	47	51	56	61	65	70	75	80	84
14	−	2	7	11	16	21	26	31	36	41	46	51	56	61	66	71	77	82	87	92
15	−	3	7	12	18	23	28	33	39	44	50	55	61	66	72	77	83	88	94	100
16	−	3	8	14	19	25	30	36	42	48	54	60	65	71	77	83	89	95	101	107
17	−	3	9	15	20	26	33	39	45	51	57	64	70	77	83	89	96	102	109	115
18	−	4	9	16	22	28	35	41	48	55	61	68	75	82	88	95	102	109	116	123
19	0	4	10	17	23	30	37	44	51	58	65	72	80	87	94	101	109	116	123	130
20	0	4	11	18	25	32	39	47	54	62	69	77	84	92	100	107	115	123	130	138

The top of the table is headed n_1 (columns 1 to 20).

SOURCE: D. Auble, 'Extended tables for the Mann−Whitney statistic' in *Bulletin of the Institute of Educational Research,* Vol. 7, No. 2, Indiana University

Table E Critical values of *t* at various levels of probability (Wilcoxon)

	Level of significance for one-tailed test					Level of significance for one-tailed test			
	0.05	0.25	0.01	0.005		0.05	0.025	0.01	0.005
	Level of significance for two-tailed test					Level of significance for two-tailed test			
N	0.10	0.05	0.02	0.01	*N*	0.10	0.05	0.02	0.01
5	1	—	—	—	28	130	117	102	92
6	2	1	—	—	29	141	127	111	100
7	4	2	0	—	30	152	137	120	109
8	6	4	2	0	31	163	148	130	118
9	8	6	3	2	32	175	159	141	128
10	11	8	5	3	33	188	171	151	138
11	14	11	7	5	34	201	183	162	149
12	17	14	10	7	35	214	195	174	160
13	21	17	13	10	36	228	208	186	171
14	26	21	16	13	37	242	222	198	183
15	30	25	20	16	38	256	235	211	195
16	36	30	24	19	39	271	250	224	208
17	41	35	28	23	40	287	264	238	221
18	47	40	33	28	41	303	279	252	234
19	54	46	38	32	42	319	295	267	248
20	60	52	43	37	43	336	311	281	262
21	68	59	49	43	44	353	327	297	277
22	75	66	56	49	45	371	344	313	292
23	83	73	62	55	46	389	361	329	307
24	92	81	69	61	47	408	379	345	323
25	101	90	77	68	48	427	397	362	339
26	110	98	85	76	49	446	415	380	356
27	120	107	93	84	50	466	434	398	373

SOURCE: F. Wilcoxon, *Some Rapid Approximate Statistical Procedures,* American Cyanamid Co., 1949

The symbol *t* denotes the small sum of ranks associated with differences that are all of the same sign. For any given *N* (number of subjects or pairs of subjects), the observed *t* is significant at a given level if it is *equal* to or *less* than the value shown in the table.

Table F Distribution of chi square

df	0.10	0.05	0.02	0.01	0.001
1	2.706	3.841	5.412	6.635	10.827
2	4.605	5.991	7.824	9.210	13.815
3	6.251	7.815	9.837	11.345	16.266
4	7.779	9.488	11.668	13.277	18.467
5	9.236	11.070	13.388	15.086	20.515
6	10.645	12.592	15.033	16.812	22.457
7	12.017	14.067	16.622	18.475	24.322
8	13.362	15.507	18.168	20.090	26.125
9	14.684	16.919	19.679	21.666	27.877
10	15.987	18.307	21.161	23.209	29.588
11	17.275	19.675	22.618	24.725	31.264
12	18.549	21.026	24.054	26.217	32.909
13	19.812	22.362	25.472	27.688	34.528
14	21.064	23.685	26.873	29.141	36.123
15	22.307	34.996	28.259	30.578	37.697
16	23.542	26.296	29.633	32.000	39.252
17	24.769	27.587	30.995	33.409	40.790
18	25.989	28.869	32.346	34.805	42.312
19	27.204	30.144	33.687	36.191	43.820
20	28.412	31.410	35.020	37.566	45.315
21	29.615	32.671	36.343	38.932	46.797
22	30.813	33.924	37.659	40.289	48.268
23	32.007	35.172	38.968	41.638	49.728
24	33.196	36.415	40.270	42.980	51.179
25	34.382	37.652	41.566	44.314	52.620
26	35.563	38.885	42.856	45.642	54.052
27	36.741	40.113	44.140	46.963	55.476
28	37.916	41.337	45.419	48.278	56.893
29	39.087	42.557	46.693	49.588	58.302
30	40.256	43.773	47.692	50.892	59.703

Abridged from Table IV of Fisher and Yates: *Statistical Tables for Biological, Agricultural and Medical Research,* published by Oliver and Boyd Ltd., Edinburgh, and by permission of the authors and publishers.

Table G (1) Values of F at $p < 0.05$

v_2	v_1											
	1	*2*	*3*	*4*	*5*	*6*	*7*	*8*	*10*	*12*	*24*	*∞*
1	161.4	199.5	215.7	224.6	230.2	234.0	236.8	238.9	241.9	243.9	249.0	254.3
2	18.5	19.0	19.2	19.2	19.3	19.3	19.4	19.4	19.4	19.4	19.5	19.5
3	10.13	9.55	9.28	9.12	9.01	8.94	8.89	8.85	8.79	8.74	8.64	8.53
4	7.71	6.94	6.59	6.39	6.26	6.16	6.09	6.04	5.96	5.91	5.77	5.63
5	6.61	5.79	5.41	5.19	5.05	4.95	4.88	4.82	4.74	4.68	4.53	4.36
6	5.99	5.14	4.76	4.53	4.39	4.28	4.21	4.15	4.06	4.00	3.84	3.67
7	5.59	4.74	4.35	4.12	3.97	3.87	3.79	3.73	3.64	3.57	3.41	3.23
8	5.32	4.46	4.07	3.84	3.69	3.58	3.50	3.44	3.35	3.28	3.12	2.93
9	5.12	4.26	3.86	3.63	3.48	3.37	3.29	3.23	3.14	3.07	2.90	2.71
10	4.96	4.10	3.71	3.48	3.33	3.22	3.14	3.07	2.98	2.91	2.74	2.54
11	4.84	3.98	3.59	3.36	3.20	3.09	3.01	2.95	2.85	2.79	2.61	2.40
12	4.75	3.89	3.49	3.26	3.11	3.00	2.91	2.85	2.75	2.69	2.51	2.30
13	4.67	3.81	3.41	3.18	3.03	2.92	2.83	2.77	2.67	2.60	2.42	2.21
14	4.60	3.74	3.34	3.11	2.96	2.85	2.76	2.70	2.60	2.53	2.35	2.13
15	4.54	3.68	3.29	3.06	2.90	2.70	2.71	2.64	2.54	2.48	2.29	2.07
16	4.49	3.63	3.24	3.01	2.85	2.74	2.66	2.59	2.49	2.42	2.24	2.01
17	4.45	3.59	3.20	2.96	2.81	2.70	2.61	2.55	2.45	2.38	2.19	1.96
18	4.41	3.55	3.16	2.93	2.77	2.66	2.58	2.51	2.41	2.34	2.15	1.92
19	4.38	3.52	3.13	2.90	2.74	2.63	2.54	2.48	2.38	2.31	2.11	1.88
20	4.35	3.49	3.10	2.87	2.71	2.60	2.51	2.45	2.35	2.28	2.08	1.84
21	4.32	3.47	3.07	2.84	2.68	2.57	2.49	2.42	2.32	2.25	2.05	1.81
22	4.30	3.44	3.05	2.82	2.66	2.55	2.46	2.40	2.30	2.23	2.03	1.78
23	4.28	3.42	3.03	2.80	2.64	2.53	2.44	2.37	2.27	2.20	2.00	1.76
24	4.26	3.40	3.01	2.78	2.62	2.51	2.42	2.36	2.25	2.18	1.98	1.73
25	4.24	3.39	2.99	2.76	2.60	2.49	2.40	2.34	2.24	2.16	1.96	1.71
26	4.23	3.37	2.98	2.74	2.59	2.47	2.39	2.32	2.22	2.15	1.95	1.69
27	4.21	3.35	2.96	2.73	2.57	2.46	2.37	2.31	2.20	2.13	1.93	1.67
28	4.20	3.34	2.95	2.71	2.56	2.45	2.36	2.29	2.19	2.12	1.91	1.65
29	4.18	3.33	2.93	2.70	2.55	2.43	2.35	2.28	2.18	2.10	1.90	1.64
30	4.17	3.32	2.92	2.69	2.53	2.42	2.33	2.27	2.16	2.09	1.89	1.62
32	4.15	3.29	2.90	2.67	2.51	2.40	2.31	2.24	2.14	2.07	1.86	1.59
34	4.13	3.28	2.88	2.65	2.49	2.38	2.29	2.23	2.12	2.05	1.84	1.57
36	4.11	3.26	2.87	2.63	2.48	2.36	2.28	2.21	2.11	2.03	1.82	1.55
38	4.10	3.24	2.85	2.62	2.46	2.35	2.26	2.19	2.09	2.02	1.81	1.53
40	4.08	3.23	2.84	2.61	2.45	2.34	2.25	2.18	2.08	2.00	1.79	1.51
60	4.00	3.15	2.76	2.53	2.37	2.25	2.17	2.10	1.99	1.92	1.70	1.39
120	3.92	3.07	2.68	2.45	2.29	2.18	2.09	2.02	1.91	1.83	1.61	1.25
∞	3.84	3.00	2.60	2.37	2.21	2.10	2.01	1.94	1.83	1.75	1.52	1.00

NB When there is no exact number for the *df*, use the next lowest number. For very large *df*s (well over 120) you can use the row of infinity (∞).

Table G (2) Values of F at $p < 0.01$

v_2	v_1											
	1	*2*	*3*	*4*	*5*	*6*	*7*	*8*	*10*	*12*	*24*	*∞*
1	4052	5000	5403	5625	5764	5859	5928	5981	6056	6106	6235	6366
2	98.5	99.0	99.2	99.2	99.3	99.3	99.4	99.4	99.4	99.4	99.5	99.5
3	34.1	30.8	29.5	28.7	28.2	27.9	27.7	27.5	27.2	27.1	26.6	26.1
4	21.2	18.0	16.7	16.0	15.5	15.2	15.0	14.8	14.5	14.4	13.9	15.5
5	16.26	13.27	12.06	11.39	10.97	10.67	10.46	10.29	10.05	9.89	9.47	9.02
6	13.74	10.92	9.78	9.15	8.75	8.47	8.26	8.10	7.87	7.72	7.31	6.88
7	12.25	9.55	8.45	7.85	7.46	7.19	6.99	6.84	6.62	6.47	6.07	5.65
8	11.26	8.65	7.59	7.01	6.63	6.37	6.18	6.03	5.81	5.67	5.28	4.86
9	10.56	8.02	6.99	6.42	6.06	5.80	5.61	5.47	5.26	5.11	4.73	4.31
10	10.04	7.56	6.55	5.99	5.64	5.39	5.20	5.06	4.85	4.71	4.33	3.91
11	9.65	7.21	6.22	5.67	5.32	5.07	4.89	4.74	4.54	4.40	4.02	3.60
12	9.33	6.93	5.95	5.41	5.06	4.82	4.64	4.50	4.30	4.16	3.78	3.36
13	9.07	6.70	5.74	5.21	4.86	4.62	4.44	4.30	4.10	3.96	3.59	3.17
14	8.86	6.51	5.56	5.04	4.70	4.46	4.28	4.14	3.94	3.80	3.43	3.00
15	8.68	6.36	5.42	4.89	4.56	4.32	4.14	4.00	3.80	3.67	3.29	2.87
16	8.53	6.23	5.29	4.77	4.44	4.20	4.03	3.89	3.69	3.55	3.18	2.75
17	8.40	6.11	5.18	4.67	4.34	4.10	3.93	3.79	3.59	3.46	3.08	2.65
18	8.29	6.01	5.09	4.58	4.25	4.01	3.84	3.71	3.51	3.37	3.00	2.57
19	8.18	5.93	5.01	4.50	4.17	3.94	3.77	3.63	3.43	3.30	2.92	2.49
20	8.10	5.85	4.94	4.43	4.10	3.87	3.70	3.56	3.37	3.23	2.86	2.42
21	8.02	5.78	4.87	4.37	4.04	3.81	3.64	3.51	3.31	3.17	2.80	2.36
22	7.95	5.72	4.82	4.31	3.99	3.76	3.59	3.45	3.26	3.12	2.75	2.31
23	7.88	5.66	4.76	4.26	3.94	3.71	3.54	3.41	3.21	3.07	2.70	2.26
24	7.82	5.61	4.72	4.22	3.90	3.67	3.50	3.36	3.17	3.03	2.66	2.21
25	7.77	5.57	4.68	4.18	3.86	3.63	3.46	3.32	3.13	2.99	2.62	2.17
26	7.72	5.53	4.64	4.14	3.82	3.59	3.42	3.29	3.09	2.96	2.58	2.13
27	7.68	5.49	4.60	4.11	3.78	3.56	3.39	3.26	3.06	2.93	2.55	2.10
28	7.64	5.45	4.57	4.07	3.75	3.53	3.36	3.23	3.03	2.90	2.52	2.06
29	7.60	5.42	4.54	4.04	3.73	3.50	3.33	3.20	3.00	2.87	2.49	2.03
30	7.56	5.39	4.51	4.02	3.70	3.47	3.30	3.17	2.98	2.84	2.47	2.01
32	7.50	5.34	4.46	3.97	3.65	3.43	3.26	3.13	2.93	2.80	2.42	1.96
34	7.45	5.29	4.42	3.93	3.61	3.39	3.22	3.09	2.90	2.76	2.38	1.91
36	7.40	5.25	4.38	3.89	3.58	3.35	3.18	3.05	2.86	2.72	2.35	1.87
38	7.35	5.21	4.34	3.86	3.54	3.32	3.15	3.02	2.83	2.69	3.32	1.84
40	7.31	5.18	4.31	3.83	3.51	3.29	3.12	2.99	2.80	2.66	2.29	1.80
60	7.08	4.98	4.13	3.65	3.34	3.12	2.95	2.82	2.63	2.50	2.12	1.60
120	6.85	4.79	3.95	3.48	3.17	2.96	2.79	2.66	2.47	2.34	1.95	1.38
∞	6.63	4.61	3.78	3.32	3.02	2.80	2.64	2.51	2.32	2.18	1.79	1.00

SOURCE: Lindley, D. and Miller, J. C. *Cambridge Elementary Statistical Tables* 10th edn. Cambridge University Press. 1973.

Table H Critical values of rho (rank order correlation coefficient)

N (number of subjects)	Level of significance for one-tailed test			
	0.05	0.025	0.01	0.005
	Level of significance for two-tailed test			
	0.10	0.05	0.02	0.01
5	0.900	1.000	1.000	—
6	0.829	0.886	0.943	1.000
7	0.714	0.786	0.893	0.929
8	0.643	0.738	0.833	0.881
9	0.600	0.683	0.783	0.883
10	0.564	0.648	0.746	0.794
12	0.506	0.591	0.712	0.777
14	0.456	0.544	0.645	0.715
16	0.425	0.506	0.601	0.665
18	0.399	0.475	0.564	0.625
20	0.377	0.450	0.534	0.591
22	0.359	0.428	0.508	0.562
24	0.343	0.409	0.485	0.537
26	0.329	0.392	0.465	0.515
28	0.317	0.377	0.448	0.496
30	0.306	0.364	0.432	0.478

SOURCE:E. G. Olds, 'The 5% significance levels for sums of squares of rank differences and a correction' in *Annals of Mathematical Statistics,* Vol. 20, The Institute of Mathematical Statistics 1949.

Table I Critical values of the Pearson correlation coefficient

	Level of significance			
df	*0.10*	*0.05*	*0.02*	*0.01*
1	.9877	.9969	.9995	.9999
2	.9000	.9500	.9800	.9900
3	.8054	.8783	.9343	.9587
4	.7293	.8114	.8822	.9172
5	.6694	.7545	.8329	.8745
6	.6215	.7067	.7887	.8343
7	.5822	.6664	.7498	.7977
8	.5494	.6319	.7155	.7646
9	.5214	.6021	.6851	.7348
10	.4973	.5760	.6581	.7079
11	.4762	.5529	.6339	.6835
12	.4575	.5324	.6120	.6614
13	.4409	.5139	.5923	.6411
14	.4259	.4973	.5742	.6226
15	.4124	.4821	.5577	.6055
16	.4000	.4683	.5425	.5897
17	.3887	.4555	.5285	.5751
18	.3783	.4438	.5155	.5614
19	.3687	.4329	.5034	.5487
20	.3598	.4227	.4921	.5368
25	.3233	.3809	.4451	.4869
30	.2960	.3494	.4093	.4487
35	.2746	.3246	.3810	.4182
40	.2573	.3044	.3578	.3932
45	.2428	.2875	.3384	.3721
50	.2306	.2732	.3218	.3541
60	.2108	.2500	.2948	.3248
70	.1954	.2319	.2737	.3017
80	.1829	.2172	.2565	.2830
90	.1726	.2050	.2422	.2673
100	.1638	.1946	.2301	.2540

Abridged from Table VI of Fisher and Yates: *Statistical Tables for Biological, Agricultural and Medical Research,* published by Oliver and Boyd Ltd., Edinburgh, and by permission of the authors and publishers.

Appendix B

Glossary of terms

This glossary may help you in different ways. It can be used as an easy means of reference while studying the various sections in the book. It can also be used as a means of revision, though it is in no way intended as a substitute for reading the book. Not every term and concept has been included in this list; other authors may have chosen differently.

Abscissa   The X or horizontal axis in a graph.

Analysis of variance   A technique which has many uses. The most important is to test whether there are significant differences between the means of several different groups of observations. The test is particularly useful where there are several means to test at the same time. Testing each separately by means of a t test would increase the probability of falsely rejecting the null hypothesis.

Arithmetic mean   The sum of values of a variable for all the observations in a data set divided by the total number of observations, i.e. $(\Sigma X)/N$.

As a measure of central tendency the arithmetic mean takes into account all the observations in the set and therefore can be influenced by atypical extreme values. It is appropriate only when measurement is at least on an interval or ratio scale.

Association   A very general term applied when there appears to be some kind of connection between the values of one variable and the values of another. This connection may take many forms: high values of one variable might be likely to go with high values on the other; high values might tend to be seen with low values; or certain categories on one variable may be associated with certain categories on another. Associations are strong when knowing the values of one variable allows good prediction of the values of the other, and weak when such a prediction is little better than a guess. Association does not necessarily imply causation. (See *correlation*.)

Assumption   A basic tenet of a theory that is taken for granted from which other tenets are derived; condition that must be met before certain conclusions are warranted (e.g. the assumptions of a statistical test).

Attitude   A relatively enduring tendency to perceive, feel or behave towards certain people or events in a particular manner.

Between-group variance A measure of the fluctuations between groups based on group means.

Bias This term can take a number of meanings. When a sample fails to reflect accurately the characteristics of the population from which it is drawn owing to systematic rather than random effects it is said to be biased (statistically). Bias is also used to refer, in a more general way, to the conscious or unconscious effects of the researcher.

Chi-square test (χ^2) A test of whether a particular pattern of frequencies in a table is likely to have occurred by chance. It is a two-tailed test appropriate for nominal data, provided that there are sufficient observations in the cells of the table and that all the observations are independent of each other. It is given by the formula:

$$\chi^2 = \Sigma \frac{(\text{observed value} - \text{expected value})^2}{\text{expected value}}$$

where the summation is over all cells of a table, observed value refers to the actual cell frequency and expected value to the cell frequency which would be expected by chance.

Communality In factor analysis, the communality of a test is that part of its variance which may be considered to be shared in common with other tests. Its specificity is that part of of its variance which is not error variance and which is specific to the test itself.

Confounding variable A variable not manipulated as an independent variable that systematically varies with an independent variable so that the effect of the confounding variable and the effect of the independent variable cannot be separated.

Continuous variable A continuous variable is one which may assume any value between two extremes. They are to be distinguished from discrete variables which can take only whole numbers or distinct values or scores.

Control The attempt to eliminate the effects of extraneous variables so that one may be sure that any results found are due only to the independent variables being tested. Methods of 'physical control' include using the same subjects under all experimental conditions, using matched pairs, keeping an extraneous variable constant and randomly allocating subjects to the different groups. A *control group* is a group of people as similar as possible to an experimental group and treated in exactly the same way, except that they are not given the experimental treatment. The control group thus furnishes a base line against which the effects of this treatment may be measured.

Correlation The extent to which two variables vary together. This is measured by a statistic called the correlation coefficient, of which there are various types. Correlation coefficients vary between $+1.0$ and -1.0. A positive correlation indicates that high scores on one variable tend to be associated with high scores on the other and low scores with low scores. Zero correlation means no relationship, while a negative correlation means that high scores on one variable tend to be associated with low scores on the other and vice versa. A correlation of $+1.0$ is known as perfect positive correlation, and one of -1.0 is called perfect negative correlation. In both these cases, given the value of one variable, the value of the other can be predicted with absolute certainty. For values between $+1$ and -1 this is not the case, and the closer the value is to zero, the less precise are predictions made from one variable to the other. Correlation does not necessarily prove causation.

Counterbalance the order A method of controlling for the effects of the order of presentation of two or more experimental treatments given to the same subjects. The subjects are randomly split into groups of equal size, each group receiving one of the possible orderings. In this way unwanted effects such as improvement with practice or deterioration due to fatigue or boredom are controlled.

Criterion A standard against which performance may be assessed. Often used as synonymous with dependent variable. Another use of the term criterion occurs in the validation of a new method of measurement. Here a criterion is a variable against which the new method is being assessed.

Cumulative frequency distribution A distribution obtained by starting at one end of a range of scores and for each class interval in turn adding the frequency in that class interval to all the frequencies which preceded it. This enables one to see how many observations fall above or below any particular value of the variable.

Degrees of freedom (*df*) Mathematically, the equation expressing the distribution of a statistic contains a parameter called the number of degrees of freedom. This number is always the number of cases in the sample less a few depending on the statistic and the circumstances of its use. Statistical tables are therefore constructed showing initial values of various statistics for the various degrees of freedom from 1 up to about 120. For samples larger than this the degrees of freedom make little further difference.

Demand characteristics Those cues available to a subject in an experiment that may enable him to determine the 'purpose' of the experiment; the cues that allow the subject to infer what the experimenter 'expects' of him, one type of confounding variable.

Dependent variable Causal statements are statements about the relationship between variables. The variable to be explained or predicted is known as the dependent variable. The variables doing the explaining are known as independent variables. In experimental research the independent variables are the ones systematically varied by the experimenter and the dependent variable is the one not under the experimenter's control but which is to be affected by the other variables being manipulated.

Descriptive statistics Statistical methods for summarizing large quantities of data so that patterns and relationships within the data may be seen. These methods include the presentation of data in tables and diagrams and the calculation of summary measures of location, dispersion, correlation and association.

Deviation   The difference between a measurement and an average for the set of measurements.

Directional null hypothesis   A null hypothesis states that two groups do not differ in a specified direction. A non-directional hypothesis is one in which no indication of the direction of the difference is given.

Dispersion   The extent to which a set of observations is spread out over a range of values or the extent to which they vary around the mean or median. There are several measures of dispersion including the quartile deviation, variance, and standard deviation.

Double-blind   An experimental procedure used to guard against experimenter bias. It is arranged that neither the subjects nor the person gathering the data are aware which of two treatments is being given to which subjects.

Error variance   The variance of the error scores on a test or other measure or, equivalently, that part of the observed variance which cannot be accounted for in any other way. The (total) error variance is given by the square of the standard error, or in the case of a stratified sample the sum of the squares of the standard errors of the individual strata.

Experiment   A study in which all the relevant variables are controlled and manipulated by the experimenter rather than simply observed in their natural setting. The experimental design is intended to ensure that an experiment affords a valid, efficient and unambiguous test of the hypotheses set up and that extraneous variables are controlled.

Factor analysis   This is a statistical technique aimed at describing a number of variables (or test items) in terms of a smaller number of more basic factors. An example is when the items of the Eysenck's Personality Inventory Test are found to be describable by the extraversion, neuroticism and lie-scale factors. A general factor is one which underlies to a varying degree all items in a test. A group factor underlies only a specific group of items. A factor loading of an item on a factor is the correlation between the factor and the item.

Frequency distribution   A set of scores arranged in ascending or descending order. The number of times each score occurs is indicated.

F statistic   A statistic used to determine whether two variances are significantly different. To apply it, the estimate of variance explained is divided by the residual variance to obtain the F value. The F table is then entered with degrees of freedom appropriate to the numerator and denominator and if the F value is sufficiently larger than the value in the table, the variances differ significantly. The main application of the F statistic is in analysis of variance. In this context the variance estimates are termed mean squares.

General population   The general population is the total population to which the researcher sees his results as relevant.

Generalizability   The extent to which research findings are true for subjects or settings other than the ones which the researcher used.

Goodness of fit   The extent to which a model or theory really fits the data it is intended to explain. If there are many exceptions or wildly incorrect predictions then the goodness of fit is poor. The term frequently crops up also when it is desired to know whether a set of data are, for example, normally distributed. Tests, such as the χ^2 test, exist which may be used to determine the goodness of fit of the normal curve to the data.

High positive correlation   A high positive correlation represents a strong, but not perfect, tendency for high scores on one variable to be associated with high scores on another variable. A correlation coefficient greater than about $+0.7$ would indicate a high positive correlation. (See also *correlation*.)

Hypothesis   An untested assertion about the relationship between two or more concepts. They may vary considerably in precision and in breadth. For example, they may be simply vague assertions, or very precise, explicitly formulated hypotheses which are capable of precise testing. Some hypotheses are derived deductively from existing theory whereas others are 'grounded in empirical observation'. Hypothesis testing is the process of testing a hypothesis in a scientific manner. The hypothesis will have been stated in terms precise enough to make a test possible, and data relevant to it will have been gathered. In social science this is usually stated as a null hypothesis, i.e. that no difference will be found with respect to a variable between two or more specified groups or that there is no correlation between the relevant variables. A statistical test is then performed to try to refute this null hypothesis. If we are able to reject the null hypothesis then we have evidence of an alternative hypothesis that a difference or correlation exists. This is the hypothesis in which we are primarily interested.

Hypothetico-deductive model   A paradigm asserting what the logic of explanation ought to be throughout the sciences. An hypothesis has empirical predictions deduced from it. These can be tested and, if confirmed, corroborate the hypotheses. Deduction must be by the strict rules of logic. The hypothetico-deductive model owes much to what is known as the natural science paradigm and many people consider that its underlying assumptions are inappropriate in attempting to understand and explain the social world. They therefore question, and in some cases reject, its use in the social sciences.

Independent variable   An independent variable is one which is thought to produce or cause changes in another variable. This latter variable is known as the dependent variable. In experimental research the independent variable is the one systematically varied or manipulated by the experimenter. The effect of this on the dependent variable is studied.

Inter-quartile range   A measure of dispersion of a frequency distribution. When a distribution is split into four equal parts the quartiles are those values of the variable below which 25%, 50% and 75% of the distribution lie. The distance between the '75%' or upper quartile (Q3) and the '25%' or lower quartile (Q1) is known as the inter-quartile range. The quartile deviation (QD) is defined as half the inter-quartile range.

Interval scale   A measurement scale in which the intervals between the scale points are equal but which has no true zero point. In an interval scale a score of say 15 is as far above 10 as 20 is above 15, but 20 need not represent twice as much of the quantity being measured as 10 does.

Kurtosis   The degree of peakedness of a distribution.

Leptokurtic   A distribution or curve that is steep.

Level of confidence   The degree of reliance that may be placed on a particular interval estimate for a population parameter. Measured as the number of times out of 100 that the interval can be expected to include the 'true' parameter value, if the research were repeated a large number of times.

Linear relationship   A relationship between two variables in which an increase in one variable is always accompanied by a constant increase or is always accompanied by a constant decrease in the other.

Likert scaling method   An attitude scaling method in which respondents indicate the extent of their agreement with each item on a scale (e.g. a five- or seven-point scale). Their score is the sum of the scores for each item.

Matched pairs design   An experimental design which seeks to remove the effects of extraneous variables by having each subject in the control group on one or more of the extraneous variables.

Mean deviation   A measure of dispersion. The sum of the absolute differences between a set of observations and their mean, divided by the number of observations. This statistic is not often used.

Measures of dispersion or variation   Dispersion is the extent to which a set of observations is spread out over a range of values. Measures of it include the quartile deviation, the variance, the standard deviation and the mean deviation.

Measures of central tendency   These are what the layman often calls an 'average'. Single-figure summary measures to show where, in the main, a whole distribution of values is located on some given dimension. Measures of central tendency include the arithmetic mean, the median, and the mode, each of which makes different assumptions about the data, is calculated in different ways, and for different reasons.

Median   If the observations in a frequency distribution are placed in rank order, the median is that value of the variable corresponding to the central observation. Thus it is the value above and below which 50% of the observations in a distribution lie.

Mode   The most frequently occurring value of a set of observations. The mode is the simplest type of average and is the only one that can be used on nominal data. The *modal category* is the category containing the greatest number of observations. When a distribution has several distinct values around which observations tend to cluster we say that it is a *multi-modal distribution,* when it has two distinct values around which the observations cluster we say that it is a *bi-modal distribution.*

Nominal scale   A system of categorization and the simplest form of measurement.

Non-parametric   Non-parametric statistical tests do not involve the estimation of a population parameter (e.g. the mean or standard deviation) and generally require no assumptions about how the scores in question are distributed. They may often be used when parametric tests are inappropriate but lack some of the power of parametric tests.

Normal distribution   A bell-shaped frequency distribution curve which is often obtained when human characteristics are measured and plotted. The normal distribution has some very useful features which are important in probability theory and which allow us to estimate how close our results from our sample are to the true figures for the population.

Null hypothesis   Before an hypothesis is tested statistically it is always stated in the form of a null hypothesis, that is, that no difference will be found between the groups being tested or that no relationships between the variables will be found. If we are able to reject the null hypothesis then we have evidence of an alternative hypothesis that a difference or correlation exists. This is the hypothesis in which we are primarily interested. (See *hypothesis.*)

One-tailed test   A procedure for testing the null hypothesis in which the entire rejection area is placed at one end of the appropriate sampling distribution.

Operational definition   A definition of a concept in terms of the operations that must be performed in order to demonstrate the concept.

Order effect   The effect of doing one treatment after another in an experiment. A practice effect is an improvement in performance with practice. A fatigue effect is a reduction in performance due to tiredness or boredom. Both these order effects must be ruled out, by counterbalancing, from experiments in which the same subjects are tested several times under different conditions.

Ordinal scale   A scale in which scale values are related by a single, underlying quantitative dimension but it is not possible to assume that the differences between successive scale values are of equal magnitude.

Parameter   A descriptive summary of some characteristic of a population, e.g. mean, median, standard deviation. The term statistic or sample statistic is used for the same type of entity when describing the value for it obtained from a sample.

Parametric A parametric statistical test involves the estimation of a population parameter (e.g. the mean or standard deviation) and involves certain assumptions about the data. These are that the data are measured on at least an interval scale and that the populations from which the samples have been drawn are normally distributed and have equal variances. In practice it has been shown that very considerable violations of these assumptions do not invalidate the conclusions drawn about the hypothesis being tested. The main parametric tests are the z test, the t test and the F test.

Pearson's product moment correlation coefficient (r) A measure of the strength of relationship between variables, each of which must be measured on an interval or ratio scale. It is theoretically given by:

$$r = \frac{\text{Cov}}{s_x s_y}$$

where s_x and s_y are the standard deviations of the variables X and Y and Cov is their covariance. Its value can only lie between $+1$ and -1, where $+1$ signifies a perfect positive linear relationship and -1 a perfect negative linear relationship. It will be zero in any situation where there is no linear relationship.

Population Any group of people or observations which includes all possible members in that category. A *population parameter* is a descriptive summary measure of some characteristics of the population. *Statistical inference* is concerned with estimating population parameters from samples.

Power (of a test) The power of a statistical test reflects its efficiency at rejecting a null hypothesis at a particular significance level. The fewer observations needed to obtain a statistically significant result, the more powerful the test.

Probability An estimate of the likelihood that a particular event will occur; the ratio of the number of favourable events to the total number of possible events if only chance is operating.

Questionnaire A set of carefully designed questions given in exactly the same form to a group of people in order to collect data about some topics in which the researcher is interested. Sometimes the term questionnaire is limited to a set of questions for completion by the subjects themselves in which case the term *interview schedule* or *inventory* is applied to a set of questions administered by an interviewer.

Random error In statistical theory random error is error or measurement which may stem from any one of a large number of uncontrolled sources. It is assumed that over a large number of cases random error will balance out, i.e. that there is no tendency for the errors to be predominantly in one direction rather then another. Thus for large samples, measures of central tendency such as the arithmetic mean will be unaffected by random error. It should be contrasted with *systematic error*, which does not cancel out over a large number of cases.

Random sampling   A random sample is one in which all members of the population have a known chance of selection, this chance for any population member being greater than zero and less than one. The process of selection is known as random selection. If this process is faithfully adhered to we meet the statistical requirements for generalizing from the sample to the total population. Random selection will often be done using random numbers which are numbers generated at random but in such a way that all the numbers appear an equal number of times in the overall table.

Randomization   The balancing up of extraneous variables when subjects are allocated to different groups at random, so that it is purely a matter of chance which person ends up in which group. Randomized variables are to be distinguished from other extraneous variables called confounding variables which are related systematically to the explanatory or independent variable.

Range   A descriptive measure of variability; the difference score obtained by subtracting the smallest score in the distribution from the largest score in the distribution.

Ranking   A technique sometimes used for getting at attitudes, feelings, meanings, etc. It involves setting a number of observations, people, statements etc. in order along some given dimension. Rankings differ from rating scales chiefly in that they make no assumptions about the intervals between the ranks – the measurement is ordinal.

Rank order   To place a variable in rank order is to put the cases in order from highest to lowest (or vice versa). If it is possible to do this then at least ordinal measurement has been achieved and certain statistical methods which require rank ordering can be used. Rank ordering does not necessarily imply that the first value is as far above second as the second is above third etc.

Ratio scale   This is an interval scale which has a true fixed zero point. On this scale not only would 20 be as far above 15 as 15 is above 10, but 20 would represent twice as much of the quantity being measured as 10. This means we can use all the usual arithmetic operations on such data.

Reliability   The extent to which a test would give consistent results if applied more than once to the same people under standard conditions. *Reliability coefficients* are correlation coefficients assessing reliability. There are various ways of obtaining these. In the *split-half method* the scores on a randomly chosen half of the test questions are correlated with the scores on the other half. This is an *internal consistency measure*. In the *test–retest method* a correlation is obtained between scores on the test administered to the same people on separate occasions. The *alternate forms method* is similar except that a second form of the test, as nearly equivalent to the first as possible, is administered on the second occasion.

Replication To replicate a research design is to repeat it exactly in order to check the results. 'Partial replication' is when the second research design is much the same as the first but not exactly so. As there is much more reliance on natural settings replication is more difficult in ethnographic research.

Representative sample A sample, drawn from a population, which accurately reflects all the important characteristics of that population. In simple terms, if a population is known to contain 50% females then the sample must also have 50% females, and so on for any characteristic of the population which is relevant to the study. This allows one to generalize justifiably one's results to the population as a whole.

Rotated solution The factors first obtained in a factor analysis often make better logical sense after rotating the reference axes.

Sampling A sample is a group selected from a larger population so that we can make statements about this population as a whole. A *sample survey* is one which is conducted on a sample of some such population. Because this is a cheap way of collecting information, sample surveys are often used in the social sciences. A *sampling procedure* is any one of a number of methods for drawing a sample. In certain types of sample, and particularly random sampling, one normally needs a *sampling frame* which is a record or set of records which sets out and identifies the population from which a sample is to be drawn, e.g. the electoral roll. *Sampling theory* is the set of assumptions and mathematical deductions which underlie random sampling procedures and which allow us to estimate from sample statistics to population values or parameters. These estimates are known as *sample estimates*. No sample, however carefully drawn, can be perfectly representative of the population from which it is selected. Any estimate of the population value made on the basis of the sample is therefore liable to be more or less wrong depending on the representativeness of the sample. Such error is known as *sampling error.*

Semantic differential technique A very flexible method of attitude measurement. Subjects rate the concepts in which the experimenter is interested on several bipolar scales (usually seven point), the ends of which are defined by pairs of adjectives opposite in meaning (e.g. 'good−bad', 'hard−soft', 'fast−slow'). Any concepts and any adjectival scales may be used.

Spearman's rank correlation coefficient An estimate of the Pearson product moment correlation coefficient appropriate to the situation where both variables being correlated are in the form of ranks. It is given by the formula:

$$rho = \frac{1 - 6\Sigma D_1^2}{N(N^2 - 1)}$$

where D_1 is the difference in rank between members of a given pair and N = number of pairs. The coefficient measures the strength of relationship and takes the value of zero when there is no relationship between the variables, + 1 if the rankings are in perfect positive cor- respondence, and −1 if there is a perfect negative correspondence; in reality the value will lie somewhere between + 1 and −1.

Standard deviation The standard deviation is a measure of dispersion of a frequency distribution. It is the square root of the variance and is given by:

$$\sigma = \frac{\sqrt{\Sigma(X - M)^2}}{N}$$

If there is no variation between values in a distribution the standard deviation will be zero and it will increase as the variation increases.

Standard error If an infinite number of samples all the same size are drawn from a population, the means, standard deviations, variances etc., of these samples will vary. The standard error of such a sample estimate is simply the standard deviation of the whole set of estimates, e.g. the *standard error of the mean* is the standard deviation of an infinite set of means of samples all of the same size drawn randomly from the same population. The standard error of the mean may be estimated from the standard deviation of a single sample of size N by the formula:

$$SE_M = \frac{\sigma}{\sqrt{N}}$$

Standardization The term 'standardize' can be applied to conditions of testing, to subjects and to observations. Standardization of condi- tions of testing covers the whole process of exactly specifying the questions to be asked, the manner of asking them, how the replies are to be scored etc. A *standardized test* is constructed to measure some definite variable and additionally has norms of performance available so that any individual who takes the test can be assessed relative to other people in the population. Standardization of sub- jects refers to the exclusion of extraneous variables by restricting the sample to only certain types of people. Standardization of observa- tions means making two sets of observations directly comparable. The problem arises when samples of different sizes are to be com- pared, possibly on different variables, for example when one wishes to know whether one person's mark of 75 in History represents as great an achievement as another person's mark of 80 in Latin. Com- mon methods of standardization include transforming both sets of data into z scores.

Standard score Standard, or z scores enable individual scores to be com- pared by placing these raw scores into the context and characteristics of the distribution from which they came. Thus standard scores take into account both the mean and standard deviation of the respective distributions.

Statistical significance The result of an experiment or a correlation between variables found in survey data is said to be statistically significant if it can be shown that it is highly unlikely to have occurred just by 'pure chance'. Usually, if the odds against 'pure chance' are more than 20 : 1 (i.e. a probability of less than 0.05), the result is accepted as statistically significant, but there is no hard and fast rule about this cut-off point. In general the larger the samples tested the smaller the difference between them which can be detected and shown to be statistically significant.

Stratification (of a sample) The division of a population into layers or strata so as to be able to draw a random sample from each layer and thereby increase the precision of the sample without having to increase its size. The variables out of which the strata are formed must be relevant to the question at issue, if precision is to be improved. This term is not to be confused with social stratification (class structure).

Student's t-test This test is used for determining whether the means of two small samples differ so much that the samples are unlikely to be drawn from the same population. It is given by the ratio of the difference between the means to the standard error of this difference. It assumes interval measurement, approximately normal distribution of the underlying variable and approximately equal variances in the two populations being compared. However, in practice the *t*-test is extremely robust and will not usually lead to false conclusions, despite some violation of these assumptions.

Symmetrical distribution In a symmetrical distribution, mean, median, and mode all have the same value. If a symmetrical distribution is divided at its mean value, the shape of each half will be the mirror image of the other. The normal distribution is an example.

Systematic error If a measurement is made on a sample of people and the errors in this measurement all tend to be in the same direction then systematic error is present. A systematic error will bias the results of the survey in a way in which random error will not.

Thurstone scaling An attitude scale consisting of items to which the respondents have to agree or disagree. Only those items with which they agree are scored. Score values for the items are determined by asking a large number of judges to rate them on a scale (usually an eleven-point scale). The median value of these opinions serves as the score for the item. A respondent's score for the whole scale is taken as the median score of the items to which he agrees.

Two-tailed test a procedure for testing the null hypothesis in which the rejection area is placed at both ends of the appropriate sampling distribution.

Type 1 error an error that occurs if the null hypothesis is rejected when it is true.

Type 2 error an error that occurs if the null hypothesis is not rejected when it is false.

Validity Validity refers to the extent to which a test, questionnaire or other operationalization is really measuring what the researcher intends to measure. A test or questionnaire is said to have *concurrent validity* if it correlates well with with other measures of the same concept; it has *content validity* when it samples adequately the domain which it is supposed to measure and *predictive validity* if it may be used to make accurate predictions of further performance. Concurrent validity and predictive validity may be classified as *criterion-related validity* as they both evaluate the test or questionnaire against some criterion assumed to be valid. *Construct validity* refers to the extent to which the test appears to conform to predictions about it from theory. Validity is also used in a more general sense to refer to the validity of a piece of research as a whole (as opposed to the validity of particular measurements). In this respect it is concerned with the extent to which one can rely upon and trust the published findings of some research and involves an evaluation of all the methodological objections that can be raised against the research.

Variability   The extent to which a set of scores spreads out around the mean value. If all the scores bunch closely around the average, the set has a low variability; if they spread out widely it has a high variability. *Variance* is a statistic which measures the variability of a set of scores. For large samples it is obtained by squaring the deviation of each score from the mean of the set of scores, adding them together and then dividing by the number of cases in the set. The *standard deviation*, another measure of dispersion, is simply the square root of the variance. *Variation* is a term which has a similar meaning to dispersion but it sometimes implies a spread of values due to some definite non-random cause – one may talk of 'variation in X due to Y'.

Variable   A variable is an entity which can take two or more values. Some people use the term to refer to the property denoted by a concept whereas others use it to refer to the observational categories which result from operationalizing the concept.

Wilcoxon test   a statistical test appropriate for analysing ordinal data obtained with within-subject designs.

Within-subject design   An experimental design in which the same subjects take part in all the different treatments. This design is very effective in controlling extraneous variables, but order effects (fatigue and practice) must be counterbalanced out by having different groups of subjects undergo the treatment in every possible order.

z score   A score obtained by expressing a raw score as a deviation from the mean score and dividing by the standard deviation of the scores:

$$z = \frac{X - M}{\sigma}$$

This transformation allows a comparison of scores measured in different scale units; z scores have a mean of 0 and a standard deviation of 1 and being pure ratios have no units.

Appendix C

Answers to Self Test Questions (STQs)

Page 27   1. (a) M = 6 σ = 3.16
               (b) M = 6 σ = 2.74
               (c) M = 18 σ = 19.13
               (c) has a greater standard deviation
                   because there is a greater dispersal
                   of scores.
           2. (b) is true. All scores are indentical.
           3. The standard deviation is 3.25
                   (a) The standard deviation is still 3.25
                   (b) $\sigma = 6.50$ The standard deviation has doubled.
           4. The mean is a poor choice as a measure of central
               tendency when there are extremely large or small
               values in a distribution. An extreme score can exert a
               disproportionate effect on the mean.
           5. If a distribution is substantially skewed, the median is
               usually preferred to the mean.

Page 32   1. The student's score was equal to the mean.
           2. John did better on maths.
               Peter did better on spelling.
               Mike did equally well on both.
               Chris did better on maths
               Betty did equally well on both.
           3. Raw Score = 91
           4. (a) 130 (b) 85 (c) 122.5 (d) 88 (e) 100
           5. (a) 2 (b) -1 (c) 0.5 (d) -2.5
           6. There is a very large deviation from the mean.
           7. The mean of a z score distribution is 0, and the stan-
               dard deviation is always 1. A z score from one distribu-
               tion may therefore be legitimately compared with a z
               score from a different distribution, because essentially
               they are standard scores and therefore a z score of a

431

particular value will always give the same relative position whatever the mean and standard deviation of the raw scores.

Page 41   (i) 49.53%   (ii) 3.59%   (iii) 95%   (iv) 80%
           (v) The distribution is bilaterally symmetrical and bell-shaped.
           (vi) 68.26%   95.44%   99.74%

Page 42   1. (a) 18   39   27
              (b) 120   50   134
           2. (a) 4772   (b) 228   (c) 918
           3. (a) 34.15   (b) 95.4   (c) 72.13
           4. (a) 9974   (b) 3415   (c) 13   (d) 15.87   (e) 15.87
           5. (a) 48.21   (b) 17.36   (c) 40.82   (d) 47.44
              (e) 11.03   (f) 49.48   (g) 35.31
           6. (a) 0.4505   (b) 0.9505   (c) 0.0495
           7. (a) 0.4713   (b) 0.0287   (c) 0.9713
           8. 68 (approx). √
           9. 54 (approx). ⁄
          10. (a) ± 0.675   (b) scores between 54 and 66 (approx).
          11. A normal distribution.

Page 51   (i) 2 in 100   (ii) 7 in 100   (iii) 1 in 4   (iv) 1 in 10; 6 in 1000   (v) 3 in 1000; 27 in 100

Page 54

Level	Probability limits	Frequency of a chance occurrence	Significance levels	Odds against a chance occurrence
NS	$p > 0.05$	more than 5 in 100	$> 5\%$	$< 19 : 1$
Low	$p < 0.05$	less than 5 in 100	$< 5\%$	$> 19 : 1$
High	$p < 0.01$	less than 1 in 100	$< 1\%$	$> 99 : 1$
High	$p < 0.001$	less than 1 in 1000	$< 0.1\%$	$> 999 : 1$

Page 59   (1) They are biased because (a) it only involves those who are present on the day; (b) pupils and students do not represent the general adult population.
           (2) (a) The mean ego strength level in the Gas Works High School Sample.
               (b) The population consists of 12-year-old males in the city.
               (c) The sample consists of 12-year-old males at the Gas Works High School.
               (d) The parameter is the mean ego-strength level of 12-year-old males in the whole city.

Page 76   1. (a) systematic sampling

   (b) opportunity sampling
   (c) stratified sampling
2. Obtain the registers and select students by some random technique – e.g., by using a random number table.
3. A random sample is defined as one in which *every* member of the population has an equal chance of being selected.
4. (b)

Page 84   The boundary scores are 107.41 and 112.59.

Page 86   (i) 2.086   (ii) 2.66   (iii) 2.042   (iv) 8.61   (v) 1.96

Page 106   (i)   A type I error is made when we conclude that the independent variable had an effect on the dependent variable when it did not have, i.e. we reject the null hypothesis when it is true.
   (ii) When we reject the null hypothesis we take some sort of positive action, such as publishing our results, or advocating some kind of behaviour. Thus, a type I error may be considered to be more serious than a type II error.
   (iii) The risk of making a type II error can be minimized by increasing the significance level, but then there would be the danger of making a type I error.

Page 110   (i)   *Table 17*

p	t-value two-tailed	t-value one-tailed
0.05	1.96	1.65
0.01	2.58	2.33
0.001	3.29	—

   (ii) (a) The advantage of a one-tailed test is that it is easier to obtain statistical significance, but you have increased the chance of making a type I error.
   (b) It is harder to obtain significance but there is less chance of making a type I error.
   (iii) One-tailed tests increase the possibility of making type I errors, whereas two-tailed tests increase the possibility of making type II errors because the significance levels for two-tailed tests require a larger critical value of t than for one-tailed tests.

Page 119 (1) (a) The independent variable is the material presented
                    to the subject.
                (b) The dependent variable is the number of items
                    recalled.
                (c) People will not find it significantly easier to
                    remember meaningful material than nonsense
                    syllables.
          (2) (a) The independent variable is practice with multi-
                    plication tables.
                (b) The dependent variable is improvement in child-
                    ren's understanding of mathematical principles.
                (c) Practice with multiplication tables will signifi-
                    cantly improve children's understanding of mathe-
                    matical principles.
          (3) (b) form position,   (v) scores on reading test.
          (4) (a) The independent variable is behavioural therapy/
                    psycho-therapy.
                (b) The dependent variable is the number of cigar-
                    ettes smoked daily after treatment.
                (c) There will be no significant difference between
                    behavioural therapy/psycho-therapy in reducing
                    cigarette smoking.

Page 124   (a) nominal (b) interval (c) ordinal (d) ordinal
               (e) ratio (f) ordinal (g) ratio (h) nominal
               (i) interval (j) nominal.

Scale	Labels	Order	Equal intervals	Absolute zero
Nominal	Yes	No	No	No
Ordinal	Yes	Yes	No	No
Interval	Yes	Yes	Yes	No
Ratio	Yes	Yes	Yes	Yes

Page 157 (i) $t = 9.18$ The null hypothesis can be rejected.
          (ii) $t = 14.70$ No.

Page 170 1. (i) d   (ii) b   (iii) b
          2. There is no systematic bias in the rankings between
             each group.
          3. There is a significant difference between scores at the
             0.5 level, one tail.

Page 196   1. Null hypothesis is rejected as t is greater than tabled t.
2. 9 *df*
3. Reject null hypothesis.
5. t is not significant at 0.05 level.

Page 199   1. The null hypothesis would be retained.
2. The null hypothesis would be retained.

Page 205   1. $T = 27$ $N = 10$ ∴ the null hypothesis can be retained.
2. The Wilcoxon test is used instead of a related t test if (a) the difference between treatments can only be ranked in size, or (b) the data are quite skewed, or (c) if there is clearly a difference in the variance of the two groups.

Page 216   2. This is not an experiment because there is no control group.

Page 229   1. (a) Among the residents, the proportion who agree, disagree or are indifferent to the council's proposals will be equal.
(b) Expected value for each category is 16.
(c) $\chi^2 = 6$
(d) 2
(e) Yes.
(f) That the distribution of responses was not due to chance.
2. No.
3. Yes.

Page 238   1. (b)
2. 31.08 : 7.185
3. 10.1 $p < 0.01$
4. Weak positive (b)
5. Not significant
6. Yes. Significant at $p < 0.01$
7. Yes. Significant at $p < 0.05$
8. Yes. Significant at $p < 0.01$

Page 269   1. (a) true   (b) false   (c) false   (d) false
2. (iv) high negative
3. (a) positive (b) positive (c) positive (d) near zero
(e) negative (f) negative
4. (b)
5. Wrong. It cannot exceed $+1.00$

6. $r = +0.116$
7. rho = 0.543
8. rho

1. (a)   2. (b)   3. (d)   4. (b)   5. (a)   6. (d)   7. (b)
8. (d)
9. (a) 150   (b) 97   (c) 75   (d) 6.7   (e) 11.9
   (f) Yes
10. $SS_w = 334$; $MS_b = 20$; $MS_w = 2$; total $df = 119$;
    $F = 10$
11. (a) F ratio   (b) F ratio increases
12. Mean square
13. (b)
14. df between = 3; $SS_w = 390$; $MS_b = 20$; $MS_w = 6.96$;
    $F = 2.87$; significant at null 0.05 level
15. F not significant at 0.05 level

1. C
2. (a)
3. C   (D is close but likely to reflect the influence of
       memory for specific items).

Index